Terry's Texas Rangers
History of the Eighth Texas Cavalry

"Now, by God, Follow your Jimtown-MarkaTime Major"

By Bryan S. Bush

TURNER PUBLISHING COMPANY
Paducah, Kentucky

TURNER PUBLISHING COMPANY
Publishers of America's History
412 Broadway • P.O. Box 3101
Paducah, KY 42002-3101
270-443-0121

By: Bryan S. Bush

Publishing Consultant: Douglas W. Sikes
Book Designer: Emily K. Sikes

Cover Description: *Harper's Weekly* print of the Battle of Woodsonville, 1861. The 32nd Indiana Infantry has formed a square formation against the Texas Rangers Cavalry attack. During this battle Col. Terry was killed.

First Printing 2002 A.D.
Copyright © MMII Bryan S. Bush
All rights reserved.
Publishing Rights: Turner Publishing Company

This book or any part thereof may not be reproduced by any means, mechanical or electronic, without the prior written consent of the author and Turner Publishing Company. This publication was produced using available information. The Publisher regrets it cannot assume responsibility for errors or omissions.

Library of Congress Control No.: 2002100542
ISBN: 1-56311-790-8
Printed in the United States of America

LIMITED EDITION
Additional copies may be purchased from Turner Publishing Company.

Contents

Introduction 5
Chapter 1: Early Beginnings 7
Chapter 2: The Battle of Shiloh 25
Chapter 3: The Siege of Corinth, Mississippi 34
Chapter 4: The Capture of Murfreesboro, Tennessee 37
Chapter 5: The Kentucky Campaign 41
Chapter 6: The Battle of Stone's River 65
Chapter 7: The Attack on Dover, Tennessee 78
Chapter 8: The Battle of Liberty, Tennessee, 1863 83
Chapter 9: The Tullahoma Campaign 85
Chapter 10: The Battle of Chickamauga 100
Chapter 11: Wheeler's First Raid October 1st-9th, 1863 110
Chapter 12: The Knoxville Campaign 114
Chapter 13: The Atlanta Campaign 125
Chapter 14: Wheeler's Second Raid 139
Chapter 15: March to the Sea Campaign 143
Chapter 16: The War's End: The Battle of Bentonville 151
Chapter 17: Twilight on Brilliant Careers 170
Chapter 18: Flags of Terry's Texas Rangers 172
Chapter 19: Pistols and Carbines 174
References 178
Special Thanks 180
About the Author 181
Index 182

Special thanks must go to the following people: Elvin Smith Jr., Judy Stephenson and the Army School Library; Fort Knox, Kentucky, Donald Bryan, The Texas State Library, Fort Harrod State Park, and The Civil War Battles of the Western Theater Museum, Bardstown, Kentucky.

Introduction

The Texas Rangers were a hard fighting body of men who were totally devoted to the cause for which they were fighting, but they were not machines, they had family at home, and they also were rowdy Texans, who knew a good laugh. The Texans were also not big on flashy uniforms, the men knew who was in command, and they were not persuaded by flashy uniforms, and speeches, but by the deeds and actions of their commanders. Hardly a man was seen in the command with an officer's rank on his uniform, except on dress parade, when Col. Harrison might show his rank on a dress coat that he kept for that purpose.

The Rangers favorite weapon was the six shooter navy revolver and the double barrel shotgun. The Union cavalry quickly learned that cavalry charges made with the gleaming saber were no match for the double barrel shotgun. Sabers were non existent among the Rangers.

The Rangers were formed when B. F. Terry, a native of Todd County, Kentucky, but a Texas resident, left his sugar and cotton plantation on the Brazos when the Civil War broke out and volunteered as a staff officer, and fought at the Battle of Bull Run. Terry returned to Texas and raised a regiment. Thomas Harrison was one of the men that joined Terry's regiment. Each man was self equipped, carrying two navy revolvers, a Bowie knife, and a double barrel shotgun, and everything for his horse, from spurs to the lariat. Members of Texas high society joined the Rangers, such as a son and nephew of Sam Houston, J. A.. McKenzie, a Congressmen from the Second District of Kentucky. Terry's Texas Rangers didn't sign up for the ninety days enlistment, but would serve until the war was over. There were 1,170 men when the regiment left Texas. By the end of the war there were only 248 men left.

Of the eight commanders from first to last, Terry was killed on the field in their first battle at Woodsonville, Kentucky, Lubbock died, Wharton was wounded several times and promoted to Major General, Harrison was wounded a number of times and promoted to Brigadier General, Ferrell was wounded and died, Walker was wounded and died, Evans was killed at Perryville, and Gustave Cook, the last Colonel fell severely wounded at the Battle of Bentonville in 1865.

The Texas Rangers began the war in the department under Sidney Johnston by charging Willich's 32nd Indiana at Woodsonville, Kentucky. They drove over rocky ground, and a part of it through a corn field, and the whole finally across the bridge to Munfordville. It was in vain that, after staggering from the shock of shot guns, these trained Union infantrymen threw themselves into groups after the regulation, and bristled all around to the command of "guard against cavalry." The crack of the Rangers navy six shooters right over the glistening steel forced them back , and yet back, they regained the bridge. During the battle Terry fell, shot in the face.

In April 1862, Confederate General Albert Sidney Johnston paid the Rangers a special visit on the eve of the movement from Corinth, Miss. to Shiloh, TN. In response to the cheers that greeted him he said, "With a little more drill you are the equals of the "Old Guard" of Napoleon." During the battle of Shiloh, the Rangers fought on the extreme left, battling Union General William Tecumseh Sherman's troops around Shiloh Church. Later the Rangers participated in the charge against the Hornet's nest. As the Confederates were falling back from Shiloh to Corinth, the Texas Rangers were the rear guard of the army. The Union army soon caught up with the rear of the army, and Tom Harrison with a red bandanna on his head charged the Union forces under Sherman. Sherman himself was almost caught during the charge. Confederate General Nathan Bedford Forrest was severely wounded during the engagement. The Union army was kept back and the Confederate army reached Corinth, Miss.

Harrison started out as a Major, commanding only a company of the Texas Rangers, but he quickly rose in the ranks to Brigadier General. He at one time commanded the Texas Rangers and later commanded a brigade, which included the Texas Rangers. He remained with the brigade until he was finally severely wounded towards the end of the war. He has been described as a short, nervous, cantankerous man. His men called him by several different names. Early in the war, Tom Harrison fell out of favor with his men because his falling back after he encountered a large Union force. Harrison was smart not to engage the Union force, but his men saw it as cowardice. His men now called him Jimtown Major. Later two of his men broke orders and Harrison was strict on orders and ordered the men to mark time. This enraged his men because they were not much on rules and regulations. His name was now Jimtown-Mark Time Major. After the Battle of Shiloh his men no longer called him Jimtown-Mark Time Major. Harrison showed courage under fire, and his men now gained respect for Tom Harrison, and would follow him anywhere. His men now gave him endearing names such as Old Ironsides. The reason for this nickname was Tom seemed to be covered in iron. It seemed like Tom could fight in any battle without being injured, but this all changed. He was injured several times during his career. After the war, most of his men spoke of him fondly.

Harrison would fight at the Battle of Perryville, Stone's River, Dover, Tennessee, Battle of Liberty, Tullahoma campaign, Chickamauga, the battle of Lookout Mountain and Missionary Ridge, The Knoxville Campaign, The Atlanta Campaign, and Sherman's March to the Sea Campaign, and the Battle of Bentonville. He served under some of the greatest cavalry Generals in the Confederacy: Joseph Wheeler, and Nathan Bedford Forrest. Harrison won high praise from Wheeler during many of the battles.

Harrison must be included in the roll call of famous Civil War Generals. His bravery, courage, and the total commitment to his country makes him an outstanding Cavalry General. His cavalry unit must also be counted in the roll call of the best cavalry units of history.

Chapter 1:
Early Beginnings

Thomas Harrison was born on May 1, 1823, in Jefferson County, Alabama, but raised in Monroe City, Mississippi. He was the son of Isham and Harriet Kelley Harrison, the former a direct descendant of Benjamin Harrison, of Virginia, signer of the Declaration of Independence, and a conspicuous figure of the Revolutionary period, and the latter the daughter of a distinguished South Carolina family, of Irish origin. The elder Harrison was a planter and when Thomas was about ten years old his family moved from Alabama to Monroe County, Mississippi. After securing a good education, Harrison took up the practice of law and settled in Texas. In 1843, Harrison established a law practice, with his brother in law, Honorable William H. Jack, in Brazoria County, Texas. William Jack was at the time a Senator in Congress for the State of Texas. After studying law, Harrison returned to Mississippi, and was admitted to the bar at Columbus, and settled temporarily in Aberdeen, where he began the practice of law. [1]

In 1846, Harrison abandoned law, and enlisted in McCluny's company, First Mississippi Rifles, commanded by Jefferson Davis. During the Mexican War, Harrison served for one year, and was involved in the Battle of Monterey. After the war, Harrison returned to Texas, and set up home in Houston in 1847. In 1850, he served as a state legislator, but resigned before his term had expired. In 1851, Harrison moved to Marlin, Falls County, remaining there until 1855, when he moved to Waco, Texas. Harrison quickly rose to the top of his profession and was the leading council in many important cases, both civil and criminal. In 1857, he ran for District Judge, which he lost. In 1858, Harrison married Miss Sallie E. McDonald, a native of North Carolina, and a niece of Governor John Ellis of that state. In 1860, Harrison was elected Captain of the State Militia, in Waco and assigned to the West Texas frontier by Governor Sam Houston to guard against Indian attacks. He served under Col. Dalrymple, along the Prairie, Dog and Canadian Rivers. While in service, he, along with Lt. Granbury, compelled the surrender of the United States troops at Camp Cooper, whose military stores assisted them largely in operations against the Indians. This is said to be the first attack by State troops on United States forces. [2]

In September of 1861, while at Millieau, Harrison was elected to the command of Company A, Eighth Texas Cavalry, Terry's Texas Rangers. He marched with his company to Houston, where he was to meet with Col. Benjamin Terry's Eighth Texas Regiment. [3]

In late March 1861, Benjamin Franklin Terry, Thomas S. Lubbock, and John Wharton were returning home from the secession convention, to which they had been delegates. All three men agreed that they should form a regiment of Texas cavalry to the Confederate government, which was then organizing in Montgomery, Alabama. All three men came from different states and different backgrounds, but all of them loved Texas.

Benjamin "Frank" Terry was born in Russelville, Kentucky on February 18, 1821, and taken to Brazoria County, Texas at the age of ten. In 1852, Terry bought Oakland plantation, which was a sugar plantation in Fort Bend County, and changed it's name to "Sugar Land", eventually his plantation covered 8,000 acres. By 1861, Terry was regarded as one of the wealthiest men in the state. [4]

Thomas Lubbock was born in North Carolina, in 1817 and reared in that state. He moved to Texas in 1836 with the New Orleans Greys. Lubbock was a veteran of the Texas Revolution and the Santa Fe Expedition of 1841. He was captured by the Mexicans, and escaped from Mexico City, and returned to Texas to participate in time for the Somervell punitive expedition of 1842.

When the Civil War broke out, Lubbock was a Houston commission merchant. His brother Francis, would become governor of Texas. [5]

John Wharton was born in Nashville, Tennessee in 1828 and had been brought to Texas as an infant. He was educated at the University of South Carolina. In 1861, Wharton was planning to open a law practice in Brazoria County, where he was a partner with Clinton Terry, younger brother to Benjamin Terry.[6]

In April 1861, Lubbock went to Montgomery, Alabama to seek a commission to raise a regiment. Lubbock went away disappointed. The Confederate government felt that raising a regiment in Texas would be too costly to transport the troops, and the war would be of short duration. While Lubbock was away, Wharton raised a company of cavalry in Brazonia, Texas. Terry also was raising a company in Fort Bend County and was corresponding with others to assemble a regiment upon Lubbock's return. In June, the two Texans, Terry and Lubbock were determined to get into the first big fight. They arrived in Richmond, Virginia: the new Confederate capital. Terry and Lubbock made friends quickly in Richmond and both became aides on the staff of General James Longstreet. During the Battle of First Manassas, in July 1861, Terry and Lubbock were Colonels serving under Longstreet. They were employed under the signal services. During the battle Terry and Lubbock made reconnaissances of the enemy's position. On July 21st, Col. Terry rode forward under the protection of Capt. Whitehead's troops, to take possession of Fairfax Courthouse. Col. Terry captured the Federal flag said to have been made in anticipation of victory and was to be hoisted over the Confederate entrenchments at Manassas. He also shot with his "unerring rifle" at the Federal flag flying on the cupola of the Fairfax courthouse. Both Col. Terry and Col. Lubbock received high praise for their "daring, and valuable reconnaissance", from General P. G. T. Beauregard and Longstreet.[7]

Terry and Lubbock again applied for a regiment of cavalry. The Confederate government gave authority for Lubbock to raise a regiment of cavalry. Terry and Lubbock returned to Texas. Operating out of Houston, they recruited ten companies, mustering them into service on September 9th, 1861. Eleven hundred strong signed up for the Eighth Texas Rangers. Major Tom Harrison was elected to the command of Company A. All the Rangers were sworn in at Houston. They took the oath that they would fight for the duration of the war.[8] Terry was to go to Virginia with his unit. All the Rangers were to bring their horses and equipment with them on their trip. The Rangers were not dressed in uniforms. They were wearing civilian clothing, and their weapons varied immensely. They carried pistols, shotguns, rifles, twenty different calibers in all. Some of the Rangers carried as many as four revolvers. Confederate General Albert Sidney Johnston, commander of the Confederate forces in the Western Theater, commented that the Rangers were a better armed unit then most.

From Houston they traveled to Beaumont by foot, covering eighty miles. While at Beaumont their horses were sent home. From Beaumont they traveled by steamboat, down the Neches and up the Sabine to Niblett's Bluff, then they disembarked and walked on foot; the next forty miles they went by horse draw carts. At New Iberia, on the Bayou Teche, they were transferred to boats and went down to Brashear. From there they pushed on to New Orleans. The trip from Houston to New Orleans took one week. In New Orleans, the Rangers learned they were heading for Bowling Green, Kentucky, not Virginia.[9] On September 27th, 1861, Confederate Acting Secretary of War, Judah Benjamin sent a telegram to Confederate General Albert Sidney Johnston that 1,200 men from Texas under Col. Lubbock were to be fully equipped except horses, these were to be provided by Johnston. Benjamin also reminded Johnston that the money to buy horses for the Rangers were not to come from the War Department.

Either at Houston or en route to New Orleans, members of the command began calling themselves Texas Rangers. This mistaken notion concerning Terry's command would be a problem. The prewar reputation of the Texas Rangers would become a common assumption for Terry's Rangers. The unit would now have to live up to the former's reputation.[10]

At New Orleans, Terry received a telegram from Confederate General Albert Sidney Johnston. Johnston and Terry's families were friends, when Johnston used to live in Brazonia County as a planter. Johnston invited Terry to bring his regiment to him for service in Kentucky. The command immediately set out for Bowling Green, Kentucky. Bowling Green, Kentucky was the headquarters for General Albert Sidney Johnston and was the central focus for his defense line. Johnston's line stretched from Columbus, Kentucky to the Cumberland Gap. Kentucky was not in the Confederacy. A whole series of events led up to Johnston taking Bowling Green, Kentucky.

Kentucky had declared her neutrality on January 21st, 1861. When Lincoln called for seventy

Early Beginnings

five thousand troops on April 15th, 1861, and the Union Secretary of War, Simon Cameron asked for troops, Kentucky Governor Beriah Magoffin wrote to Cameron: "Your dispatch is received. In answer I say, emphatically, Kentucky will furnish no troops for the wicked purpose of subduing her sister Southern States." Magoffin refused to honor a Confederate requisition for a regiment of infantry, but many Kentuckians were joining the Confederacy. In the spring of 1861, large numbers of the State Guard resigned, and entered the Confederacy. The neutrality of Kentucky was slowly eroding. In May 1861, a supply of five thousand muskets with bayonets and a quantity of ammunition was sent by the U.S. War Department to Cincinnati for distribution to the Union men of Kentucky. The Home Guards who were loyal to the Union cause were beginning to form. The arms were delivered on May 18th. Magoffin issued an armed neutrality proclamation and warned both Union and Confederate States to stop recruiting in this state. On May 24th, the state legislature provided for the arming of the state under supervision of five commissioners, including Governor Magoffin. An appropriation of $750,000 dollars was made for the purchase of arms to be distributed to the Home Guard and the State Guard. Both groups were not to use their arms against the Union or Confederate government, unless it was for protecting Kentucky's soil. On May 28th, the U.S. War Department established the Military Department of Kentucky. Lincoln kept Kentucky's neutrality by placing native Kentuckians in command. Union General Robert Anderson was given the Department of Kentucky.[11]

In June 1861, Newport was formally occupied and Anderson's headquarters was set up in Louisville, Kentucky. Early in June, Inspector General of the Kentucky State Guard, Simon Buckner went to Cincinnati for a conference with Union General George B. McClellan. It was agreed that Kentucky would not be invaded unless the Confederates occupied the State first. In that event Buckner was to try and preserve Kentucky's neutrality without Union aid. In June the Congressional elections went for the Union, as did the August elections for the legislature. The June election in Kentucky provoked a Confederate determination to seize strategic river points. General Buckner ordered Col. Lloyd Tilghman, with six companies of State Guards to be stationed at Columbus, Kentucky, with the purpose of preserving Kentucky's neutrality. On June 24th, Col. Tilghman and six companies of the State Guard took up duty at Columbus, Kentucky. Tilghman resigned from the State Guard and joined the Confederacy and Col. Ben Hardin Helm, Lincoln's brother in law, was put in his place.[12]

In late June and early July many more members of the Kentucky Militia, including the State Guard were casting their lots with the Confederacy or Union. The Union enlistments were being made at Camp Clay, across the river from Newport, Indiana, or at Camp Joe Holt in Indiana. The Confederate recruits were enlisting at Camp Boone in Montgomery, Tennessee.[13]

After the battle of Manassas in July, 1861, the Confederacy began to accept all troops from Kentucky. The establishment of recruiting stations in the state was provided for by an act of the Confederate Congress on August 13th.[14]

In August Camp Dick Robinson was established in Garrard County, Kentucky by Brig. General William "Bull" Nelson, in direct violation of Kentucky's neutrality. After violations of Kentucky's neutrality Confederate troops were moved from Tennessee to Hickman and Columbus, Kentucky to fortify and hold these points for control of the Mississippi River navigation.[15]

Conditions now started to heat up in Kentucky. Union General John Fremont put Union General Ulysses Grant in command of all Union forces in southeastern Missouri, and let the Confederates know that he was going to take Columbus, Kentucky. On September 2nd, Union troops occupied Belmont, Missouri, across from Columbus. Confederate General Leonidas Polk ordered General Gideon Pillow to Columbus, which he occupied on September 5th. Hickman had been invaded the day before. The people of Columbus had asked the Confederacy to occupy their city as early as April. On September 7th, General Grant occupied Paducah, and then Smithland. The House of Representatives in Kentucky on the same day voted to raise the U.S. flag on the State Capitol. On September 18th, the legislature declared war on the Confederacy, and that Union General Robert Anderson should expel the Confederate forces from the state. Magoffin vetoed the resolution, but the legislature passed over the veto. By August and September, the Kentucky State Guard joined the Confederacy. Col. Roger Hanson, Col. Lloyd Tilghman, and even General Simon Buckner resigned their commissions in the State Guard to the join the Confederacy.[16]

In mid September Confederate General Albert Sidney Johnston ordered Confederate General Simon Buckner to occupy Bowling Green, Kentucky with four thousand troops. The fortifications the Confederates built were named Fort Johnston, named after General Albert Sidney Johnston, who was now the commander of the Western Department of the Confederate army.[17]

9

In late September the Rangers boarded a train at New Orleans and arrived in Nashville, Tennessee. At Nashville, they encamped on the Fairgrounds. While in Nashville, the Rangers borrowed some horses and put on a show for the ladies of Nashville. The men would ride sideways on the saddle and pick up coins that the public would throw on the ground. They also would ride wild horses until they were broken, just like they did at home in Texas, although this didn't happen too much in Nashville, since wild horses weren't in abundance in Nashville. The men were becoming restless in Nashville. During their stay in Nashville, the men went to see a play, during the play the actor portraying an evil villain was about to injure the damsel in distress. The Rangers got upset, and fired a round into the playhouse. The public panicked. The cops were called out, and two police officers ended up getting killed by the Rangers, and one wounded. The Governor of Tennessee wrote a letter to General Albert Sidney Johnston and the Rangers were ordered to be put on rail and sent to Bowling Green.[18] At Bowling Green, Johnston assigned Terry a camp area near Oakland, fifteen miles to the northeast.

On October 28th, 1861, Johnston moved his headquarters from Nashville, Tennessee to Bowling Green, Kentucky and assumed immediate command of the Army of Central Kentucky, which consisted of the First Division under Major General William Hardee, and the Second Division under Brig. General Simon Buckner.

In November the regiment's members elected Terry Colonel and Lubbock Lieutenant Colonel, and Thomas Harrison as Major. In late October, the regiment became mounted. The horses the Rangers left in Beaumont were driven by detail to Nashville, and then to Bowling Green. The rest of the horses may have come from a rich benefactor in Kentucky who bought the rest of the horses for the regiment, although documented evidence does not exist, and it still remains a mystery. The unit was also equipped with tents, camp utensils and wagons. Corporal J. W. Rabb wrote on October 22nd, 1861 that the horses have arrived in camp. "I got me a good charger. He is a sorel of medium size and has good gate" wrote Rabb. He goes on to say "We have very good tents. We draw ammunition today."[19] During the winter months, the elements took a heavy toll on the Rangers. The men came down with measles, mumps, and pneumonia. At any one time, half the regiment was down with illness. According to Rangers Chaplain Robert Bunting, by the end of January 1862, eighty four Rangers had died, but only five from wounds inflicted from battle. On December 13, 1861, Private C. W. Love wrote that seventy five to one hundred men had died from disease.[20]

During the month of November, while the Rangers were at Bowling Green, Kentucky, they were sent on a reconnaissance mission. Capt. Ward McDonald, 4th Alabama Cavalry, who was a member of the Buckner Guards, had scouted three Federal camps, one at Jimtown, another at Tompkinsville, and the last at Glasgow. After he reported his findings to Confederate General Simon Buckner, Buckner sent Major Tom Harrison and one hundred men from the Eighth Texas Cavalry on a reconnaissance trip to Jamestown. The Rangers referred to Jamestown as Jimtown, Kentucky. Captain McDonald was sent as their guide. Jimtown was a village forty miles east of Bowling Green. The town was very pro Union and didn't like the Confederates. According to McDonald, the men and women, who lived by the Jamestown road, fled to the woods. On the second day of their trip, the men stopped at every house on the road to get buttermilk, eggs, etc. The houses were almost totally deserted. At one house a women decided to stay at her residence and when the Rangers entered her house, she was petrified with fright, and gave the Rangers all the buttermilk they wanted. She was shocked when one of the men thanked her and handed her the pay for the goods they had took. At the next house, about half a mile down, there were two old men, an old woman, and some children. The two men went out to the fence, but the old women remained on the porch with a pistol in her lap and knitting in her hands. She never even looked up at the approaching cavalry. When some of the Texas Rangers dismounted to go in the house, the old woman looked up "with a face full of defiance", and cried out, "I will shoot the first man that comes in!" The men halted, and all the men began to laugh. The old woman kept up her warlike attitude, with pistol in hand and the knitting needle by her side on the floor. Just then a younger women entered from the back yard and approached the old woman. She cried out "Mother, mother! Treat those men right, they are perfect gentlemen, they came to my house and never hurt a thing!" "It don't make any difference, I'll shoot the first man that comes in." Some of the men again tried to enter the yard, but old woman again aimed her pistol and the men backed down. The Rangers laughed out loud at the way the old women kept back the Rangers.[21]

They continued on until they came across a Federal force of about three hundred strong.

The Rangers were about three miles from Jamestown. The Federals had placed their men so that they could have raked the Rangers with their fire and wipe them out, but the cavalry made a "big show," and the Federals out post ran and told the main force that there were a thousand Rangers approaching the town. At this information the Federals fell back to an old barn in the center of a field. Harrison gave the order to dismount and form a line of battle. The men were about ready to charge the barn through the open field, when it was suggested by one of the Captains that Harrison should flank it under cover of the woods, which was nearer to the barn then the men were. This checked Harrison's movement, and Harrison, after some parlaying and a little reconnaissance, gave orders to mount and fall back to Bowling Green. Harrison decided to pull back two compa-

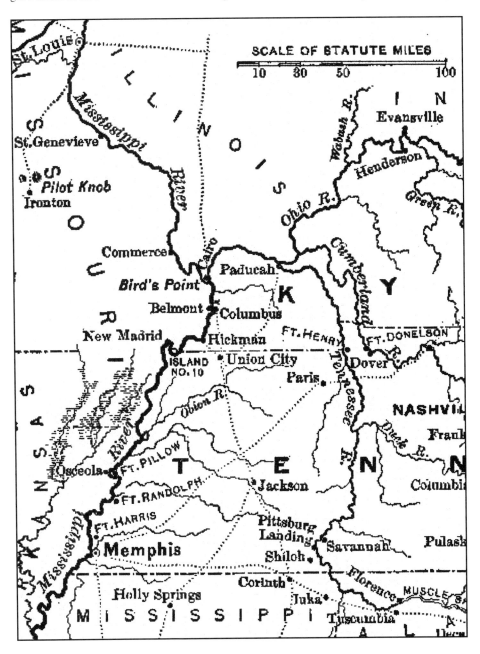

nies. The withdrawal was prompt, and Harrison's men thought it was a little too premature to pull out so quickly. The men were ready for a fight, and they thought that old Tom Harrison got scared, and yelled all along the road , "Hurrah for the Jimtown Major". The men would not stop there, they continued to call out Jimtown Major all the way back into camp.[22] On November 13th, 1861, Confederate General Patrick Cleburne's advance division of infantry, including the Texas Rangers marched from Jamestown to Tompkinsville, Kentucky. Along the way he found that the houses were abandoned, and the country deserted. He saw a few woman and children, but when they saw the Confederates coming they would run and hide. He said that he met one old woman "with an open Bible in her hand, said she was prepared to die, and would not be convinced that we meant no harm." As Cleburne as his force entered Tompkinsville, he ordered the advance guard to fall back and ordered fixed bayonets, with the bands to the front to make the biggest show possible as they marched through town. The town was abandoned. There was a rumor that ten thousand Union troops under General Lovell Rousseau was advancing a few miles from where Cleburne was located. At 12 midnight, Cleburne left Tompkinsville and headed for McRea's Crossroads, nine miles away. Two miles from town, his advance guard surprised the Union pickets. The Texas Rangers, ten in front, gave chase for four miles, when they suddenly came upon forty U.S. Cavalry. They fell back and sent for reinforcements. Cleburne sent twenty more men to join them, and ordered sixty more in advance of his infantry. Cleburne soon discovered that the Crossroads was sixteen miles away not nine miles, and the Union scouts were seen on his flanks and rear.[23]

Cleburne halted the main column, took up strong positions on Skagg's Creek. Cleburne could not tell if the approaching Yankees were an entire army or just a mere scouting party. He knew nothing of the movements of the Federals. Cleburne set false camp fires on every surrounding hill, and a wide line of pickets. In the mean time, Cleburne's cavalry pressed the Yankees in the direction of the Crossroads so closely that they got confused and dispersed in the woods at McRea's Crossroads. Cleburne' cavalry fell back on the main column of the Federal cavalry, about one hundred strong, and after a skirmish, in which the Union cavalry broke and left. Two Union soldiers were killed, with no loss to the Confederates. Cleburne' cavalry fell back five miles to camp for the night.[24]

During the night, Cleburne captured a number of U.S. dragoon horses, fully accoutered, a number of muskets, pistols and sabers. Cleburne commended Major Harrison "for the way (he) managed to disorganize and disperse this large body of the enemy's cavalry in an unknown country in the night, and without one friend among the country people." "The truth is, the rush of the Rangers so dispersed and confused the enemy that they got lost and were wandering about in every direction, and this accounts for their appearance on the Confederate flanks and rear." [25]

Major Harrison was ordered to fall back to Cleburne's camp. By accident, Bankhead of the Rangers was shot by accident when he rode into the Confederate pickets.

The next morning, Cleburne and his force marched back to Tompkinsville. The Rangers advanced to and beyond the Crossroads and up the Glasgow road, They heard artillery fire in the direction of Columbia, and believed a force was advancing along that road. They left the Crossroads and rode twenty three miles, but later returned to Tompkinsville. [26]

During November the Union army made it's first strategic move on Kentucky and testing Confederate General Albert Sidney's Johnston's line of defense. On November 6th, Grant with 3,114 men, made ready to attack Belmont, a key Confederate stronghold, defended by heavy guns and a huge garrison. Grant and his men left their camp at Cairo, Illinois and boarded transport boats for the trip to Missouri. Grant landed his men just north of the hamlet of Belmont, and found himself facing a Confederate force of five thousand men, 2,330 manning the garrison and Gideon Pillow's 2,300 men. Polk learned of the Union force shortly after daybreak. Polk ordered Pillow's division to move to support Col. Tappan, who was in command of the force at Belmont, with only four regiments. Col. Russell, Col. Wright, Col. Pickett, and Col. Freeman's regiments of Tennessee troops were sent. Col. Tappan had the 13th Arkansas, Capt. Beltzhoover's Watson Battery, and a squadron of Lt. Col. Miller's battalion of cavalry. Grant's men attacked Belmont at 8:30 AM, November 7th, 1861. Polk expected an attack to come from the Columbus side of the river. General McCown had charge of the left flank, and moved a long range battery under Capt. R. A. Stewart, of the Louisiana Point Coupee Battery. At the fort in Columbus, the heavy siege battery, under Capt. Hamilton opened a heavy fire upon the Yankees. The cannon fire was returned. After half an hour, the boats were driven up the river. But the Union boats again dropped down and renewed the cannonade. This artillery duel continued for an hour, and again the Union boats had to fall back. [27]

At 10:20 A.M. the Yankees advance guard began to fire upon the pickets, and within forty minutes the entire Union force had arrived to the scene. Pillow sent for help. Polk sent him Col. Knox Walker's regiment and a section of artillery. Capt. Beltzhoover's battery had ceased firing from the lack of ammunition, and the Yankees began to fire with a heavy battery. The battery never made it to the opposite shore, because their were no stage planks to unload the guns onto the shore. Capt. Polk's battery was landed, but was too late for the battle.[28]

Col. Carroll and Col. Mark regiments were sent forward. Col. Marks was ordered by Polk to land his regiment higher up the river, with a flank movement. General Pillow ordered Col. Russell with his brigade to support the flank movement. The Confederate troops were falling back at Belmont. Polk ordered further reinforcements. General Cheatham, with the First brigade, under Col. Preston Smith was ordered down to the transports, which they boarded and headed for Belmont. The Yankees soon set the camp tents on the Belmont side on fire, and the Union batteries were advancing near the river bank and opening fire on the Confederate transport ships. The Confederate boats Prince, the Charm, the Hill, and the Kentucky were transporting 2,000 troops across. Polk ordered Capt. Smith's Mississippi battery to the river bank, opposite the battle, and to open fire on the Yankees. Polk also ordered Maj. A. P. Stewart to open the guns at the fort to fire down on the Yankees. The fire was so heavy that Grant and his troops had to fall back to his transport ships. Grant then ran into Col. Marks and then General Cheatham in his flanks.[29]

Polk arrived on the field and ordered Capt. White's company of Lt. Col. Logwood's battalion of cavalry, across the river, with two regiment of General McCown's division to follow. On landing General Pillow and Cheatham met Polk . Polk ordered them to push the Yankees to their boats. The route over which Polk passed was strewn with the dead and wounded from the battle between Col. Marks and General Cheatham and Grant. [30]

When Polk arrived at the point where Grant's transports were, he ordered the column, headed by the 154th Tennessee, under the cover of a corn field to deploy along the river bank within range of the boats. A heavy fire was now opened upon the Yankees. Under this fire Grant had his lines cut and retreated from the shore. Grant was surrounded and had to fight his way back to his transports. Once the Union troops had boarded the transport ships, the Confederates were fired upon by the cannons from the gunboats, as they headed for Cairo, Illinois. Polk ordered his men to retire. The Confederates counted Belmont as their victory. Grant said that Belmont was a victory for the Union. In fact, neither side won or lost. There were 607 Union casualties and 641 casualties for the Confederates. The Battle of Belmont was General Ulysses Grant's first Civil War Battle, and would not be his last. [31]

Also in November of 1861 Union General William Sherman was replaced with Don Carlos Buell. Buell began to concentrate his forces in the direction of Bowling Green. Union General George Thomas, who had been operating in the Cumberland Gap, was moved to Somerset, Kentucky and also occupied points on the upper Green River, which was immediately situated on Johnston right flank. Preparations were being made to advance on Johnston's front by repairing the Green River bridge at Munfordville, Kentucky. General Felix Zollicoffer's command was moved to Monticello, placing him closer to Johnston and protecting his right flank. Johnston also increased his force. Confederate General George Crittenden, brother of Union General Thomas Crittenden, was assigned to his command. [32]

In early December, Johnston ordered Terry's Rangers to the Green River to help support General Thomas Hindman's brigade. Sickness, leaves and details depleted Terry's ranks to no more than two hundred and fifty men. Lt. Col. Lubbock was ill at Nashville with typhoid fever. Harrison was either ill or on detail. On December 17th, Brig. Gen. Thomas Hindman moved out for the Green River, reaching Woodsonville. The command consisted of three hundred cavalry, four pieces of artillery and two regiments of Arkansas Infantry, in all two hundred men. When he reached the stream he found the Yankees on the north bank. Hindman deployed some infantry skirmishers, who engaged the Yankees at long range but with little effect. Hindman decided to ride to the front, where he left Col. Terry in charge with instructions to decoy the Yankees up the hill and away from support to a point where the Confederate infantry and artillery could be used to better advantage. The Yankees allowed themselves to be decoyed. Terry sent Ferrell, commander of Company D, with seventy five men against their left. Terry led the rest against the right. Ferrell charged, yelling, each man riding as fast as his horse could carry him. Ferrell charged the skirmishers of the 32nd Indiana Volunteers. The Texans got within twenty yards and opened fire with their rifles and revolvers. As the story goes, while Terry was watching Ferrell, another Federal party was hiding in a blackjack thicket, and opened fire on Terry's men. Terry yelled out "Charge, my brave boys, charge!" and taking the lead, Terry dashed toward the thicket. The Yankees broke and ran. But after a few moments, Terry noticed a small group of Yankees in some bushes a short distance away, and he called "Yonder is a nest of birds." Terry and five men charged the Yankees in the bush. Terry shot two of them with his pistol. The one Yankee remaining raised his pistol and fired point blank into Terry's face. The bullet struck Terry in the face and came out at the back of his head. Capt. Evans is said to have shot the last Yankee.[33]

Meanwhile, Ferrell continued to lead his force into an open field against the body of Yankees, who rallied behind a makeshift breastwork made from straw stacks and fences. They were pouring musket fire into the Rangers ranks. A disorderly charge of undrilled men was sent into one of the best drilled regiments, the 32nd Indiana Infantry. Union Col. Willich of the 32nd Indiana reported that the fight now became one of the "most earnest and bloody part of the struggle. With lightening speed, under infernal yelling, great numbers of Texas Rangers rushed upon our whole force. They advanced to fifteen or twenty yards of our lines, some of them even between them, and opened fire with rifles and revolvers. Our skirmishers took the thing very coolly, and permitted them to approach very close, when they opened a destructive fire on them. They were repulsed with severe loss, but only after Lt. Sachs, who left his covered position with one platoon was surrounded by about fifty Rangers several of them demanding of him three times to give up his sword and let his men lay down their arms. He firmly refused and defended himself till he fell with three of his men, before the attack was repulsed. Lt. Col. Von Trebra now led on another advance of the center and left flank, when he drew down upon his forces a second attack of the Rangers in large numbers, charging into the very ranks, some dashing through to the rear. In the fight participated three field officers, one staff and sixteen officers of the line, twenty three sergeants and 375 men. Our loss is one officer and ten men dead, 22 wounded and five missing." Ranger losses were four killed and eight wounded. The regiment elected Lubbock to take Terry's place.[34]

Sergeant Benjamin Frank Batchelor, Company C, described the battle with vivid detail. He said that the "*morning was clear and we started for the River at 9 A.M. arriving at the scene of action about 11 A.M. To give you a better idea of our maneuvers I must first state the enemy have some 20,000 soldiers on the opposite side of the river and the object of our advance was not to occupy this side, but merely to ascertain their strength and damage any detachment of their army from this side. A range of hills on this bank of the river completely hides their forces which are seen only by ascending those hills. The Railroad Bridge had been blown up by a party of Southerners to prevent the enemy from attacking Bowling Green before it was fortified; but there are three fords on the river each having a road leading into the Turnpike at from one to three miles back from the bridge. Over these fords they can pass everything but their heavy siege cannon. Now as we came down the turnpike these roads lay in our rear, and left us subject to flank movements, and to be attacked in the rear. When within a mile or so from the river Capt. (J. G.) Jones, (Company I) was sent to the left to ascertain if the enemy were in that direction; detachments from three other companies were sent out in other directions and in front; this done, the main body of our Regiment led by Col. Terry moved forward on the Turnpike till we reached a bridge about one mile from the river and halted. Here we examined our arms and divested ourselves of everything that would encumber us in battle. In about 10 minutes the sharp crack of the Minnie Rifles was heard to the left and in front and our advance scouts came in reporting the enemy had crossed the river and were rapidly advancing-About 125 of our men were then ordered to advance obliquely to the left and take position to meet the enemy in that quarter while a courier was dispatched to hurry forward the Arkansas Infantry. We had not advanced more than 40 yards before the enemy, 250 strong, armed with Minnie and Enfield rifles, opened upon us from a thick woods and fence, which concealed their advance. At the first fire Col. Terry's horse was slightly hurt, and raising in his stirrups Terry shouted in a clear loud voice "Charge them boys! Charge!' then bending low with drawn revolver he dashed forward toward the enemy; his words were hardly uttered before a wild shout broke from our ranks and with spurs closely pressed the column made the charge. Firing from both sides in an instant became general, filling the air with whizzing lead and powder smoke. Our charge was not made in front, but on a line; our column running closely outside the fence, which served the enemy as a sort of* breastwork and rest for their guns-Nothing could exceed the brilliancy and daring of that impetuous charge. Our Shot Guns threw up a blaze of fire and shot almost into their faces-the distance between our lines did not exceed ten or fifteen feet and in some instances the boys did not fire until the muzzles of their guns were within a few inches of the Enemy's heads causing horrible mutilation. Shrieks of their wounded filled the air, still they stubbornly held their position till our guns and six shooters were nearly exhausted, and more than half their number were either killed or wounded. They stood their ground like brave men, but shot too low, killing more horses than men; in fact we were so close, and rushed along their line in such headlong fury-yelling like Demons-that they could no more draw a sight on us than they could a Meteor. Our lamented Colonel fell very soon after the action began, shot with a Minnie ball through the head; his horse fell at the same moment pierced by three shots-The first thing that arrested my attention in the charge was the situation of Capt. (Mark. L.) Evans, (Captain Company C); when the charge was ordered he was in command of Wharton's company and ours-and was riding near Col. Terry-as I rushed on heading our company I saw Mark engaged in close quarters with a Big Dutch soldier who had got over the fence and was trying to run bayonet him-Mark had just shot the soldier who killed Terry and turning round saw his peril in time to get a tree between himself and the shining steel as his antagonist fired tearing a hole in the tree-the fellow then tried to run the captain through as mentioned. I drew up and was in the act of letting my gun speak when a Ranger passed between us and I had to hold fire-a second more and I heard the report of Mark's pistol which put an end to the struggle. In a moment after a fellow near me fired and then started to run, but my double barrel pet was allowed to report and he sprang into the air and then fell forward to rise no more. Unable longer to stand the rain of bullets from our six shooters the enemy began to run across the field but we leaped the fence and pursued, shooting as we came to them till we reached a ravine swept by their artillery and we returned to our position before the first fire." [35] Frank estimated the Union loss at sixty killed. He reported that very few prisoners were taken. The reason being that once the Rangers found out that Terry was killed, the men were overcome with rage and killed the prisoners.

During the battle, a detachment under Stephen Ferrill, Co. D and John T. Holt , Co. H, engaged the Yankees on the right of the turnpike in a corn field and drove them back "with great slaughter killing about thirty and wounding as many more." According to Batchelor, at about the same time two companies from Arkansas, the Red Rangers and the Young Guards, attacked the Yankees on the left and killed sixteen and captured eight prisoners. General Hindman ordered the regiment to take position in some woods on the right of the Turnpike and hold their position. After a couple of minutes the scouts came in reporting the Yankees were rapidly crossing the river above and below the Rangers and throwing out skirmishers on both sides to flank and cut the Rangers off in the rear. A meeting was held and the regiment was sent out to hold the Yankees in check until the wagons retired to the main branch of the road leading to Bowling Green. The Rangers made it to the road, but Union soldiers kept out of range and the fighting ended after a fight of about two hours and a half. Frank Batchelor said that one hundred Federals were killed and eight prisoners. The Rangers according to Batchelor estimated their loss at four killed and one mortally wounded and eight "who would probably never recover." [36]

Lt. Issac Fulkerson, of the Texas Rangers, also was involved in the battle and wrote to his brother Frank, from Cave City, Kentucky, "*Eight Companies of our Regt. left out camp the morning after you left, we were accompanied by Gen. Hindman's Legion, and have been busy ever since between our camp (where you saw us) and Green River collecting grain, horses and hogs, scouting, skirmishing, and tearing up the R.R. track. We have been nearly all the time in sound of the enemies drums. You thought we were living well when you were with us and we were. Since that time we have had no cooking utensil in our mess except a coffee pot. We eat crackers and cook our meat on a stick, and live that way until we get back to our camp. Our headquarters are now at this place six miles from Green river where the RR crosses, but we do not expect to stay here long, as the enemy have possession of the RR Bridge, which they are repairing, and are on this side of the river in force, and as I write the cannon are firing in that direction. Our horses are saddled and we are ready. Breckinridge's Brigade is coming to join us. they staid at our camp last night. Last Sunday we attacked their pickets at five different places, killing four, wounding three, taking two prisoners. On Tuesday a part of our Regt. about 250 and all of Hindman's went up the river. Our advance and their pickets met on top of a hill a mile this side of the river. We, the advance, run the pickets in and in turn were driven back by about six hundred of the enemy. All of our Rangers then charged them with a shout but they having posses-*

sion of a fence and a wooded hill, held their position bravely for about ten minutes, when they were forced to retreat through a field, back to the main body under the cover of their batteries. It was a brilliant little fight and would have been perfectly satisfactory to us, but for the death of Col. Terry. He was the first man killed. He was shot in three places and his horse at the same place. Five other horses and one of our men were killed in a few yards of where the Col. fell and the dead Dutch were to thick to count. We suffered a great loss in the death of Col. T. He knew not what fear was.

Three of our men were killed, five or six wounded, about seventy five of the enemy were killed and wounded and twelve prisoners. The position and strength of the enemy being too great, we fell back to our camp. The cannons fired a few shots, all the balance was done by the Rangers. The word charge was given and every man went to fighting on his own hook. I went up the fence and tried to get a shot at one in the field, but he got behind a peach tree and I got over this fence and overtook him, but my horse was so restive that I could not shoot, but I hit him on the head with my gun. When he surrendered I took his gun, and told him to turn back, and turned my horse to go with him, but he started the other way, when a young man with me shot him."[37]

Chaplain Ganter, of the 15th Ohio, also wrote an account from the Union perspective. He writes: "The noted Texas Rangers have been for some time dodging, sneaking, dashing about us in a desperate manner. Sunday last we had a skirmish with them in which Col. Willich had two men wounded and one sergeant taken prisoner. Yesterday (Tuesday 17th,) Colonel Willich sent over one or two companies to watch them. About noon the trumpeter came to the bank on the opposite side of the river and blew the signal for reenforcements. Immediately four or five companies (of Colonel Willich's regiment) crossed the river at double quick (across the bridge which they had just completed). They ran in eagerness to fight, stimulated to rage, to revenge their wounded comrades of Sunday last. When they crossed the river they deployed as skirmishers and doubled quicked it over fences, through the woods, when all at once one of their men cried halt, and seeing a horse in the woods near by, he fired, and the horse fell. Immediately a yell echoed through the woods, and about one hundred and fifty Rangers issued forth, and came within ten feet of the muzzles of the guns of our men. Here they halted, and did not stir or budge one inch until each one of their number had fired fourteen shots, being armed with a pair of revolvers and double shot guns apiece. But while this was going on our men were not idle. Rangers dropped-Rangers yelled, groaned, and cursed-horses Rangerless, riderless, were galloping in all directions. When the Rangers had performed their shooting in a cool, careless way, they just as cooly turned around and retired. They had no sooner disappeared, and our men were once more advancing, than another company of Rangers galloped up, and performed the same remarkable fourteen shot feat in the same cool, determined manner, and were met by the same sturdy, brave German square. Once more Rangers and Germans mingled dying groans, when at length, after the Rangers had gone through this exact program several times, three or four hundred of them made on grand rush, with the evident intention of breaking the German carrere, or square. They came up with the same dash, and fired their shots with the same apparent neglect of life, some were literally lifted from their horses on the point of the bayonet, some were knocked off with butts of guns. It became a hand to hand fight, Rangers retreating and Germans following up. Lieutenant Saxe of this point of the fight was somewhat in advance. He was surrounded by Rangers-they asked him to surrender-but instead of replying he rushed at the man who made this request, but before he reached the object of his attack dropped dead in his tracks, receiving five bullets in the chest and about twenty buckshot in the abdomen. Then the struggle became fiercer and hotter, when all at once the Germans found themselves in a net. On the right came the firing from concealed infantry; on the left the boom of cannon from a masked battery startled the heroes. Seven hundred cavalry at once came into view in front. We could see the whole affair from the high bluff on this side of Green River. Reenforcements were hurried across-Cotter's batteries opened from our bluff-Germans slowly, but unwillingly, retired to the woods, and just by chance, the merest in the world, escaped from a dreadful slaughter. The Forty-ninth Ohio and Thirty Ninth Indiana formed in line of battle, and double quicked it over the field; but the enemy had retired. Our loss was eleven killed, twenty one wounded, and five missing (when I say wounded, I mean severely). Among the killed was one officer, Lieutenant Saxce, a Jew, an old country soldier, and a brave man. The loss of the enemy (I am giving you the lowest figures) was thirty three killed; wounded we cannot positively tell, for they were carried off the field. Colonel Terry, their brave and celebrated Colonel of Rangers, was killed. And now with regards to numbers engaged: We had about five hundred men (all of Colonel Willich's command) actually engaged at one time or another. They had seven hundred Rangers, one regiment of infantry (six hundred men) and four cannon."[38]

Chaplain Ganter also said the Germans from the 32nd Indiana also described the Rangers appearance. *"They described them as swarthy complexioned, a mixture of creoles, trappers, desperadoes, with long hair and shaggy whiskers, and even when lying wounded, upon the ground exhibiting the fierceness of a wounded tiger."*[39]

After the battle Chaplain Ganter described the aftermath. He wrote that he had visited the hospital to see the wounded. *"Number one had his ear shot off, number two is minus the bridge of his nose, four or five wounded in the arms, four or five in the legs, four in the chest, one in the abdomen, another has a quantity of buckshot in his side. I saw the latter gentlemen as the doctor was cutting out the shot. He remarked 'tat dey didn't shoot mit buckshot in de old country,' but hoped the rebels would 'shoot buckshot all de times. They all took great pleasure in explaining their wounds, and most of them did not wince under the doctor's dressing. One poor fellow comforted himself with the reflection that if had to lose his leg he would join the cavalry."*[40]

Chaplain Ganter also visited the funeral and burial site. He said the dead were *"laid out in the field, neatly dressed; graves were dug on the top of a knoll, in a semicircle. The regiment formed around them. The Colonel made a speech, and then remarked, 'that as their brave comrades had fallen in the struggle for human rights and liberty, and were now on their journey to immortality, they would give them three cheers;' and cheer they did, and then the band played the Marseilles Hymn, and the soldiers marched around graves, each throwing a handful of earth into each of the graves. No salutes were fired on account of the close proximity of the hospital."*[41]

In mid January of 1862 Private August Bloedner of the 32nd Indiana placed a memorial for his comrades killed in action at the Battle of Roweltt's Station, at Fort Willich, in Munfordville, Kentucky. On June 6, 1867 fourteen bodies along with the monument were moved to Cave Hill Cemetery in Louisville, Kentucky, where it remains to this day.

Captain John Walker, of the Eighth Texas, and those who were able to travel, escorted Col. Terry's body to Nashville, Tennessee to the State Capitol where funeral services were held. The Legislature, Masonic fraternity, and the military paid Terry their final respects. [42] Terry's body was put on a train and taken to Houston. When his body arrived in Houston a large military escort and a regimental band joined the Masons of Holland Lodge #1 and formed a prosession that occupied twelve blocks. They accompanied Terry's body to the Tap and Harrisburg Depot and then to his plantation in Sugar Land. In 1880 Terry's body was moved to Houston.

By December 21, 1861, Confederate Albert Sidney Johnston began to concentrate his forces at Bowling Green against Union General Don Carlos Buell's forces. The Confederate forces under Confederate General John C. Breckinridge, who was under Simeon Buckner's Division in December 21, 1861, were moving towards Munfordville, Kentucky, heading toward Bowling Green, Kentucky. General Buckner and the rest of his force were crossing the Great Barren River and was also heading towards Bowling Green. Conf. Major General William Hardee was moving towards the Great Barren River Bridge, including General Thomas Hindman's brigade The Eighth Texas Cavalry, under Major Harrison, along with Brig. Gen. Charles Phifer's battalion of cavalry, was covering Hindman's front. Lubbock was ill from typhoid fever and was at Nashville. Lubbock later died from his illness on January 23, 1862. Captain John Wharton became Colonel and commanded the regiment. John Walker was made Lieutenant Colonel.

Private George Turner, Company C, Eighth Texas Rangers, was ill of chronic diarrhea, and was hospitalized at Nashville. On December 29th, 1861 he wrote to his sister, Charlotte (Batchelor) Winne and Mrs. Eugenia Wilkins, that the Rangers had been hard at work since the fight at Woodsonville and were constantly dodging the Yankees and watching them, sleeping every night with their boots on and their horses saddled so that they could be ready at a moments notice.[43]

On January 5th, 1862 Frank Batchelor wrote that Confederate troops were crowding into Bowling Green from Missouri and Virginia. Confederate General Ben McCulloch from Missouri and General John Floyd from Virginia arrived. The Federal forces were increasing also. *"It is evident this place (Kentucky) is to be the scene of their bloody struggles and that speedily. Meantime the fortifications around Bowling Green have been completed, properly tested, and General Johnston says he is now "ready". Nearly every hill is fortified and it makes one feel strong and defiant to look up at those towers of strength with their long iron arms pointing ominously out upon every approach to the city."*[44] Batchelor mentioned that Generals Albert Sidney Johnston, William Hardee, Simon Buckner, Thomas Hindman, William Preston, Ben

McCulloch, and John Floyd, John C. Breckinridge were all at Bowling Green. He knew the immense pressure that was beginning to build in Kentucky. *"Both sides are aware of the immense importance of victory, and the crushing effects of defeat...If we whip them we have force enough to push on to Louisville and drive the last Lincolnite in arms from the state, and this will be such a reverse that newspapers cannot conceal, not the Federal government bear up under. All Europe will clamor and force our recognition. But on the other hand should they prevail, Nashville is gone and Tennessee becomes a battlefield, and the war must, I suppose, go on."*[45]

Private C. W. Love wrote to his father and mother about the conditions in Kentucky. There is *"plenty of clothing and bedding to be comfortable and plenty to eat of beef. Flour, bread, genuine coffee and sugar and whatever else we may be able to purchase when we have the money which just at this time is very scarce generally and with me the last of the $48.00 with which I left home was spent this morning for the unnecessary comfort called tobacco. I think it will however be but a few days until we will be paid about one months wages which will be about sufficient to feed a man a few times on butter and eggs, chickens and some other little things bought with this money at from thirty five per. Ct. Discount and with Tenn money at a Discount of 40 to 50 pt ct Discount.. This is because the whole trade of the country of almost all kinds is in the hands of the Unionists with whom this whole country is cursed. I am fully of the opinion that is the war is brought into this region of the country it will truly be a war of brother against brother and of son and against father and in many instances the children of the same family are in both armies-there are several cases in this region one family in particular the father being rabid Unionist has two sons in the Northern army and one in the Southern army at Bowling Green-there are numberless instances of this kind in this Christian County. It appears now that the Northern forces have begun the long threatened simultaneous movement against us."*[46]

Private Cyrus Love was right, Union forces were beginning to make their moves against the Confederate forces. By January General Albert Sidney Johnston's hold on Kentucky would slowly slip away. On January 19th, 1862, at Mill Springs, Kentucky, Union forces under Brig. Gen. George Thomas battled Confederate forces under General George Crittenden and crumbled the Eastern defense.

Brig. Gen. Felix K. Zollicoffer's main responsibility was to secure East Tennessee and to protect the railroad from Chattanooga to Knoxville. In September 1861, Zollicoffer made a bold move by seizing the Cumberland Gap, invading Kentucky, and setting up his headquarters at a ford on the upper Cumberland River. With no real opposition to his front, he continued on his march into Kentucky. Union infantry was well entrenched on a densely wooded hill near the Rockcastle-Laurel county line. Zollicoffer approached well fortified position and the Union troops attacked and drove Zollicoffer back. The battle between the two forces became known as the Battle of Wildcat Mountain, which was fought on October 21, 1861. In November 1861, Zollicoffer left five thousand men and his artillery at the Cumberland Gap, and advanced west into Kentucky with four thousand men, to strengthen control in the area around Somerset, Kentucky. He found a strong defensive position at Mill Springs and decided to make this his winter quarters. He fortified the area, especially both sides of the Cumberland River. Union Brig. Gen. George Thomas received orders to drive the Rebels across the Cumberland River and break up Maj. Gen. George B. Crittenden's army. Thomas left Lebanon and slowly marched through rain soaked country, arriving at Logan's Crossroads on January 17th, where he waited for Brig. Gen. A. Schoeph's troops from Somerset to join him. Zollicoffer took the time to reconnoiter the north bank of the river opposite Mill Springs. The south bank had many advantages, including fresh water, a grist mill, a sawmill, and a supply line by river to Nashville. Zollicoffer was ordered to remain on the south side of the river, but he disobeyed orders and moved his force across the river to the north bank, and put his cannons on the bluffs opposite Mill Springs, called Beech Grove. Zollicoffer's men now set to work building cabins, rifle pits, and setting up defenses. Union General George Thomas decided to strike first and on December 31, 1861, Thomas and his men marched forty miles, but the weather turned to rain and the roads soon became a quagmire of mud. What should have taken a few days, ended up taking two and a half weeks! Thomas arrived at Logan's Crossroads on January 17th, 1862. Thomas set up his headquarters at the Jamestown and Columbia roads. Eight miles separated Thomas from his rear column, and to make matters worse, the Fishing Creek was so swollen from the recent rains, Albin Schoepf's brigade was separated from Thomas. He was located on the high bluffs on the east of the creek. Schoepf's men did not link up with Thomas until January 18th, 1862. [47]

Early Beginnings

In early January, Maj. Gen. George Crittenden, Zollicoffer's superior, had arrived at Mill Springs and taken command of the Confederate troops. A council of war was held, and it was decided that the best defense was to hit the Federals first. There is some evidence that Zollicoffer may have objected to the attack, because Crittenden and Brigadier General William Carroll drank heavily before and during the council of war and that Zollicoffer doubted the mental capacity to make rational decision sunder such conditions. The Rebels formed their lines of march and as they were moving out it began to rain heavily. Zollicoffer and his 4,000 men now headed towards Logan's Crossroads. Zollicoffer's men slowly made it down the narrow, twisting road, surrounded by dense woods. Unbeknownst to the Confederates, some of Schoeph's troops had arrived and reinforced the Union troops which now numbered around 4,000 men. [48]

On January 19th, just shortly after daybreak, the Rebel cavalry under Sander's attacked the 10th Indiana and Wolford's 1st Kentucky Cavalry (U. S). Sergeant George Thrasher, Company C, 1st Kentucky fired the first shots of the battle. Lt. Jonathan Miller, Company H was sent to support Company C. and was mortally wounded. Union pickets began to retire to a house west of the Mill Springs Road and opened up on the approaching Rebels. Zollicoffer placed his skirmishers and formed his brigade for an attack. The 15th Mississippi drove the Union pickets from the house and ran to the east side of Mill Springs Road, taking cover behind a fence. The 15th Mississippi under Walthall came across an unknown unit in the mist and fog. Walthall cried who is was and the other unit gave out the secret password "Kentucky". Walthall thought it was a friendly unit, but it was the 1st Kentucky Cavalry. A rain of fire came down on Walthall's men, but he managed to escape. Walthall along with the Battle's 20th Tennessee attacked the Yankees and they fell back. Col. Cummings of the 19th Tennessee moved up the west side of the road, then crossed to form a front with Walthall and Battle. The Confederates overran the 1st Kentucky Cavalry's camp, pushed their way over the fence, and ended up into William Logan's cornfield. The Rebels were now on the edge of the 10th Indiana's camp. [49]

Rain, fog, smoke all added to the "Fog of War". It was very difficult to make out which side was which. The heaviest part of the battle was now raging in a cornfield. The Rebels took cover in a deep ravine southeast of the field, the Federals took refuge behind a fence to the northwest. Wolford's dismounted cavalry and Speed Fry's 4th Kentucky Infantry rallied their men and kept back the Confederate advance. Thomas now arrived on the field and directed movements, taking a position near the intersection of Mill Springs and Somerset roads. Fry began to counterattack, driving the Confederates back across Logan's field, over the branch and up the hillside. The 4th Kentucky reached a fence to take cover. Both sides hammered away at each other. At 7:00 A.M. Fry moved beyond a fence up the hill and into a clump of trees. At the same time, Zollicoffer also rode to a clump of trees. He was nearsighted and rode up to a Union officer. The officer was none other than Col. Speed Fry. Zollicoffer thought that the 19th Tennessee was firing on their own men. He ordered the 19th Tennessee to seize fire and rode to the Yankee officer on the crest of the hill. Zollicoffer pointed to the 4th Kentucky and yelled at Fry "those are our men!" Suddenly a Rebel officer rode up and screamed, "General, it's the enemy!" Fry immediately rode down the hill but turned and fired his pistol. The entire line of the 4th Kentucky fired a volley at Zollicoffer. Zollicoffer, who was clad in a white raincoat, fell from his horse dead. Major H. M. R. Fogg, Zollicoffer's aide, also fell from his horse with a mortal wound. After Zollicoffer was killed, Crittenden took over and rallied his men to attack. Crittenden's men were armed with flintlock rifles that didn't shoot well in the rain, and his men began to retreat. The Federals were equipped with percussion capped rifles. Union counterattacks on the Confederate right, led by Col. Samuel P. Carter's brigade, and the left, led by the 9th Ohio Infantry, were successful, forcing the Confederates from the field. Crittenden never deployed two Confederate regiments. [50]

By 9:00 A.M. the battle was still raging where Zollicoffer had fallen, but the Confederates were now only holding back the Yankees. Thomas moved the 2nd Minnesota into the Union center to relieve the exhausted 4th Kentucky and 10th Indiana. Union artillery from Ohio, under Kenney, now fired fifty six rounds into the Confederate line. Standart's 1st Ohio battery also began to rain down death upon the field. They fired an additional twenty rounds. [51]

The 9th Ohio Infantry now moved through a field and into the woods west of the Mill Springs Road and flanked Carroll's brigade. The Confederate left now collapsed. The 2nd Minnesota attacked the Confederate center, and Battle's and Walthall's troops began to leave the field. Lt. Balie Peyton, Company A, 20th Tennessee tried to rally his men, but they fled fro the field. Peyton charged the Union lines with his revolver firing round after round. He fell dead

19

immediately from a hail of fire. Crittenden ordered a withdrawal and had to abandon twelve cannon and large quantities of stores in Beech Grove, and then crossed the Cumberland River by the use of the Noble Ellis, which was a boat provided to Crittenden by General Albert Sidney Johnston. Crittenden headed toward Knoxville. Crittenden lost 439 men, Federal losses were 232. The Battle of Mill Springs, along with one at Middle Creek, broke whatever Confederate strength there was in eastern Kentucky. This battle now exposed Confederate General Albert Sidney Johnston's right line. Mill Springs was less than eight miles from Bowling Green. [52]

News of the disasters had already reached the Rangers. Private Cyrus Love wrote home to his parents that *"about 27,000 of them (the Northern forces) have taken Murray in Tennessee (actually Kentucky) and it appears are getting in the rear of Fort Henry. There is hardly any doubt now of their having whipped Crittenden and Zollicoffer up in the mountains of East Ky. And that they the last that was heard of them were retreating towards Knoxville, Tenn and that the enemy were possibly in Tenn in pursuit of them."*[53]

During the month of January the Rangers had been patrolling constantly for a month. The men and horses were worn down and rendered unfit for further service. The Rangers had lost their beloved Colonel Terry, Lt. Col. Lubbock and Major Harrison were sick, and the half of the Captains and other Commissioned officers were also down with illnesses. The Rangers had to be reorganized. General Albert Sidney Johnston ordered the Rangers to retire from active service for two weeks to rest and reorganize. The Rangers moved to Oakland Grove, which was near Woodburn twelve miles west of Bowling Green. The Rangers took only their clothes on their backs, forty rounds of ammunition, coffee pot and frying pans. They camped at Oakland Grove for three weeks. Frank Batchelor commented that after the three weeks were up, the Rangers looked worse as well as wear. They were "a hard looking set." Frank described the camp at Oakland Grove consisting of tall red oaks, the trees break off the wind, and *"we brake off the limbs, to warm out limbs, and keep timber...The ground is rolling and picturesque and a fine bold spring rises about fifty yards from our line of tents, but the most favorable item to us, in relation to camp, is plenty of oats and corn for our jaded horses."*[54] While at Oakland Grove the Rangers were called out for General Inspection and dress parade, which took place every two months. Since all of the officers were sick, a Colonel of the Regular Confederate army was sent to superintend the function. Frank Batchlor said that *"if there is anything that a Texan Ranger hates particularly it is a man in Uniform and the Colonel's appearance on the field was the signal for all sorts of squibs at his expense; he had not gone far with the inspection when a man let his thumb slip from the hammer of his gun and sent a bullet whizzing close to his ears, another spurred his horse who sprang forward and nearly unseated him, another wanted to bet a brass button, "as big as the Colonel's" that he could rope his plume and these pleasantries made the inspection quite brief and the officers disgust was profound when upon the announcement of "Dismissal" the battalion set up a hideous "Yell" and pell mell, helter skelter for camps they charged leaping log fences and ditches on the way; in less than three minutes "brass buttons" was the only horsemen on the ground."*[55] Frank Batchelor reported that his company was reduced to sixty eight men, nine died, and eighteen had been discharged.

During the month of January Union forces under General Ulysses Grant started to move on Fort Henry. Fort Henry was located on the Tennessee River between Columbus and Bowling Green. Johnston immediately sent eight thousand men under John B. Floyd and Buckner to Fort Henry and Donelson.

On February 1st, 1862 the Rangers camped at Bell Station, Kentucky. The Rangers scouted in the direction of the Green River, intending to go to Rowlett's Station, but came upon some Union pickets two miles of Horse Cave and six miles from Rowlett's Station. Small detachments of three were sent out to the right and left to ascertain the strength and purpose. The scouts returned and reported the Union strength at eight hundred. On the Rangers approach five hundred Union infantry were thrown into a thick timber, while three hundred cavalry took position to cut off the Rangers retreat and then they stood waiting for the Rangers advance. The Rangers had only two companies, A and C, numbering about fifty six men and quietly withdrew a mile or two and kept the small parties on the hills watching their progress until nightfall, when the Yankees counter marched and returned to Woodsonville on the River. Batchelor assumed that the Union force was sent to protect their men who were busy repairing the Turnpike and Railroad torn up by General Hindman. [56]

While the Rangers were near Munfordville, Kentucky, J. B. Seawell, of the 4th Tennessee Cavalry relates a story about Private Charley Howard, of Terry's Texas Rangers. Howard was as familiar with the use of a lasso as he was with a revolver, and was an expert with both. He was out foraging, and riding carelessly along a country road. Suddenly there sprang up before him a Dutchman, who shouted: "Halt-surrender, got dam." Taken completely by surprise, and with the Dutchman's bayonet at his breast, there was nothing to do but surrender. "Now, down on der ground dot gun trow, and dose peestols trow down, too, got dam." Down went the carbine and pistols. "Now git you back some." As Charley reined his horse back, and the Dutchman stooped to pick up the weapons, he got out his lasso, and instantly out it spun, settling around the Ducthman's neck. Putting spurs to his horse at the same instant, poor Dutchy was jerked off his feet, and dragged some hundred yards before he realized what had happened to him. Not wishing to strangle his enemy, Charley stopped his horse and gave the Dutchman time to breathe, at which he blurted out, "Mein Got in himmel, dot vas no vay to fight mit von tam rope." "Well, Mr. Dutchy," replied Charley, "you have had your 'lead', it is now my 'deal'." Recovering his arms, and the Ducthman's as well, he drove the latter into camp at the end of a lasso. As this was among the first Federal prisoners captured, nearly as great excitement was created as if an elephant had been bagged.

During the night the Rangers traveled ten miles to Bear Wallow, Kentucky and came back through the town of Horse Cave, gathering intelligence of the Union force's visit from the citizens of the town. Batchelor said that the Rangers had just learned of Zollicoffer's death and defeat at Mill Springs. The Federals sent word to the Confederates that Zollicoffer's body and that of Bolie Peyton would be delivered to the Confederates under a flag of truce at Woodsonville by 4 P.M. General Hindman immediately started forty men from the Regiment to meet them before they passed the Confederate's outside pickets knowing they would improve the occasion to see their position and defenses. The men from the regiment arrived at twelve midnight and found the Union escort, thirty in all, three miles from Horse Cave. They were halted there and kept waiting until General Hindman and staff, and Colonel Wharton and five Captains of the regiment came up. According to Batchelor, a friendly conversation was carried on between the regiment's officers and the Union officers for about an hour. Several sharp cuts and repartees passed between the officers, one of which was from Union General Lewis Johnson and Capt Evans. Johnson said: "You see captain that our Government is generous in their sending the body of your General. "Yes" returned Mark Evans, but you shall find us not behind in courtesy. I hope we shall soon have the opportunity of returning the like kindness!" Speaking of the ability of their government to crush the rebellion Mark Evans asked General Johnson why they did not come down in force and test the strength of the armies in this part of Kentucky. Johnson replied "We are waiting till fully prepared and when so, we will come in a hurry." "Yes" replied Mark Evans, "you will rush down in a hurry, and like the herd of swine the Devils will get into you and you'll never get back again." [57]

The Rangers camp was ten miles from Mammoth Cave, Kentucky and some of the Rangers rode to the town and found the Hotel closed and all the valuables carried two or three miles into the cave. The proprietor was a Union sympathizer and the Rangers helped themselves freely to the liquor, cutlery, bedding, and cooking utensils. While the men were gathering up their booty they heard firing on the river and rushed out supposing that a Union force was upon them. Upon closer inspection it was Conf. Col. John Hunt Morgan's cavalry shooting at a body of Federals on the opposite side of the river. [58]

On February 4th, 1862, Frank Batchelor wrote about the frustration that many Confederate soldiers had with Kentucky. On November 16th, 1861 in Russellville, Kentucky, a convention was held to compose delegates from the counties within the Confederate line. The session was held three days and adopted an ordinance of secession and a provisional state government. George W. Johnson, of Scott County, Kentucky was elected Governor. The Confederate Congress admitted the State as a member of the Confederacy on December 10th, 1861.[59] Batchelor would have supposed that since Kentucky had a Confederate Governor the young men of Kentucky would have flocked to Brig. General John C. Breckinridge's standard by the thousands, but the months had gone by and General John C. Breckinridge was ten miles below the Rangers with no more than four thousand troops and no more recruits coming in, while on the other hand twenty eight regiments from Kentucky swell the Union ranks. Batchelor said that the only way that the Confederates are going to win the war was through guerilla warfare. "*In this way a large part of our fighting men would sustain themselves and lessen government expenses, it would change the burden to the shoulders of the scoundrels who conceived this war, and prove a great stimulus to the daring men of our Army and throw terror into the enemy's camp. In a country like Kentucky one Regiment cut up into small bands-say 30 strong-would do more execution than ten regiments moving in a body. they could wear an army out in short time by stealing upon them at midnight shooting pickets and throwing their army into alarm. In this our Regiment annoyed the Yankee army-20,000 strong-for more than a month, besides killing quite a number."* He knew that was going to be a *"severe and prolonged one."*[60]

On February 7th, Johnston next line of defense would collapse in the Western half of the state. Grant's gunboats under Andrew Foote captured Fort Henry and the commander of Fort Henry, Confederate General Lloyd Tilghman surrendered. Johnston sent General Pillow with four thousand men on February 9th to Fort Donelson. On February 12th, General Floyd and Buckner, with eight thousand men were also sent to Fort Doneslon. On February 11th, 1862, General Albert Sidney Johnston knew that Fort Donelson was doomed. With the depletion of his forces in Bowling Green and the necessity to protect Nashville, Johnston decided to pull out of Bowling Green, and fall back to Nashville, Tennessee. Frank Batchelor described the scene as they were pulling out of Bowling Green: *"On the morning of the 12 instant we were aroused at 3 A.M. and told to cook two days provisions and be ready to march at daylight none knew our destination, but having heard the enemy was advancing by flank movement through Glasgow (Kentucky) we supposed we were going out with Generals Hindman and Breckinridge's brigades to engage them-Great was our surprise when formed on the Turnpike to receive orders to march to Bowling Green for we then thought the enemy must be advancing on that place-we arrived at the first Fort about 4 P.M. to our utter astonishment found it was dismantled and that the city would be evacuated, in fact, that all troops had been withdrawn leaving us the rear guard. We rested there two days while the frequent scream of the cars told the rapid movement of cannon and public stores. A severe snow storm raged all the time and finally rendered the rail road impassable leaving the streets choked up with government and private stores. "*[61]

On February 14th, Grant attacked Fort Donelson first with his gunboats, but the gunboats took several hits, so it was up to Grant's infantry to attack the Fort. A fierce battle raged for several hours between both sides. General Nathan Bedford Forrest had secured a escape route, but Confederate General Gideon Pillow ordered a withdrawal back into the Fort.

On the night of February 15th, Confederate Generals John Floyd, with Pillow's approval, decided to surrender the Fort, but neither wanted to surrender so they appointed Confederate General Simeon Bolivar Buckner to do the actual surrender. Floyd and Pillow along with 2,500 men, escaped in boats, while Forrest and his cavalry left by the backwaters.

Meanwhile back in Bowling Green on the 15th, the Rangers received orders to march and had barely gotten into their saddles when the pickets came *"dashing in and reported the enemy planting cannon to shell the city, in a few minutes more and when within a half a miles to town the Yankees opened fire; they saw our advancing column and threw shells and balls like hail at us. Some busted high above our heads others barely passed over our heads making the air whir with the sound of rushing iron-two buildings were struck within 30 or 40 yards of us but not a man was hit except Generals Hindman's aide de camp, who lost one ear and was wounded in the arm. The bridges had been fired at daylight, but a courier reported the enemy crossing the river on pontoon bridges, our Regiment was thrown out to intercept and beat them back and we held this position with orders to charge them for about three hours while the infantry and trains left the city in the rear. Wagons were furiously driving through the streets strewing lose baggage as they went-foot soldiers going almost in a run,, even the sick pale and haggard with fear striving to keep up with the retreating army; but the most distressing sight of all was that of women ringing their hands or rushing through the streets carrying their little ones in their arms. Every kind of conveyance from carriages to carts were crowded with fugitive citizens who fled as from prisons. The roaring cannon and whizzing balls had no terror to us then for our hearts rung with anguish at the grief of the helpless, and no force could have driven us back from them. The enemy surveyed our position and did not deem it prudent to advance but continued the cannonade. At 4 P.M. the citizens had got out of the city and our last train passed out when we went to the Railroad depot, and public buildings and set them on fire agreeable to Generals Johnston's orders and retired in good order.* [62]

On February 16th, Fort Donelson fell to Grant's army. Kentucky and Tennessee west of the Cumberland Mountains were open to invasion by the Union forces. The last of his defense line had crumbled before General Albert Sidney Johnson's eyes. He had lost the Cumberland Gap

Early Beginnings

with the battle of Mill Springs, and then Forts Henry and Donelson. It was time to pull his remaining troops out of Columbus, located in western Kentucky protecting the Mississippi River.

The Rangers, who were under Hindman's brigade, fell back to Nashville without incident.

The Rangers were camped around Nashville, when they learned the news that Fort Donelson had surrendered. They were immediately ordered down toward Donelson to cover the retreat of the army leaving Fort Donelson. They were to guard in that direction and to provide protection for the men trying to escape and make their way south. Batchelor described the scene: *"Next morning at 3 A.M. were directed to load our arms, put some provisions in our haversacks and be ready to start at day light. We obeyed with alacrity supposing the enemy had appeared and that the battle would begin that morning-All along the road to Nashville the troops cheered us as we passed calling out-"give them h_ll boys we'll be with you in a short time." In the city our welcome was a perfect ovation-ladies from balconies and windows waived their handkerchiefs and cheered us as we pranced along proud of the honor of opening (as we supposed) the fight. I noticed some grey haired matrons who alternately wept cheered and prayed saying: " go on brave Texans and may God preserve your lives; but never, never surrender." " "We continued the march for six miles when the object of our mission began to appear. It was to cover the retreat of our troops that had escaped from Fort Donelson.-When the Fort was about to be surrendered General Floyd determined to save his Brigade and instructed the Cavalry to cut their way through the enemy's lines while with a steamer he crossed his Infantry over the river and told them to scatter and make their way best they could to Nashville where he could join them. We continued toward the Fort 40 miles to the Town of "Charlotte" and stayed there till the last of the Infantry came in, then collected all stray horses and mules owned by the government and returned to this place, covering the retreat of the stragglers and carrying the weary on our horses behind us. We have been for days in the cold drenching rain without tents, but stood it very well."*[63] The Rangers returned to their army in Nashville, but found Union General Don Carlos Buell's army was hot on the trail of Johnston's army, and Johnston had to leave the city. If it weren't for the quick thinking of General Nathan Bedford Forrest's cavalry many of the ammunition arsenals, and supplies such as uniforms, rifles, and food would have been captured by Union General Don Carlos Buell's army.

The Rangers found the main Confederate army at Murfreesboro, Tennessee, but the Rangers, along with Johnston's army, continued to move onto Shelbyville, Huntsville, and Decatur, finally arriving at Corinth, Mississippi. The Rangers were the rear guard for the army. On the way to Corinth, Tom Harrison again fell out of disfavor with his men. Harrison came across two men who had not gotten permission to go into town, and he ordered them to return to camp immediately. They refused. When he returned to camp he ordered the men to be arrested by the guard and placed on the Shelbyville pike, and put to marking time. As the story goes, friends of the two men were furious at Harrison, and one of them went to the two offenders and led them back to camp, telling them that no such disgraceful punishment should be inflicted on them. Major Harrison let the incident pass. But the men would not let it go. Every time Harrison would pass by the men he would get a angry look. Harrison lost his temper. He turned to the crowd of men and yelled out, "Is there an officer of my regiment present who will execute my orders?" Lieutenant S. P. Christian of Company K, stepped out and said: "Major, I will." then Harrison ordered him to take a group of men and get the two men and bring them back and set them again to their punishment. The friends of the two men, who were being punished, were not so bold as to defy the authority of Harrison and Lt. Christian outright. Things quieted down but they didn't forget what Harrison did to the two men. Harrison was now known by his nickname "Mark Time Major".

[1] Texas State Archives: Memorial and Biographical History of McLennan, Falls, Bell and Coryell Counties, Texas, 1893
[2] Ibid.
[3] Ibid.
[4] Terry Texas Rangers, Lester Fitzhugh, 1958
[5] Ibid.
[6] Ibid.
[7] Series I-Vol. II The Bull Run or Manassas Campaign, Va. No. 100 Report of Gen. James Longstreet, C. S., commanding the 4th Brigade
[8] Terry's Texas Rangers, A.P. Harcourt, Southern Bivouac, P.89
[9] Terry's Texas Rangers, Leonidas Giles; The Civil War Letters of J. W. Rabb

[10] Terry Texas Rangers, Lester Fitzhugh, 1958
[11] Confederate Military History, P. 19-29
[12] Ibid. P. 29-48
[13] Ibid.
[14] Ibid.
[15] Ibid.
[16] Ibid.
[17] Ibid.
[18] August 14th, 1861, Terry's Ranging Regiment, Weekly Telegraph, Houston, Texas.
[19] The Civil War Letters of J. W. Rabb
[20] The Civil War Letters of C. W. Love, May Counts Burnett Library, Special Collections
[21] Sensations in Kentucky Backwoods, Ward McDonald, Captain 4th Alabama Cavalry, Confederate Veteran. P. 143
[22] Ibid. P. 143
[23] O.R. Series I-vol. IV Chapter XII Correspondence, Orders & Returns Relating Specially to Operations in Kentucky, Tennessee, from July 1 to November 19, 1861. Confederate Correspondence, Etc. #4
[24] Ibid.
[25] Ibid.
[26] Ibid.
[27] Early Battles in Kentucky: The Road to Shiloh, P. 48-49, 52-57, 78-88, 90-101; Civil War Cards The Battle of Fort Henry and Fort Donelson; Civil War Sites Advisory Commission Reports: Fort Henry & Donelson.
[28] Ibid.
[29] Ibid.
[30] Ibid.
[31] Ibid.
[32] Confederate Military History
[33] O.R. Series I-vol. VII December 17, 1861, Action at Rowlett's Station, (Woodsonville} Green River, Ky. No. 3 Col. August Willich, 32nd Indiana, No. 4 Brig. Gen. Thomas Hindman, C. S. Army, with congratulatory orders from Major Gen. Hardee.
[34] Ibid.
[35] The Batchelor-Turner Letters, P. 2-3
[36] Ibid. P. 3-4
[37] Navarro College, The Pearce Civil War Letters Collection, The Isaac Fulkerson Letters
[38] Anecdotes, Poetry, and Incidents of the Civil War: The Civil War in Song and Story, 1860-1865, p. 252
[39] Ibid. P. 252
[40] Ibid. P. 252-253
[41] Ibid. 253
[42] The Batchelor-Turner Letters, P. 1
[43] Ibid. P.7
[44] Ibid. P. 10
[45] Ibid. P. 11
[46] Civil War Letters of C. W. Love, Mary Counts Burnett Library, Special Collections.
[47] Blue & Gray Magazine, The Battle of Mill Springs, p. 13-52; Civil Battles of the Western Theater, P. 19-20
[48] Ibid.
[49] Ibid.
[50] Ibid.
[51] Ibid.
[52] Ibid.
[53] The Civil War Letters of C. W. Love, Mary Counts Burnett Library, Special Collections.
[54] Batchelor-Turner Letters
[55] Ibid. P. 7-8
[56] Ibid. P. 14
[57] Ibid. P. 14
[58] Ibid. P. 15
[59] Confederate Military History
[60] The Batchelor- Turner Letters, P. 16
[61] Ibid. P. 19
[62] Ibid. P. 19-20
[63] Ibid. P. 2

Chapter 2:
The Battle of Shiloh

During the months of March and the early part of April 1862, Terry's Texas Rangers relaxed at Corinth, Mississippi while Confederate General Albert Sidney Johnston reorganized his forces. Some additional recruits from Texas arrived, including Clinton Terry, younger brother of Ben Terry. Private Cyrus Love wrote home to his parents on April 1, 1861 while in Corinth, Mississippi of the events taking place. "*I have learned from men just from Texas that there are reported to be upwards of hundred of the enemy's gun boats inside of the bar at the mouth of the Mississippi and that the troops on the other side of the river at New Orleans had been immediately put over on this side-they bring also the news that all of the troops on our coast had been ordered to Missouri and that new troops were being raised to supply their places. Our forces burned all the bridges on the R.R. down to their present position which is said to be a much better one than formerly occupied. The bridges all along down from Nashville to the Cumberland Gap have also been burnt. There will no doubt be a tremendous fight near here in a few days. The rangers were on scout day before yesterday and got back yesterday. They saw movements on the part of the enemy but do not know they were advancing this way but suppose they were. They heard cannon firing all day yesterday which they thought were from the enemy's gunboats-I myself heard a cannon two or three times yesterday evening about dark and took them to be cannon of a land battery if so the enemy are in a few miles of us or were the cannon fired-let all this be as it may there is no doubt we are on the point of fighting a great battle.*"[1] Private Love couldn't have been more correct in his assumptions. The Battle of Shiloh was about to take place.

Once Fort Henry and Fort Donelson had been taken, General Ulysses Grant was free to move into Tennessee. Grant's army arrived at Pittsburgh Landing in March 1862. Union General Henry Halleck, commander of all forces in the West, ordered Union General Don Carlos Buell's army at Nashville to join Grant at Pittsburg Landing, and then to attack Corinth, Mississippi. Confederate General Albert Sidney Johnston concentrated his forces at Corinth to oppose Grant. By the end of March, he had 44,000 men, commanded by Lt. Gen. Leondias Polk, Maj. Gen. John Breckinridge, Gen. Braxton Bragg and Maj. Gen. William Hardee. They would be facing Ulysses Grant's 39,000 men. Johnston knew that he must attack Grant before Buell's 36,000 men reached Pittsburg Landing. Grant was not expecting an attack, so no defensive plans were formulated and no trenches or earthworks were dug. Sherman set up his headquarters at a place called Shiloh church. Since Grant assumed that there would be no attack, he placed Sherman's raw recruits in the advance position. [2]

On April 3rd, Wharton was ordered forward by General Albert Sidney Johnston to scout on the road from Monterey to Savannah between Mickey's and it's intersection with the Pittsburg-Purdy road. They were to "annoy and harass any force of the enemy moving by the latter way to assail Cheatham's division at Purdy." [3]

Before Confederate General Leonidas Polk left Corinth for Shiloh, he paid the Rangers a visit. The Rangers cheered Johnston and he was moved to say a couple of words. He told the Rangers that "with a little more drill you are the equals of the 'Old Guard' of Napoleon."[4]

On April 4th, the Rangers reached the front at Shiloh and were ordered to guard the left wing of the army. In detachments, the Rangers guarded every road, trail, and opening around the whole left front, and flank with strict orders that none of them were to be allowed to sleep at all. Soon after nightfall, it began to rain. It poured down in torrents, and the night was pitch black. It was a long dreary night, but the morning was bright and sunny. Col. Wharton gave one man permission to discharge his wet gun. To his amazement the whole regiment had wet guns, and they all went off. General Leonidas Polk quickly rushed a brigade of infantry over from their hiding place to discover if the Federal army had been alerted. Luckily Grant's green troops headed no alert to the firing. Polk arrested the entire regiment. [5]

Because of the rain, and a lost division under Confederate General Braxton Bragg, Johnston was not able to reach Pittsburg Landing until April 6th. Johnston's troops were now less than two miles from the Federal camps. [6]

At 5:00 A.M. on Sunday morning, April 6, 1862, Johnston gave the order to attack. The battle began when Union Major James Powell of the 25th Missouri and three hundred men scouted the area, and collided with Confederate Major Aaron Hardcastle's 3rd Mississippi Infantry Battalion, the advance guard of Wood's brigade, Hardee's Corps in Fraley field. The Confederates began to fire, and the Federals under Powell stood their ground as reinforcements were brought up. Jesse Appler of the 53rd Ohio, deployed his men, but soon fell back before the massive Confederate onslaught. He called up Col. Hildebrand's brigade, and the battle was now escalating.

The Rangers would do most of their fighting on April 6th on the Sowell and Jones fields, which was the position held by Union Generals William T. Sherman and James McClernand.

At 8:00 A.M. the Rangers, along with the 38th Tennessee Infantry, the Crescent Regiment, and a section of Ketchum's artillery were instructed by General P. G. T. Beauregard to protect the left flank of the army. Terry's Rangers rode to the bridge across Owl Creek, near Hurly's, on the Purdy and Pittsburg road. Clinton Terry, and J. M. Weston were sent to Beauregard to inform him of their position, and to receive orders for further movements. The order was given to cross Owl Creek. The 16th and 18th Louisiana, Orleans Guard Battalion, and the remaining guns of Ketchum's battery moved toward the Shiloh Branch, with the Rangers protecting their front and flank. General Ruggles ordered to advance the entire line. The brigade moved forward in double columns, over difficult ground, trying to stay in contact with General Anderson's brigade and guard the flank on Owl Creek. After advancing six hundred yards the brigade was halted near some houses, with a large field on the left and a field in the front. Union skirmishers were seen towards Owl Creek, and Col. Looney's regiment, with a section of Captain Ketchum's battery, were sent to the left, and ordered to command Owl Creek road. Col. Looney sent word back that the Yankees were ambushed in his front, so the Crescent Regiment, under Col. M. J. Smith, was sent to report to Col. Looney. Two sections of Ketchum's battery was ordered to Col. Pond, jr.. Ketchum took charge of this battery with four pieces leaving the third section with Lt. Bond. [7]

Hardee sent a message for the left to advance. The 16th and 18th Louisiana Infantry and the Orleans Guards advanced until they reached the line occupied by the Second Brigade, commanded by Gen. Anderson, which was already engaging the Union troops in their camp. The Union camp was taken and the whole line advanced through a narrow strip of woods and across a field until they reached the Union main and last camp, which was already abandoned. As they approached this camp a few of the Yankees were seen on their left, who fired a few rounds at them. Ketchum's artillery had arrived and unlimbered. They fired at the log house, in which the Yankees were firing from and dispersed them. When Col. Preston Pond, Jr.'s Third Brigade entered the edge of the field in which their main camp was situated they saw what they thought was the entire Union army in retreat on their right. The left of Pond's brigade was ordered forward and the whole brigade was marched at the double quick to cut the fleeing Yankees off, but when they were almost across the field a deadly fire fell upon Pond's right, killing and severely wounding several members of the 18th Louisiana, under Col. Mouton.[8]

The brigade was halted and retreated one hundred yards to the edge of the woods. When the Confederate troops on the right advanced across the opening Pond's brigade also advanced, passed through the main camp, and through a deep ravine. At this time Pond's brigade was moving a little in advance of the front line, which was commanded by General William Hardee.[9]

Upon rising the crest of the hill the brigade encountered a heavy firing of grape shot about four hundred yards away. The brigade fell back under the cover of the hill, and Captain Ketchum's battery was placed on the hills to the rear, to silence the Union guns. While waiting for Captain Ketchum's battery to get into position, Pond reconnoitered and found the Yankees in a camp some two hundred yards to his front and left, and in another camp immediately to his front and right, from which the fire of the Union battery was coming from. Hardee rode up and ordered

Ketchum to the left. On arriving at an eminence on the road, commanding a camp on the right of the one they had just shelled, they found the Yankees in large force, and the woods in the gorge below, between his battery and the camp, filled with sharpshooters. Some of the Texas Rangers, who directed Ketchum, lost four or five men from these sharpshooters while pointing out the Union position. Ketchum opened fire on the camp, advising the Rangers to dismount and enter the woods as skirmishers, while Ketchum shelled the camp. [10]

At 4 P.M. Col. Ferguson brought a order to charge the Union battery with his brigade. The Washington Artillery was brought up and placed to the right of the Union infantry's main camp and tried to silence the Union guns, but failed to do so.[11]

General Hardee ordered Pond to move up a deep ravine, in a direction flanking the Union battery, and while the head of the column was some three hundred yards in front of the battery, he ordered a charge. Pond's brigade was raked by cannon fire and his troops fell back from the destructive fire.[12]

The 18th Louisiana suffered the most in the charge. As Pond's troops were advancing to charge they again received fire from his own troops on the right, which, added to the fire of the

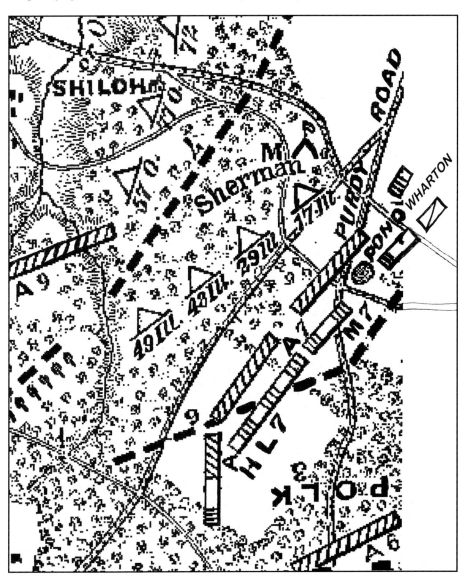

Yankees, almost disorganized the entire command. In order to reform, Pond was compelled to fall back one hundred and fifty yards to the Yankee's main camp, where he was joined by Col. Looney with his regiment. Looney had been ordered to leave his position on Owl Creek road and unite with Pond. The camp on Pond's right was abandoned and occupied by Confederate troops. The Yankees by this time had withdrawn their battery. [13]

Pond heard firing on the right of the Union camp, in which the 38th Tennessee was engaged before it united with the brigade. The camp on Pond's left continued to be occupied in considerable force, and as the duty of guarding the left was placed in his hands, and being separated about a quarter mile from the force immediately on his right, he concluded that any rash advance might result in the exposure of the Confederate left and rear, and no attack was made on it. Pond stopped his attack and fell back, resting his right on the Union main camp and extending his left to Owl Creek. [14]

After protecting Ketchum's battery, Wharton was ordered by General William Hardee, who was in command of the left flank, to pursue the Union troops and intercept their retreat. Wharton ordered his men to mount. Wharton rode through Sowell Field and toward the northwest corner of Jones Field. Wharton pursued what he thought was the fleeing enemy, but as soon as he had ridden no more than three yards, a heavy fire erupted from a large Union force who laid in ambush, and opened up on Terry's Rangers. Having been forced to cross a ravine in single file, the rear of Wharton's cavalry was four yards away. Wharton and about twenty others who were in front of the column, received the fire of Union troops no more than forty yards away, and positioned at right angles. The Federal fire raked the Rangers from one end to the other. Five of Wharton's men were killed and twenty six were wounded, including Wharton, who was shot in the leg and had his horse hit three times. Wharton decided to ride two hundred yards, formed his men, and dismounted. The Confederate infantry in his rear were ordered forward, and after a severe struggle, the Union troops were driven back. Wharton then quickly rode to the extreme left, where Ketchum's Confederate battery was exposed, with no support. Wharton told his men to dismount and help the Confederate battery. Wharton advanced his men towards the Union troops who were advancing on the helpless battery. Having five companies, Wharton threw them at the enemy as skirmishers. The Yankees were driven back to their camps. After the battle, Wharton and his men encamped upon the extreme left, near Ketchum's battery which they helped to protect. Wharton threw out a heavy picket.[15]

While Wharton was protecting Ketchum's Alabama battery and protecting Col. Preston Pond Jr.'s Third Brigade, on the Confederate left, the battle was raging on all around them. Earlier that day Confederate General Patrick Cleburne advanced his 2nd Brigade, under Hardee's Third Corps, his goal was to seize the crossroads at Shiloh church. Confederate General Braxton Bragg, commander of the 2nd Corps, moved up to support William Hardee. Grant now called for Union General Don Carlos Buell's Army of the Ohio, who had arrived in Savannah the day before, and were on the east bank of the river. Grant also called for Lew Wallace's Third Division to get his men ready to move out. At 9:00 A.M., Grant rode from his headquarters to the front. By 10:00 A.M., the Confederates had driven through the camps of three Union divisions, sending the surprised blue-clad soldiers reeling back toward the river. Union General Benjamin M. Prentiss's division was pushed back almost a mile. The Confederates now stopped at Prentiss' camp and began to eat the food that Prentiss's men had been cooking for their breakfast. This gave Prentiss time to take up a good defensive position on high ground along a sunken road. About 1,000 men formed along the road, which was about a mile behind their original position. Other units formed on either side of Prentiss: General Stephen Hurlbut sent two brigades on his left, and W. H. L. Wallace aligned three brigades on Prentiss flanks, two on Prentiss right and one to his far left, beyond Hurlbut. Union Gen. Ulysses Grant looked over the new line and ordered Prentiss to "maintain that position at all hazards."[16]

General Benjamin Cheatham's Second Division, Polk's First Corps, now advanced upon the new Federal line, and when they came within one hundred and fifty yards, the Federals unleashed their artillery. At thirty yards, Union Col. William Shaw and his 14th Iowa, fired at the oncoming Confederates. The Confederate line fell back. On Cheatham's extreme right, Union Brig. Gen. Jacob Lauman's brigade of Hurlbut's division, took on the Confederates. His men opened fire on the Rebels at one hundred yards, but the Confederates approached until they were within ten yards of the 31st Indiana before they were stopped. The Rebel troops under Braxton Bragg continued crashing and screaming through the woods, toward the Federal position. Bragg ordered the 4th, 13th, and the 19th Louisiana and the 1st Arkansas to attack the Federals on the

The Battle of Shiloh

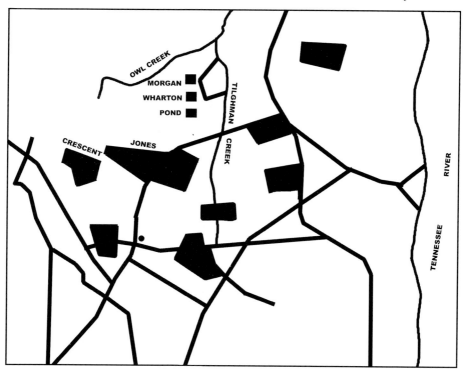

sunken road. Charge after charge, twelve in all, were made against Prentiss position, and each was repulsed with great slaughter. "It's a hornet's nest in there!" cried the Rebels, recoiling from the blasts of canister and case shot and the fire from the 8th Iowa's eight hundred rifles. By 2:30 PM, after two hours of fighting, the Confederates were no closer to taking the Federal lines at the Hornet's Nest than they were at the Sunken Road, and the Confederate onslaught began to grind to a halt. There were massive problems on the field. There was no overall Confederate commander, and no coherent plan of attack. The Confederates had seventeen thousand men against Grant's four thousand men under Prentiss, but the Confederate troops were sent in piecemeal. Orders were given and then countermanded by different generals. At some points along the line Confederate companies halted because there were no further orders for them. Beuregard was in the rear and did not know what was going on at the front and only sent men where he heard fighting. Corps commanders reduced themselves to small unit commanders.[17]

A Confederate attack led by Gen. Albert Sidney Johnston broke through Union troops in the Peach Orchard on Prentiss left, led by the Kentucky troops under Gen. John C. Breckinridge, and the Rebels pushed back the troops on his right, leaving what was left of Prentiss's division without support. Johnston led the Kentucky Confederate troops toward the Peach Orchard, but about half way there he was struck in the leg by a bullet that severed a major artery and the blood was flowing into his boot. Johnston soon became disoriented and dismounted. Johnston had a field tourniquet in his pocket, but his officer's didn't know how to use it, and earlier in the battle he had sent his personal surgeon, Dr. Yandell away to tend to the wounded soldiers. General Johnston soon bled to death.[18]

After Albert Sidney Johnston's death, Gen. P. G .T. Beuregard took command of the Rebel forces. Beuregard now was obsessed with the Hornet's Nest also. He could have gone to the flanks, and driven the Federals right into the river at Pittsburg Landing, but he chose not to. Beuregard soon massed the largest assembly of cannon in the war up to that point, 62 in all, and he aimed them at point blank range at the Hornet's Nest and the Sunken Road. At about 4:00 PM, he began a bombardment with shell and canister that was like "a mighty hurricane sweeping everything before it." The Hornet's Nest exploded under the fire, but still Prentiss and his men held on, their lines bending back into a horseshoe shape as more and more pressure was applied to their flanks. By 5:30 they were completely surrounded and being attacked on all sides. According to A. P. Harcourt, the Rangers rode away from Owl Creek up a slope, over acres of ground, down the road through lanes of Confederate infantry, around a point of woods into an opening and across a ravine into line, and the regiment confronted the Federal General Prentiss. Separated by a rail fence and half concealed by timber and undergrowth, the Federals under Prentiss used their defense well. Wharton and the two Terry's, which was Terry's son and brother, fell, the last mortally, and thick and fast horses and riders were dropping, when a rush was made forward, and the Federals's front line gave way, followed by the Rangers, who began tearing away and leaping the fence. Just then the Federals opened with grape and canister. The command was now exposed to a brutal fire. But a wild yell and rattle of small arms is heard in the Federal rear. Hardee came charging down. Unable to do any more to obey Grants order to hold his position, Prentiss ordered cease-fire and surrendered his remaining 2,200 men at 6:00 PM. The Rangers escorted General Prentiss and his men to the rear.[19]

Prentiss gallant defense had given Grant the time he needed to construct a new line to the rear. Grant's new line ran inland at a right angle from the river above Pittsburgh Landing northwest toward Owl Creek. The line was three miles long and strongly defended. Col. J.D. Webster grouped cannon on the left of the line while Sherman and McClernand protected a road that ran north parallel to the Tennessee River. Lew Wallace arrived at 7:00 PM and set up at the far right of the new line. Col. Jacob Ammen's brigade, from Buell's corps arrived. The division commander, Brig. Gen. William Nelson and his men followed Ammen's brigade across the river and took their positions on Grant's new line.[20]

The Confederates had been fighting for twelve hours and were exhausted and hungry, having not eaten since 3:00 A.M. that morning. Many of the Confederates refused to go on and sat down in the abandoned Federal camps and began to eat. Most of the Confederates believed they had won a great victory and thought they had beaten most of the Union forces. Bragg and Polk tried to rally the men for one more attack before darkness set in. Bragg, on the left, could only gather Chalmers troops and John Jackson's men, who were already out of ammunition. Bragg's two divisions tried to rush the new line, but Federal artillery ripped Bragg's men to pieces. As twilight settled, Beauregard suspended the assault on the Federals, and recalled Polk and Bragg.[21]

During the night, Confederate Col. Nathan Bedford Forrest's cavalry scouted the Federal lines. Forrest reported to Hardee that Grant now had about forty five thousand men, against their twenty thousand Confederates. Grant decided that he would attack the Confederates the next day.[22]

During the night, Union General Ulysses Grant had been re-enforced by Union Generals Don Carlos Buell, and Lew Wallace, which made Grant's force around 60,000 Union strong.

The next day, Ketchum's battery and the Texas Rangers awoke to a chilled morning. The men had no tents and few if any blankets. A Union battery suddenly opened fire. Ketchum's battery immediately replied. A duel broke out between the artillery teams for half and hour. The Union guns soon found Ketchum's range, and began to shell his position with dead accuracy.

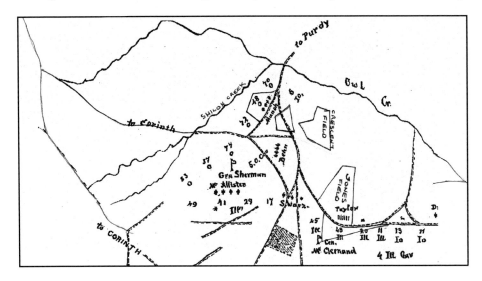

Ketchum fell back one hundred yards. Ketchum again unlimbered and began to shell the Yankee guns, and succeeded in silencing them after another half hour's duel. They then opened upon a body of infantry which appeared near the position occupied by Col. Pond the previous evening. During this engagement, Wharton remained on Ketchum's right, witnessing the artillery duel, and ready to charge the Yankees if any of them were so bold as to take Ketchum's battery. [23]

At this time Ketchum was ordered to fall back. Wharton left Ketchum's battery and was ordered by Confederate General Beauregard to charge the Union right, which was pressing their left heavily. Wharton was compelled to file through some woods down the sides of a ravine. This threw the head of the regiment four hundred yards in advance of the rear. Wharton selected ground upon which to form a charge of the Union right flank, which was stationed in the woods, engaging in a severe struggle on their left. Wharton ascended the ground to command a better view of the ground. He soon found a Union reserve, full two regiments strong, of Thayer's brigade, advancing in line of battle. Thayer's brigade was circling to the right near Sowell's field. These troops were not engaged. When the Union troops saw Wharton's men ascending the hill they let out a murderous fire, killing and wounding many of Wharton's men. Wharton's horse was disabled. Wharton tried to engage the Union reserve, until the rest of his rear could arrive, but his thirty men against a regiment was suicide. Wharton knew that as his rear guard moved up to the hill, they would be in full view of the Union advancing lines and be mowed down, Wharton withdrew a short distance, dismounting the entire regiment, and advanced upon the enemy as skirmishers. Wharton informed Beauregard of the Union reserve, and that his command was fighting them on foot. While fighting, the Confederate left fell back upon Shiloh Church. Wharton withdrew from his position, and fell in with the infantry. Around 3:30 P.M. General Beauregard sent a message to Wharton to move to the right of the Confederate army and support the retreat.[24]

During the day's battle Union General Ulysses S. Grant managed to push the Confederates from the field which they had won just the previous day.

During the evening, Wharton took a position next to Licking Creek, and then finally once night had fallen, Wharton encamped near the Confederate rear, throwing out pickets in connection with Col. Nathan Bedford Forrest, Wirt Adams, and Robert Lindsay. During the two days fighting, Wharton lost Lt. Lowe, and six privates. Four privates were missing, Among the wounded were Col. Wharton himself, Clinton Terry, severely, Capt. R. T. King, Capt. M. L. Rayburn, 2nd Lt. M. L. Gerom, severely, Capt. Cooke, and fifty non-commissioned officers and privates. Total killed, wounded, and missing, sixty six. They lost fifty six horses. On April 6th, Colonel Wharton had received a wound, and turned command over to Major Tom Harrison. Lt. Col. Walker was on sick leave. [25]

On April Eighth, the Confederate army fell back to Corinth, Mississippi. Terry's Rangers were to cover the army's rear. Later that evening, Harrison was informed by Col. Nathan Bedford Forrest's cavalry that a small body of the enemy's cavalry had appeared on his right flank. Major Harrison sent J. K. P. Blackburn to General John C. Breckinridge's Headquarters, who was commanding the rear of the retreating army, to tell Breckinridge that a large body of Yankees were approaching and to ask him for orders or aid. General Breckinridge reply was: "Give Major Harrison my compliments and tell him to hold the enemy back awhile for I can't move from here yet."[26] Blackburn rode back to Harrison to inform him of the message. Harrison proceeded with two hundred and twenty Rangers, accompanied by forty of Col. Forrest's cavalry, to the point occupied by the enemy. Harrison found the enemy in considerable force and did a personal reconnaissance of the enemy's lines. Harrison determined that the enemy had three hundred cavalry, with a line of infantry in it's rear, which Harrison could not determine because of thick brush. Harrison also figured that there were artillery, although it could not be seen. Harrison decided that the position his forces had taken was too dangerous and decided to pull back to a better position. The enemy tried to pass his flank, so Harrison again fell back. Harrison met with Capt. Isaac Harrison of Col. Wirt Adams cavalry, commanding about forty men. Wirt informed Harrison that the his regiment was positioned so that the enemy could not out flank Harrison. Harrison along with Wirt returned to a hospital where they found Col. Forrest commanding his own regiment. Wirt, Forrest, and some Kentucky cavalry under Capt. John Hunt Morgan constituted a force of about three hundred and fifty troopers. Forrest formed his lines on the ridge. The two battalions of cavalry and one infantry charged the Confederates line. The Union soldiers encountered some confusion while crossing a stream. Forrest after consultation with Harrison, determined to charge the oncoming Union infantry. Harrison rode up in front of their line, telling the Rangers to prepare for the charge, and added, "Boys, go in twenty steps of the Yankees before you turn your shotguns loose on them." Forrest's bugler sounded the order "Charge". Harrison called out to his men, "Now follow your Jimtown-Mark Time Major!" Harrison flew down the field with his large bay, and a red bandanna tied around his head since he had lost his hat in the dark of the preceding rainy night. The 77th Ohio Infantry prepared their bayonets, with butts of their rifles on the ground, the bayonets at right angles and the rear lines with bayonets extended between the heads of the men of their first line. At twenty paces the Confederates gave a huge volley with their shotguns, and rushed in with their sabers and pistols. Before the Union infantry and cavalry had time to prepare it was too late. The Yankees scattered "like quail."The front line of the infantry's and their cavalry in it's rear were put to flight. A portion of the Union cavalry engaged in a hand to hand combat, but the "superior skill in the use and management of pistol and horse" drove the enemy from the field. Mass confusion arose on the field, as Union cavalry, under Col. Dickey's 4th Illinois Cavalry quickly overran the infantry in retreat. Harrison's men having no sabers and had run out of ammunition ordered a retreat, when the appearance of a strong line of infantry under Hildebrand's Infantry Brigade, formed to his front. Harrison rallied and reformed his men on the ridge where the charge had begun. The Union troops did not advance. Forrest got caught up in the moment and had ridden right into Hildebrand's brigade, without realizing that he had advanced too far ahead of his men. Harrison had already fallen back. Forrest found himself alone, within fifty yards of the Union infantry's main line. The Union troops soon realized that Forrest was alone, and began to assault him. Union soldiers cried out "Kill Him!", "Unseat Him" Stick Him". Forrest was being fired upon by all sides. A musket ball from a Austrian rifle hit Forrest on the left side, just above the point of his hip bone. The bullet penetrated his spine, and lodged in his left side. His right leg was useless. His horse also suffered a mortal wound. Forrest still managed to wheel his horse around, fire a path with his revolver, and at a break neck speed, rode back to his lines, with a hail of hundreds of bullets whizzing past him. Forrest managed to make it back to his lines, with no further injuries. Forrest rode to the hospital. Forrest was the last casualty of the Battle of Shiloh. It is of some interest to note that J. P. Blackburn of the 8th Texas said that Forrest and his command never fired a shot in the battle. He claims Forrest was struck in the back by a bullet as he rode urging his men to move forward quickly.[27]

During the Battle of the Fallen Timbers, Harrison lost two killed and seven wounded, among them Capt. G. Cook, Lt. H. E. Storey, Lt. Joel McClure, and Gordon. Private Ash was listed as missing. After the battle, Harrison was no longer called "Jimtown-Mark Time Major."[28]

During the two day battle the Union losses were 13,047. Confederate losses were 10,694.

While the battle of Shiloh was raging, Island No. 10 on the Mississippi fell on April 7, 1862, and the capture of New Orleans took place on April 25, 1862. The Mississippi River was slowly being controlled by the Union army. This would have dramatic effects on the Confederacy in the Western Theater. It cut off all trade for the South with the North. It was also cutting off another means of transportation for the Confederacy. The Battle of Shiloh was close to being a Confederate victory on the first day of battle, but total victory would be snatched from the Confederates hands on the second day of battle. Confederate General Albert Sidney's Johnston's fears had come to bear. Union reenforcements had arrived and greatly outnumbered the tired and weary Confederate troops. It also did not help that the Confederates lost their overall commander on the first day of battle. Poor coordination also played a major role in the defeat of the Confederates.

But there would be rising stars that would emerge from this battle. Men like Nathan Bedford Forrest, John Hunt Morgan, and John Wharton were becoming legends of the saddle. Even Tom Harrison had gained favor with his men.

[1]The Cyrus Love Letters, Mary Counts Burnett Library, Special Collections
[2]The Civil War Battles of the Western Theater, P. 29
[3]Series I-Vol. 10 Special Order No. 8 Inclosure A Pittsburg Landing or Shiloh, Tenn.
[4]Southern Bivouac, P. 91
[5]Ibid. 91-92
[6]The Civil War Battles of the Western Theater, P. 29
[7]O.R. Series I-Vol. 10 Pittsburg Landing, or Shiloh, Tenn. No. 180 Report of Col. Preston Pond, jr., 16th Louisiana Infantry, commanding Third Brigade; O.R. Series I-Vol. 10

Pittsburg Landing, or Shiloh, Tenn. No. 185 Report of Capt. William H. Ketchum, Alabama Battery.
[8] Ibid.
[9] O.R. Series I-Vol. 10 Pittsburg Landing, or Shiloh, Tenn. No. 180 Report of Col. Preston Pond, jr., 16th Louisiana Infantry, commanding Third Brigade
[10] O.R. Series I-Vol. 10 Pittsburg Landing, or Shiloh, Tenn. No. 180 Report of Col. Preston Pond, jr., 16th Louisiana Infantry, commanding Third Brigade; O.R. Series I-Vol. 10 Pittsburg Landing, or Shiloh, Tenn. No. 185 Report of Capt. William H. Ketchum, Alabama Battery.
[11] O.R. Series I-Vol. 10 Pittsburg Landing, or Shiloh, Tenn. No. 180 Report of Col. Preston Pond, jr., 16th Louisiana Infantry, commanding Third Brigade
[12] Ibid.
[13] Ibid.
[14] Ibid.
[15] O.R. Series I-Vol. 10 Pittsburg Landing, or Shiloh, Tenn. No. 229 Report of Col. John A. Wharton, Texas Rangers (unattached)
[16] Civil War Battles of the Western Theater, P. 29
[17] The Civil War Battles of the Western Theater, p. 29
[18] Ibid., p. 29-30
[19] The Civil War Battles of the Western Theater, p. 30; The Southern Bivouac, Terry's Texas Rangers, P. 92.
[20] The Civil War Battles of the Western Theater, p. 30
[21] Ibid. P. 30
[22] Ibid. P. 30
[23] O.R. Series I-Vol. 10 Pittsburg Landing, or Shiloh, Tenn. No. 185 Report of Capt. William H. Ketchum, Alabama Battery.
[24] O.R. Series I-Vol. 10 Pittsburg Landing, or Shiloh, Tenn. No. 229 Report of Col. John A. Wharton, Texas Rangers (unattached)
[25] Ibid.
[26] Terry Texas rangers Trilogy, J. P. Blackburn
[27] The Southern Bivouac, P. 93; Terry Texas Rangers, J. P. Blackburn; Appendix April 8, 1862-Reconnaissance from Shiloh Battlefield. Report of Thomas Harrison, Texas Rangers, (unattached)
[28] Appendix April 8, 1862-Reconnaissance from Shiloh Battlefield. Report of Thomas Harrison, Texas Rangers, (unattached

Chapter 3:
The Siege of Corinth, Mississippi

After the battle of Shiloh, Tom Harrison was ordered by General John C. Breckinridge to the rear of his infantry and artillery. After the Battle of the Fallen Timbers Col. Nathan Bedford Forrest was granted a forty day leave to recover from his wounds and returned to Memphis, Tennessee.

The Confederate army now fell back to Corinth, Mississippi. The Rangers remained in Corinth for two or three weeks performing routine cavalry chores. During the remainder of April, the Yankees inched their way from Pittsburg Landing to Corinth. The Confederate troops escaped Corinth by rail. On April 26th the Texas Rangers were camped at Reinzi, Mississippi. They had left Corinth on the 23rd. Reinzi was only fifteen miles from Corinth and was on the Mobile and Ohio Railroad. The Rangers were sent to Reinzi to forage and procure new horses. It had been raining ever since the Rangers left Bowling Green. Their horses were thin and worn out because of the lack of food. Confederate General Sterling Price's division were camped with the Rangers at Reinzi. Frank Batchelor commented that many of Price's men had no shoes, and were thinly clad. Sickness still reined high over the Rangers. Batchelor commented that Wharton was absent because of illness, Lt. Col. Walker would never return, and had been absent for over four months, and Major Harrison had been sick and absent three fourths of the time. The Adjutant Martin Royston was sick and out of ten captains, only four were present for duty. Col. John Hunt Morgan filled the place of Wharton temporarily. [1]

In early May Gen. P. G. T. Beauregard brigaded the Rangers with the 1st Kentucky Cavalry under Col. John Adams as a senior Colonel. This small command was ordered on a raid into Middle Tennessee. The purpose of the raid was to surprise a party of 350 Yankees, in and about Bethel, which was a small town on the Elk River. On May 8th, Lt. Col. T. G. Woodward, 1st Kentucky Cavalry, left Lamb's Ferry, Tennessee with 350 men of his regiment and a detachment of eighty men from the Texas Rangers, under the command of Captain Houston.

The next day, on May 9th, 1862, Lt. Col. Woodward rode into Bethel but found no Yankees, except some stragglers. He learned that the Yankees were guarding a trestle work on the railroad on the opposite side of the river. Woodward decided to capture them, and began to divide his command, placing one squadron of his regiment with the Texas Rangers, under Captain Houston, with orders to cross the ford below the trestle work and cut off the Yankee retreat in that direction, while Woodward's force would cross at the upper ford and make an attack from above. The movement was successful, resulting in the capture of the entire force stationed at the trestle work. The Union troops made a "gallant defense" under the cover of some buildings, but after ten minutes they surrendered. Woodward managed to capture two captains, two Lieutenants, and 43 non commissioned officers, and privates. Woodward's loss during the battle was five killed, including Capt. A. D. Harris of Texas Ranger Co. I. Seven men were also wounded. Woodward commended Captain Houston for "much credit for his able manner in which he cooperated, and the conduct of the men as extremely gallant and praiseworthy." [2]

During the raid, Col. John Adams fell back to Chattanooga to obtain a battery of artillery. Wharton refused to cooperate and would only stay in Middle Tennessee.

Later in the month, Wharton crossed the Tennessee River below Chattanooga and went into camp around Lookout Mountain. On June 14th, 1862 Private Cyrus Love wrote a letter while in camp near Chattanooga, Tennessee. He wrote in detail about Terry's Texas Regiment progress since leaving Corinth. "*We started from Corinth about 6 or 7 weeks ago and camp up to Lamb's Ferry where Scott's cavalry had just had a brush with some of the enemy near Athens on or near Elk River-they became after a while too strong for him and compelled him to recross both the Elk and Tennessee-when we got to the ferry (on the Tennessee) river it took us about two days to cross our forces and wagons after crossing some four or five hundred of our Regiment and the Kentucky 1st Regiment went on a scout and killed and made prisoners of 69 of the enemy at a place on Elk River about thirty miles from where we crossed the Tenn a few days afterward the most of the Ky 1st & our Regiment (the 1st Texas Rangers or Eighth Texas Cavalry) went on another scout up Elk River and were cut off from our wagons by about 400 of the enemy's forces consisting in part of infantry & cavalry & we started immediately toward Winchester Tenn picking up their couriers and spies as we went until we got to Winchester. We lay about that place a few days when we learned that some 1500 or 1800 of the enemy had come from Huntsville on the hunt for us. We started about day light with the intention of surprising them but had not gone far when we learned that they after marching a good part of the night were at Winchester. We turned about and returned toward Winchester but were going in South of town when the enemy discovered us and shot a few shells at us doing however but very little harm. We returned to our camp and scouted about the town for some days and finally about 250 of us in making a scout concluded to attack the town or rather the enemy that were in it. In the charge we were in view of the town for more than half a mile-we caught 7 of their pickets in about 200 yrds of the Public Square and charged on till the front of the column who were Kentuckyans and a few Rangers were up in the square. One of the Ky.'s was killed and 3 or 4 wounded. One of them mortally. There was but little firing done when we retreated as we at first intended we do not know whether we killed any of them or not. Someone said three were killed on the bridge as we were going in-another fellow said he saw one lying under the bridge but I saw none there-it was also said that some of them were killed in the Court House but there is no way of knowing the truth about it unless the enemy tell it themselves which they are not likely to do as they reported that they killed 36 of us which they knew to be false in as much as they could not have known that they killed but one of us-we camped that night in about 6 miles of them-they were so badly scared that they threatened to kill the people of the town if they were attacked that night-they started during the night at double quick for Huntsville 45 miles distant where they arrived before night of that day-we passed back through the town next day and returned to our old camping place with the view of crossing the mountains to Chattanooga. We crossed the mountains the next day into Sequatchie Valley and the next day we crossed the Tenn river. General Adams with the Ky. Regiment remaining in the valley-in a few days a force of 4000 or 5000 of the enemy came very near surprising the Ky.'s having crossed the Mountains behind us a strong force came up from Huntsville between the River and the Mountains with the intention no doubt of hemming us up in this valley and they would possibly have hemmed the Ky.'s if we had not been watching them from this side of the river. We sent a few balls from some of our cannon at them and our boys were frequently giving them a taste of Enfield and Sharps rifle balls-from appearances they got in a notion it was not good policy to show themselves very much where our boys had a chance to shoot at them-they however would get behind shelter and fire back at us very frequently but did no damage at all whether our boys hit any of them is not known. A part of their force came up opposite Chattanooga and shelled the town a couple of days but did but little harm wounding only one or two men and injuring a few houses to the amount of about fifty dollars worth-no one knows what harm we did them-it is reported in camp though that somebody went over after the enemy left and found three graves in two of which there were 15 men one of whom was thought to be a field officer and in the third two cannon that had been dismounted by our guns-this may or may not be true.* [3]

On June 9th, at Tupelo, Mississippi, Beauregard promoted Nathan Forrest to Brigadier General and ordered him to North Alabama and Middle Tennessee and assume command of the cavalry regiments in that section, commanded by Colonels John Scott, Wharton, and Wirt Adams. Forrest reached Chattanooga, Tennessee on the third week of June. Wharton accepted Forrest as the commander of the raid. Forrest by this point in the war already had a reputation as a ruthless fighter. At the Battles of Fort Henry and Donaldson he helped save valuable cavalry from capture. At the Battle of Shiloh, his exploits during that battle would give rise to stories of myth and legend. Nathan Bedford Forrest was born in Bedford City, Tennessee and came from a background of poverty. His father was a blacksmith in the backwoods. Forrest had to help raise a large family at sixteen. Forrest later became a successful slave trader and planter by 1861. He enlisted as a private in 1861. At the Battle of Forts Henry and Donelson he was promoted to Colonel. Forrest was known for his ability as a tactician and his firm grasp of strategic considerations. His style of fighting was ruthless and was brought down on his enemy with lighting speed. It is no doubt why the Confederacy was in awe of a man who had no military background whatsoever, but was beating back the Yankees every time he went into battle. [4]

On July 9th, Forrest left Chattanooga, Tennessee. He took with him Col. Wharton, and Col. Lawton, of the 2nd Georgia Cavalry. They made a forced march of fifty miles, reaching Altamount on July 10th, 1862. After resting for the night, Forrest rode onto McMinnville, where he was joined by Col. Morrison, of the 1st Georgia regiment, two companies of Col. Spiller's battalion, under Major Smith, and two companies of Kentuckians, under Capt. Taylor and Waltham. Forrest's force consisted of about 1,400 men. [5]

[1] The Batchelor-Turner Letters, P. 27-28
[2] O.R. Vol. 10, Skirmish on the Elk River, Tenn., Reports No. 2 Lt. Col. Woodward, First Kentucky Cavalry (Confederate)
[3] The Love Letters, Mary Counts Burnett Library, Special Collections
[4] Historical Times Illustrated Encyclopedia of the Civil War; Who's Who in the Confederacy.
[5] The Campaigns of General Nathan Bedford Forrest and of Forrest's Cavalry

Chapter 4:
The Capture of Murfreesboro, Tennessee

On July 12th, Forrest and his units arrived at Woodbury, Tennessee, nineteen miles from Murfreesboro. The women of the town told Forrest that the Union provost marshal at Murfreesboro, Col. Oliver Rounds, had rounded up most of the town's men and locked them in the Murfreesboro jail. Forrest decided to move onto Murfreesboro, Tennessee, and take the city. On that same day, Union General Thomas Crittenden took command of the 1,400 man Union garrison stationed there. Crittenden found that the Union soldiers at the garrison were poorly disciplined and broken into two camps. He was in the process of reorganizing the force, when the attack came the next day. [1]

Forrest and his force approached Murfreesboro about 4:30 a.m. Nearing the town, his scouts reported a fifteen man Union picket force ahead. Forrest ordered Wharton to circle behind the picket and capture them. Wharton's men quietly snuck around the Union pickets and captured them without firing a gun. Forrest learned from the pickets that there were two regiments in and near Murfreesboro, one was the Ninth Michigan Infantry, and the other the Third Minnesota, along with two hundred of the 7th Pennsylvania Cavalry, one hundred of the Eighth Kentucky, and Capt. Hewett's Kentucky battery of four guns, numbering 1,400 men, under the command of Brig. Gen. Thomas Crittenden, brother of Confederate General George Crittenden. There were two camps; the first was the composed of five companies of the Ninth Michigan Volunteers and one squadron of the Fourth Kentucky Cavalry, which were camped about a mile east of town near the Liberty turnpike; the other Ninth Michigan Infantry and a detachment of the 7th Pennsylvania Cavalry under Col. William Duffield was camped on the eastern edge of town that included the jail and courthouse. The Third Minnesota Infantry, under Col. Lester and Hewett's First Kentucky Battery, was located 1 1/2 miles north of the city, on the Nashville Pike. Captain Oliver C. Rounds, of the 9th Michigan commanded the troops at the courthouse. Some of the officer's were in the court house and private houses around the public square. [2]

Forrest decided to immediately attack the camp in town and the buildings, while the artillery should be held in check until the first was stormed and captured. Col. Wharton was ordered by Forrest to charge the camp of the Ninth Michigan in town, which was under the command of Lt. Col. Parkhurst. Wharton moved forward "in gallant style" at the head of his men. During the charge four companies became separated and fell in with Morrison's Georgia cavalry. Unaware of what had happened Wharton, with two companies, charged over the tent ropes right into camp. Col. Parkhurst, who was sleeping in his tent, was aroused by the yells of the Rangers and was informed that the Confederates were approaching. He at once gave the alarm in camp. Before Ninth Michigan had a chance to form in line of battle, Wharton had already made into the camp approaching from three directions. Some of the Ninth Michigan gave way, but most of them stood their ground, and returned a heavy fire upon Wharton's weakened force. Col. Wharton was severely wounded, and left his command to Col. Walker. Wharton's small force was pushed out of the camp and fell back four miles back on the Woodbury Pike. Forrest was unaware that his rear had now been exposed. Col. William Duffield was also severely wounded during the charge and was taken to a local house. Col. Parkhurst took command. [3]

One of the companies that became lost during the charge, was under the command of Capt. Ferrel. He led the men through the suburbs of town towards the right or north of where they thought they would find Wharton's command. They were passing through a cornfield, when the artillery of Captain Hewett's artillery opened upon them. The first shot struck William Skull of Company G, taking off both legs and passing through his horse, killing them both instantly. They found the two companies of Rangers under Wharton about a half mile east of town, on the Woodbury Pike. When they arrived they found out the charge under Wharton was unsuccessful and that he was wounded. [4]

While Wharton was making his charge on the Ninth Michigan, Col. Morrison, along with a portion of the 2nd Georgia Cavalry, was ordered to storm the court-house while the rest of the Texas Rangers would attack the private buildings. The Federal soldiers in the jail saw the oncoming Confederate cavalry and realized that they were about to be surrounded. Several of the Union soldiers in the jail tried to shoot the Confederate sympathizers that were being held in the jail. Luckily the Federal soldiers were not able to shoot the prisoners. Before leaving the prison, one of the guards set some papers on fire and shoved the lite papers into the loose planks on the floor, and threw the keys away. The fire spread rapidly, but Lt. Col. Arthur Hood, of the Second Georgia, with a portion of the his force, stormed the jail, was able to bend a grate on the doors and dragged the prisoners to safety. The Federal soldiers in the jail fell back to the courthouse. [5]

The court house contained the Ninth Michigan Infantry, Co. B under Col. Oliver Rounds. The ladies of the town were awakened by the fighting. They quickly rushed into the streets just as the Georgians came up. Pointing to the courthouse, they begged them to attack the Yankees which they hated immensely. With a "Hurrah for the Women!" Col. Morrison's men rode towards the courthouse and as they approached the Yankees in the courthouse opened a galling fire from the windows. They made several attempts to storm the courthouse but failed. Forrest arrived and changed the assault tactics. He ordered the men to dismount and form storming parties and told the men to move forward in a single file, with the lead man in each party armed with an axe and the man behind prepared to grab it if the man in front fell, until the doors of the courthouse were battered down. The door was smashed down but the Yankees would not give up. The Federal troops had to be smoked out from the second floor, by using burning cloth and manure. The Yankees finally surrendered.[6]

The Rangers found Col. Oliver Rounds hiding between two featherbeds in one of the local homes. General Crittenden was found in the local tavern.[7]

Col. Lawton, with the First Georgia, the Tennesseans, and Kentuckians, were ordered to attack the second camp, of Third Minnesota and Hewett's artillery, under the command of Col. Lester. Col. Lawton attacked the Union artillery camp for several hours. The Tennesseans under Major Baxter Smith, and Kentuckians, under Capt. Taylor, Capt. Dunlop, and Major Harper charged the cannon all the way to it's muzzles. After fighting them for two or three hours, Forrest took personal command of this force and charged the rear of the Union artillery camp. Forrest burned their camps, and stores. Col. Lester's men were pushed back and took up a position on a hill. Forrest decided not to attack Lester any further and moved back to Murfreesboro. [8]

Adjutant M. H. Royston, of the Texas Rangers, under Wharton's force, rode up to Forrest and told him of the failed attack on the Union camp of the 9th Michigan, and that Wharton had fallen back to the Woodbury pike and awaited further orders. Forrest told Royston "Tell him to bring his men up here." [9]

After the charge of the Texas Rangers, under Wharton, Parkhurst marched his force into a garden in front of his camp, which was inclosed by a cedar post fence, and made use of the local forage to barricade Maney Avenue, which was to his right, and made use of transportation wagons for the protection of his left. Forrest arrived in front of Col. Parkhurst's forces. The fight had lasted almost six hours. Forrest decided to prepare his whole force one last charge. A flag of truce was brought out to the Union camp. A message was given to Parkhurst "demanding an unconditional surrender of your force as prisoners of war or I will have every man put to the sword." [10] Parkhurst informed Col. Duffield asking for his advice. Col. Duffield left the matter in Parkhurst's hands. Col. Parkhurst met with the officers and discussed the situation. They all agreed to surrender. [11]

Forrest also sent the same message to Col. Henry C. Lester. Lester asked for an interview with Col. William Duffield, who was severely injured and was a prisoner of war at the house of

Col. Maney. Forrest sent Col. Strange with him to receive his final answer. Forrest made sure that his entire command was along the road that Lester was traveling to make it look like Forrest had greater numbers. Col. Lester decided to surrender. Forrest captured 1,765 prisoners, six hundred horses and mules, forty wagons, five ambulances, four pieces of artillery (one Parrott and three brass pieces), and twelve hundred stands of arms, and 30,000 uniforms ready for Buell's army. Forrest surmised that the enemy lost nearly a half million dollars worth of supplies. He decided to carry away $300,000 dollars worth of supplies, and burned almost $200,000 dollars worth of supplies. Forrest lost twenty five killed and forty to sixty wounded. Crittenden's force lost about seventy five killed and one hundred and twenty five wounded. The capture of Murfreesboro was a nice birthday present for Forrest's 41st birthday. [12]

While leaving Murfreesboro Forrest did not have enough men to drive the wagons of captured booty, so he told his enlisted Union prisoners that if they would drive the wagons, he would parole them once they arrived at McMinnville. The Union soldiers agreed. Col. Wharton and the Texas Rangers were in charge of General Crittenden and 250 prisoners. [13]

After the raid on Murfreesboro, Forrest continued on towards McMinnville, burning bridges, along the way. Forrest finally arrived in McMinnville on the 18th. He released his Union prisoners, and some of the Union soldiers cheered Forrest. Forrest next headed towards Nashville, for the purpose of making a reconnaissance. On his arrival at Alexandria with a portion of his command, which was the Texas Rangers, he learned that a strong Federal army of about three thousand five hundred men had been sent from Nashville to Lebanon and were looking for Forrest. Forrest immediately ordered forward the balance of his command, being portions of the First and Second Georgia Cavalry and the Tennessee and Kentucky squadrons, and by a forced march reached Lebanon. They rode into Lebanon, but found no Union troops. When Forrest arrived in Lebanon, the Federal cavalry were leaving at a break neck speed. While at Lebanon, the people of the city received the Rangers royally. They feed them with chickens, hams, roast pig, cakes and pies, "All like mother used to make." They left Lebanon with their haversacks filled with food. [14]

Forrest rode to Stone's River, seven miles east of Nashville, and captured the Federal pickets. Forrest moved around the city, until he arrived at the Mill Creek bridge, four miles from the heart of the city. Forrest charged the Yankees at the bridge and captured twenty prisoners, Forrest continued towards the next bridge, and forty Yankees were captured. Forrest reached the next bridge at Antioch Station. The Yankees tried to make a stand, but were routed by Col. Walker, and Terry Rangers. Thirty five Yankees were captured, including some small arms and railroad cars, which were burned. [15]

On August 10th, Forrest rested at McMinnville. After leaving McMinnville, Forrest moved in the direction of Altamount. They camped in a cove near the mountain. The Federal troops advanced in force on all the roads. Forrest and the Rangers had to take the dry bed of a creek which ran parallel to one of the roads on which the Union troops were advancing. On August 31st, Forrest and his force rode along the creek for a mile or two and then emerged into the open. A battery of Federal artillery opened up on them. [16] The force belonged to Union Brig. General Thomas Wood. He had already been informed that Forrest's command was crossing the railroad three miles west of his camp, going northward. He sent out three regiments of infantry and four pieces of artillery, under Col. Fyffe, 26th Ohio, to cross the north side of Barren Fork, and move out to the Murfreesboro road, take the road, and try to cut off Forrest. Col. Fyffe reached the junction of the crossroads. He then deployed a part of his command, immediately ordered up the artillery, and opened fire of shell and musketry. [17] The Union artillery divided Forrest's command, and routed them. The Rangers along with the rest of Forrest's command soon out rode the range of the guns.

Forrest and his force marched to Sparta, and joined the forces under Confederate General Braxton Bragg's army, which was making plans for the invasion of Kentucky.

The capture of Murfreesboro was a major embarrassment to the Union army. Forrest had managed to travel 200 miles, took 1,200 Federal soldiers, four pieces of artillery, 40 wagons, 300 mules and 150 horses. They also carried away $300,00 dollars worth of badly needed supplies, and another $200,00 dollars worth of supplies were burned, including 150,000 rations for Union General Don Carlos Buell's army, which led to his army being put on half rations. The railroad was so torn up that it was put out of commission for two weeks. This action delayed Buell from attacking Chattanooga. Col. James B Fry, Buell's Chief of Staff believed that the

Federal force at Murfreesboro could had repelled Forrest's force. He said that the capture was "one of the most disgraceful examples of neglect of duty and lack of good conduct in the history of all wars."[18] Leonidas Giles of the Texas Rangers also agreed that "a more resolute commander could have beaten us."[19]

[1] The Campaigns of General Nathan Bedford Forrest,
[2] O.R. Series I-Vol. XVI No. 8-Report of Lt. Col. John C. Parkhurst, Ninth Michigan Infantry
[3] O.R. Series I-Vol.. XVI No. 8 Report of Lt. Col. John C. Parkhurst, Ninth Michigan Infantry
[4] Terry's Texas Rangers, Leonidas Giles, P. 35-39
[5] O.R. Series I-Vol. XXVIII-No. 12 Report of Brig. Gen. N. B. Forrest, C. S. Army, commanding Cavalry Brigade.
[6] Terry's Texas Rangers, Leonidas Giles, P. 35-39; Surrender or Die, William R. Brooksher and David Snider; The Campaigns of General Nathan Bedford Forrest, P. 166
[7] Terry's Texas Rangers, Leonidas Giles, P. 35-39
[8] The Campaigns of General Nathan Bedford Forrest, P. 170-171; Surrender or Die, p. 32; O.R. Series I-Vol. XXVIII No. 12 Report of Brig. Gen. N. B. Forrest, C. S. Army, commanding Cavalry Brigade.
[9] Terry's Texas Rangers, Leonidas Giles, P. 35-39
[10] O.R. Series I-Vol. XVI No. 8 Report of Lt. Col. John G. Parkhurst, Ninth Michigan Infantry
[11] O.R. Series I-Vol. XVI No. 8 Report of Lt. Col. John G. Parkhurst, Ninth Michigan Infantry
[12] The Campaigns of General Nathan Bedford Forrest.
[13] Ibid. P. 175
[14] Terry's Texas Rangers, Leonidas Giles, P. 40-48
[15] The Campaigns of General Nathan Bedford Forrest, p. 177
[16] Terry's Texas Rangers, Leonidas Giles, P. 40-48
[17] O.R. Series I-Vol. XXVIII, No. 1 Report of Brig. Gen. Thomas J. Wood, U.S. Army, of skirmish at Little Pond.
[18] Surrender or Die, William r. Brooksher and David Snider, p. 33
[19] Terry's Texas Rangers, Leonidas Giles, P. 3

Chapter 5:
The Kentucky Campaign: The Battle of Bardstown & Perryville, Kentucky

When we last left the force under Forrest they were in Sparta, Tennessee. General Forrest and the Texas Rangers finally arrived in Woodbury, Tennessee, which was in the rear of the Federal force, under Union General Don Carlos Buell. Confederate General Braxton Bragg was in Chattanooga, massing his "Army of the Mississippi", and planning his invasion of Kentucky. Confederate General Braxton Bragg and Major General Edmund Kirby Smith met in Chattanooga, Tennessee, July 31st, 1862 to plan their invasion of Kentucky. Both Generals were hoping to bring Kentucky into the fold of the Confederacy. Braxton Bragg had high hopes for Kentucky. Kentucky Confederate Calvary General John Hunt Morgan promised that Braxton Bragg would be able to pick up twenty five thousand men if he entered this state. Bragg was also looking for badly needed supplies. Edmund Kirby Smith was the first to enter the state on August 9th, 1862. His objective was to move against Union General George W. Morgan's ten thousand men in the Cumberland Gap. General Edmund Kirby Smith changed his plans on August 13th, and decided to take Lexington, Kentucky. Smith marched with nine thousand men, under Heth, Cleburne, and Thomas J. Churchill. He left General Carter Stevenson's division to take on Union General Morgan's force. When realized that he had been outflanked Morgan abandoned the Cumberland Gap. On August 24th Smith advised Bragg to move north across the Cumberland Mountains in order to distract Buell's Federal force from Smith's operations. On August 28th, Bragg's Army of the Mississippi headed north from Chattanooga towards Kentucky, heading up the Sequatchie Valley to Pikeville and then across the Cumberland Plateau toward Sparta, twenty miles northeast of McMinnville. Buell's Army of the Ohio was at McMinnville. [1]

Union General Don Carlos Buell received word at his headquarters at Decherd that Bragg was entering Chattanooga, Tennessee. Buell gave word for Union General Alexander McCook to march his division between Chattanooga and McMinnville and watch and oppose the Rebels on the Anderson or Thurman road, in the Sequatchie Valley. Union General Thomas Crittenden's division was to follow him. McCook was unable to move up the Sequathcie Valley. McCook and Crittenden both organized at McMinnville, Tennessee.

Bragg ordered Forrest to leave Woodbury, and ride towards the Cumberland Gap, and secure the road. Forrest, along with Wharton, Captain Bacot of the Alabama Cavalry, Major Baxter Smith's 4th Tennessee Cavalry, and the Kentucky Cavalry, were riding along the Manchester McMinnville Road when they came upon one hundred men of the 18th Ohio Volunteer Infantry, Company A, and I, under Captain Charles Ross, and the 9th Michigan Volunteer Infantry, Company D, under Lt. Wallace, who were located near the Short Mountain Crossroads. The Union soldiers had just completed a stockade thirty feet by forty feet square, of round timber, and twelve feet high. The Yankees were eating dinner at 1 o'clock when they heard the hooves of Forrest's force. When Forrest and his men got to within one yards of the stockade, he formed his men in line of battle along the skirt of the woods extending from the railroad along the south side of the stockade at the distance of two hundred yards, and rapidly extended his line on the east

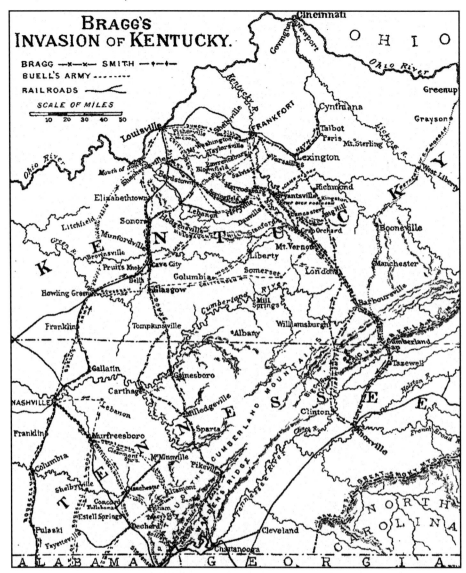

and west sides. Captain Henry R. Miller, commander of the 18th Ohio Infantry, ran his men quickly to the stockade, and at the same time, Forrest ordered his men to dismount and attack. Forrest quickly tried to cut off the Yankees from reaching fort. Miller's men kept up a running fire on the way to the stockade, checking Forrest's men. All but ten of Company I reached the stockade. The men that were cut off kept up a constant fire from the railroad and woods during the engagement and got to safety. Once inside the stockade, Miller at once sent three parties of six men each, one from each company, to bring in the ammunition. They succeeded in their mission under a heavy fire from Forrest's men. [2]

Forrest next made an attack from three directions approaching the stockade to within fifty feet. Miller's men kept up a constant and well directed fire upon Forrest for ten minutes. Forrest soon realized that it would be impossible to dislodge the Yankees inside the stockade, he fell back to the woods and out of range. Forrest next tried to destroy the railroad above Miller's stockade by setting it on fire, but Miller sent out a party to stop Forrest. Forrest was driven off and the fire was quickly put out. According to Miller's report, he buried twelve of Forrest's men, and wounded forty one. Among the dead were Captain W. Y. Houston, and Lt. Butler of the Texas Rangers. Miller lost nine men wounded, five of which were seriously wounded. He also captured eight horses, three saddles, and thirty guns. [3]

After the attack on the Yankees along the McMinnville-Murfreesboro turnpike, Forrest headed for Sparta. Again Union troops would be waiting his arrival. On August 31st, Col. Edward P. Fyffe, of the 26th Ohio Infantry, was ordered by Union General Wood to cut off Forrest and his command. Fyffe marched his men through the woods towards the Murfreesboro-McMinnville road, which was six miles from his camp. Fyffe's men came into an open field and saw Forrest's column across the same field. Forrest immediately saw the 26th Ohio entering the field. Forrest and the Yankee infantry made a race for the crossroads. Fyffe discovered, when about 400 or 500 hundred yards away from the junction of the crossroads, that Forrest had formed his command in line of battle to receive Fyffe's attack. Fyffe ordered the Eighth Indiana Battery to take a position on an elevated position in the field to the left of the road. The advance companies of Company A and F of the 26th Ohio were ordered forward and deploy in front of the artillery on the low ground and advance. Lt. Col. Young of the 26th Ohio formed his regiment in rear of the advance guard and followed it closely. After firing a few rounds Forrest soon fell back. His right wing, comprised of the Texas Rangers and Alabama cavalry, were forced back to the left, while Forrest, with his left wing, headed toward Murfreesboro. Fyffe ordered Lt. Jervis forward on the main road with one section of artillery to fire on Forrest's detachment, and ordered Lt. Col. Gorman, commanding the 17th Indiana, to support him with his regiment. Fyffe next ordered Lt. Voris, with the other section, supported by the 58th Indiana, Lt. Col. Buell commanding, to follow up and to fire on the Texas Rangers, leaving the 26th Ohio to occupy the center. Soon Fyffe's force scattered Forrest's command. Fyffe followed Forrest's command to Murfreesboro road, but darkness soon ended the chase. Fyffe claimed that he killed or wounded about twenty men. [4]

Forrest reached Sparta on September 3rd. By this time, Kirby Smith had already taken Lexington, and Frankfort, Kentucky; the capitol of Kentucky. Five days earlier, on August 30th, 1862 Kirby Smith's forces had totally demolished any opposition in the state of Kentucky by defeating and routing Union General William Nelson's Federal force at Richmond, Kentucky. [5]

Forrest personally met with Bragg at his headquarters and he told Forrest to get in the rear of Buell's army which was retreating westward to Murfreesboro. General Don Carlos Buell arrived at Murfreesboro on September 5th. He then headed toward Nashville.

On September 4th, Col. Scott, with a brigade of cavalry, was ordered to push on as near to Louisville, and destroy the Louisville and Nashville Railroad. General Heth, with a division of infantry and a brigade of infantry and a brigade of cavalry, marched north, and on the 6th, some of Heth's men reached Covington, Kentucky. Smith immediately went about concentrating his supplies and start a recruiting drive.

On September 6th, Buell had learned that Bowling Green, Kentucky was threatened. Two divisions were moved across the river at Nashville on the 7th, one to go to Bowling Green, and the other was to head for Gallatin, Tenn.

On September Eighth, 1862, Union Col. John T. Wilder assumed command of the forces at Munfordville, Kentucky. He immediately set about building fortifications for the defense of the railroad bridge over the Green River. Wilder's force consisted of the Sixty-Seventh and Eighty-ninth Indiana Regiments, one company of the Eighteenth Regulars, two hundred and four recruits of the 17th Indiana, two companies Seventy-fourth Indiana, one company of cavalry, Louisville Provost Guard, Lt. Watson commanding, one 12 pound heavy gun, one 12 pound Napoleon, one 12 pound howitzer, and one three inch rifled gun, under Lt. Mason, Thirteenth Indiana Battery; sixty men Thirty-third Kentucky, Capt. Wilson. On September 9th, the railroad bridge at the Salt River was burned by the Rebels. No supplies were able to reach Wilder's men and he had only one days rations, so he set about collecting flour, and bacon from the surrounding area and bought bread from Bowling Green, Kentucky. He was able to collect fifteen days worth of rations. At the same time, Wilder ordered all Home Guard companies and recruits for the Thirty-Third Kentucky, who were not equipped with arms, to act as scouts. These men informed Wilder of Confederate General Braxton Bragg's arrival into Kentucky from the Cumberland River. [6]

With the scouts watching Bragg's approach, Wilder learned Bragg's numbers, pieces of artillery, and his direction. On Saturday September 13th, Col. John S. Scott, of the 1st Louisiana cavalry and a battery of five mountain howitzers, came down the north side of the river from

Greensburg and at 8:00 P.M. demanded that Wilder surrender Fort Craig. Wilder refused. That night, Brig. Gen. James Chalmer's Mississippi Brigade, which was comprised of the 7th, 9th, 10th, 20th, 29th, and 44th Mississippi, and Garrity's and Scott's Louisiana batteries, arrived, and at three o'clock the next morning, Col Scott and Chalmer's men fired on Wilder's pickets. Chalmer's sent three regiments against the western Union stockade and two regiments against the eastern blockhouse. Artillery was brought up. [7]

At daybreak a furious attack was made on the pickets on the south side of the river by a large force of infantry. Wilder sent out Company K, 74th Indiana, out to a belt of woods about a quarter mile in advance, to act as a reserve, for the pickets to rally on. They held their ground until surrounded, and fell back only when ordered by Major Cubberly of the 89th Indiana, who had charge of the pickets and skirmishers on the south side of the river. Wilder's advance line fought the Confederates for an hour, and entered back into the fort when ordered by Wilder. At 5:30 A.M., the fighting broke out along the whole line. The Confederates advanced within 200 yards of Wilder's works. At 6:30 A.M. the Confederates advanced in line of battle upon the west, or main work, Wilder ordered his men to fix bayonets and prepare for an assault. The Rebels came screaming into the works. When the Rebels came within thirty yards, Wilder ordered his men to fire. Wilder said that a "very avalanche of death swept through the ranks", causing the Rebels to first stagger and then run in disorder to the woods in the rear, having left their field officers on the ground either killed or wounded. The regiments that made the charge were the Seventh and Tenth Mississippi and Seventh Alabama. [8]

Another attack was made on the redoubt by the Ninth and Twenty-ninth Mississippi and a battalion of sharpshooters. Wilder said that the Rebels were "murdered by a terrible fire from the gallant defenders of the work."

Maj. Augustus Abbott sprang upon the parapet, with his hat in one hand and a drawn saber in the other, urging his men to stand to the work, until he was shot dead under the flag he was defending. The flag had one hundred and forty six bullet holes shot through it and the staff was struck eleven times. [9]

Lt. Mason, of the Thirteenth Indiana, commanding the artillery, was riddling the Confederates with grape and canister, when the Confederates broke and ran in all directions, fleeing the scene. Wilder sent Col. Emerson, of the Sixty-seventh Indiana, with one company, to reinforce the redoubt and to take command. The Confederates rallied, and kept up a constant fire. They charged again, but it was repulsed. At 9:30 A.M. the Chalmer's sent in a flag of truce, and sent a message to Wilder. The note said "You have made a gallant defense of your position, and to avoid further bloodshed I demand an unconditional surrender of your forces. I have six regiments of infantry, one battalion of infantry sharpshooters, and have just been reinforced by a brigade of cavalry, under Colonel Scott, with two battalions of artillery. I have two regiments on the north side of the river, and you can't escape. The railroad track is torn up in your rear and you can't receive reenforcements. General Bragg's army is but a short distance in the rear." Wilder wrote back: "Your note demanding the unconditional surrender of my forces has been received. Thank you for your compliments. If you wish to avoid further bloodshed keep out of the range of my guns. As to reenforcements, they are now entering my works. I think I can defend my position against your entire force; at least I shall try to do so." Chalmers than asked if he could remove the dead and wounded from the field. Wilder gave him permission to do so.[10]

Wilder's telegraph line was still uncut and immediately called for help. At 9:00 A.M. Wilder was re-enforced by six companies of the Fiftieth Indiana, under Col. Cyrus Dunham, who had come up on the railroad from Louisville. Before arriving to Munfordville, the train was thrown off the track six miles back. Luckily, Dunham and his men arrived into the works with only one man lost. [11]

By this point, Chalmer's had become frustrated with the situation. He came to the conclusion that the Fort could not be taken by infantry or light artillery. He also was deceived by reports saying that there were only 1,200 to 1,800 men in the fort, that the strength of the works was only rifle works, and that the Yankees could not be re-enforced. But in reality, their were 2,500 men; their works were extensive and complete and mounted with heavier guns that what Chalmer's had, and that Col. Dunham, with his six companies had arrived. [12]

As night was falling upon the battlefield, Chalmer's and Wilder collected their dead and wounded. Wilder had lost 37 killed and wounded. The Confederates loss was three officers and 32 men killed, 28 officers and 225 men wounded, including Lt. Col. James Bullard, Col. Smith, Lt. Col. Moore.[13]

With the arrival of Dunham, the whole force amounted to 4,076 men. Since Dunham was Wilder's superior, he took command of the Fort. Bragg was prepared to attack. He was talked out of attacking the town by Confederate General Simon Buckner, who was a native of Munfordville. By this time Confederate General Leonidas Polk, of Bragg's command had crossed the river ten miles above with the right wing of Bragg's army, and coming down on the north side took up a position on the hills on the south side. Bragg had to take Munfordville quickly before Buell's army caught up with him. Buell was at Bowling Green, approaching Bragg's west flank. Confederate Major General William Hardee's men were placed in front of Fort Craig. On September 16th, Bragg asked for Dunham's surrender. Dunham refused at first but then asked if he could consult with his superiors. General C. C. Gilbert telegraphed instructions from Louisville removing Dunham from command and Wilder was put back in command. Wilder wrote to Bragg that after a consultation with his officers it was agreed upon that if satisfactory evidence is given of Bragg's ability to make good on his assertions of largely superior numbers, so as to make the defense of this position a useless waste of human life, Wilder will treat as to terms of an honorable surrender. Bragg wrote back that he had 20,000 men were waiting to attack. He gave Wilder one hour in which to make his decision.[14]

Buckner asked if Wilder would met with him under a flag of truce. Wilder agreed and met with the Rebel commander. Buckner showed Wilder some of the Confederate positions, pointed out superior gun emplacements and the extent of the besieger's lines. Wilder was told that he would get no help from Louisville, his ammunition for small arms was running out, and his men were worn out by constant work and fighting for four days and nights, being satisfied that further resistance was "no less than willful murder of the brave men who had so long contested with overwhelming numbers" and after counting forty five cannon and surrounded by 25,000 men, Wilder decided to surrender at 2:00 A.M. , September 17th, 1862. At 6:00 A.M., Wilder and his men marched out of the works with "all the honors of war, drums beating and colors flying, we being allowed by the terms of surrender our side arms and all private property and four days rations." Officer and men were paroled and they started for the Ohio River. Wilder and his men reached Louisville. General Buell commended Wilder for his stand at Fort Craig by saying: "By this brilliant and gallant defense Colonel Wilder gained due credit as a gallant and determined officer in whom confidence could be placed in time of need. Wilder was a year under my command and was distinguished for the push and untiring devotion with which he met every duty."[15]

Bragg left Munfordville on September 20th to rejoin Smith, but by this time, Buell's army had moved north to reinforce Louisville, Kentucky and Bragg missed Smith. By taking time to capture Munfordville, Bragg had lost time, supplies, and had lost an opportunity to seize an important military objective: Louisville.

While the Battle of Munfordville was raging, Forrest continued to harass Buell's rear. At Tyree Springs, Forrest made another attack upon Buell's army. Forrest rode ten miles to the north of Buell's army to try and strike a blow to his Federal force. By accident, Forrest rode into Major General Joseph Wheeler's cavalry. Wheeler was trying to hit the Federal force upon the Nashville-Bowling Green turnpike, striking the Federal flank. Forrest tried to help Wheeler, but a Federal force appeared to his right. Forrest ordered Lt. Col. Walker, and his Terry's Rangers, to charge the front while Forrest moved around with the rest of the command to the Federal force's flank. Col. Walker formed his men, when to his surprise it was General Wheeler's command, falling back and in confusion. But Wheeler thought the enemy was in front of him, and quickly ran away in great confusion. Forrest was getting ready to attack Wheeler, when he realized what had happened. Forrest arrived at Glasgow, Kentucky on September Eighth.[16] The rest of Bragg's army arrived in Glasgow on September 14th. Forrest met with Bragg, and Bragg told Forrest to report to General Leonidas Polk. Polk ordered Forrest to secure the Elizabethtown-Bardstown Road.

When Buell arrived in Louisville, he picked up recruits and brought his army to 58,000 men. Bragg had about fifteen thousand men and Smith had the main army of about twenty five thousand. Buell now secured Louisville and was awaiting Bragg.

Upon reaching Munfordville, the Texas Rangers learned about the Confederate victory at Munfordville. Private Cyrus A. Love wrote to his parents in Texas about the battle, he called it a "foolish and wicked affair."[17] Bragg assembled his army at Munfordville. More than making a stand he continued on towards Bardstown, Kentucky. Forrest was ordered to Bardstown to secure the roads.[18]

45

On the 25th, Forrest was ordered to General Polk's headquarters. Forrest learned that he should head back immediately to Murfreesboro, and command the new troops being formed in Middle Tennessee. This force was to harass the Yankees in Nashville. Forrest turned the command over to Col. John Wharton. Forrest took four Alabama companies with him, as well as his staff. Forrest visited Bragg on the 27th at Bardstown, and was told that the troops that he was raising was to be for Bragg's command only. Wharton was also ordered to Bardstown.

While in Bardstown, Col. Wharton was informed that he was now in command of the brigade, and Major Tom Harrison now took command of the Eighth Texas Cavalry. Lt. Col. Walker, who would have been next in command, had never recovered his use of the arm that had been injured by a bayonet at Woodsonville, Kentucky and had resigned.

On September 27th, Wharton's headquarters was near High Grove, Kentucky. At the time, the brigade was divided over several areas. Captain M. L. Evans, of Company C, with 160 men was at Taylorsville; three companies under Captain C. H. Ingles, 4th Tennessee Cavalry, was at the Salt River, on the Louisville and Bardstown Pike; ten men guarded the mills at Bloomfield. Ten men were protecting the mills at Fairfield; four companies under Major C. A. Whaley, Second Georgia Cavalry, were at New Haven; two companies were guarding a wagon train under order from Col. Obannon; one company with engineer corps under order from General Polk; thirteen men were at Danville; three companies were sent to Bragg; six companies were at Sear's Mill, on the Shepherdsville road, and one company was on police duty. Wharton only had forty men from the Second Georgia Cavalry and two hundred of the Rangers with him at High Grove. This made Wharton very nervous. He felt that his force could not withstand an attack from a Union force, because of his fragmented forces. [19]

Private Cyrus Love, who was under the command of Captain Shannon, was one of the Rangers that was doing picket duty between the Confederate infantry and Louisville. He was near Boston, Kentucky, when he had heard that three thousand Yankees were at Lebanon Junction. The reconnaissance scouts went out to investigate. A local citizen led the men to Lebanon Junction, but when they got there the Yankees had burned everything and had left. The next morning Love and the rest of the scouting party followed the Louisville & Nashville Railroad for about a mile. They stopped and decided to lay down and get some sleep since they had gone for a whole day with no rest or sleep. It was a bad decision. While they were sleeping, the Yankees came down upon the party and caused a stampede among the horses. Twelve or fifteen of the men were captured immediately, most of them from the Georgia Cavalry. The Yankees chased the remaining pickets for six miles, where twenty men from Love's group decided to make a stand. Ten of the Yankee cavalry arrived on the scene, and the Confederate scouting party charged the Yankees wounding three of them and capturing seven. Love and another Georgia cavalrymen pursued one of the Yankees through a corn field to the top of a hill and saw the fleeing Yankee about 150 yards away and about forty other Yankees standing in the road. There were about three hundred Yankees and only about sixty from the picket group that Love belonged too. Part of the Union cavalry group knew the countryside better than the Rangers and Georgians and cut across from the road leading to Boston and Bardstown. They were hoping to cut the picket group off. Four of the Yankees, according to Love, made it to the road at a place where General Frank Cheatham's Division's wagons were passing. They managed to capture and stop the wagon train. Seven or eight of the Rangers and Georgians went back one at a time to see what was the reason for the wagon train stopping. All seven of the scouts were captured by the Yankees. [20]

On September 28th, the Army of the Mississippi was put under command of General Leonidas Polk. According to Polk, Bragg had ordered him to hold onto Bardstown, unless a large force approached the city. He was then to fall back to Harrodsburg, Kentucky.

By October, Buell's force was ready to move out. His army soon moved out of Louisville towards Bardstown, Kentucky. On October 4th, 1862, Wharton and his men were posted four miles on the Louisville pike, occupying and guarding the town of Bardstown and it's approaches. Wharton received information that the Yankees were in force and were within a half mile, to the east of the pike, between Wharton and Bardstown, cutting him off from Bragg's main army. Wharton ordered his battery to follow him as soon as possible and put himself at the head of the Rangers and rode at half speed to the point of danger. In thirty minutes, Wharton passed the four miles and then found the First and Fourth Kentucky, U. S., the Fourth Ohio, and the Third Indiana regiments of cavalry-four times Wharton's strength-drawn up on the road and behind houses to receive him. In their rear, but not in supporting distance, was a battery of artillery and a heavy force of infantry. The Yankees cavalry was drawn up in columns of eight, prepared for a charge, and the rest as a reserve. Wharton called in his outposts threw his command into column, Rangers in front, Company D, leading. The Yankees were allowed to approach within forty yards, when Wharton ordered a charge. The Rangers bugle sounded the charge and they went at them as fast as their horses could carry them. The Yankees broke almost at once, firing only a few shots. It was now a chase for several miles.[21] Private Dunbar Affleck, of the Texas Rangers, was a witness to the battle and wrote to his parents on November 1st, 1862 about the engagement. He writes "...*the Yankees cut us off with three thousand of their cavalry; they were two miles ahead of us drawn up in sections of eight in a lane which we had to pass through; we got up in about a hundred yards of them when Col. Wharton ordered a charge. Co. B in advance; we raised a yell and charged them at full speed; one end gave way and then the whole column broke through the woods at full speed with us after them. I shot both barrels of my gun at a crowd of Yankees in a lane about 30 yards distance. I stopped my horse and took deliberate aim at the bunch and I think I either killed or wounded some. My gun was loaded with a ball and three buckshot in each barrel.*"[22]

L. S. Ferrell, of the 4th Tennessee Cavalry, Company K, Cedar Snaggs, was also a witness to the battle and wrote his version of the events that took place. He writes: "*Our Company (K), afterwards a part of the Fourth Tennessee Cavalry, composed mostly of boys who had never been under fire, was serving as escort to General Wharton, and occupied the village. Our Commissary sergeant had purchased a wooden bucket of nice yellow butter, and we were getting ready for a "good time", when the bugle call, "You'd better saddle up, you'd better saddle up, you'd better saddle up your horses!" brought every man with his "quippages" to the side of his horse. Soon there was mounting in hot haste, and a dash was made to the front. Some Federal cavalry had driven in our pickets and retired. ...We advanced some distance beyond our picket line and to a large brick house on the left of the pike. A splendid looking old gentlemen-I understood his name was Preston-and General Wharton had a lengthy consultation. I over heard this remark distinctly: "I have just received this morning a note from my niece in Louisville saying that Buell will move early tomorrow morning with nearly a thousand men.*

The "ball" opened next morning, and we began our retrograde movement. The usual tactics were observed-skirmishing, planting our guns in every available position to check the enemy. When within a mile or two of Bardstown a rumor reached us that a heavy force of Federal cavalry had slipped in between us and the town. Of citizens who passed us, some said there were no Federals between us and the town; and others reported "a Yankee line of battle across the pike at the fair grounds." To settle the question, General Wharton directed Capt. Anderson to take his company and ascertain the facts. We went at a gallop, and soon found them in line and "ready for business." Sending a courier hurriedly back to General Wharton, Capt. Anderson called at the top of his voice: "Form fours, my brave boys!" This was to mislead the enemy and gain a few precious moments of time. Meanwhile the Yankees began firing. They shot over our heads at first, but soon secured good range. The captain, knowing our threatened annihilation, ordered the fence on our right pulled down so we could pass into a growth of timber. I sprang from my horse and lowered the fence. As the boys rushed through one rode between me and my horse, and I was forced to turn him loose. The company kept on and left me, striking the enemy's flank. Just then I wished that horse was somewhere else, and I honorably with my wife and babies.. Forty kingdoms would I have given for a horse-for my own little roan. I secured him with nerve, and just as I caught him I heard the hoof beat and muttering roar of Wharton's column as it advanced down the pike in a headlong charge. 'Rough riders" they were, sure enough."

"*Standing in his stirrups, bareheaded, his hair streaming behind, and whipping his gray mare, fanny, across the withers with his hat, Gen. Wharton led the charge, shouting: "Charge'em boys!" I fell in with the Texans.*"

"*When the head of our column struck the enemy the rail fence on our left went down in a moment, and we charged through an open woodland. Capturing a prisoner, Col. (afterwards General) Tom Harrison ordered me to take him up behind me, and carry him to headquarters.*"[23]

Private Cyrus Love was another witness to the battle and wrote to his parents writing that the Rangers were "*five miles of Bardstown when the Yankees came to the conclusion they would surround and capture us there was enough of them to do this as they had a whole division of infantry and several thousand cavalry to effect it with-they succeeded in getting fifteen hundred* cavalry between us and Bardstown and formed in seven or eight sections across the road and their infantry and artillery were coming up on each side and in six or eight hundred yards of the road. Their artillery lacked about ten minutes of getting in position. We had been waiting for them to approach us on the road and Wharton being in error supposing Wheeler's Brigade were guarding about Bardstown left his rear unguarded when we learned that the enemy were in our rear. We started at once and went four miles in thirty minutes-the Cedar Snaggs (a Tennessee Company) and the Texas Rangers ahead when we began the fight and not more then two hundred and fifty of our men were engaged before the enemy were entirely routed and running for life- according to report about fifty of them were killed. We also took forty two prisoners."[24]

According to the Rangers they captured two hundred Union soldiers, and "strewed the woods with their dead and wounded."[25] Union General George Thomas, who was second in command to Buell, says that they lost twenty killed and wounded with a great many missing.[26] Officially the Confederates claimed that fifty Union soldiers were killed and forty prisoners were taken, among them a Major. According to Leonidas Giles, Texas Rangers, if the Yankees had taken a strong position at the mouth of the lane in which the Rangers were traveling, and had the Yankees had the same amount of courage as their numbers, the battle might have been much different than it's outcome.

After the long chase, the Rangers were scattered as much as the Union force was. John Rector, of the Texas Rangers, seeing a lone Federal officer, rushed upon him and demanded his surrender. "Surrender yourself", replied the man leveling his pistol. Rector surrendered and discharged every chamber of his pistol. Just then Bill Davis, another member of the Texas Rangers, dashed up. He was a large fierce looking man, on a powerful horse not less than sixteen and a half hands high. He broke out, "John, Why the hell don't you disarm that God d_____ Yankee?" "I am a prisoner myself, Bill, he replied." Quick as a flash Davis was at the Yankee's side and bringing his pistol against his head broke out, "Give up them pistols, you_____ _____ blue bellied_____ _____." The shooting irons were promptly handed over and the prisoner escorted to the rear. It was pure bluff all around for all the firearms were empty.[27]

After the battle L. S. Ferrell, of Company K, 4th Tennessee Cavalry still had his prisoner to escort to headquarters. He continues with his story: "*As we had to retrace our steps and get on the pike to find headquarters, and as our forces had move on and the Yankees were expected every minute, I thought it foolhardy to risk my prisoner with the advantage he would have behind me, and for once disobeyed orders and made my prisoner double quick. We had not proceeded very far when we encountered another Reb having charge of a prisoners. He asked me what I was going to do with my Yank. "Take him to headquarters," I replied. "Yes, and we will both be captured. I'm going to kill mine right here," he rejoined. At this the prisoner began begging for his life. I told Johnnie not to do so cowardly a deed as that, and requested him to turn his man over to me. "Take him, and go to h__ with him!" he shouted, and, putting spurs to his horse, was quickly out of sight, leaving me with both prisoners, who readily ran until we were out of danger.*"[28]

Wharton was highly recognized for his bravery at the Battle of Bardstown. General Leonidas Polk said of the Battle of Bardstown: "*To this gallant action not only were the dangerous consequences of surprise obviated, but a severe chastisement was inflicted on the enemy and new luster added to the Confederate army. In complimenting Col. Wharton and the brave men under him for this daring feat of arms, the general commanding can not but mark the contrast with that which resulted so differently at New Harbor a short time before. Col. Wharton and the Texas Rangers have wiped out that stain. Their gallantry is worthy of the applause and emulation of their comrades of all arms in the army.*"[29] For Wharton's charge at Bardstown, he was made a Brigadier General by Braxton Bragg. Frank Batchelor also wrote home about Polk's compliment to the Rangers. He wrote: "*General Polk-who by and by is, in the opinion of many, the General of our Western Army-paid our Regiment a high compliment for gallantry at Bardstown, Ky.* "[30]

The only known wounded soldier from the Eighth Texas was W. G. Mitchel. He was shot between the eyes during the battle. L. S. Ferrell of the 4th Tennessee Cavalry saw Mitchell as he rode to the front. "*On our way to the front we met one of the Eighth Texas, who had a bullet hole in his forehead from which the blood flowed freely. He presented a ghastly sight to beginners. As he passed us, he pointed exultingly to his wound and wanted to know of Capt. (afterwards, Colonel) Paul Anderson if that would entitle him to a furlough?*"[31] The bullet would remain in Ferrell's head and was still there when he died in 1899.

Top Left: Original badge belonging to E. H. McKnight
Top Right: Tom Harrison's saddle bag
Center Left: Tom Harrison's rare Texas Hope saddle, with original equipment, including binoculars, bit, and harness.
Center Right: Dance Revolver belonging to E. H. McKnight, 8th Texas
Right: Tom Harrison's jacket

Terry's Texas Rangers

Brigadier General Thomas Harrison

Union General Ulysses S. Grant

Col. Ben Franklin Terry, first commander of the 8th Texas Cavalry, killed at the Battle of Woodsonville in 1861.

Confederate Gen. Simon Bolivar Buckner, a commander of the army in Kentucky in 1861, and also at Perryville. The photo, taken early in the war, depicts Buckner in his Kentucky State Guard uniform.

Confederate General Joseph Eggleston Johnston

Major General Joseph Wheeler

Major Genaral John A. Wharton

Union General William Rosecrans, commander at the Battle of Stone's River

Terry's Texas Rangers

Confederate General Braxton Bragg, commander of the troops at Perryville

Edmond Kirby Smith, commander of the army of East Tennesee during the Kentucky Campaign

Union Col. John Wilder, commander of the famous 17th Indiana mounted infantry; later commander of the "Lightning Brigade."

Later war picture of Simon Bolivar Buckner wearing a Confederate General's uniform.

Union General William T. Sherman

Union General Thoma Crittenden, who was captured during the raid on Murfreesboro.

Union General Don Carlos Buell, commander of the Union troops at Perryville.

Confederate General Albert Sidney Johnston

Confederate General Frank Armstrong

Col. Gustave Cook, commander of the 8th Texas.

C.D.V. of Confederate General Felix Zolli Coffer, K.I.A., Battle of Mill Springs.

Courthouse in Murfreesboro, Tennesee

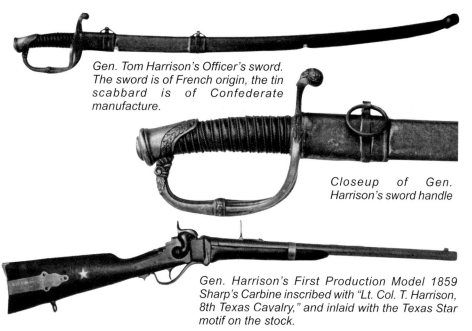

Gen. Tom Harrison's Officer's sword. The sword is of French origin, the tin scabbard is of Confederate manufacture.

Closeup of Gen. Harrison's sword handle

Gen. Harrison's First Production Model 1859 Sharp's Carbine inscribed with "Lt. Col. T. Harrison, 8th Texas Cavalry," and inlaid with the Texas Star motif on the stock.

Union soldiers repairing the rails in Murfreesboro, Tennessee. (Courtesy of the Old Bardstown Civil War Museum and Village)

Present day photo of the cornfield, Perryville: view from Parson's Battery towards Starkweather's Hill. The Rangers were to the right of the field and crossed to the left during the battle.

Elmwood Inn, Perryville. Amputated limbs from the soldiers after the Battle of Perryville were thrown from the windows and piled up reaching the window sill.

The Kentucky Campaign

After the battle, Polk marched his force on the Springfield and Perryville pike. Polk was trying to link up with another Confederate force under General Edmund Kirby Smith, who was moving along the north side of the Kentucky River. Polk arrived in Perryville on October 7th, 1862. Polk informed Bragg, who was in Harrodsburg, Kentucky that his force had arrived in Perryville, and he was securing the water source. During the month of September and October, Kentucky was going through a severe drought. Both armies were desperately looking for water. There was still a water source in Perryville, mainly the Chaplin River. Once in Perryville, Polk ordered General Ben Cheatham, who was in control of the right wing of the army, to advance and take position on the far side of the town. General William Hardee was ordered to halt Confederate General Simeon Buckner's division near Perryville, and to post Brig. Gen. James Anderson's division on the Salt River between the two towns.

Buell's army was kept at bay by Col. Wharton and Wheeler. Col. Wharton's 1st Cavalry Brigade consisted of the 1st Kentucky Cavalry (three companies) under Captain Cyrus Ingles, the 4th Tennessee Cavalry, under Major Baxter Smith, the Eighth Texas, under Lt. Col. Tom Harrison, the 2nd Georgia (five companies) under Lt. Col. Arthur Hood, and Major John Davis Tennessee Battalion (four companies). The Second Cavalry Brigade was under General Joseph Wheeler. His force consisted of the 1st Alabama, under Col. William Allen, the 3rd Alabama, under Col. James Hagan, the 6th Confederate, under Lt. Col. James Pell, the Eighth Confederate, under Col. W. B. Wade, the 2nd Georgia Battalion, under Major C. A. Waley, the 3rd Georgia, the 1st Kentucky (six companies), under Major J. W. Caldwell, Bennett's Battalion, 12th Tennessee Battalion, four companies, under Major T. W. Adrian, 6th Kentucky (two or three companies), Georgia Cavalry battalion (Sumner Smith's Legion).[32]

The Confederate cavalry force under Col. Wharton and General Wheeler had bought into Buell's deception. Buell fooled Bragg into thinking that his whole force was concentrating on Edmund Kirby Smith's force, which was in Frankfort, but in actuality Buell's entire force was heading straight for Polk's Army of the Mississippi in Perryville.

Hardee told Polk that the Union forces were arriving in the town and that the Army should attack. On the 7th, that evening, Hardee ordered Anderson's division, of Hardee's wing, to return to Perryville, and ordered Confederate General Benjamin Cheatham, with General Daniel Donelson's division on his wing, to follow it immediately, and take charge of the forces and attack the Union army in the morning. Bragg objected to Polk's orders of placing the main force of the army in Perryville more than Harrodsburg. Bragg still thought the main Union force was going to attack Edmund Kirby Smith. Wither's, who made up the rest of the Army, was ordered to Harrodsburg. Confederate General Benjamin Cheatham and Anderson were given permission to follow Polk's orders and set up in line of battle. Bragg arrived that night, and did his own reconnaissance that morning. According to Dunbar Affleck, Eighth Texas Cavalry, on the evening of the 7th, "*a division [was] made from each company of eight men for a patrol to guard the left wing and I was one of them; such relief of twenty men had to ride four hours. We went through the enemies line and in a hundred yards of their pickets but did not fire on them.*"[33]

Bragg that morning decided to take a defensive-offensive position, meaning that if the enemy attacked, then the Confederate army should attack in defense. The line of battle chosen was on the Chaplin Fork of the Salt River, on the banks of where the army was posted. General Simon Buckner of the left wing, occupied the extreme right, General James Anderson the center; that of General Donelson, of the right wing, under General Ben Cheatham, the left. General Wharton's brigade of cavalry covered the right wing, General Wheeler the left. General McCown arrived by forced march with a cavalry force, and was directed by Bragg to turn his command over to Wheeler. Bragg's force at Perryville was fifteen thousand men. Polk, from his intelligence, figured that Buell's army consisted of eighteen thousand under Generals Alexander McCook and Gilbert, and that of General Thomas Crittenden, with a Corps about eight miles outside of Perryville.

On October Eighth, 1862, General St. John Liddell's brigade, of Buckner's Division was ordered to advance about a mile in front of Perryville, between the Springfield and Mackville Roads.

At 10:00 o'clock Liddell became heavily engaged, and the Union army was pressing in their right. Polk ordered Buckner to retreat Liddell's brigade and fall back to the main Confederate line. General Ben Cheatham was then ordered to move the whole of his line from left to right. It was now 1 o'clock. General Bragg had now arrived from Harrodsburg, and took command.

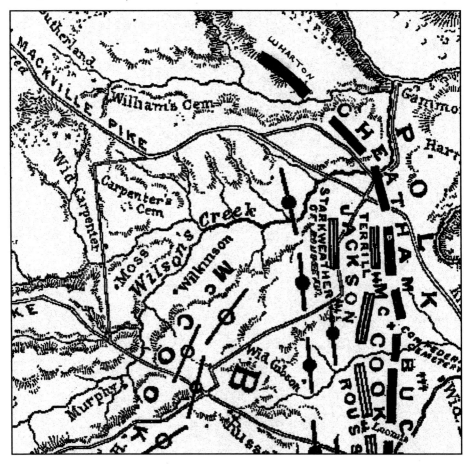

Bragg ordered a offensive. General Cheatham's column of brigades, along with Col. Wharton's cavalry including Col. Tom Harrison and the 8th Texas, were informed that they should attack as soon as possible. Col. Wharton informed Polk that Yankee infantry was seen by the Mackville road supporting the Union left. Polk waited for his reenforcements and then ordered the attack. By 1:30 P.M. Wharton and his cavalry were ready to move out from his position on the Dixville Road. A.B. Briscoe, Texas Rangers, describes the movements of the 8th Texas Cavalry: "*The Yanks were on the west side of the creek and our army on the east. The valley between was open field and the tops of the hills covered in places with timber. There were no breastworks, but the hills on both sides were crowned with artillery. Polk expected the Yanks to attack and waited for them until 2 P.M. The artillery was making the very earth tremble with a duel of nearly 100 guns. We lay in the little valley a few hundred yards to the rear, partially sheltered from this storm of shells. At 2 P.M. we were moved in column, through the lines of infantry and the smoking batteries to the front. The open valley was before us with a deep creek spanned by a wooden bridge. Down we charged in columns of fours across the bridge.*" The wooden bridge that Briscoe is referring to was on the Chaplin River. Once over the bridge, Wharton and his men proceeded west along the Benton Road. Captain David Stone of Stone's Battery saw Wharton's force and began shelling his position. Briscoe continues with the story: "*After crossing, each squadron formed left front into line, which made us present five lines, one behind the other, and in this order we charged up the hill, into the woods and among the Yanks... The Yanks were brushed back from the hill and woods and when the bugle sounded the recall and we returned, our own infantry and artillery had crossed the creek and were taking position on the hills from which we had driven the enemy. Lt. Col. Evans was killed.*" [34] Once Wharton had crossed the bridge and

The Kentucky Campaign

formed into lines, he followed a road across the top of the bluff and out of the range of Stone's Battery. The "Yanks" that Briscoe was referring to were Montgomery's skirmishers from the 33rd Ohio. Wharton and his men easily pushed back the small force, but soon came upon the main body of the 33rd Ohio, and the shot and shell from Harris' Battery. As Briscoe alluded to after the bugle was sounded for recall of the troops, Wharton's force returned to the Chaplain River and watched the battle begin.

According to the Texas Rangers, the charge on the right of the battlefield, which was the main part of General Wharton's cavalry force, along with the Eighth Texas Cavalry, was one of the greatest cavalry charges they made during the war. During this charge, Lt. Col. Mark Evans was severely wounded while leading the regiment and would later die of his wounds on October 18th, 1862.

During the battle, the brigades of Confederate General Benjamin Cheatham now came up, under Donelson, Stewart, and Maney. The Confederate troops crossed the Chaplin River and moved forward upon the Union position. They were met with shot, shell, and musketry from Parson's battery's eleven cannons, and Yankee infantry from the 105th Ohio. The Confederate troops under Stewart, Maney, and Donelson continued to advance, although mowed down by the cannon fire along the ridge where Parson's battery was located. Maney decided to move to the extreme Union left, and approached a bluff. They came upon the Yankee's and totally caught them by surprise. Union General James Jackson, who was the division commander, was with Parson's battery, and the 105th Ohio, when he was killed by a Confederate volley. His last words were: "I'll be damned if this isn't a particular situation," and was hit by two bullets in his chest, he died instantly. The green troops from Ohio broke and ran. The Yankee line collapsed, and Parson's battery was captured, except for one cannon that had not been unlimbered yet. The Union line was pushed a mile back. The Confederate troops now advanced down the ridge, through a corn field and approached the next ridge held by Starkweather and the batteries of Bush and Stone. [35]

Sergeant Frank Batchelor, of the Texas Rangers, was a witness to the Battle of Perryville and wrote home about his experience. He wrote: "*General Cheatham who stood the fiercest of the fight on the bloody field of Perryville speaks in highest terms of our Regiment in that battle– we were on the extreme right where the hard fighting was done and made the first charge on the ground where [Union] General James Jackson was killed and 13 pieces of cannon taken–in our charge we drove back the Federal Cavalry also one Regiment of Infantry and charged up to their strong reserve of two brigades of Infantry supporting their cannon. While this was being done and the enemy's fire turned upon us General Cheatham's Division double quicked it across an open space of 600 yards and came up in time to make the charge entirely successful and we continued driving their broken lines for two miles and until night.*" [36]

According to Dunbar Affleck, Eighth Texas, who was a witness to the battle said that on the morning of October Eighth "*we had a fight with Yankee cavalry and whipped them; we then went to look for our regiment, we went up on a hill on the other side of town and remained there all day, until evening when the Yankees shelled us out. We could see fighting going on all day.*" [37] According to Leonidas Giles, of the 8th Texas Rangers, he was also involved in a small detachment of Texas Rangers who were sent to the left, while the main part of the regiment were on the right. Some light may be shed on what this small detachment did. According to Major John Wynkoop of the 7th Pennsylvania, under Col. Edward McCook's Cavalry Brigade, they may have become engaged with a part of Wharton's Cavalry Brigade, serving under Wheeler on the left of the battlefield. As Major George Wynkoop wrote: "*McCook's corps had engaged the enemy's right wing early in the morning. As we advanced we heard the loud roar of artillery and the sharp cracking of the musketry. By nine o'clock our line was formed, with Wolford's (Union 1st Kentucky Cavalry) in the advance. Our battalion supported the artillery. Scarcely was the line complete when we heard our pickets firing. Co. A of our battalion was ordered to take the advance and skirmish. Fifteen minutes later Co. F was ordered to help Co. A (Co. A. numbered 36 men, commanded by Lieut. Jones). The respective platoons were commanded by O. Sergeant Price and Peter Kelly. Co. F. numbered 28 men commanded by Lieut. Heber S. Thompson. (The 1st platoon by O. Sergeant Geo. F. Steahlin). Our position was on a ravine. Co. A was deployed and under fire at the time we arrived. My platoon was sent to the right. Lieut. Thompson deployed to the left under a heavy fire. Three men and a corporal went on the hill in my rear. As my platoon advanced, the rebels poured a volley of musketry over our heads. A gate was reached.*

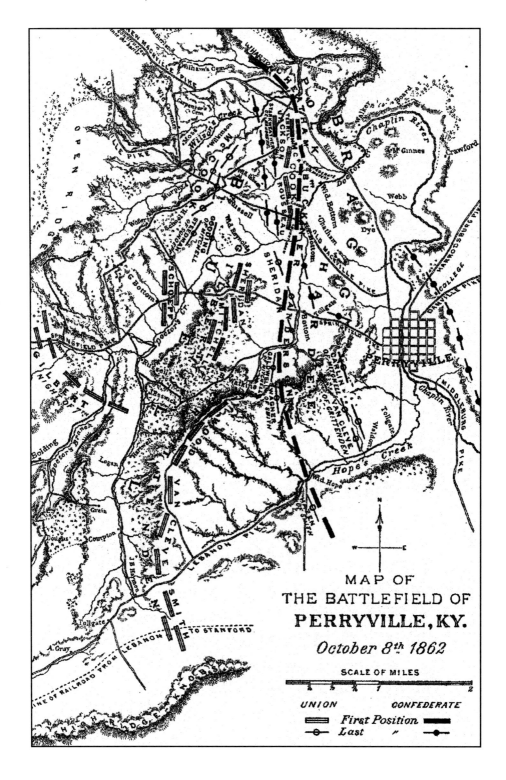

Here we halted a second or two. They took advantage of the pause by sending a little grapeshot at us just as the last man entered the gate; a few yards more to make, we were safe behind six hay stacks. I dismounted four men to act as sharpshooters. They opened the artillery upon us. We were too low to do us any damage, except taking the cap off our hay stack, and blowing the limbs off the trees behind us, which caused the corporal's squad to shelter behind the trees.

"The skirmish became general. Ten men of Co. A sheltered themselves behind a house. From there they killed eighteen (18) men and one Major. We had the position for 30 minutes under a galling fire of musketry and artillery. We did too much execution for them, so they prepared a column of cavalry to charge upon us. Our skirmishers on the left could see them preparing. The distance was but 150 yards. The charge was made. Lieut's. Jones and Thompson's men took to the woods with the Rebels on their heels. I heard them yell. Gave the order to retreat. As were turned, the artillery opened. A column was on my right and left. We would have been captured had I not ordered a man (James A. Wilson) to open the fence behind us. He did not reach his horse; but made good time on foot. The horse followed us. James took shelter under a hay stack. The Rebels passed him. Our artillery opened and knocked the hay stack over. James was again put hors du combar. He came in carrying the colors of the 1st Ky. Cavalry, which they left behind as the rebels charged upon us. The 1st Ky. Cavalry behaved anything but bravely. The rebels were close enough to use the saber, and came near taking two pieces of artillery and three Generals, all caused by the 1st Ky. Cavalry balking. Their Colonel took the lead and begged them to charge, but alas, they turned their backs to the rebels. Our loss was four men taken prisoners...I have since learned from a prisoner, that we killed about sixty men and wounded some forty. Their force at that point was 5,000 cavalry, under General Wharton, late Col. of the Texas Rangers, two regiments of infantry, and one battery of artillery from Louisiana." [38]

It is interesting to note what the Union 1st Kentucky Cavalry, under Col. Wolford, had to say about this same incident. According to Sergeant E. Tarrant, historian for the 1st Kentucky Cavalry, the 1st Kentucky along with Col. Edward McCook's cavalry brigade reached the Lebanon and Perryville Road and was ordered on a hill to the right of the Lebanon road, being on the extreme right of the Union forces. Capt. Silas Adams, Company A, 1st Kentucky Cavalry, was ordered to dismount and advance his men to the left of the road into some woods below the brow of the hill. The Captain soon encountered a large force of Wheeler's cavalry, who advanced up a hill so rapidly on the Yankee cavalry that Captain Adams had to quickly fall back to the main line. About the same time, the General Thomas ordered to the left of the 1st Kentucky's line a piece of artillery, which was endangered of being captured from the Confederate cavalry charge. General Thomas, Crittenden, and Col. McCook and Col. Wolford of the 1st Kentucky Cavalry were on a high position in the rear of the line and was watching the Confederate cavalry charge. They immediately ordered a countercharge. But the field officer in command of the line, mistaking the order, ordered the line to right about wheel by fours, and fell back under the hill, as the Confederates were then shelling the Union line with their artillery. Capt. N. D. Burrus of Company K, 1st Kentucky Cavalry, was the only line officer who understood the order, charged, and with a Union infantry advance on the left, stopped the Confederate advance. Captain Adams men were exhausted. According to Sergeant Tarrant the main body of the 1st Kentucky Cavalry obeyed the field officer with reluctance, but before the men made the right wheel, when Col. Wolford came down the Union line, ordered an about face, and charged, and the Confederates retreated for the time being. General Thomas went past the 1st Kentucky amid cheers from the men. No sooner had he come to the advance line, when a company of rebel cavalry from the woods in the Union cavalry's front came up the slope in full charge to capture the General and his staff. As they wheeled and put spurs to their horses, the 1st Kentucky opened fire on their advance, and the Rebels fell back. [39]

Meanwhile, Bragg informed Polk that the Confederate right was now in danger. Polk ordered Stewart and Donelson to shift to the right to help Confederate General Patrick Cleburne's troops. Cleburne pushed the Yankees back almost a mile and a half.

On the left wing, Hardee attacked the same time that the right wing attacked. Buckner was ordered to move forward his division and unite with the attack under General Cheatham. With the combined movements of two brigades under General Anderson's division the whole Union line collapsed and was driven a mile to the rear, reaching Cheatham's left. Night fall ended the pursuit of the fleeing Union army.[40]

With night fall approaching, it was difficult to make out who was who, and Polk ordered the troops to cease firing and set up camp for the night. Cheatham had lost 1,466 men, and Hardee lost 1,930 men, for a total of 3,396. Union losses were 4,211.

Polk in his official report praised Col. Wharton and Wheeler for their "*Vigilance and activity in protecting our flanks and for the vigorous assaults made by them upon the enemy's lines.*"[41]

During the night, the Eighth Texas Cavalry went looking for shoes and boots among the dead since many of them were barefoot. Mullins of Co. D, found a nice pair of boots on what he thought was a dead soldier. Mullins decided to take them and grabbed one of them and jerked it off the soldier. To Mullins surprise the soldier wasn't dead but sleeping. The soldier cried out "What in the hell are you doing there?" Mullins replied "Nothing, damned you, I thought you were dead and I needed those boots." Mullins next found out that the soldier he tried to get the boots off of was none other than Confederate General Joe Wheeler himself! Wheeler probably kept his boots and Mullins went barefoot that night. [42]

With the great victory won by the Confederate troops, Bragg decided to pull Polk's army out of Perryville and fall back to Harrodsburg, Kentucky. Once the two armies had linked up, Bragg decided to leave Kentucky and crossed back into Tennessee. The Confederate troops couldn't understand why Bragg was pulling out of Kentucky, they thought they had won a great victory. The seed of distrust was laid in the men's minds. The reason for Bragg's evacuation and refusal to take a stand at Harrodsburg, was that Bragg was disgusted with Kentucky. He only got a fraction of the recruits promised to him, because of the drought there was no food in the state, and the Kentuckians did not rally to his side like he thought they would.

The day after the battle Dunbar Affleck saw first hand the carnage of the battlefield. He writes: "*The next day we rode over the battle field under a flag of truce which the Yankees sent in [and] we took off about three thousand arms. I saw more dead men in an hour than I saw in my life before[;] about two thirds of them were Yankees [and] they were lieing in every position[,] some shot in too by cannon balls some with their head and legs shot off, they were killed in every position. It made me sick when I first went in but I got used to it very soon. The Yankees were so thick in some places that I could hardly keep from riding over them[.] I saw six Yankees in one field. We went in amongst the yankeys and talked to them a while [part of the letter was torn] left, we took out several yankey prisoners we [letter was torn] were I there with their guns.*"[43]

Once the Terry's Rangers fell back to Harrodsburg they were made part of the rear guard which covered Bragg's withdrawal from Kentucky, and back into Tennessee. Dunbar Affleck writes; "*We went on Harrodsburg and we stayed in line of battle for two days and nights without anything to eat and without sleep, we then went on to the wagons and stayed one night. I had a fever for two days before that so I remained with the wagons but old Bragg made us stay in the rear of all the wagons about twenty of us under a Lieut., but we managed to get our wagons again. We turned off the main road and went by Big Creek gap, going over the Mountains the "Bush whackers" fired on us every day. I am sorry to say I lost old Perry. (Perry was Dunbar's body servant, who had belonged to Dunbar's mother. He had served as house servant or as assistant to the elder Affleck at the Mississippi nursery.) I think bush whackers got him. I told him to try and get me something to eat and I think he must have turned off the road and some whire and got lost from us, he may be with some of our infantry but I have not heard from him yet.*"[44] The Rangers followed the army back into Tennessee by the way of the Cumberland Gap. The Confederate army cleared the land until no food was left for the Rangers. A story is told that one day when the Rangers were foraging for food, Confederate General Ben Cheatham came up riding among the Rangers with eight ears of corn tied to his saddle. At the sight of Cheatham, one of the Rangers cried out, "Old man, I'll give you a dollar a piece for those ears of corn." In reply, the General with a haughty look, said, "Do you know whom you are talking to?" The Ranger replied, "No, and I don't give a damn, but I'll do what I said I would about that corn." The General must have been amused by the soldiers reply, because he decided to give the corn to the Ranger. [45]

Bragg was expected to make a stand at Camp Dick Robinson. It was easily defended against an approach in front by a few batteries on cliffs which line Dick River, but was easily flanked. General Buell planned to make a feint in front and a strong attack on the flank of the Confederate position. Union Generals Alexander McCook and Charles Gilbert were to approach by different roads, so as to cut off the escape of Bragg and leave him no choice to fight or surrender. On October 11th, Camp Dick Robinson was evacuated, and Bragg headed for the Cumberland Gap. On the 12th, Buell ordered an advance. At 1 P.M. his army started for Stanford, nine miles from

Danville. The advance saw the Confederate rear guard pass unmolested. Two or three regiments of cavalry, one of which was the Texas Rangers, and two howitzers, was the Confederate rear guard. They stopped the Federals from advancing and then retired toward Crab Orchard.[46] By October 12th, the entire Army of the Ohio was within a mile of Danville, Kentucky.

On October 13th, Wheeler was made the Chief of Cavalry and commanded all the Confederate cavalry, including the Texas Rangers. Wheeler re-crossed Dick's River and finding the Union army was moving toward Lancaster and Stanford, Wheeler left a small force to guard the fords and the Bryantsville road, and with the main cavalry force, and Wharton's brigade moved over the roads leading from Danville to Lancaster and Standford. The Union army was pushing forward and were continually fighting them, and in return the Yankees repeatedly deployed in line of battle. [47]

Wheeler arrived at Lancaster and after a fight, in which they disabled a battery, prevented the Union army from approaching nearer than two miles of the town. Wharton was near Standford and was being pushed back by the enemy. Wheeler rode out to Wharton's help. When Wheeler arrived, he allowed Wharton to move in toward the main army, while Wheeler engaged a large Union force, falling back slowly through Crab Orchard. At this time Union General Alexander McCook's corps and part of Gilbert's were at Crab Orchard, and all the cavalry had been ordered to the rear on the hills in the defiles between Mt. Vernon and the Kentucky border. The army had become too strung out and it was decided to call off the pursuit. The Union army stopped at Rock Castle.[48]

On October 22nd, Wheeler and Wharton arrived at London. After guarding the roads at London and Barboursville, the Confederate Army of the Tennessee arrived and had reached the Cumberland Gap. Wheeler along with Wharton moved on to Tennessee. [49]

During the Kentucky Campaign, the Rangers were in Kentucky for thirty eight days and had been under Yankee fire forty two times. Lt. Issac Fulkerson wrote to his sister Kate about his experiences in the Kentucky Campaign. He writes: *"We arrived at this place yesterday off of one of the longest, hardest, and most dangerous trip our Regt. has been on since the war commenced. I think I can safely say that I have been under the fire of the enemy at least forty times since I last saw you. At one time a shell struck a man and horse near me killing both and covering me all over with blood and flesh. At another, four horses were killed by one ball, just one set of four behind me. At Bardstown my horse ran off with me and got nearly into the enemies lines before I could stop him. I feel really thankful that I have escaped with my life. We were at the battle of Perryville and took quite an active part in the fight. Our Regt. made the first charge and really opened the fight. The fighting at Perryville was for a while I think harder than Shiloh. We staid eight or ten days in twenty miles of Louisville and went frequently in ten or twelve miles of the place. The people of the "Blue Grass" counties were really glad to see us and done everything they could for us, and we lived better there than at any place we have been. We had no news from the South while we were in Ky. except what we got from the Yankee papers which are received nearly every day. Gen. Bragg is much abused for leaving Kentucky. I think it probably that it was the best, and that the trip to Ky was an advantage to us. We fed the Army two months, besides the supplies brought away. We got supplies of cloth & clothing and we got possession of Cumberland Gap which alone I think was worth the trip. We came through Cumberland Gap and turned to the right, down the Mountain and I did not see any of our relations in that region...Coming through the mountains, our Army was reduced to short rations, and I saw biscuits sell for a dollar a piece and corn for .25 cents an ear...I expect we will be here three or four days and will then expect go to Middle Tenn."*[50]

All the Rangers agreed that the Kentucky Campaign was one of the most fiercest campaigns that they had ever been involved in. They were proud of their service, but as the rest of the army they could not understand why they had left such a great victory after the Battle of Perryville. Private Cyrus Love sums up the whole campaign" "It was a long and apparently useless trip."[51] This was just the beginning of Bragg's failures as a commander.

[1] The Struggle for Tennessee, P. 44-45
[2] O.R. Series I-Vol. XXVIII No. 2 report of Capt. Henry R. Miller, 18th Ohio Infantry, of skirmish at Short Mountain Crossroads
[3]. O.R. Series I-Vol. XXVIII No. 2 report of Capt. Henry R. Miller, 18th Ohio Infantry, of skirmish at Short Mountain Crossroads

[4] O.R. Series I-Vol. XXVIII No.3 Report of Col. Edward P. Fyffe, 26th Ohio Infantry, skirmish at Little Pond.
[5] The Campaigns of General Nathan Bedford Forrest, P. 182; The Struggle for Tennessee, P. 50
[6] O.R. Series I-Volume XVI/1 September 14-17, 1862-Siege of Munfordville and Woodsonville, Ky. No. 1 Report of Col. John T. Wilder, Seventeenth Indiana Infantry.: O.R. Series I-Volume XVI/1 September 14-17, 1862-Siege of Munfordville and Woodsonville, Ky. No. 4-Report of General Braxton Bragg, C. S. Army, commanding Department No. 2.: O.R. Series I-Volume XVI/1 September 14-17, 1862-Siege of Munfordville and Woodsonville, Ky. No. 5 Report of Brig. Gen. James R. Chalmers, C. S. Army, commanding Second Brigade, right wing of Army of the Mississippi, including operations September 12-17.
[7] Ibid.
[8] Ibid.
[9] Ibid.
[10] Ibid.
[11] Ibid.
[12] Ibid.
[13] Ibid.
[14] Ibid.
[15] Bid.
[16] The Campaigns of General Nathan Bedford Forrest, P. 183
[17] The Cyrus Love Letters, Mary Counts Burnett Library, Texas Christian University
[18] The Campaigns of General Nathan Bedford Forrest, P. 184-185
[19] O.R. Series XXVIII Correspondence, Etc.-Confederate.
[20] The Cyrus Love Letters, Mary Counts Burnett Library, Texas Christian Library.
[21] Terry's Texas Rangers, Leonidas Giles, p.40-48
[22] With Terry's Texas Rangers: The Letters of Dunbar Affleck, Vol. 9, 1963
[23] Reminiscences of Fighting In Kentucky, Vol. VIII Conf. Vet. 1900, P. 59
[24] Cyrus Love Letters, Mary Counts Burnett Library, Texas Christian University.
[25] Terry's Texas Rangers, Leonidas Giles., P. 40-48
[26] O.R. Series I-Vol. XVI Oct. 4, 1862, Skirmish near Bardstown, Kentucky. Report of Maj. Gen. George H. Thomas, U.S. Army.
[27] Terry's Texas Rangers, Leonidas Giles, P. 40-48
[28] Reminiscences of Fighting In Kentucky, Vol. VIII Conf. Vet. 1900, P. 59
[29] Major General John A. Wharton, Conf. Vetertan
[30] The Batchelor-Turner Letters, P. 33
[31] Reminiscences of Fighting In Kentucky, Vol. VIII Conf. Vet. 1900, P. 59
[32] The Battle of Perryville, Ken Haffendorffer
[33] With Terry's Texas Rangers: The Letters of Dunbar Affleck, Vol. 9, 1963
[34] Terry's Texas Rangers, Leonidas Giles, p. 45
[35] The Civil War Battles of the Western Theater
[36] Batchelor-Turner Letters
[37] Ibid.
[38] The Pottsville Miner's Journal, The Civil Letters of the 7th Pennsylvania Cavalry. Interpreted by Larry Flyer
[39] The Wild Riders of the 1st Kentucky Cavalry
[40] The Civil War Battles of the Western Theater
[41] O.R. Polk's Report
[42] Terry's Texas Rangers Trilogy, J. P. Blackburn
[43] With Terry's Texas Rangers: The Letters of Dunbar Affleck, Vol. 9, 1963
[44] Ibid.
[45] Terry's Texas Rangers Trilogy, J. P. Blackburn
[46] O.R. Series Report of Union General Don Carlos Buell.
[47] O.R. Series Report of Union General Don Carlos Buell.:O.R. XXVIII Operations of Wheeler's Cavalry. Report of Brig. Gen. Joseph Wheeler, C. S. Army.
[48] O.R. Series Report of Union General Don Carlos Buell:
[49] O.R. XXVIII Operations of Wheeler's Cavalry. Report of Brig. Gen. Joseph Wheeler, C. S. Army.
[50] The Letters of Issac Fulkerson, The Pierce Collection, Navarro College.
[51] The Cyrus Love Letters, Mary Counts Burnett Library, Texas Christian Universit

Chapter 6:
The Battle of Stone's River

After crossing the Cumberland Gap, the Rangers along with the rest of the army fell back to Knoxville, Tennessee. While in Knoxville, it snowed three inches. It was an unusual sight, considering green leaves were still on the trees. For more than a week the Rangers were ordered not to unsaddle. On October 29th, the Rangers were camped twenty miles from Knoxville, Tennessee. Their horses needed shodding. A falling out occurred between Sergeant Frank Batchelor and Col. Tom Harrison. Col. Wharton appointed Batchelor on the staff, but Col. Harrison gave strong opposition to the appointment, who had his heart set of appointing his nephew Charles Pearre, of Co. A.. Because of this falling out, Batchelor would have ill feelings for Col. Harrison throughout the whole war. [1]

According to Frank Batchelor, the Rangers had up to this point in the war, captured over one thousand breech loading guns and six shooters. Since most of the Rangers were equipped with only shotguns at the beginning of the war, this must have been a huge change for those that now possessed these breech loading guns. [2]

From Knoxville, the Rangers marched into Middle Tennessee, camping at Nolensville, fifteen miles southeast of Nashville. In November, Tom Harrison was promoted to a Colonel. For two months, the Rangers stayed in Nolensville. While in Nolensville George Turner wrote to his father about the conditions in their camps around Nolensville. *"We are still frolicking with the Yankees about Nashville our pickets stand 8 or 9 miles from the city and within a mile and a half of their pickets. We picket by Companies and about five miles from the Brigade. 3 days on duty and 3 off but we no sooner get back to our tents and prepare for a good rest and Lem (George's personal black servant) sets his good things before us, than the bugle sounds to saddle and mount and off we gallop to the Yankees lines and skirmish the rest of the day but we generally get to sleep in our tents on our three days rest. Most of the Infantry is kept at Murfreesboro and we seem to be awaiting something, probably the enemy's advance so that we can draw them far enough from Nashville to make a victory complete. We have plenty to eat and wear, though there are some of us that don't get a roast turkey every day for dinner nor an overcoat to wear, but most of us are lucky enough to get it. Sometimes we are reduced to the necessity of eating hard butter on cold biscuit, yes and on more than one occasion we have had to eat everything cold, chicken, sausages, ham, but such hardships are cheerfully borne by our gallant boys. Thompson, Frank, Stribling, Lattimer, Moore, Pace, and I. Stribb presides over the culinary department, is excellent on a fry, but marvelous on a stew. Yea, the great Ayer would hang his head in despair could he but sniff the savory incense from under the kiver of Stribbs skillet, the removal of which none dares attempt while it's great artisan presides over it."* [3]

George Turner, of the Eight Texas cavalry, wrote a detailed letter as to what a typical Texas Ranger was carrying in his saddlebags. He described Frank Batchelor's saddlebags. The saddle had *"the outside flaps torn to frazzles, and they bore evidences of having been shot out of a mortar. As I promised to report you everything concerning him I'll open these same bags for you; here first is a roll of jeans to be made into pants (probably after the war), a piece of a splendid sword belt, an old muslin shirt with a calico bosom and a lot of dirty socks. In the other side, a fine pair pants, 2 flannel shirts one blue, the other red, 2 pair of drawers, 2 pair check shirts, the tin box you filled with thread, needles, etc. was full of pistol balls and caps and buttons, a pile of our letters and an onion. His wardrobe consists of flannel and calico shirts, two* pair of pants velvet vest coat (Confederate uniform) a beautiful Yankee Officers sash a very common black hat, boots (so so) and fine overcoat and you have Lieut. Batchelor, our bed furniture may be summed up thus, to wit Frank's one hoosier (?) counterpane called by the original owners Kiverlid, one spread (light but woolen) and one blanket. Mine one quilt line with a blanket, one sheepskin and 2 blankets."[4]

George also goes on to say how the women of Nashville helped the Rangers acquire their goods and clothing while they were in camp at Nolensville. He writes that *"The Ladies of Nashville are our best friends, they slip into Nashville and bring us our boots, clothing, etc. concealed about their persons. One of them smuggled out a pair of six shooters hid in the collar of her buggy horse. They go out to the Yankee pickets and get the latest papers for us, the last they brought us was a Harper's Weekly, full of Yankee camps and Yankee Generals."*[5]

The Federal army had quickly caught up with the Confederate army. The Federal force was now assembling at Nashville, Tennessee, while Bragg's forces were in Murfreesboro, Tennessee. Union General Don Carlos Buell was relieved of his command and replaced with Union General William Rosecrans.

In early December, Union forces made their presence known to the Confederate forces. The Rangers were quickly put to work doing reconnaissance work, scouting the Union positions. The first encounter was on December 1st, near Nolensville, Tennessee. Wharton reported that he had a skirmish with the Yankees and his battery drove them from their position.[6]

On December 3rd, Union Brigade Quartermaster D. B. Sears, Regimental Quartermaster S. B. Hood, and Lt. O. A. Clark were with a forage train under the command of Lt. Col. Walworth. The wagon train was on the Hardin pike. Three miles from the pike they began to load supplies. The wagons were well loaded. While the officers were eating dinner in a local house, used by the Yankees, the Texas Rangers began firing on the train and escort. Forage Master Bruce, of General John Palmer's division train, mounted his horse, and escaped. The other officers, seeing the Rangers between them and the train, remained in the house, and were taken prisoner. The Rangers charged on Sergeant Huerson, of Company E, 42nd Illinois, and seventeen men, of the same regiment, who were posted as a lookout. But the Sergeant formed his men and fired into the Rangers by volley, advanced on them, still firing, dared them to come on, and completely drove them back. The Rangers managed to wound eight mules.[7]

Several days later, on December 9th, the Rangers under General Wharton made a forced reconnaissance on the Owen and Wilson, or Liberty Pike.. While Wharton was making his reconnaissance, the 25th Illinois Infantry, under Lt. Col. McClelland, and the Eighth Kansas Infantry, under Captain Block, were also making a reconnaissance and were heading in the direction of Franklin. Wharton ordered his one artillery piece to fire into the camp of the Union forces, which were camped on the junction between the Liberty pike and Nolensville pike. Another Union regiment and a section of artillery were sent out after the Rangers. The 81st Indiana and two pieces of artillery under Captain Carpenter's Eighth Wisconsin Battery joined the Union reconnaissance. Col. McClelland deployed four companies of the 25th and Eighth as skirmishers on each side of the road, and these units had a running fight with the Rangers. Col. John Martin, of the Eighth Kansas, ordered up his battery. Captain Pease, of Union General Jefferson Davis staff, arrived on the scene and reconnoitering to the right and front. The whole command was then ordered forward, until they were five miles beyond Brentwood, when a considerable body of Confederate cavalry were seen in the road about a mile ahead. The Eighth Wisconsin was unlimbered and fired several rounds at them. The Confederates disappeared. The Yankees returned to camp. Only one private of the 25th Illinois was wounded.[8]

On December 12, 1862, Brig. General David Stanley, commander of the Union cavalry, was approaching Brentwood, along the Franklin pike to Murfreesboro, Tennessee. Stanley had only passed Brentwood for two miles when Stanley's advance guard encountered Wharton's cavalry brigade. Stanley attacked Col. Baxter Smith, 4th Tennessee Cavalry, Wharton's 1st Cavalry brigade, who had about four hundred men with him. Stanely's men forced Baxter Smith to retreat south towards a pike due west from Triune. After driving Smith's men almost two miles, Stanley tried to pass, but Wharton ordered a force of four hundred men and one more regiment to assist Smith. Smith ordered his men to dismount and fight on foot. Stanley tried to close in on Smith, but Smith fell back. Wharton ordered Col. Harrison and Major John Davis Tennessee battalion of cavalry on the Franklin-Nashville Pike to hold the Union forces in check until Confederate General Patrick Cleburne's infantry could arrive. Stanley decided that this battle was causing a delay in his plans and he took the old Liberty road to Franklin. Night stopped Stanley from any further movements. He camped on the Widow Water's plantation. One of the Confederate pickets fired on Stanley's men, wounding a private in Captain Julian's company, 1st Middle Tennessee Cavalry. At midnight, the Confederates again opened upon Stanley's pickets.[9]

The next morning, on December 13th, Stanley's force headed for Franklin, he arrived at Franklin at about noon. Stanley found Wharton's force on the banks of the Harpeth River, in the mill and houses. The 4th Michigan, and the 7th Pennsylvania, were dismounted and engaged Wharton's men. Wharton's men retreated. Col. McCormick, of the 7th Pennsylvania relates the story that *"We marched across the country and after dark (December 12th) fed our horses in a corn field, took a lunch and a rest and at day light (December 13th) we were banging away at Franklin, where we had surprised the enemy. They made a stand and our Regt. fought them for about half an hour on foot. The fight was sharp while it lasted; several of our horses fell. We drove them back into the town. Then came the grand charge. 3000 cavalry dashed through with a yell that might have been heard for ten miles. We captured a good number of prisoners, a large number of horses, bacon, flour, and other army stores and returned to Nashville."* [10] Stanley destroyed the machinery and burrs of the mill, which was making one hundred barrels of flour for the Confederate troops. He also destroyed one wagon load of whiskey and brandy which was heading for the Confederate troops. Once Stanley had left, Col. Baxter Smith returned to Franklin and re-occupied the town. Col. Smith had lost three men killed and six wounded. The Yankees lost one man killed.[11] Private Cyrus Love, Captain Shannon's Company, Eight Texas Cavalry, wrote home to his parents mentioning the attack on the flour mill. He wrote that "the enemy forage near our pickets everyday or two-they destroyed the machinery of a large flour mill at Franklin a few days ago-our scouts go in and annoy them near Nashville every now and then. It is impossible to tell when a fight will take place here if it does at all."[12]

Another skirmish occurred between Union forces and Wharton on December 23rd, 1862. A detachment of Texas Rangers and the 2nd Georgia Cavalry, under Lt. M. L. Gordon, and John Trippe, captured an advance picket, comprised of one sergeant and nine men, under General Phil Sheridan on the Nolensville pike. The Rangers had no losses during the capture. The Union prisoners were taken to Murfreesboro. Wharton reported to the Chief of Cavalry, Brig. General Joseph Wheeler, that Union General George Thomas's Army had arrived and were encamped on the Charlotte and Granny White pikes. He also reported that they had annoyed the Union foraging parties so much that a heavy supporting Union force was sent out. [13]

On December 25th, Col. Sidney Post, of the 59th Illinois Infantry, commanding a brigade, started out with two hundred wagons. He proceeded to Brentwood and then to the Wilson Pike, where they drove in the Confederate pickets. Two miles farther Col. Sidney post came to a crossroads leading to Nolensville, on which the Confederates were camped about a mile away, and at another point about two miles away. The Texas Rangers abandoned the nearest camp. Col. Post stationed the 59th Illinois Infantry and one section of the 5th Wisconsin Battery in position to command the road, and prevent the Rangers from Nolensville, which was five miles away, establishing themselves in the rear. Col. Post then proceeded two miles farther with the wagon train, placing the 15th Wisconsin Infantry and once section of the artillery on the right, and commanding the road coming from Franklin, and the 22nd Indiana Infantry, the 74th Illinois Infantry, and one section of artillery in front. The Union force moved on the Rangers. The regiment was mounted. The Yankees opened fire with their artillery. The Texans moved in columns of two's. The Rangers moved to the left to avoid the artillery fire, then dismounted and formed a line and moved out toward the left of the battery, but soon a Union flanking command was moving to the rear on the right, and the Rangers returned to their horses and rode over to the right. The Rangers quickly became hotly engaged with a Federal unit on the right. Another Federal unit, equally as strong as the first, was approaching from the front. The Rangers had to fall back and form a new formation. Col. Harrison said, "Form your company on this rise and hold the position while I form the regiment behind you in supporting distance." J. K. P. Blackburn called his men into line, but they had turned towards the rear and heavy firing from the Yankees from two different points made it impossible for men and horses to wheel around and get into position and stand still. Blackburn told three men to turn around and make a halt and then move forward toward the enemy. Gabe Beaumont of Co. A, Eighth Texas, formed the men around him, Blackburn then rushed his men in line. Gabe was injured. Col. Harrison told Blackburn to withdraw. This ended the battle. The Union wagons were completely loaded. But the wagons for the Confederate forage were not loaded, but at least they were not captured. Wharton reported that three of his men were wounded. Six of the Yankees were killed and fourteen wounded. [14]

After the battle Col. Post returned to camp. Col. Post made a comment that "the enemy are so near and from every hill top estimate the number of the escort and the value of the train, is attended with considerable risk. Our train could not be made to move in a less space than four miles, and if it were not possible to throw a superior force in rear of foraging expeditions it would not be difficult to suddenly attack so long a train and destroy some portion of it, especially while threatening it in the rear, as they did much of the way in today, unless the escort were very large." The Confederate cavalry in the area were making it extremely difficult for the Union forces to look for forage. But the Confederates cavalry under Wharton were also experiencing difficulties in attacking the Union forage parties. "The country is very hilly and covered with cedar brakes, which renders it totally unfit for cavalry, and the infantry here has orders to risk nothing." Wharton's men were also tired. "My force in camp has to be moved forward every day to sustain the pickets, and never return until dark, so, whether on picket or off, they have no rest." [15]

The day after Christmas 1862, Union General William Rosecrans, with over half his Army of the Cumberland, advanced southeast from Nashville, Tennessee. Rosecrans attempted to fool Bragg by moving in three different directions. Union General Thomas Crittenden came from the Murfreesboro Pike, Maj. Gen. Alexander McCook parallel to and fifteen miles west of Bragg, and Maj Gen. George Thomas was to move straight south on McCook's right, then turn east and strike the Confederate flank. The ruse worked and Bragg was confused.

From December 26th to December 30th, the Yankee army moved ahead in separate columns the thirty miles to Confederate Gen. Braxton Bragg's position in front of Murfreesboro. With thirty eight thousand men from his Army of Tennessee, Bragg was deployed along a four mile front arching inward. About one and a half miles west and northwest of Murfreesboro, his lines covered the Nashville Pike, and the winding Stone's River, which passed behind his men, under the pike, then meandered northwest along the east of the pike. Recent heavy rains had raised the level of the river. Bragg put Confederate General Patrick Cleburne's division on the far left resting on the westward bend of the river, with a brigade of cavalry extending south. In the wood's to Cleburne's right was Leonidas Polk's Corps, extending a mile and a half across the open side of a wide eastward bend of the river, then resting on the stream. Breckinridge's division was on the east side. His left meeting with Polk's right across the river, and extending at right angles east across the northern approach to Murfreesboro. Breckinridge was in a good position to cross the river and reinforce Polk's center, but several hundred yards to his front was a commanding position called Wayne's Hill.

Rosecrans troops skirmished daily with Bragg's cavalry and advance infantry until arriving before Bragg's main line on December 30th. Rosecrans was only a few hundred yards from Bragg's army. The Federal commander believed that if he could push Bragg from Murfreesboro, he could secure Nashville's supply lines and eliminate threats from the Army of Tennessee until spring. Bragg hoped to do the opposite, and used the days of Rosecrans' slow advance to plan the coming battle. By late on the 30th of December, facing the Confederates from right to left, he had deployed Maj. Gen. John C. Breckinridge's division (east of the pike and the river), Lt. Gen. Leonidas Polk's corps (from the pike river crossing to a point about 1 1/4 mile west) and Lt. Gen. William Hardee's Corps (from Polk's left, west about 1 3/4 mile). He planned on assaulting Rosecrans right with Hardee's Corps and turning the entire Union force, putting it's back to the river, and ideally, cutting off its northwest line of retreat on the Nashville Pike. A second road, the Wilkinson Pike, traveling west-northwest, cut the intervening ground between the Confederate left and the Nashville Pike, and intersected and ended at the Nashville Pike about a quarter of a mile behind the Southern lines. Bragg established headquarters at the intersection and ordered an attack for daylight December 31st. The Federal force continued towards Murfreesboro along three separate roads. The Yankees moved out of Nashville on December 28th arriving outside of Murfreesboro on December 30th. Bragg prepared for the battle. On December 31st, 1862, Lt. Gen. William Hardee ordered Brig. Gen. Wharton that on the morning of the 31st, the Confederate left wing would attack the Federal right. Wharton was to move to the extreme far left, and reach the enemy's rear as soon as possible, and attack them creating as much damage as possible. [16]

On December 31st, Wharton assembled his command. His brigade was divided into three commands: the Texas Rangers, the 3rd Confederate, and the 2nd Georgia were under Col. Harrison. The 1st Confederate, Davis Battalion, Malone's battalion, and Murray's regiment were under Col. Cox, and the remainder were to support a battery, and act as reserve.[17]

At daybreak, Wharton dashed forward at a gallop and soon reached the Wilkinson turnpike, two and half miles in the rear. Wharton reached the Wilkinson pike. The Union troops were to his front. Col. John T. Cox of the First Confederate Cavalry, formed for a charge. Captain White was instructed to open up his battery upon the Union force. After the artillery began to fire, Cox ordered a charge. Cox captured the 75th Illinois Infantry.

At the same time that Cox was charging, Captain S. P. Christian of the Eighth Texas, Co. K, with four companies, charged a Union battery of four guns and captured it.

Wharton's force had captured 1,500 prisoners. Wharton swept around toward the Nashville turnpike, and noticed a supply wagon train moving along the Nashville pike in the rear of the Union army. The Confederate infantry by this point had driven the Union troops across the Wilkinson pike. A heavy Union cavalry force was parallel to the pike, facing Wharton. The Union force saw Wharton and prepared for battle. Wharton unlimbered his guns, and pointed them towards the Federal's supply train. Ashby's regiment and Hardy's company formed in front of the Union cavalry. Col. Harrison formed on the right flank. The Confederate battery opened up on the Union cavalry. Once the artillery had fired, Ashby and Hardy charged, but were countercharged by the Union cavalry. At the same time, Harrison was ordered to charge. The Rangers met the Union cavalry and routed them, relieving Ashby's command. Wharton next ordered the entire brigade to charge the Union force, which was now formed in a line a half mile in the rear of their main line of battle, protecting their wagons. The charge was given and two thousand soldiers descended upon the Yankees. The cavalry quickly rode up on the Yankees, and a short hand to hand battle ensued. Pistols ruled the day, and the Yankees fled in terror. The Yankees were pursued to Overall's Creek, a distance of two miles. After the Union force crossed the Overall's Creek, the Union troops reformed out of range.[18]

After the battle, Wharton captured several hundred wagons, many pieces of artillery, and one thousand infantry. The wagon train was sent by Wharton to Murfreesboro.

During the charge, a Federal cavalry force was massing to Wharton's rear, threatening his battery. Wharton realized that his battery was unsupported, so he and two staff members, rode to the battery, which at the time had just twenty soldiers under Col. Baxter Smith protecting the guns. About three hundred cavalry were four hundred yards away, barreling down towards the battery. Several shells were fired at the oncoming juggernaut, that exploded in their mists. The Union cavalry retreated. The Union cavalry force that they had just repulsed headed towards the supply train. The force that had been driven off in the Overall Creek also reformed and attacked the wagon train. Since Wharton was busy protecting his battery, he was not able to direct movements to hold off the force approaching his newly captured wagon train. Wharton's men were only to carry off a portion of the wagons, five pieces of artillery, and about four hundred prisoners, and three hundred and twenty seven cattle. According to Wharton the Yankees lost several officer's and men killed. Wharton lost one hundred and fifty men, including Captain R. J. C. Gailbreath, of Murray's regiment; Lt. William Ellis, Company G, Texas Rangers, and Lt. Sharp, Company B. Adjutant N. D. Rothrock of the 3rd Confederate was killed.[19]

According to Union Captain Henry B. Teetor, of the 4th Ohio Cavalry, Captain Peter Mathews, of Companies A, B, C, of the First Squadron, 4th Ohio Cavalry, ordered his men to charge down the road and drive back the Rangers. The Rangers were "severely repulsed, driven back, the two pieces of cannon saved, and the ambulance and the six Government wagons." Teetor lost one man killed, one man wounded, and one taken prisoner.[20]

Dunbar Affleck was involved on the first day of battle and relates his story: *"We went in the rear of the Yankey army....to capture a train of five hundred wagons—Our infantry opened the fight on the left wing about day light, and we went around them while it was going on. I saw our infantry made a charge just as we passed them, they got [within fifty yards of the yanks [before the latter] fired a shot, when they poured the heaviest volley into them that I ever saw or heard, but they did not flinch. they ran thin about four miles [and] scattered them in every direction, and we took nearly all of them prisoners—we went on and soon came in sight of about two thousand yankey cavalry and a battery of two guns, we charged them and ran them over a mile, taking their battery and killing a great many, and [capturing] a great many more. about a dozen of us charged through an open field where I got two shots with my gun, but only killed a horse.*

the Yankees charged us in return, and I only out ran them by fifty yards, they made the balls whistle around every jump, but they did not touch me—We got behind a house and shot at them with long range guns, and then left—

We rode about two miles and came in sight of their wagon train and more than our equal number of cavalry, the 2nd Georgia charged them, and were repulsed-the Rangers charged them and drove them back, and run them in every direction. I had eight shots, and killed two Yankees. one of them, I am certain that I killed, shooting him in the back with sixteen buck-shot about ten steps from him, the other I shot in the body somewhere, with my pistol, he fell off his horse, but [I] did not stop to see whether he was dead or not—I went on to the wagons and captured a negro, and a sutler wagons, and about fifty prisoners. I made the negro drive the wagon out in an old field, and then stopped to take out a piece of artillery which was with the wagons, it had four horses on it but they could not pull it. I made them take two mules out of one of the wagons and hitch to it, and just as I had every thing fixed and started-about three hundred Yanks came up [with] in about a hundred yards and shot at me before I saw them.

I turned my horses head toward a heavy woods, and was joined by two of our boys, who were shot off of their horses. The Yankees shot at me thin every jump my horse made but none of them touched me or my horse although one went through my pants-I also captured a pistol and an over coat. I could have got anything else I wanted but did not have time, the wagon I captured was loaded with everything nice belonging to a sulters store, such as clothing sweat meats, tobacco, cigars, boots, hats, etc, it was a light wagon and had four fine mules in it, it would have been worth a great deal if I could have got it to camp—My horse gave out, and I had to come to camp to get another horse and am going out again in the morning...."[21]

After returning to Murfreesboro with his captured supplies, Wharton again headed off towards the Union rear around the Nashville pike, and continued to fight the Union troops until night fall. Wharton was camped for the night less than one mile away from the Federal force.

Lt. General William Hardee commended Wharton for his actions on the first day of battle. He writes: "The conduct of Wharton and his brigade cannot be too highly commended. After a day of brilliant achievements, he covered the left of my infantry at night."[22]

The first day of battle was a great success for Bragg. Bragg's plan for the battle was to assault Rosecrans right with Confederate General William Hardee's Corps and turning the entire Union force, putting it's back to the river, and ideally, cutting off its northwest line of retreat on the Nashville Pike. A second road, the Wilkinson Pike, traveling west-northwest, cut the intervening ground between the Confederate left and the Nashville Pike, and intersected and ended at the Nashville Pike about a quarter of a mile behind the Southern lines.

Rosecrans plan of battle was for McCook to hold the right, for General George Thomas' center troops to begin with skirmishing, and Union General Thomas Crittenden's left wing to maneuver to Stones River and cross two divisions, and then assail Bragg's right. Rosecrans intelligence revealed that Breckinridge's lone division held the Confederate line east of the river. With two divisions to Breckinridge's one, he would thrust the Confederates back, attain Bragg's rear and flank, and with the Union line wheeling to its left, push the Confederates west and southwest, out and away from Murfreesboro. To ensure an overextension of the Confederate lines, he ordered McCook to send detachments farther to the left after dark on December 30th, and to build campfires to give the illusion of a longer Union line. He then ordered an attack for 7:00 A.M. on December 31st.[23]

Deceived by the false extension of Rosecrans lines, Bragg pulled his lone reserve division, commanded by Maj. Gen. John McCown, and a second line division of Hardee's, led by Maj. Gen. Patrick Cleburne, and threw them out on his left against McCook's phantom troops. Bragg attacked at 6:00 A.M., before Rosecrans had a chance to attack and his assault caught the Federals unprepared. McCown moved forward as Cleburne put his division five yards behind the first line to attack Rosecrans right flank. Willich's brigade saw the Rebels coming and fired when they got within two hundred yards of the Federals. Union Brig. Gen. Edward Kirk was wounded. Willich, who had been away, rode up only to be captured by the Rebels. Rosecrans right totally collapsed. McCown was pulled off course in his wheel movement, and Cleburne had to fill in where McCown's position was. Cleburne now faced Union Jefferson Davis's 1st brigade under Col. Sidney Post. Post couldn't handle the assault and gave way. At 7:30 A.M., the Federals reformed with fresh regiments and held until Confederate assaults broke their lines. All of Rosecrans five brigades collapsed and Rosecrans line was pushed a mile back on the right flank. The Rebel assault now hammering against McCook's left wing pushed McCook's troops back on George Thomas. Polk forged ahead, startling the Federals. Polk sent Cheatham's division to attack Union General Phil Sheridan's division, under Brig. Gen. Joshua Sill, and Brig. Gen. Jefferson Davis Division, under Colonels William P. Carlin and William Woodruff. Woodruff was on the edge of woods on the south side of a rise. Brig. General Sill was on Woodruff's left, facing east and making a sharp angle with Woodruff's line at the top of the wooded slope. Woodruff's infantry, the 25th Illinois, 30th Illinois, and 81st Indiana with the help of the Eighth Wisconsin Battery, managed to fight back attacks from Confederate infantry under Col. Loomis, comprised of the 26th, 39th, and 25th Alabama. His right three regiments, the 1st Louisiana, 19th Alabama, and 22nd Alabama hit Sill's line. Col. Loomis was injured in the heavy fighting and his men retreated. Confederate Col. Vaughan sent in his infantry after Loomis men fell back. Woodruff's line had taken back lost ground and fell in on their old line at Sill's right. Vaughn attacked Woodruff's battered regiments, but Woodruff held, and Vaughn retreated. On Loomis right, Col. A.M. Manigault attacked Sill. Sill was killed when he was riding over to Bush's guns to aid in the advance and his men fell back on Woodruff. Woodruff was now flanked on both sides and Woodruff had no choice but to retreat. Sheridan ordered a fighting retreat. [24]

Sheridan's men reformed their position on the Wilkinson Pike, west of a farm. Brig. Gen. James Negley's division, of General George Thomas' center corps, was linked on Sheridan's left and extended northeast toward the Nashville Pike. Sheridan's position was a cedar forest that was so dense no one could see where his men were hidden. Sheridan supplied his men with ammunition, and under the cover of the forest, he massed 57 pieces of artillery. Sheridan's strong position now provided Rosecrans with an anchor for his right.[25]

As the Federals fell back on the Nashville Pike, the first Union division sent across Stone's River to assault Confederate General John C. Breckinridge was recalled. Rosecrans moved the line of George Thomas to form another division in front of the massed artillery that Sheridan had assembled on the Nashville Pike. The Chattanooga and Nashville Railroad ran parallel to the pike on the east, and around it grew a four acre wood called the Round Forest, dubbed by soldiers "Hell's Half Acre". Rosecran pulled his artillery to an elevation behind these woods. Now protected from attacks from the south by Union Maj. James Negley's division, Sheridan's division held the Federal center. The Union line resembled a narrow V, its right and left being pressed back on one another. By 11:00 A.M., Sheridan's troops had fallen back, with Negley's men following quickly behind him, and the new line was created with the Round Forest forming a sharp salient. The forest itself was held by five brigades, under Col. William Hazen, Brig. Gen. Charles Cruft, Col. William Grose, Brig. Gen. Milo Hascall, and Col. George Wagner. Supported by the massed artillery in their rear, they withstood repeated Confederate attacks by Polk's men. Chalmer's was wounded during the attack on the Round Forest and was replaced by Donelson, who was immediately attacked, but Col. William Hazen stood firm. Two brigades under Breckinridge were sent in, but the attacks were piecemeal, and were not successful in dislodging the Federals from the Round Forest. Darkness ended the assaults by the Confederates. At nightfall, a thin line of Union divisions held the road to Nashville, and additional troops stretched around to the east of the Round Forest, facing Stone's River and Breckinridge's Confederates.[26]

During the first day of battle, Bragg had managed to push back the Yankees for almost two miles behind their lines. Dunbar Affleck was well aware of the first days success. He writes; *"...I came out safe, and unhurt from the battle which has been going on here for several days and in which we are again victorious, having driven the enemy back with heavy loss. So far we have taken about 7,500 prisoners, killed about four thousand, and wounded about 20,000, that is about the estimate I have made, from what I have seen and heard. Our killed and wounded is about half their number. We had a great many more wounded than killed. The rangers suffered more in this fight than they ever have yet, having had some fifteen or twenty killed and a great number wounded amongst who were several of our best Lieutenants. Co. B had six wounded, and our 2nd Lieut., who was mortally wounded."*[27]

On Thursday January 1st, 1863, neither side renewed the battle. Rosecrans had pulled his troops from the Round Forest salient during the night, establishing a new line to the north. Still retaining some of its V shape, it covered both the Nashville Pike and the river. Bragg expected Rosecrans to retreat north on the pike and had his cavalry ready to disrupt any attempts at resupply. Wharton was ordered to attack the Union force at any point along the Nashville and

Murfreesboro pike. The cavalry under John Wharton, Joseph Wheeler, and Abraham Buford moved around to La Vergne. A large wagon and some artillery were moving along the pike with a strong cavalry escort in the direction of Nashville. General Wheeler attacked the train a mile below La Vergne. Wharton attacked the front, having dismounted most of his men. They captured one hundred wagons, one hundred and fifty prisoners, and three hundred mules, and one piece of artillery. Wharton then captured a Federal fortification under the command of Col. Dennis. During this battle, Col. Harrison was injured in the hip by a bullet. [28]

Previous to this battle, Harrison had escaped injury from shot and shell. His men started to call him "Old Ironsides" because they said he was "Sheathed with iron and no bullet could penetrate his body." During the battle, Billy Sayers, Harrison's adjutant, sat on his horse beside him under heavy fire. Col. Harrison leaned over to Sayers and whispered, "I am wounded, but don't say anything about it on account of the men." Sayers wanted Harrison off the field, but he wouldn't go. Luckily it was just a flesh wound in the hip. Harrison stayed on the field with his command, until the battle was over. [29]

Wharton headed back for Murfreesboro during the night and reached the city at 1 a.m. After dark, Union Col. Samuel Beatty led Crittenden's 3rd Division across Stone's River and established it on a ridge facing Confederate General John C. Breckinridge's men.

On Friday, January 2nd, 1863, Bragg ordered Wharton to the right. Wharton fell in with Pegram's battery along with Co. K and Co. D of Terry's Rangers. That morning Confederate General John C. Breckinridge scouted the Federal lines and noticed that reinforcements and artillery were being brought up. While he was scouting, he was recalled to Bragg's Headquarters. Bragg ordered John Breckinridge to drive the Federals out of his front and back across the river. The assault would be sheer suicide and everyone knew it. Breckinridge drew on the ground with a stick and tried to explain to Bragg that the Federals were on higher ground and could sweep his men with fire from cannon and rifles. Polk and Hardee also argued against the attack. Bragg was punishing Breckinridge for not arriving in time to help out in his Kentucky Campaign in 1862. Poor railroads and politics in Knoxville kept Breckinrigde in Tennessee and he was too late for the battle of Perryville. Bragg ordered Breckinridge to assault Beatty's position and Breckinridge massed 4,500 men for the assault. He was to move in two lines-Hanson on the left in the first line with Gideon Pillow's brigade on the right, Col. Randall Gibson's brigade on the left in the second line and Preston's brigade to his right. The second line formed one hundred and fifty yards behind the first and served as a reserve. Each line was two regiments wide and six miles deep. Breckinridge crashed into Price's men and overran their position as Price fell back. Breckinridge now went up against the 35th, 44th, and 86th Indiana and the 30th Ohio. Breckinridge then turned off to face the 99th Ohio, 21st Kentucky, and the 19th Ohio. Fyffe fell back to the low ford on the river. Grider and Price fell back before Breckinridge's powerful onslaught. The 23rd Kentucky (US) and the 24th Ohio were routed, but Grose's final line tried to stop the Confederates. The battle was being observed by Union General Thomas Crittenden from a distance. Crittenden ordered his artillery çhief, Maj. John Mendenhall, to mass his guns at the ford where Beatty had crossed. Breckinridge now advanced up the hill. Hanson advanced and chased Beatty across the river. The Confederate attack was supposed to stop at the heights, and then Breckinridge was to bring up his guns, but his men wanted to get the battle over with and advanced further. Hanson was struck in the leg by a bullet, and later died of his wounds. At 4:45 PM, Mendenhall opened on Breckinridge with the concentrated fire of 57 cannon. The Confederates were ripped to pieces. Breckinridge pressed on and reached a cornfield, behind a hill. Union Col. Miller, of Negley's Division, was on the other side of the hill and surprised Breckinridge's men when they climbed the hill and fired a thousand rounds into Breckinridge's troops. Miller's troops then charged across the ford and by nightfall had driven Breckinridge back to his original position. On the left, the 2nd and 6th Kentucky (C. S.) followed the retreating Federals across the river. The Union brigades counterattacked across the river and Fyffe led his brigade forward. Beatty now rallied his men as Gibson retreated and the Federals took back the ridge. Soon it began to rain, and darkness ended the fighting. Breckinridge soon discovered that he had lost over twenty five percent of his division, and was heard to say, "My poor orphans! They have cut them to pieces."[30]

While Confederate General John C. Breckinridge and his Kentucky brigade were making their assault upon the Union left, Pegram would not fire his cannon to help support Breckinridge for fear of hitting his troops, so Wharton took charge of the battery and ordered it to fire upon the

Federal forces which were massing to Breckinridge's right. The fire directed by Wharton was so accurate, that the Union standard was shot down and the force was put into disarray. Wharton's horse was shot and when he went to look for another horse, Pegram's battery had already limbered up and rode off. Leonidas Giles, of Company D, saw Breckinridge's assault, he saw *"that gallant officer and his splendid division move forward through an open field with the precision of parade, under a furious cannonading from the Federal batteries strongly posted in a cedar wood. The shells plowed great gaps though their ranks. When the colors fell other hands seized them and bore them onward. When they reached the position of the enemy they wavered and began to give way, in order at first, but as they retreated under a distressful fire of artillery and musketry, they broke into a run. We stood there and could not help them, although every man of us would have gone to their aid with a whoop."* [31] Breckinridge's division soon collapsed and were retreating. Wharton ordered Col. Harrison to dismount and support Robertson's battery in the verge of the woods until General Breckinridge's men had safely retreated a mile to the rear. Giles sight of Breckinridge's assault upon the Union position would forever be remembered. He said the charge of Breckinridge's men was similar to the charge of the light brigade "it was magnificent, but it was not war."[32] This charge in his opinion should rank with Malvern Hill, Franklin and other useless waste of life. Breckinridge lost one third of his brigade during the fateful charge, and the men of Breckinridge's brigade would never forget what Bragg did to them. After the failure of Breckinridge's assault, Wharton's regiment supported a battery on the extreme right the rest of the night.

On January 3rd Bragg ordered a retreat that evening, believing falsely that Rosecrans had been reinforced. Left in possession of the field, Rosecrans declared Stone's River a Union victory. The stalemate cost him 1,730 dead, 7,803 wounded, and 3,717 missing. Bragg lost 1,294, 7,945 wounded, and 1,027 missing. Bragg withdrew to Shelbyville, Tennessee, while Rosecrans declined to pursue and occupied Murfreesboro instead.

On January 3rd, Wharton stayed on the right flank, making sure that the Union forces did not turn their flank. On January 4th, Wharton moved his command into Murfreesboro. Dunbar Affleck said that *"our brigade was drawn up in line of battle for nearly two hours in the cold rain and then went back to camp, with orders to start by three o'clock next morning-It was still raining when we started-when we got to Murfreesboro, we found the town deserted not a man to be seen, we saw several ladies leaning out of their windows crying, and not till then did we suspect that we were retreating-I must close for the present as we are ordered to mount our horses, the enemies cavalry are four miles this side of Murfreesboro and I expect we will have a fight before night."* [33]

After a severe fight on the 5th and 6th, Confederate General Wheeler was compelled to fall back five miles south of Murfreesboro. Union General George Thomas on the 5th reported the Confederate rear guard cavalry was overtaken on the Manchester Pike and after a severe skirmish for two or three hours were driven from the Federal front.

Frank Batchelor wrote to his wife on January 10th, 1863 about the battle of Murfreesboro in vivid detail. He writes: *"The great battle of Murfreesboro is over adding another brilliant victory to the Confederate arms and through the Infinite Mercy of God George (Turner) and I came out unharmed-The Abolitionists began their advance upon Nolansville on Christmas day and met with a spirited resistance from our Brigade but being as numerous as the Egyptian locusts we were driven back from day to day till Monday 29th ult when they had advanced to within 8 miles of Murfreesboro-here were had sharp skirmishing with their Cavalry and Infantry till night fall resulting in considerable advantage to our Brigade. They charged the Georgians and were driving them in some confusion when our Colonel (Harrison) ordered the Rangers to rescue-Like tigers they rushed at the blue coats and were soon among them shooting right and left-nothing could withstand their impetuosity and in less than five minutes Yankeedom were in full flight with our boys after them. We captured 20 prisoners in this charge with pistols and sharp shooters which we kept as our "perquisites" on the principle that "to the victors belong the spoils"-Our impetuous brother mounted on imperial Gallinipper (George Turner's horse) got so absorbed in the chase that we became separated and as he did not return till the last man came in I was alarmed fearing he had been wounded or killed, but he soon came in flushed with excitement bringing a Yankee prisoner. As we were returning to our main lines we were mistaken for the enemy and Robinson's battery (Frank may have meant possibly Robertson's Louisiana battery, under Wither's Second Division) opened up on us killing one and severely wounding* another before we could make ourselves known-Next day 30th the fighting was confined to our Infantry and Artillery on the left wing and ended with no material advantage to either side-Daylight had hardly broken on the memorable 31st Wednesday when the Texas Brigade (Infantry) (Frank Batchelor may be talking about Brig. Gen. Ector's 1st Brigade of dismounted Texas Cavalry, under J. P. McCown's Division) and Wharton's Brigade (Cavalry) were in rapid motion toward the enemy-Soon the charge was ordered and it would have made a heart of stone leap with enthusiasm to see the gallant boys double quicking with shining bayonets while the "bonnie blue flag" proudly fluttered in the breeze and a long simultaneous yell reverberated along the line-As the ripened grain bends before the driving blast or mower's sickle so the Abolition hordes fell before the charge-in 20 minutes we had captured several fine batteries and had the enemy's right wing turned and in full flight-their Cavalry showed ours their backs and we were running after them with the speed of a steeple chase-By dint of great exertion their Cavalry were rallied to support a battery planted to protect their train of wagons then retiring toward Nashville. Capt. (Samuel) Christian, (Co. K), with four companies (including C) charged the battery and took one fine rifled Parrott gun-in this affair it affords me pleasure to say that George Q fought by the Captain's side and received his warm commendation before the command in these words-giving him a warm grip of the hand-"George by G-d you're a trump-You'll do to tie to old fel" and as a testimony of his appreciation during the day Capt. Christian put George twice in command of his Company-surely no higher compliment has been paid any private in this war and in no case has it been better merited-When near the enemy's wagons the Cavalry made another stand and the Georgia Regt. were ordered to charge them-which they did in good style, but the Yankees outnumbered them and drove them back-as we rose the hill an exciting scene presented itself-the poor Georgians who are mostly armed with long Enfield Rifles and nothing else had fired and being unable to load in face of the advancing foe had turned and with heads smartly stretching froward like "Turkey in a drive" were kicking their horses for dear life, while Mr. Yankee had drawn his Shining sword and was bending forward in hot pursuit making the air whiz with saber cuts and close upon them-it needed no word to charge-the boys "went in" pell mell-and were soon thinning the enemy's lines and doing a thriving six shooter business when Mr. Yankee turned and fled in utter confusion-we drove them through their train and one mile beyond it and captured about 400 wagons and 800 prisoners-but unfortunately we carried the pursuit too far-The enemy came up in large force while the greater part of our Regt. had gone off with prisoners and re-took the train and artillery and our men had to make off with what prisoners they could hurry on before them-it was however a brilliant exploit and only failed because we undertook too much for our force-During the day our brigade captured 1,500 prisoners, 1000 Beeves-8 wagons-and any amount of overcoats, boots, hats, gun, pistols, blankets, etc., and also three beautiful brass rifled cannon-in all we made 6 distinct fights and were victorious in them all. The Rangers won Golden opinions of all and the lasting gratitude of the "Georgian Dragoons"-Thursday we made a circuit in rear of the enemy and attacked their train at Lavergne destroying 120 wagons and capturing 150 prisoners and a large amt. of mules-we brought off another fine piece of cannon and 7 wagons."[34]

After the Battle of Murfreesboro, Bragg withdrew to Shelbyville, Tennessee, while Rosecrans declined to pursue and occupied Murfreesboro instead. Most of the men learned about the slaughter of Breckinridge's men, and the distrust and hate of Bragg was mounting. Even Dunbar Affleck related the distrust that the men in the Eighth Texas were feeling for Bragg. He writes "*I can't understand why Bragg retreated from Murfreesboro-he had the Yanks completely whipped, and if he had followed them up, they could have not made another stand between here and Nashville, and there we could have starved them out-Instead of that we are in full retreat for Mississippi]-I suppose-Yesterday the Yankees were retreating, before they heard of our leaving—*" He was also becoming tried of the war and all the bloodshed and loss of life. "*I am sick and tired of this war, and , I can see no prospects of having peace for a long time to come. I don't think it ever will be stopped by fighting, the Yankees can't whip us and we can never whip them, and I see no prospect of peace unless the Yankees themselves rebel and throw down their arms, and refuse to fight any longer. There is a strong peace sentiment in the north, and I have no doubt but they will stop the war themselves.*"[35]

Frank Batchelor also didn't understand why Bragg pulled out of Murfreesboro, but he still supported Bragg. He wrote: "*We are all at a loss to know why Bragg retreated on Sunday, but suppose he had good reasons-that his is a great General none can deny and history will no doubt* clear up all mysteries." "*Many seem to criticize Bragg's retreat from Murfreesboro after whipping the enemy but I think it unjust to censure a man who acts from the light of surrounding circumstances, at the time. Our army was much smaller than that of Rosecrans, our men were worn out with 6 days constant fighting in bad weather, and it was supposed the enemy were reenforcing. Our Generals were unanimous that we had better retire: Bragg maintained his position till informed his troops could stand it no longer. Breckinridge had been fearfully repulsed on Friday, another such reverse would have ruined his army and inflicted a ruinous blow on our Country-what else could Bragg do than he did, and how unjust to censure because it turns out the enemy were in bad or worse condition and were also retreating?*"[36]

Private Cyrus Love, Captain Shannon's Company, wrote "Bragg got the best of the fight."[37]

After the week long fighting at the Battle of Murfreesboro, Wharton commented on the Eighth Texas and how they were the best unit to handle the Federal cavalry. He said that the revolver was the proper weapon for cavalry. During the Battle of Murfreesboro, the Eighth Texas Cavalry would prove how reliable the revolver was when charged by Union cavalry with swords. According to J. P. Blackburn, Eight Texas Cavalry, Col. Harrison was standing in front of his line, ready to make or receive a charge. He was looking through his field glasses at a Union cavalry force some distance off. Harrison exclaimed to his men, "Now boys, we will have some fun. There is a regiment out there preparing to charge us, armed with sabers. Let them come up nearly close enough to strike and then feed them on buckshot." The Union cavalry force came up with noise and yelling hoping to demoralize Harrison's men, scatter them, and then they would chase the Rangers, with their sabers. But the Rangers stood their ground, the Yankees rode up to within a few steps and halted. The Rangers let off one volley from their double barrel shotguns, which scattered the entire Union cavalry force, and brought the Federal attack to a grinding halt. Many of the Yankees surrendered. The results were so devastating to the Yankees, that the Rangers threw their swords away. The Rangers asked the captured Federals "Why did you stop?" "Are your sabers long ranged weapons?" "How far can you kill a man with those things?"[38] Every Ranger now carried between three to four revolvers, and a Bowie knife. Wharton also commended Col. Harrison for his gallantry and judgement. During the fighting, Wharton lost one hundred and eight killed and wounded and one hundred and seven captured, along with one hundred and fifty horses killed. Harrison lost fifty men in the Eighth Texas Rangers.[39]

Frank Batchelor wrote to his wife about the reputation of the Rangers after the Battle of Murfreesboro. "*Since the Battle of Murfreesboro, where the acts of our Brigade were performed mostly under the eyes of the infantry, the praise of the Rangers is on every tongue, from the Commanding General down; and Bragg said in a note to Wharton that when he made his official report he would do us justice if the English language could express his full approbation. Wharton stands high with our leading Generals, but he failed to get the promotion of Major General and evidently feels nettled, though he is too polite to show it openly.*"[40]

One of the more amusing stories that has been handed down about the Battle of Murfreesboro or Stone's River, was when the Rangers captured Union Brig. General Willich, who had killed Terry months before. Good humor at this capture was reflected in kind treatment to the German born Federal who had been wounded and Willich was quoted as saying he "would prefer being a private in the Texas Rangers to a General in the Federal army."[41]

After the battle of Murfreesboro Wheeler and six hundred men marched on the Federal line of communications. As to whether any men from the Texas Rangers were included in this raid is not known. Wheeler and his force of six hundred captured and destroyed a locomotive and a train of cars on the Nashville and Chattanooga Railroad and the bridge over Mill Creek was burned.

Wheeler's force next rode to the Cumberland River, which was Rosecrans chief source for supplies, since Wheeler had captured most of his wagons and trains. In Nashville a fleet of transports had been built and gunboats were ordered to convoy them down the river. Wheeler and his men rode to the river. On the 14th the Confederate cavalry under Wheeler fired into the Charter and another transport with commissary and quartermaster stores. After capturing the guards and paroling them, they set fire to the boats and destroyed them.

The next day three steamers, the Trio, Parthenia, and Hastings, convoyed by the iron clad gunboat N. H. Sidell were attacked. The transports surrendered. The prisoners were paroled and the boats and cargoes burned. The Sidell was firing shot and shell at Wheeler's men but his men acted as sharpshooters and fired into the port holes of the iron clad, picking off the gunners. Wheeler's battery was also placed on a high bluff and began to fire down on the gunboat. A flag of truce was seen appearing out of the gunboat, and Lt. W. Van Dorn, 69th Ohio, surrendered the gunboat. The gunboat was soon set aflame and the gunboat sunk. They lost three six pounder guns.

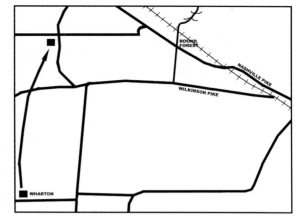

A number of other steamboats, which had run aground on the Harpeth Shoals, and guarded by gunboats, took flight when they heard of the attacks on the Sidell, and the transports. they threw their cargoes overboard and steamed away.

At Ashland, on the north bank of the river, the Federals had collected immense supplies for the Federal army. Wheeler's men swam across the river and drove away the guards, composed of a regiment of infantry, and destroyed the stores, which covered several acres of ground. Four hundred and fifty Federals were captured during the raid.

Wheeler returned to Bragg's headquarters. He destroyed a locomotive and a train of cars and captured 150 prisoners.

Private Cyrus Love, Captain Shannon's Scouts, Eight Texas Cavalry, wrote home on January 12th, 1863, that the Rangers were in and around Holly Springs. They had captured Federal overcoats at Holly Springs. He relates his experience of being in Tennessee. The ladies of Tennessee thought that "we were Feds until we told them better or they found out themselves for it was very hard to fool them long they would then open their doors and come out on the streets and get as close to us as they could without getting in the way of our horses and some would shout while others would laugh and told some would run and being everrything they had cooked for us to eat while they would put every body on the premises to cooking more. I don't think I ever saw any people as highly elated in my life. They were perfectly beside themselves with joy, but there was one drawback to the enjoyment of soldiers. It was because we knew we could not stay there for we were not strong enough and the thought that all those pretty girls had to be left to the tender mercies of the Feds put a damper on our enjoyment. But I hope it will not be long before we can drive the hierling hosts north to their homes and never be interrupted by them more when all can live in peace at home."[42]

On January 23rd Wheeler became commander of all cavalry in Middle Tennessee, which included the Texas Rangers.

On Monday January 29th, the entire force was engaged with a Federal cavalry force on the Franklin dirt road and the Wilkinson pike. Col. Harrison and the Texas Rangers charged in and saved one regiment of the brigade from complete rout.

By January 25th, 1862 the Rangers were camped near Shelbyville, Tennessee. They were informed by General Wharton that the Brigade would be sent to the enemy's rear to operate against their transportation by rail and water. The Eighth Texas could only field 250 men. By this point in the war, the Rangers had been involved in seventy five engagements. The brigade learned that the 11th Texas and 14th Texas were to be mounted. The 11th Texas would eventually be added to Colonel Tom Harrison's brigade.

The Rangers next engagement would become the most controversial campaign and would lead to the falling out of two of the most influential leaders of the Confederate Cavalry. The place where this would occur would become the Battle of Dover.

[1]Batchelor-Turner Letters
[2]Batchelor-Turner Letters
[3]Ibid.
[4]Ibid.
[5]Ibid.

[6] O.R. Series I-Vol. 20 Ky, Mid and E. Tenn., Northern Ala., and SW Va. P. 28 Skirmish near Nolensville, Tenn. Dec. 1st, 1862
[7] O.R. Series I-Vol. 20 December 3, 1862-Attack on Union forage train on the Hardin pike, near Nashville, Tennessee. Report of Col. George W. Roberts, 42nd Illinois Infantry.
[8] O.R. Series I-Vol. 20 December 9, 1862-Reconnaissance toward Franklin, and skirmish near Brentwood, Tenn. Report No. 1 Col. John A. Martin; Report No. 2-Brig. Gen. John A. Wharton, C. S. Army, commanding Cavalry Brigade.
[9] O.R. Series I-Vol. 20 December 11-12, 1862-Reconnaissance from Nashville to Franklin, Tenn., and skirmishes on the Wilson Creek pike (11th) and at Franklin (12th) Report No. 1 Brig. Gen. David S. Stanley, U. S. Army, commanding Cavarly; No. 2 Col. Edward McCook, 2nd Indiana Cavalry, commanding brigade; No. 2 Brig. Gen. John A. Wharton, C. S. Army, commanding cavalry brigade.
[10] The Letters of Col. Charles McCormick, 7th Pennsylvania Cavalry, Interpreted by Larry Flyer
[11] O.R. Series I-Vol. 20 December 11-12, 1862-Reconnaissance from Nashville to Franklin, Tenn., and skirmishes on the Wilson Creek pike (11th) and at Franklin (12th) Report No. 1 Brig. Gen. David S. Stanley, U. S. Army, commanding Cavarly; No. 2 Col. Edward McCook, 2nd Indiana Cavalry, commanding brigade; No. 2 Brig. Gen. John A. Wharton, C. S. Army, commanding cavalry brigade.
[12] The Cyrus Love Letters, Mary Counts Burnett Library, Texas Christian University
[13] Series I-Vol. 20-December 23rd, 1862-Skirmish near Nashville, Tenn. No. 1 Maj. Gen. Alexander McCook, U. S. Army; No. 2 Brig. Gen. John A. Wharton, C. S. Army.
[14] Series I-Vol. 20-December 25, 1862-Skirmish on the Wilson Creek pike, between Brentwood and Petersburg, Tenn. No. 1-Col. P. Sidney Post, 59th Illinois Infantry, commanding brigade; no. 2 Brig. Gen. John A. Wharton, C. S. Army, commanding cavalry brigade; Terry Texas Rangers Trilogy J. P. Blackburn.
[15] Series I-Vol. 20-December 25, 1862-Skirmish on the Wilson Creek pike, between Brentwood and Petersburg, Tenn. No. 1-Col. P. Sidney Post, 59th Illinois Infantry, commanding brigade; no. 2 Brig. Gen. John A. Wharton, C. S. Army, commanding cavalry brigade.
[16] The Civil War Battles of the Western Theater
[17] O.R. Series I-Vol. 20 No. 305 Report of Brig. Gen. John A. Wharton, C. S. Army, commanding Cavalry Brigade.
[18] Ibid.
[19] Ibid.
[20] O.R. Series I-Vol. 20 No. 181 report of Capt. Henry B. Teetor, 4th Ohio Cavalry, of operations December 31st.
[21] With Terry's Texas Rangers: The Letters of Dunbar Affleck.
[22] O.R. Series I-Vol. 20 No. 224 Report of Lieut. Gen. William J. Hardee, C. S. Army, commanding Army Corps.
[23] The Civil Battles of the Western Theater
[24] Ibid.
[25] Ibid.
[26] Ibid.
[27] With Terry's Texas Rangers: The Letters of Dunbar Affleck.
[28] O.R. Series I-Vol. 20 No. 305 Report of Brig. Gen. John A. Wharton, C. S., commanding Cavalry Brigade.
[29] Terry Texas Rangers Trilogy, J. P. Blackburn
[30] The Civil War Battles of the Western Theater
[31] Terry's Texas Rangers, Leonidas Giles, 49-52
[32] Ibid.
[33] With Terry's Texas Rangers: The Letters of Dunbar Affleck.
[34] The Batchelor-Turner Letters
[35] With Terry's Texas Rangers: The Letters of Dunbar Affleck.
[36] Ibid.
[37] The Cyrus Love Letters, Mary Counts Burnett Library, Texas Christian University
[38] Terry's Texas Rangers, J. P. Blackburn.
[39] O.R. Series I-Vol. 20 No. 305 Report of Brig. Gen. John A. Wharton, C. S., commanding Cavalry Brigade.
[40] The Batchelor-Turner Letters
[41] Terry's Texas Rangers, J. P. Blackburn.
[42] The Cyrus Love letters, Mary Counts Burnett Library, Texas Christian University

Chapter 7:
The Attack on Dover, Tennessee

On January 25th, 1863, Wheeler slipped away from Union General William Rosecrans army near Shelbyville, Tennessee and rode three days and nights hard riding. General Joseph Wheeler was on an expedition to attack Fort Donelson, Tennessee. He took with him Forrest's and Wharton's divisions, including Tom Harrison's brigade and two sections of artillery, in all six thousand men.[1] Maj. Gen. Wheeler was hoping to interrupt Yankee navigation on the Tennessee river as much as possible.

The Yankees had discovered Wheeler's plan and decided not to send any more ships along the Tennessee River. Wheeler brought little food with him, and it wasn't long before the troops ran out of food. The weather was bitterly cold. Leonidas Giles, of Company D, reported that they crossed one little stream fifteen or twenty times in one day. The water froze on the legs of their horses until they were encased in ice above the knees; their tails were solid chunks of ice.[2] Giles says that the weapons were so cold at Dover, that if the soldier touched his gun barrel or bridle bit their hands would stick to the metal. Giles felt sorry for the horses because they had to put those cold bits into the horses mouths. Forrest did an inspection of the troops when he arrived fifteen miles from Dover. He noticed that Wharton only had fifteen rounds of ammunition for small arms and forty five rounds for his four pieces of artillery, while he only had twenty rounds for small arms and fifty rounds for two field guns. Wheeler also could not make it across the Tennessee river, because all the ferry boats at Dover, Tennessee had been burned. Wheeler decided to attack Dover anyway.[3] It is interesting to note that Wheeler in his official reports says that after he "maturely considered the matter, we concluded that nothing could be lost by attack upon the garrison at Dover, and, from the information we had from spies, citizens, and other sources, we had good reason to believe the garrison could be easily captured."[4] Forrest in his report says that he and Wharton disagreed to the attack. Forrest told Wheeler that he thought the attack on Dover did not have promising results and would only lead to heavy losses and possible disaster. Forrest said that the most they could capture is five hundred men, while they might lose three hundred men. Forrest also pointed out that if they did capture the works, they would not be able to hold onto them because of the gunboats. Forrest pointed out that if the attack was not successful during the first attack, the men would run out of ammunition.[5]

On February 3rd, 1863, Wheeler's expedition approached Fort Donelson. Union Col. A. C. Harding, of the 83rd Illinois Infantry, who was the commander of Fort Donelson, was waiting for Wheeler's force. He had 750 men. Nine companies of the 83rd Illinois Infantry were present, Flood's battery of four rifled guns, and from ten to fifteen mounted men. At 11:30 A.M. a citizen rode to the fort and reported Wheeler approaching. Harding sent out his remaining cavalry on the different roads approaching the fort, to ascertain where Wheeler's force was. They soon returned, and reported that Wheeler was within one mile of their pickets on two different roads. At 12 noon, Harding prepared for battle. He ordered Captain P. E. Reed, with Company A, 83rd Illinois to deploy his men as skirmishers on the ridge southward near his outposts. At the same time he ordered Captain J. McClanahan, with Company B, to deploy his men on the ridge eastward, near the outposts there, thus guarding the two main approaches to his position.

Forrest approached the east side, along the river road via the Cumberland Iron Works. Forrest had eight hundred men, along with four cannons. General Wharton, with two thousand men and two artillery pieces, would approach the west and southwest sides of Dover. Wheeler, along with

Forrest, and Wharton arrived in Dover at 1:30 P.M., February 3rd, 1863. Wheeler sent a flag of truce to Col. Harding demanding his surrender. Harding refused. While Wheeler was preparing to attack, Harding ordered his gun No. 2, of Flood's battery, supported by Company I, Captain J. B. Donley, and Company F, Captain J. T. Morgan, of the 83rd Illinois, to take a position on the hill, near the graveyard, three hundred yards from the southwest corner of his base, and on the Fort Henry road, which position overlooks Harding's encampment as well as the surrounding area. Lt. J. C. Gamble, of Company C, 83rd Illinois, was sent to support this gun and the two companies. Harding also ordered gun No. 1, supported by Companies H, Captain W. G. Bond, and K, under Captain G. W. Reynolds, of the 83rd Illinois, to take a position at the east end of his rifle pits. Harding called in his skirmishers and placed gun No. 4 behind a little redoubt at the southwest corner of his base.

Wheeler set the attack for 2:30 P.M.. Col. Tom Harrison was sent to Fort Henry to make sure that Yankee reenforcements from Fort Henry would not attack Wheeler's force. The artillery from both Wharton and Forrest fired upon both sides of the Union rifle pits, and earthwork garrison. Union Lt. Col. A. A. Smith, who was commander of the gun and companies in the graveyard, became hotly engaged with Wharton's and Forrest's four guns. Harding deployed the remaining companies of the 83rd Illinois in the deep ravine west of his base, in which they were completely sheltered from the Confederate artillery.

Wheeler and Forrest began to shell Harding from the east, south, and southwest. Harding ordered the gun at the east end of the rifle pits to move to the assistance of Lt. Col. Smith, at the graveyard. He then ordered gun No. 4 to be moved from the redoubt near his headquarters, and put along side the 32 pounder siege gun, which was located near the old courthouse in Dover. Forrest charged down the slope, and across the ravine upon the Yankee entrenchments. Forrest captured them, while under heavy fire from musketry and from two brass field cannons, and a 32 pound cannon, which was in the redoubt. The Yankees fell back to the redoubt, and some adjacent buildings. Forrest rode on, his horse being shot out from under him. His men thinking that Forrest was killed fell back to the ridge. Forrest got up and hurried back to his men.[6]

Wheeler arrived on the scene and explained that Wharton was not able to attack along with Forrest and another assault should be made. Forrest ordered his men to dismount and make the assault by foot. The Union troops had now rallied in the works. But two of the Confederate guns had been placed on the ridge as to enfilade a part of the line, and the Union troops were driven from the position and Forrest's men rushed toward the town. The 32 pounder was loaded with double canister shot, and turned upon the oncoming Confederates. At the same time Harding ordered his infantry out of the ravine from the west to meet the charge. They met Forrest's men at the crest of the ridge, and three hundred Springfield rifles and the double canister shot from the siege gun forced Forrest's men back.[7] Forrest at this time lost several valuable officers and a number of his best fighting men. Forrest lost another horse while leading the assault. The men were low on ammunition and had to fall back. Forrest then dismounted and advanced on foot. Forrest's men occupied the houses on the east side of the town, and Forrest kept up a heavy fire on the enemy. At that moment, the Union forces came running out toward the river, and the men under Forrest saw the Yankees running, and thought they were trying to get Forrest's horses. Forrest abandoned his position, and rushed back to protect his horses. Wheeler blamed Forrest for losing the chance to capture the garrison, he figured that the garrison would have surrendered in a very few minutes. General Forrest withdrew and discontinued his action.[8]

On the left General Wharton's force consisting of the 11th Texas, 2nd Georgia, and the 4th Tennessee, charged dismounted and attacked Lt. Col. Smith, in the graveyard. Wharton easily drove the Yankees into their works, overrunning a battery, and capturing several prisoners, small arms, and other munitions and stores. The Yankees had cut the harness and stampeded the horses, which prevented Wharton from carrying off the battery. Wharton had also exhausted his ammunition. The Union troops were driven into a small space and continued to pour a heavy fire into Wharton's men.

Wheeler reported that soon after the battle had began, the men were out of ammunition. By nightfall, Wheeler's force occupied the west side of town, and had secured a secure position not more than ninety yards from the main rifle pits of the Yankees. While occupying this position, Sam Maverick of Co. G, Eighth Texas, swam across the Cumberland river, and burned a barge full of hay.

At about this time, Forrest arrived and a conference was set up with Wharton and Wheeler, leaving his force at some distance from the town. Wheeler, Wharton, and Forrest all agreed that the earthworks and garrison were too strongly defended and it would be better to retreat.

Union Major General Granger and six thousand men were coming by transports, protected by a fleet of gunboats had been sent to relieve the fort. A brigade of Federals had marched from Fort Henry and had also arrived on the field.

At 8 o'clock, Wheeler sent another flag of truce, and demanded the surrender of the fort. Harding refused. Wheeler decided to abandon Dover. Forrest, Wheeler, and Wharton all re-mounted and moved off slowly. Wheeler managed to bring off a section of the captured battery. The gunboats saw the Confederate force leaving and fired their cannons, but with no effect. The Confederates camped three miles south east of Dover for the night. The Yankee force arrived that morning just as Wheeler's main body was leaving the town. The Yankees decided not to pursue.

Wheeler soon learned that the five thousand man Yankee force, under Union General Jefferson Davis, was in his rear, and was closing in rapidly. Wheeler decided to move south of the Duck River and pick up more supplies. A scout was sent by the way of Charlotte to deceive the enemy, while the main force was sent over the river at Centreville. The entire force arrived at Columbia, and Wharton continued on with Wheeler's force.

According to Wheeler, he lost one hundred killed and wounded. He also captured eighty prisoners, including three captains, two lieutenants, and two wagons and an ambulance, and about one hundred horses and mules. They also captured a 12 pound brass rifled gun. Harding reported that he lost thirteen killed, fifty one wounded, and twenty were taken prisoners. Captain von Minden and his twenty six men were also captured by Wharton. Harding also lost twenty five mules, six horses. Flood's battery lost forty one horses killed and disabled.

The Rangers would forever remember the attack on Dover as the worst suffering they ever had to experience during the entire war. George Turner was a witness to the battle and wrote a vivid description to the battle. On February 20th, 1863 while camped at Lewisburg, Tennessee wrote to his father: *"Our trip has been down to Fort Donelson where we were fairly whipped, although the newspaper account will no doubt give quite a different story and color up our back out until it will seem we were called off from the Yankee entrenchments out of pure pity for them. we left Shelbyville with a portion of Forrest's and Wheeler's commands and our brigade amounting to between 5 and 6 thousand cavalry and eleven pieces of artillery. The Yankees were about 1500 strong according to the statements of citizens. We found the old fort abandoned and the Yanks in the little town of Dover close by which they had strongly fortified with the guns from the old fort. We stopped about 7 miles from the fort to warm our feet (it was an awful cold day) and take a bite to eat. We were starting when we heard two signal guns from the fort, they had heard of us and were calling in the gunboats, jumping into our saddles we dashed off for the river. When close to town most of us were dismounted and charged the Yanks who had come out to their entrenchments and rifle pits about 300 yards in front of town. We drove them back to town and into their earthworks, but we were losing so many men, we concluded that it was going to cost more than it came to, and the gunboats coming up commended at perilous shelling of the woods, so were retired leaving our dead on the field and our wounded in the neighboring houses all of whom fell into the enemy's hands. Only one company of the Rangers were put into the fight-Co. B who are General Wharton's body guard, they were sent to support the Artillery and had two men killed and a few wounded. The Regiment was held in reserve, but near the river we made us fires in the snow and I took a little nap while the fight was going on. One of the gunboats had a keelboat loaded with hay towing up the river she dropped her and Young Maverick (of San Antonio, Co. G) jumped into the river, got aboard of her and set her afire, for which act of gallantry he was promoted to 2nd Lieut. of the "Scouts". Our boys fought as gallantly as they have done at any time in the service, but it was a rash and senseless fight for us for we could not have held the place an hour had we have taken it, as it was under the guns of the gunboat. It was the first time I had been up against heavy guns, cannon to which field pieces were mere popguns. Our horses well knew the difference and as those great shells went howling over us we could scarcely hold them...Since the fight none of the Generals seem to take the credit of the affair and try to saddle it on the other but as Wheeler ranked Forrest and Wharton he has to shoulder the glory. We suffered dreadfully from the cold, a great many had their feet frostbitten and we had to leave a Tennessean who was taken from his horse senseless and almost frozen in fact the Texians seem to stand the cold better than the natives here. On our return we got to Duck River about 3 o'clock in the morning and the ferry boat was on the opposite side, and of our whole brigade there were* but two men and they were Rangers (Capt. Christian and Baker of our Co.) that would volunteer to swim over and get the boat. When they brought the boat over and we carried them out of it the fire their hair and beards were solid ice." [9]

By Special Order No. 50, issued on February 25, 1863, by Confederate General Braxton Bragg, commander of the Army of Tennessee, the cavalry under Forrest and Wheeler were broken into two separate divisions. Brig. Generals John A. Wharton, John Hunt Morgan, and Hagan would comprise one division, under Wheeler. Forrest would have control over the other division.

During the early part of March, Brig. General John Wharton became division commander, while Col. Tom Harrison became commander of Wharton's old brigade. The Eighth Texas Cavalry, Harrison's old unit would go through some changes of it's commanders. Lt. Col. Ferrell commanded the Rangers until May or early June. He then resigned. Rayburn also resigned. Gustave Cook became the new commander of the Eighth Texas.

On March 18th, 1863, Wharton, along with Harrison moved towards Murfreesboro. His force was sent to see if the Yankees were leaving Murfreesboro. Wharton saw that the Yankees were camped at the junction of the Murfreesboro and College Grove pike, and his men engaged the Yankees about a mile and a half from Salem. On the 19th, two hundred and fifty men from Wharton's command along with the support of Roddey, drove the Yankees away from the new bridge that the Yankees had constructed over the Harpeth river, near College Grove, and burned the bridge. The battle lasted several hours.[10]

Four days later, on March 21, 1863 Wharton sent Captain Gordon, with forty men to perform reconnaissance work. Wharton also sent two regiments to feel the Union army at the forks of the roads. Two men were sent to La Vergne and twelve to capture couriers riding between Murfreesboro and Triune, Tennessee. It didn't take long before the reconnaissance men met up with the Union army. A battle broke out and the Yankees were driven to within one mile of Triune. Their outpost was comprised of cavalry, three and a half miles from Triune. They were driven from their reserve camp, chased by Company C, of the Texas Rangers, and two companies of the Third Confederate, to their infantry. Union General Steedman's division was at Triune, on the north side of the town. They were drawn up in line of battle but Wharton saw that the Union force was much too strong to take on with his meager force. [11]

Most of the month of March was spent on reconnaissance work for Bragg's army. Private Cyrus Love, Captain Shannon's Scouts, Eighth Texas Cavalry, wrote home to his parents from Shelbyville, Bedford County, Tennessee on March 25th, 1863. He writes about his experiences in camp. *"I am not well at this time and have not been for some time past but have not felt much debilitated until within the last three or four days. I have been having diarrhea with loss of appetite and slight inward fever. Almost the entire regiment are in a similar condition."* Strict rules and regulations were also being enforced in camp, which must have been quite a change for the Rangers. Love writes: *"on account of the conduct of some of the men of the various cavalry regiments about this army we are now under lighter orders than ever before-We now have Roll Call five times a day whether in camp or on the march. Any man missing roll call three times in succession without leave of absence from a Brigade or Major General is to be put in irons sent to the rear of the army, his horse and arms to be taken from him and he put into the nearest Infantry Regiment from his State and other instances where they are absent without leave for a few days they are to be considered deserters and shot accordingly."* [12]

It would not take long before the Rangers would be sent on another mission. Wheeler decided to attack the Union supplies on the Louisville and Nashville Railroad. The reason for the attack was hunger. Private Cyrus Love wrote: "There will be no doubt be an important move here in a short time. Forage is getting very scarce in the vicinity of the army and it is very hard to get in some places at all. In fact considerable districts are destitute and it has to be hauled to them from a considerable distance." [13]

[1] Southern Bivouac, Terry's Texas Rangers.
[2] Terry Texas Rangers, Leonidas Giles, 53-57
[3] The Campaigns of General Nathan Bedford Forrest, p.225
[4] O.R. Series I-Vol. XXIII February 3, 1863-Attack on Fort Donelson, Tenn. No.5 Report of Maj. Gen. Joseph Wheeler, C. S. Army, commanding expedition.
[5] Ibid. 225
[6] The Campaigns of General Nathan Bedford Forrest, P. 228

[7] O.R. Series I-Vol. XXIII February 3, 1863-Attack on Fort Donelson, Tenn. No. 4 Report of Col. Abner C. Harding, 83rd Illinois Infantry, commanding Fort Donelson.

[8] O.R. Series I-Vol. XXIII February 3, 1863-Attack on Fort Donelson, Tenn. No.5 Report of Maj. Gen. Joseph Wheeler, C. S. Army, commanding expedition.

[9] The Batchelor-Turner Letters.

[10] O.R. Series I-Vol. XXIII March 19. 1863-Skirmish near College Grove, Tenn. Report of Brig. Gen. John A. Wharton, C. S. Army.

[11] O.R. Series I-Vol. XXIII Skirmish near Triune, Tenn. Reports of Brig. Gen. John A. Wharton, C. S. Army;

[12] The Cyrus Love Letters, Mary Counts Burnett Library, Texas Christian University

[13] Ibid

Chapter 8:
The Battle of Liberty, Tennessee, 1863

In the early part of April, Wheeler decided to attack the Louisville and Nashville and Chattanooga Railroads. On April 4th, Wharton was relieved of outpost duty at Unionville, and headed towards Shelbyville arriving at McMinnville on the 6th of April. On April Eighth, Wharton's Division was near Blew's, three miles from Mechanicsville, on the Liberty road, where Wharton learned that ten thousand Yankees, under the infantry brigades of Union Col. John T. Wilder's Mounted Infantry and Matthews, and General Stanley's cavalry division had retreated, thinking that General Wheeler's force was larger than theirs. Confederate General Basil Duke had about seven hundred men at Smithville, and the remainder of the cavalry was under General John Hunt Morgan at Rock Island, between McMinnville and Sparta.

Wheeler was encamped at Alexandria, and later General Wharton's Division arrived. Wharton had about one thousand nine hundred strong. The remainder of the Confederate cavalry under Wheeler, were with Generals W. T. Martin and General Gideon Pillow. The next morning Wheeler's force moved on to Lebanon, where Basil Duke's six hundred men arrived. One hundred men were left to defend Snow Hill. Wheeler decided to attack the Louisville and Nashville Railroad and Murfreesboro Railroad. Wheeler sent two companies to Auburn and a small scout to Black's shop, seven miles from Murfreesboro, to guard the approaches from that point, and proceed onto Hermitage, detaching five hundred men, under Lt. Col. S. C. Ferrill, commander of the Eighth Texas cavalry, with orders to cross Stone's River and attack the railroad trains, and return to Lebanon; leaving Duke to picket and defend the approaches near Hermitage. Wheeler with the rest of the force proceeded to a narrow bend to a point about nine miles a little northeast from Nashville, where the railroad runs down to the river bank. Wharton placed his cannons in position between two stockades.

On April 11th, Lt. Col. Ferrill came to the road near Antioch Station, at Mill Creek. His men were ordered to spread the track and he placed his men in ambush. Several of the men crawled down to the track and tore up one of the rails just around a bend in the road. The rest of the men lay in ambush along a fence that ran parallel with the road and about fifty yards distant. After waiting two hours, a locomotive came into view, drawing eighteen cars loaded with horses and other stock. The train approached at full speed, the tops of cars crowded with about 40 or 50 Union soldiers, who were standing or sitting on the top of the cars. The Union infantry on the cars were under the command of Lt. Frank M. Vanderburgh, of the 10th Michigan Infantry. The cars were full of passengers. Just as the Engineer saw the broken track and whistled on the breaks, the Rangers fired at the cars at distances of ten to fifty yards, some at the guards on top and the rest at the windows and platforms. The first three shots broke open the boiler and the train stopped. The guards from the top of the cars jumped off and rallied behind the cars. They were about to make a stubborn fight, when the "old Colonel" Tom Harrison ordered a charge, and down the bank the Rangers rushed with a yell, which made the Union soldiers take to an open field. Some of the Rangers chased them across it into the woods killing several in the pursuit. Lt. Vanderburgh was wounded twice, and then finally a third shot brought him down. Vanderburgh was trying to get over the fence. According to George Turner, one of the men from the old 11th Texas was after the Federal officer and ordered him to surrender but he only replied by hacking at him with his sword, and the Texan shot him in the fence corner with his six shooter. The rest of the Rangers dragged the wounded out of the cars, secured the prisoners, ripped open the mailbags, trunks, and boxes, and broke open with a rock a Adams Express safe. They also helped out two Michigan ladies and took them to the first house. Ferrill took seventy prisoners, including twenty officer's, including two colonels, one major, and three of General Rosecrans staff. Ferrill also captured $30,000 dollars and a silver mounted pistol said to have belonged to Rosecrans. Ferrill also managed to re-capture forty Confederates who were on their way to Camp Chase prison, unfortunately two were killed by friendly fire by mistake during the attack on the trains. Col. Ferrill destroyed the train and broke up the telegraph office. One man was wounded. The Rangers had just recovered their horses when the Union infantry from the stockade came up and poured a volley into the Rangers. Taking the Union prisoners up behind, the Rangers galloped out of the way. George Turner was sent ahead and was in charge of a picket to watch the pike which they had to cross. Turner threw out scouts up and down the pike. There were large forces of cavalry near by and the Rangers had to work with caution. The Union prisoners thought they were going to be recaptured, so as the Rangers crossed the river and the prisoners were trotting behind the Rangers on foot for about fourteen miles, half of the Officers refused to be paroled.[1]

Wheeler discovered that he could not cross the river, so he brought his cannon to bear upon another locomotive, and shot through it several times. Wheeler shot the horses in the cars, and left. On April 11th, the Confederate forces under Wheeler, Wharton, and the others, arrived at two o'clock in the morning five miles from Lebanon. On April 12th, Wharton received dispatches telling of the results from Col. Ferrill's raid on the Murfreesboro and Nashville Railroad. Wharton was more than pleased with the results.

On May 2nd, 1863, Col. Harrison was ordered to guard a wagon train in the direction of Liberty. Wheeler also wanted Snow Hill held. On May 3rd, Confederate General John Hunt Morgan, and Basil Duke, second in command to Morgan, arrived in Liberty. Four companies of Texas Rangers were also ordered to Liberty, including two light 6 pounders. On May 7th, Harrison's cavalry brigade was ordered to Snow Hill or Liberty. Harrison reported to General Joseph Wheeler that he thought Liberty of little value as a defensive position, since it is turned by roads on the left and right. Harrison also reported back that there was no longer any forage left in the area. Harrison was ordered to stay in the area.

On June 4th, Col. Paramore, with the Third, Fourth, and Tenth Ohio Regiments, went on a reconnaissance mission, along with Col. Wilder's brigade of mounted infantry. The Union force skirmished with Harrison's cavalry brigade at Snow Hill, twenty five miles from Murfreesboro. The Confederates were driven from their position. The Union force now occupied Liberty.

The next day, on June 5th, Col. Paramore moved with his brigade and two regiments of mounted infantry toward Smithville, twelve miles from Liberty. Just below Liberty, the Union force encountered Rebel skirmishers, under Col. Harrison. At Smithville, Harrison attacked Col. Paramore. The battle lasted for several hours. The Union force drove Harrison back a mile, but Harrison reformed in the woods and attacked again with renewed resilience, but Harrison was again driven back. Harrison fell back in confusion. Col. Paramore lost two men of the Third Ohio during the fighting.[2]

[1] O.R. Series I-Vol. XXIII April 7-11, 1863-Wheeler's raid on the Louisville and Nashville and Chattanooga Railroads, including the affair (April 10) at Antioch Station, Tenn. No. 3 Report of Lt. Col. Christopher J. Dickerson, 10th Michigan Infantry, of affair at Antioch Station, Tenn.: No. 5 Report of Maj. Gen. Joseph Wheeler, C.S. Army, commanding cavalry; No. 6 Report of Brig. Gen. John A. Wharton, C. S. Army; Batchelor-Turner Letters, p. 49

[2] O.R. Series _Vol. XXIII June 4-5 Scout to Smithville, Tenn. Abstract from "Record of Events" 2nd Brigade, 2nd Cavalry Division, Department of Cumberland, commanded by Col. Eli Long

Chapter 9:
The Tullahoma Campaign

After the Battle of Stone's River, Union General William Rosecrans and his Army of the Cumberland was re-grouping around Murfreesboro. Confederate General Braxton Bragg's Army of Tennessee was covering the Duck River from left to right, from the town of Shelbyville to Wartrace on the Nashville & Chattanooga Railroad. Confederate infantry and cavalry under Lt. Gen. Leonidas Polk and Brig. Gen. Nathan Forrest held the line's left: infantry and cavalry under Maj. Gen. William Hardee and Maj. Gen. Wheeler took the right. Four approaches led through the mountains: Guy's Gap on the west, then Bellbuckle Gap, Liberty Gap and Hoover's Gap to the far east. Hoover's Gap was the most difficult to travel by, so Bragg sent most of his strength to the left, where the other three gaps were more negotiable and led directly to Bragg's lines. Bragg expected the main Union thrust to come at Shelbyville. Bragg's set up his headquarters at Tullahoma, on the railroad fifteen miles southeast of Wartrace. Bragg was hoping to prevent Rosecrans's army from controlling Middle Tennessee and reaching Chattanooga. [1]

The Union government feared that Bragg might help Major General John Pemberton's forces at Vicksburg and break the siege to the southwest, and ruin Union General Ulysses Grant's plans. By late June, the War Department ordered Rosecans into action. Rosecrans had 70,000 men against Bragg's 47,000. [2]

Rosecrans devised a plan. His main objective would be the capture of Manchester and the right flank. His first movement was to plan a feint against Shelbyville with Major Gen. Gordon Granger's corps. While Granger was moving on Shelbyville, Union General George H. Thomas's 14th Corps would move on Hoover's Gap, then turn towards Manchester. General Alexander McCook's 20th Corps would move on Liberty Gap, and then move on Manchester. Union General Thomas Crittenden's 21st Corps would move against Bradyville and McMinnville, on Bragg's extreme right. Crittenden's move was to fool Bragg into thinking that his move was a feint to distract attention from Granger's advance on Shelbyville, which was also a deception. After fooling Bragg, Crittenden was to move south towards Manchester. Rosecrans hoped to turn Bragg's right and expose his headquarters at Tullahoma. [3]

On June 21st, Wharton was on picket in front of Shelbyville. Forrest was at Spring Hill with three thousand men, and General William Martin had about 930 men. Three days later on June 24th, Union General Alexander McCook's corps began it's march towards Liberty Gap. McCook drove in the Confederate cavalry pickets under Confederate Col. Featherstone, and McCook was advancing rapidly. Soon Col. Featherstone was heavily engaged with McCook. Confederate Col. J. E. Joey's regiment was on the right of the gap, and Featherstone was on the left. Capt. L.R. Fisk, of the Fifth Arkansas was killed during the battle. There were no supports, so both commanders fell back. Artillery could not be used because the Yankees kept under the cover of hills and woodlands out of view, using only skirmishers to press the Confederate lines. The Yankees continued to advance, and soon were approaching the rear of Col. Featherstone's regiment. The commander of the brigade, Brig. Gen. St. John Liddell, ordered the regiment to fall back to the next range of hills. [4]

By 5 P.M. the rest of the brigade came up through the rain and mud. Liddell placed one section of artillery on a little eminence in the valley on his right, and the other section on the slope of a hill oh his left. The cannons prevented the Union force from advancing any further, but the Union skirmishers still advanced and were constantly reenforced causing Liddell's skirmishers to fall back. The Union force had pushed back his skirmishers a half mile from the entrance to the gap. Liddell decided to withdraw his force and fall back to a position behind intervening hills.[5]

During the night, Liddell was reenforced with a cavalry company. It was placed on the hills just south of Wartrace, in sight of the gap, with instructions to report any movement of the enemy. The infantry pickets were also thrown out in the rear. [6]

On June 25th, McCook renewed his attack, and Col. John H. Kelly's Eighth Arkansas Regiment was left to cover the approaches to Bellbuckle by the way of the railroad gap. Col. D. C. Govan's regiment was placed on a hill south of the Wartrace, and Col. Featherstone's and Joey's regiments were on the knobs on the left of the stream. The battery was put on the left of the next hill in the rear, commanding a view of the gap, about one mile away. The Sixth and Seventh Arkansas were kept in reserve with the battery.[7]

No fighting occurred until 4 o'clock in the afternoon. Liddell received a message reporting that the Union force was moving away toward Millersburg. Liddell ordered Featherstone to advance his skirmishers. Featherstone soon became engaged with the union lines. Liddell ordered Col. Josey to support Featherstone. The Union skirmishers were driven back from under cover of the woods on the hill into the field beyond and to the next gap. The Union forces now brought up more reenforcements and advanced in line of battle with two regiments. Liddell now sent the skirmishers of Col. Govan's regiment to move down to the base of the hill on the Wartrace Creek, and divert his attention by throwing a galling fire upon his left flank. The Union force continued to press the skirmishers of Liddell's left wing with their line of battle until the Union skirmishers were compelled to retire to their old position. Both sides discontinued their firing after falling back to their old positions.[8]

The Union force resumed their battle on Col. Govan's skirmishers, and a fresh regiment was rushed rapidly forward from the cover of timber in the valley, with a line of skirmishers in it's front, both of which were driven back. This attack was made across an open cornfield. The fire of Govan's skirmishers and the line of battle on the hill was so intense as to cause the Union force to double up in confusion and retreat to the opposite side of the corn field. Again two more regiments were moved successfully forward to the attack, both of which were repulsed. A fourth line of two regiments now advanced, and this time succeeded in gaining the base of the hill at Wartrace Creek. The main body of Govan's regiment was fired upon by the shattered lines of the Union force at different distances at the same time. Govan's men kept up a heavy fire and halted the Union advance up the hill. The 6th and 7th Arkansas were ordered up to support the 2nd, at that moment Govan informed Liddell that his ammunition was exhausted. Liddell told Govan to hold his position, until reserves could be brought.[9]

Meanwhile, the 6th and 7th Arkansas were engaged heavily. Two color bearers of the 2nd were killed, and the third, was fatally struck. The flag fell close to the Union line. The regiment retired over the crest of the hill, and having no ammunition it was too late to save their flag.

The 6th and 7th Arkansas were now six to one, with no reserves. Liddell withdrew his line on the right to a position to the next range of hills, about four hundred yards distant, where the battery was placed.

The next morning, Liddell discovered that the Union force was now positioned to left of the 2nd Arkansas. General Wood, the division commander, arrived and ordered the entire force to fall back to Bellbuckle.

On the 26th, the command resumed it's positions of the previous day, except Liddell's brigade took post on the heights on the left of the Wartrace. About seventy skirmishers advanced across the open field toward General Wood, but were repulsed. At 10:00 o'clock Wood ordered Liddell to place a regiment immediately at a point designated by him in his rear, to relieve one of his own regiments on the Bellbuckle Road. Liddell was informed that the Union force, under Maj. General George Thomas, was trying to get in the Confederate rear from Fairfield, having forced General Stewart back from Hoover's Gap to that place. General Wood withdrew his force from Bellbuckle, and Liddell ordered Colonel Kelly, of the Eighth Arkansas, to cover his rear with his regiment on the Bellbuckle road. After midnight, Liddell camped his command on the left flank down the railroad to Bellbuckle. It was here that he received orders to cover the retreat of the division on Tullahoma, and remained in place until 8 A.M., on the 27th., when he was relieved by Col. Tom Harrison's cavalry brigade, including the 8th Texas. Liddell joined the rear of the division on the road to Schoefner's Bridge. During the fighting, Liddell lost one hundred men. Liddell finally reached Tullahoma on the 28th.

The Union forces now had control of Liberty Gap. Bragg now believed that the main Union thrust was going to attack Shelbyville.

While Union General Alexander McCook was fighting Liddel for control of Liberty Gap, Union General George Thomas corps was sent towards Hoover's Gap. Union General Joseph Reynold's division led the advance down the Murfreesboro-Manchester pike. Col. John T. Wilder's Lightening Brigade, of mounted infantry skirmished with Confederate cavalry, under the 1st Kentucky Cavalry, posted seven miles southeast of Murfreesboro, drove them back on their reserves, and stormed the gap. Wilder and his 1,200 men, armed with Spencer repeating rifles, force the Confederates to McBride's Creek, near the southern end of Hoover's Gap. Hoover's Gap was now in the hands of the Union.

On June 25th, Granger's cavalry had a run in with Wharton at Guy's Gap. Granger reported that Wharton's division of cavalry was at the gap. General William T. Martin's brigade of cavalry left for Chapel Hill. The Eighth Texas cavalry left for Manchester. Union General Mitchell had beaten the Eighth Texas Cavalry on June 24th at Middleton. Granger reported that Mitchell had killed ten or fifteen men and fifty horses during the skirmish. [10]

On June 26th, Bragg finally realized the full extent of his mistake in judgement. On that day Wilder led Thomas Corps south toward Manchester. Bragg was about to be cut off from Chattanooga. Bragg immediately ordered Polk and Hardee to fall back to Tullahoma. Confederate General Joseph Wheeler was ordered to Bragg's Headquarters, and was ordered by Bragg to protect the Confederate left. Wheeler ordered General John Wharton at Wartrace to protect the Confederate right flank, and directed General William Martin's force of nine hundred men to reinforce Col. Malone on the Murfreesboro Pike, and sent orders to General Forrest to come quickly to his assistance, since the Federal cavalry corps which was supported by infantry, was pushing down on the Confederate front. [11]

On the 27th Martin with one thousand men arrived at Shelbyville. There were twelve thousand Union cavalry, supported by infantry under General Stanley and Granger approaching from Murfreesboro. Wheeler was aware of the Union force coming his way. Martin took position behind breastworks. Wheeler soon joined him, but unfortunately two hundred of Martin's men, which were placed one mile to the left, had been captured by the Federals. Two hundred more men were captured to the right of Martin's line. Wheeler took personal command of the remaining six hundred men and withdrew to the town, which he determined to hold until Forrest arrived with his force.[12]

Wheeler had not heard from Forrest in some time so he sent two of his staff to go find Forrest and urge him to quickly move to help General Martin. Both officers found Forrest at a halt, but he told them to tell Wheeler that he would quickly move to the direction of firing and would join Wheeler on the pike or attack the Federals flank.[13]

At 11 A.M. Col. Malone, with a heavy picket, was driven from his position by a large force of Federals. Wheeler met and charged and pushed back the Federals. Wheeler managed to maintain his position for several hours.

The rear of Confederate General Leonidas Polk's wagon train had just left Shelbyville entirely unguarded, while the greater part of the wagon train was broken down over impassable roads of less than five miles from the Federals. Wheeler attacked the Federals. On reaching the town, the Federals charged Wheeler, but Wheeler countercharged and stopped the Federal column even though it was three times his size. Two hours had passed and the Federals were deploying their forces as they came up until more than five thosand men faced Wheeler's small force. The Federals didn't charge, so Wheeler decided to withdraw across the Duck River. Wheeler almost completed his task when ten men, consisting of staff officers and commissary details from General Forrest, told Wheeler that Forrest was only a few hundred yards away and coming to his assistance. Wheeler returned and placed his troops in position. This movement was observed by the Federals.[14]

Wheeler formed his command in front of the courthouse and attacked. Finally a column was seen moving rapidly down the road upon which Forrest was expected. Suddenly, as the column drew nearer, it was discovered that they were Federals not Forrest. Three heavy columns were thundering down the road towards Wheeler's force. One of the columns charged a portion of Wheeler's men and driven them over the Tullahoma bridge. Wheeler's men were soon surrounded. The rest of the command rode out of town, and Wheeler remained with his escort and stopped one column which threatened their total destruction. Charge after charge was made upon Wheeler's small force.[15]

Wheeler soon saw that a portion of his force had been cut off, and the Federals held the bridge over Duck River, which would allow the Federals to attack the Confederate wagon trains. Wheeler managed to gather about fifty or sixty men and charged the Federals flank, driving them back into town, opening the road for the escape of his command, and placing the wagon train out of danger. The Federals quickly rallied and charged again and again, but Wheeler met them and the Federals were soon repulsed. It was now sundown and the battle stopped.[16]

Wheeler had saved the Confederate wagon trains. Everything of value was now across the Duck River. Wheeler saw another Federal column advancing and was about to charge again, when a officer pointed out that another Federal force was forming to his rear. Wheeler charged through the column and plunged into the Duck River and made it to the opposite bank. Of the sixty men that plunged into the river with him, only thirteen made it across. [17]

While Wheeler was trying to protect Polk's wagon trains and fighting the Federal cavalry, Wilder's mounted infantry had captured Manchester. That afternoon, Union General George Thomas Corps had arrived at Manchester. On June 28th, Rosecrans sent a column to strike Bragg's rear. Col. Wilder's force reached Decherd, a junction on the Nashville & Chattanooga railroad. The mounted infantry tore up hundreds of yards of track. Wilder fell back when Confederate reinforcements arrived.

On the 29th, the Federal force advanced along the Lynchburg road leading to Tullahoma. Five companies of Anderson's cavalry, the 15th Pennsylvania cavalry, and fifteen men from the 2nd Kentucky Cavalry U.S., proceeded within four miles of Tullahoma, when they captured a Rebel picket post. The men who escaped fell back to a reserve, and formed into line of battle, but they were charged by Captain Betts with the advance guard. The Rebels broke and ran, Captain Betts pursued the Rebels for two miles, until Capt. Betts reached the advance force of the Rebels. The advance was halted, formed in line of battle, and a reconnoitering party was sent out. The party reported that a large Rebel force was to their front, less than two miles from Tullahoma. Col. Charles Lamborn, of the 15th Pennsylvania Cavalry, learned that a regiment and half of Col. Tom Harrison's brigade, and Stranes Cavalry, were to his left toward the railroad, with numerous roads leading to his rear. Col. Lamborn decided to return to camp. Col. Lamborn managed to capture Col. Estes, from the 3rd Confederate Cavalry which was under Tom Harrison's brigade. He also captured three Enfield rifles, one Colt carbine, and one Colt revolving rifle.[18]

Major General Thomas Crittenden, who was on the Union left and rear, occupied Bradyville, while Granger's was on the right, and made it's way to Shelbyville. Union cavalry, screening Granger's corps, pushed the Confederate cavalry from Guy's Gap into the Shelbyville entrenchments.

The next day, on June 30th, Wheeler and his men fought Rosecrans entire army and kept it from Bragg's position at Tullahoma. At night Bragg withdrew his army to Elk River, leaving Wheeler to cover the retreat and check the advancing Federals. At noon Rosecrans advanced, driving back Wheeler, and his men, who finally yielded the town and forts at Tullahoma. Union General George Thomas was hoping to capture Bragg's wagon trains and artillery at Elk River bridge. Union General James Negley's entire division was deployed and with heavy supporting columns with flanks covered by cavalry, they moved forward. Wheeler fought at every point and at one point charged their skirmish line, and at dusk Negley fell back from the field. Bragg's infantry, artillery and wagon trains were now south of the river, and at dark, Wheeler's forces withdrew and destroyed the bridge, and placed guards at the river.[19]

Rosecrans was unable to strike at Bragg's flank or line of retreat, or force him to battle in crossing either the Elk or the Tennessee River. Every wagon and all material had been removed and since leaving Hoover's Gap, Bragg's infantry had never been nearer than within five miles of the Federals.

On July 1st, Rosecrans, after a fight, succeeded in forcing a crossing, and advanced, opposed by Wheeler's men. At New Church their cavalry attempted to push ahead of their infantry, which Wheeler attacked and totally defeated.

On July 4th, Col. Tom Harrison was still engaging the Yankees forces near University Place, and charged the Yankees driving them back. Bragg's army had crossed the mountain and was able to cross the Tennessee River without incident.

Karrick House was used as a hospital and officer's quarters after the Battle of Perryville, Merchants Row.

Bloody Pond, Shiloh, Tenn., the site where the Orphan Brigade charged the Union position. Confederate General Albert Sidney Johnston was killed during the charge.

Terry's Texas Rangers

Right: Merchant's Row: church used as a hospital after the Battle of Perryville.

Union guns on the Peach Orchard, Shiloh, Tenn. The Kentucky "Orphan" Brigade led the charge towards this position.

Left: Monument to Confederate mass grave, Perryville, Kentucky.

Monument to Confederate Dead in Bowling Green, Kentucky.

Monument to Confederate dead, Bowling Green, Kentucky.

Monument to Confederate dead, Bowling Green, Kentucky.

Chattanooga from the North

To the left of the picture, Peach Orchard. Photo taken from Sunken Road, behind Sunken Road is the Hornet's Nest. Union General Prentiss surrendered his 2,200 men in the Hornet's Nest. The Rangers escorted Gen. Prentiss to the rear.

Battlefied of New Hope Church, Georgia

Battlefield of Atlanta, Georgia, July 22, 1864

Savannah, Georgia

The New Capitol, Columbia, South Carolina

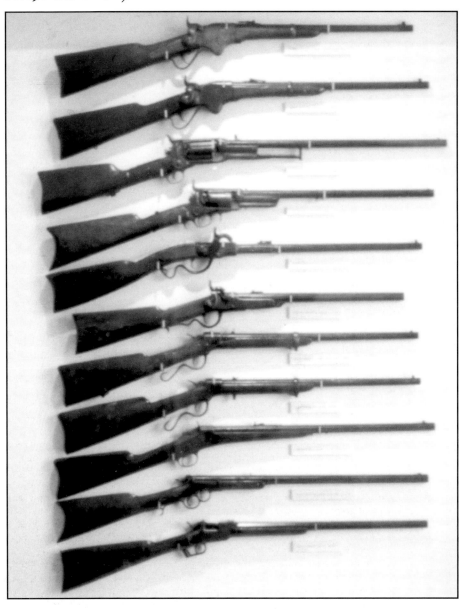

(A-B) Carbines used in the Civil War (Ft. Harrod Collection):
Spencer Breech load .50 caliber Repeater Model 1855
Spencer Breech load .50 caliber Repeater Model 1865
Colt 6 Shot Rifle .56 caliber Model 1855
Colt 6 Shot Rifle .45 caliber Model 1855
Cosmopolitan Breech load Lever Action .50 caliber
Gallager Breech load Carbine .50 caliber
Ballard Breech load Carbine Single Shot .45 caliber
Ballard Breech load Carbine .45 caliber
Remington Rolling Block .22 caliber Model 1873
Wesson Breech load Carbine Single Shot .32 caliber
Allen & Wheelock .44 caliber Repeater

The Tullahoma Campaign

After the Yankees crossed the Elk River, Bragg fell back to the Cumberland Plateau and took position behind the Tennessee River. Rosecrans ordered his men to halt. Rosecrans had lost five hundred and sixty men, and outmaneuvered Bragg, compelling Bragg to withdraw eighty five miles and evacuate several formidable positions with the loss of 1,634 prisoners, and eleven cannon, and large quantities of supplies.

On July 7th, 1863 George Turner, of the Texas Rangers, wrote to his father about his experiences in the Tullahoma Campaign. George Turner along with the rest of the Confederate Army of Tennessee, realized the huge blunder that Bragg had made, and what he lost in return. "*Old Rosey is too many for us. We expected to fight him at Tullahoma but he flanked us in spite of the mountains. We have from learned him the efficiency of Cavalry and he has immense bodies of mounted Infantry which enables him to make his movements with a rapidity that is quite uncomfortable and kept us for weeks jumping from one wing of our line to the other like the puppet figures of cavalry on a chess board. Now just glance at your map and see what an ample and delicious slice of Tennessee we have given up. The brigade headquarters were at Liberty about the center of our lines and about 18 miles distant. We pushed 3 miles of Liberty we met a courier on his way to call in the pickets, he told us the Yanks were making an advance, had run into camp and had very nearly captured the Staff. Here was a dilemma-we were cut off from the Regiment we had left in the morning and all the roads leading to the mountains were swarming with Yanks. We turned and struck up a deep hollow where we found an old saw mill and got very ambiguous directions to Snow Hill where some of Morgan's men had been captured a few weeks before, so up the mountain we crawled. As we went along I secreted my watch and money about in my clothes and gave Lem direction what to do in case he was captured, which was to go to Mrs. Jackson in Nashville and she would help him to get away etc. but the Negro was so frightened that I don't think he would have remembered a word. It was nearly sundown when we commenced our retreat and the night caught us about half way up the mountain. It was dark being cloudy and we were in a dense forest. We could only proceed by following the barking dogs which we made for regardless of fences, rocks or creek...At last we came out on the broad pike leading over Snow Hill to Smithville where the Brigade had gone luckily for us the Yanks thought we would be picketing the place and stopped a few miles short of it and we came in just ahead of their videtts. We found the Staff in town at the hotel. Next morning our pickets were run in just as we were getting up from breakfast and we drew up our lines to meet the enemy. I volunteered my aid on the Staff. We had but parts of three Regts. and no artillery so could make only a running fight. We fought them for three hours until their artillery came up and began killing our horses. When we drew off, we came on to McMinnville, drew our rations and went on to Hoover's gap where we were joined by the Rangers, from here went over to the Shelbyville Pike and then back again. Wherever the Yanks would run in the McGruders we were sent for. Once they thought they would dash in on them but it happened to be our boys and we checked them and fought them nearly all day without giving an inch. We had a rocky hill on them skirmishes on foot getting so near them sometimes as to talk with them. One of us told a Yank-grant hasn't got Vicksburg yet!- No, replied Yank, but he caught h_ll a trying-We had two or three wounded, a few horses, but we killed several of them and wounded a great many, the citizens told us. After the grand advance commenced and wherever we would form to meet them they would engage us at a distance and flank around us no matter how we would extend our lines they would out stretch us. When we got to Tullahoma and saw the magnificent defenses we were told here we will make a stand and we all were determined to make it another Vicksburg for them. But after waiting two days they had crossed the mountains with Cavalry and Artillery and were marching on our rear. Bragg will be censured much for this move but there was no alternative for him. And the manner in which he brought off his army stores, wagons, etc. deserves the highest commendation. Our and the 11th Texas was the main stays and the "forlorn hope" and through every mountain pass trees were felled in our footsteps and bridges burned as our rear guard passed over so to us belongs the honor of shutting the door on Old rosy and of fighting the last battle on the soil of old Tennessee. They were determined not to let us go without a fight and fell upon our pickets the day before yesterday morning. Companies D & H were on duty, it was on the top of the last mountain that walls in the valley of the Tennessee River. they charged the pickets but they moved off slowly firing their pistols as they went for 3/4 of a mile giving the reserve (only the rest of our Regt.) time to form and meet them. When the Yanks came up we fell back once to draw them on and then charged them. It was no place for Cavalry being just what you would imagine a mountain top to* be cut up with ravine thickets and great plies of rocks, but we made them get farther and gather their dead and double quick down to their lines. As we were covering a retreat and not making a battle and did not know what force they had we were contented by being let alone. We sent a scout back in the evening, who went to a citizen's house about 2 miles back from where we fought them, who told them that we killed a Colonel and 8 men, mortally wounded a Lt. and otherwise wounded 25 or 30. One of our company was either killed or captured. Pvt. Perry Guinn of Co. E was killed-4 or 5 others wounded and about 8 or 10 horses killed and wounded. What we are going to do now is a mystery."[20]

Frank Batchelor, of the Texas Rangers, also related his experience during the Tullahoma Campaign. On July 7th, 1863 near Trenton, Georgia he wrote his wife Julia: "*On the 24th ult our pickets notified us that the enemy had appeared and was pressing them vigorously about 15 miles from Shelbyville. Our Brigade was soon in readiness and went to the front to support them. On arriving there we found him in strong force with Cavalry, Infantry, and Artillery while his long train of wagons, to be seen stretching as far as the eye could reach up the pike, convinced us that something more than an ordinary skirmish was intended. The firing opened briskly and continued until about 4 P.M. when couriers from the right and left flanks came in reporting the enemy advancing in like heavy force on all the approaches from Murfreesboro, and driving our inadequate picket force before them. Finding the two wings had been driven back two or three miles we had to retire also, though the enemy had been unable to drive us a foot from our position. It had then been raining several days and the roads were in dreadful condition but our men were in fine spirits for they thought the time had come when another battle and victory would give us the possession of Tennessee. It would be tedious for me to detail the numerous skirmishes and marches, some of them in the night, the rain pouring in torrents, which ensued until the 27th when it was found that General Rosecrans with an immense army divided into three columns was vigorously passing down on our right flank towards Tullahoma via Manchester, thus dividing our fortifications in front of Shelbyville. Our military men think General Bragg ought to have attacked the crops nearest our position and thus forced the enemy to stop and fight or destroy that part of his army, but I am not sufficiently skilled in the science of war to say whether such a move was practicable or not; probably our force had been too much weakened by reinforcements sent General (Joseph) Johnston to justify it. It now became evident that we had to fall back and we ordered over to the right to protect the retreat of our army. No one unacquainted with service can properly estimate the task of the Cavalry on a retreat. Theirs is the duty of scouring the enemy lines night and day reporting his movements. they are constantly in sight of the advancing foe, fighting him at every favorable position, hurrying up the jaded Infantry, obstructing the roads, and often standing under severe fires of his Artillery, or resisting the charges of his Cavalry. On the 29th we reached tullahoma and found it teeming with our foot soldiers. It was fortified as well as we expected to find it but the works were being rapidly strengthened and none doubted our ability to maintain the place if it was attacked. We were thrown out on the right towards Manchester and guarded it till the evening of the 1st inst when it was found the enemy were still passing to the rear and flanked Tullahoma and threatened to cut off our retreat across Elk River. In haste General Bragg was compelled to put his army in motion and abandon his fortifications at that place. From this time till we crossed the Tennessee River at Bridge Port we were in the saddle, and wet to the skin by the rain-fighting the enemy several times each day. The Cavalry did excellent service and punished the enemy severely on many occasions. In one instance the 11th Texas held their position three hours against a superior force of the enemy's Infantry and drove them back. In another the glorious Rangers were attacked about daylight by three Regts. of Cavalry (as stated by prisoners captured in the fight) and after two charges drove them back and held them in check till our reserve lines were formed and they were ordered to fall back. We protected the retreat of our Army so effectively that not a man of the Infantry fell into the hands of the enemy after leaving Shelbyville. We are now on this side of the Tennessee River, and it is understood we are ordered to this pleasant valley of Georgia (called "Wills Valley") to recruit our horses and remount those whose horses have been killed in action, or worn out with hard service.*"[21]

The last fight the Rangers had with Rosecrans army was on July 4th, 1863. It would be the last time the Federals could engage the Confederates before they crossed the Tennessee River. The Union cavalry followed the Rangers up the mountain on which the Southern Episcopal University was located, which was in Sewanee, Tennessee. The Federal force attacked the Rangers at about sunrise with a yell and laughing at the Rangers when more than half of their guns snapped at the first fire, but the Rangers then drew their pistols and charged at the Yankees driving them three miles down the mountain killing Col. Ruffan of the 5th Kentucky Union Cavalry. Other Yankees wounded during the battle were a Lieutenant Colonel, a Lieutenant, and eight Union men were killed and a good proportion wounded. But the last hurrah for the Rangers came with disheartening news. They soon learned that Vicksburg had fallen to Grant's army on that same day, and that Confederate General Robert E. Lee and the Army of Northern Virginia had suffered a loss at Gettysburg. The morale in the South came to an all time low. But in the North, the two victories at Gettysburg and Vicksburg invigorated the North. Unfortunately for Rosecrans, one of the greatest campaigns in the western theater had been overlooked. Rosecrans had tricked Bragg out of Tennessee and into Georgia. The Union push was now on for Chattanooga.

[1] Blue & Gray Magazine, The Deception of Braxton Bragg: The Tullahoma Campaign, June 23-July 4, 1863, by William B. Feis; The Fight for Chattanooga: Chickamauga to Missionary Ridge, P. 22-25
[2] Ibid.
[3] Ibid.
[4] O.R. Series Vol. 23 June 23-July 7-The Middle Tennessee or Tullahoma Campaign. No. 92 Report of Brig. General St. John Liddell, C. S. Army, commanding brigade.
[5] Ibid.
[6] Ibid.
[7] Ibid.
[8] Ibid.
[9] Ibid.
[10] Series I-Vol. 23 The Middle Tennessee Campaign. Ky., Mid. And E. Tenn., N. Alabama, and Sw. Va. No. 59 Reports of Maj. General Gordon Granger, U. S. Army, commanding Reserve Corps.
[11] Campaigns of Wheeler and His Cavalry, 1862-65 Chapter IX.
[12] Ibid.
[13] Ibid.
[14] Ibid.
[15] Ibid.
[16] Ibid.
[17] Ibid.
[18] Series I-Vol. 23 The Middle Tennessee Campaign. Ky., Mid. And E. Tenn., N. Alabama, and Sw. Va. No. 59 Reports of Maj. General Gordon Granger, U. S. Army, commanding Reserve Corps. .
[19] Campaigns of Wheeler and His Cavalry, 1862-65 Chapter IX.
[20] Batchelor-Turner Letters
[21] Ibid.

Chapter 10:
The Battle of Chickamauga

Between July 12th and August 3rd the Rangers were camped in Rome, Georgia. Although food prices were high the men were fortunate to be in Georgia during harvest season. The men were able to forage for food and managed to fill their plates with blackberry or Peach Cobblers, snap beans, cabbage, cucumbers, onions, tomatoes, Irish potatoes, beets, squash, and fruits and melons. The Rangers camps were filled with farm people who travel by foot, with baskets, on horseback, and in carts, with food for sale. After a while the food prices came down and the men were able to buy bacon for a dollar a pound. The state of Georgia was full of refugees from Tennessee and Kentucky. During the month of August, the Texas Rangers, under Col. Tom Harrison, recruited their strength and for two months they enjoyed activities such as barbeques, religious revivals, and even organized a Masonic Lodge. The Rangers had also learned from the Yankee newspapers that General John Hunt Morgan had been captured on July 26th at New Lisbon, Ohio. The Rangers could not believe the news.

On August 5th, a through breed horse and a $1,000 dollar saddle was bought for General Wharton. John Rector, of the Texas Rangers, made the presentation speech. By accident he offended the Georgia regiments that was with his division. In his speech he said that the best fighting units were from Texas and the next best was Tennessee. Other members of the Rangers made speeches such as Capt. William Jarmon, of Co. F, General Wharton, Col. Harrison, Capt. William Sayers, of Co. D., and Private W. S. J. Adams, of Co. C. There was a great crowd. Many of the speakers thanked the ladies of Tennessee, which offended the Georgia ladies. According to George Turner "the Rangers heart throbs when a Lady tells him she is from old Tennessee." Frank Batchelor had been promoted to acting Captain, and his uniform was "blazing with lace and button." According to George Turner, Frank Batchelor was one of the best dressed Officers in the Army. A ball was held by Wharton's division in Rome, Georgia. The music was provided by the "Bloody Sixth Arkansas" band. The ball was followed by presentation of the saddle to Wharton. The saddle's mountings were of solid silver, with silver plated stirrups, and the quiltings were of gold and silver threads, and on the points of the holsters were two gold knobs about an inch in diameter. The saddle was bought by the men in Mexico City, and shipped to Georgia. During the closing days of August, the Eighth Texas numbered four hundred and twelve men.[1]

After Bragg' army was pushed out of Middle Tennessee, Rosecrans next objective was Chattanooga, Tennessee. Chattanooga commands the southern entrance into East Tennessee, the most valuable if not the chief sources of supplies of coal for the manufactures and machine shops of Confederate States and is one of the great gateways through the mountains to Georgia and Alabama. Rosecrans began to repair the Nashville and Chattanooga Railroad and bring it forward to Tullahoma, McMinnville, Decherd, and Winchester for forage and supplies, which was impossible to transport from Murfreesboro to those points over the horrible roads the Yankees traveled on their advance to Tullahoma. On July 13th, the main road was open to the Elk River Bridge, and the Elk River Bridge and the main stem to Bridgeport was completed on the 25th and the branch to Tracy City was completed by August 13th. As soon as the main stem was finished to Stevenson, Union General Phil Sheridan's division was advanced, two brigades to Bridgeport and one to Stevenson. On August 16th Union General Thomas Crittenden's corps entered the Sequatchie. Union General John Palmer headed for Dunlap. Union General Van Cleve headed toward the Sequatchie Valley, Col. Robert Minty's cavalry left Sparta to drive back Dibrell's cavalry toward Kingston, where the troops under Forrest were concentrated, and then were to cover the left flank of Van Cleve's column, and proceed to Pikeville, The 14th Corps under General George Thomas from University was to move by way of Battle Creek and take a post concealed near it's mouth. The 20th Corps under Maj Gen. Alexander McCook was to move near Stevenson. The three brigades of Union cavalry by Fayetteville and Athens was to cover the line of the Tennessee from Whitesburg up. General Thomas Crittenden arrived in the Sequatchie Valley and sent a brigade of infantry to reconnoiter the Tennessee near Harrison's Landing and take position at Poe's Crossroads. Col. Minty was to reconnoiter from Washington down and take a position at Smith's Crossroads, and Col. John T. Wilder's mounted infantry was to reconnoiter from Harrison's Landing to Chattanooga and be supported by a brigade of infantry. These movements were completed by August 20th. Union General William Hazen took position at Poe's Crossroads on the 21st. Union General Wagner, with his brigade, supported Union Col. John T. Wilder in his reconnaissance on Chattanooga, which they surprised and shelled from across the river. Rosecrans army had passed the first great barrier between it and the objective point, and arrived opposite the Confederates on the banks of the Tennessee. The Federal army now began to cross the Tennessee River. [2]

On August 27th, Wheeler's Corps comprised of Wharton's and Martin's Divisions, and Roddey's brigade. Estes Regiment, under Col. Tom Harrison's brigade was located picketing the Tennessee River from Bridgeport to Guntersville; Wade's regiment, Martin Division, from Guntersville to Decatur, and detachments from Roddey's brigade from Decatur to the mouth of Bear Creek. The main body of Wharton's Division was stationed near Rome, Georgia.; of Martin's division near Alexandria, Alabama, and of Rodney's brigade, near Tuscumbia, Alabama. Two regiments of the corps were on detached duty with General Pillow. [3]

On the 27th, Gen. Martin's command, numbering 1,200 men, was ordered to Trenton, and General Wharton's division was sent to the vicinity of Chattanooga.

On the 29th, the Union forces were crossing the Tennessee River in force, driving back the pickets of Col. Estes regiment. About five hundred men of General Martin's division, under Lt. Col. Mauldin, moved up Will's Valley, and placed on picket duty below Chattanooga.

Wheeler now realized that the Union force was moving with two divisions of cavalry and McCook's corps of infantry over Sand Mountain and into Will's Valley, by the Caperton Road. Wheeler was ordered to take post in Broomtown Valley for the purpose of picketing the passes of Lookout Mountain. General Martin, with 1,220 men, guarded the passes from the Tennessee River to Neal's Gap, and General Wharton from Neal's Gap to Gadsen. These divisions kept the Union force under constant observation, and full reports were sent back to Wheeler. Several columns of Union cavalry were pushed over the mountain, all of which were driven back.[4]

On September 8 and 9th Union General Crittenden was ordered to reconnoiter the front of Lookout Mountain, sending a brigade up an almost impracticable path called Nickajack trace to Summertown, a hamlet on the summit of the mountain overlooking Chattanooga, and holding the main body of his corps either to support these reconnaissances to prevent a sortie of the Confederates over Lookout, or to enter Chattanooga in case the Confederates evacuated the town, or make feeble resistance. The Union cavalry was ordered to push by way of Alpine and Broomtown Valley and strike the Confederate's railroad communication between Resaca bridge and Dalton. [5]

On September 9th Crittenden informed Rosecrans that the Confederate army had left Chattanooga and he had taken the city. His whole corps passed around the point of Lookout Mountain on the 10th and camped at Rossville, five miles out of Chattanooga. Negley's division advanced to within a mile of Dug Gap, which was heavily obstructed and Baird's division came up to his support the next day. Negley fell back after a sharp skirmish, in which General Baird's division participated, and fell back to Steven's Gap.

By the 11th, Crittenden had occupied Ringgold, pushing Wilder's mounted infantry as far as Tunnel Hill, skirmishing with the Confederate cavalry. Hazen joined Crittenden near Ringgold and the whole corps moved across the Gordon's Mills. Union General George Thomas had reached the eastern foot of Lookout Mountain. [6]

On September 12th, Union General Alexander McCook's corps of infantry and Union General Stanely's corps of cavalry moved over the mountain at Alpine and after a severe fight Wheeler's cavalry, under Col. Avery, was compelled to fall back. Wilder's mounted infantry had a severe fight with the Confederates at Leet's Tanyard. Union Generals Reynolds and Brannan were to close up to the support of Generals Negley and Baird's divisions. On that same day, it was learned that the Confederate army was concentrating all their forces, both cavalry and infantry, behind Pigeon Mountain, in the vicinity of La Fayette, while the corps of Rosecrans army were at Gordon's Mills, Bailey's Crossroads, at the foot of Steven's Gap, and at Alpine, a distance of forty miles, from flank to flank, by the nearest roads, and fifty seven miles by the route taken by the 20th Corps. It had also been learned that the main body of Confederate General Joseph Johnston's army had joined Bragg and was a matter of life and death to concentrate his army. General Alexander McCook was already directed to support General George Thomas, but was ordered to send two brigades to hold Dougherty's Gap, and to join General Thomas with the remainder of his command. McCook closed up with Thomas on the 17th, with General Jefferson Davis at Brook's, in front of Dug Gap, Johnson at Pond Springs, in front of Catlett's Gap, and Sheridan at the foot of Steven's Gap. As soon as General Alexander McCook's corps arrived General Thomas moved down the Chickamauga toward Gordon's Mills. Meanwhile, to bring General Crittenden within reach of General Thomas, he was withdrawn from Gordon' Mills and the 14th corps and ordered to take position on the southern spur of Missionary Ridge, his right connecting with Thomas, where he remained until General McCook had joined with General Thomas.[7]

Union Col. Robert Minty's cavalry reconnoitered the Confederates on the 15th and reported them at Dalton, Ringgold, and Leet's and Rock Springs Church. Union General Thomas Crittenden was ordered to return to his old position at Gordon's Mills, with his line resting along the Chickamauga via the Crawfish Spring.

On the 17th the Union army was ordered to move northeast down the Chickamauga, with a view covering the La Fayette road toward Chattanooga, and facing the Confederates front. Bragg gave orders on the same day to attack the Federal forces. He believed that the center of the Union force was centered around Lee and Gordon's Mills. He decided that a force comprising three infantry corps would cross Chickamauga Creek, and turn the Union left and sweep up the Chickamauga, toward Lee and Gordon's Mill. As they would drive south they would find additional fords permitting Confederate Generals Polk's and Hill's Corps to enter the battle. Bragg believed that the chosen crossing points of the three corps would place them on the Federal left flank. His attack would hopefully drive Rosecrans away from Chattanooga and towards McLemore's Cove.

During this time skirmishing occurred every day for the Rangers until the 17th, when Wheeler was ordered to move into McLemore's Cove by Dug and Catlett's Gaps and attack the Union force, which was moving in that direction. On September 17th Wheeler's force fought for some hours, driving the Union force for some distance, but finally a larger Union force made it impossible for Wheeler to dislodge them.[8]

On the 18th, Wheeler's force moved to Owen's ford on the Chickamauga River, leaving heavy pickets at all the gaps of the mountain as far as Gadsden. At 2:00 P.M., Wheeler learned that the Union cavalry were moving up McLemore's Cove. Wheeler moved across the river and attacked their flank, dividing the column and driving the Yankees in confusion in both directions.[9]

During the day, Union Col. Robert Minty was attacked on the left in the area of Reed's bridge by General Nathan Bedford Forrest's cavalry and Confederate John Bell Hood's Infantry, and Union Col. John T. Wilder's mounted infantry were attacked by Confederate General W. H. T. Walker and Simon B. Buckner's infantry and driven into La Fayette road. Rosecrans quickly learned that the Confederate army was massing on his left, crossing Reed's bridge and Alexander's Bridges while he had threatened Gordon's Mills. Rosecrans ordered General George Thomas to relieve General Thomas Crittenden's corps, posting one division near Crawfish Springs, and to move with the remainder of his corps by the Widow Glenn's house to the Rossville and La Fayette road, his left extending obliquely across it near Kelley's House. General Crittenden was ordered to proceed with Generals Van Cleve's and Palmer's divisions to drive the Confederates from the Rossville road and form on the left of General Wood, then at Gordon's Mills. General Alexander McCook's corps was to close up on General George Thomas, occupy the position at Crawfish Springs, and protect General Thomas Crittenden's right, while holding his corps mainly in reserve. Thomas pushed forward to where General Baird's division was posted. Union General Brannan followed, and was posted on Baird's left, covering the roads leading to Reed's and Alexander's Bridges. Bragg's lines of battle was Confederate General Hill's Corps was on the extreme left, with the center at Glass's Mills; Confederate General Leonidas Polk was at Lee and

Gordon's Mill; Confederate General Simon Bolivar Buckner's Corps was at Byram's Ford; Confederate General John Bell Hood's was at Tedford's ford. On the early morning of the 19th Confederate General Benjamin Cheatham's division of Polk's Corps was detached, moved down the Chickamauga, and crossed at Hunt's Ford at around 7:00 A.M..[10]

Col. Daniel McCook, of General Granger's command, who had made a reconnaissance to Reed's Bridge the evening of the 18th, and had burned Reed's bridge, met General Thomas and reported that an isolated brigade of Confederates was this side of the Chickamauga, and the bridge being destroyed, a rapid movement in that direction might result in the capture of the force that was isolated. General Thomas ordered General Brannan with two brigades to reconnoiter in that direction and attack any small force he should encounter. The advance brigade, supported by the rest of the division, soon encountered Forrest's dismounted cavalry, who were screening Confederate General W. H. T. Walker's infantry crossing the creek, and attacked it and drove it back more than half a mile, where Ector's brigade was found, with the evident intention of turning the Union left and gaining possession of the La Fayette road between the Yankees and Chattanooga. Forrest and Walker's men came up and drove Brannan back to his starting position, and overran Brannan's artillery. But Baird's division was sent in to help Brannan and between the two divisions, drove Forrest and Ector back. The Union infantry halted and the battery deployed forward to a low ridge. Confederate St. John Liddell's division with two thousand men strong, hit the right flank of Brig. Gen. John King's Third Brigade, Baird's division, capturing Loomis's battery, commanded by Lt. Van Pelt. Bush's Indiana battery was captured at the same time. Baird's and Brannan's men were falling back to the rear, when Liddell encountered the Federal troops of Brannan's reorganized troops and R. W. Johnson's division, McCook's Corps. Liddell was pushed back and had to abandon his captured Union guns.

At 11:00 A.M. Bragg ordered Ben Cheatham's to the relief of Liddell. Before Cheatham's division, ordered to his support, could reach him, Liddell had already been pressed back to his first position by the extended line of the Yankees assailing him on both flanks. The two commands united were soon able to force the Yankees back again and recover the Confederate advantage, though the Confederates were yet greatly outnumbered. These movements on the Confederate right were in a direction to leave an opening in the Rebel line between Cheatham and Hood. A. P. Stewart's division, forming Buckner's second line, was thrown to the right to fill this, and it soon became hotly engaged, as did Hood's whole front. Stewart's division attacked Palmer's division of Crittenden's corps, which was flanking Cheatham's division, and drove it back, and soon met Van Cleve's division, but it pushed it back also. Stewart, by a vigorous assault, broke the Union's center and penetrated far into his lines, but was obliged to retire for want of sufficient force to meet the heavy enfilade fire which he encountered from the right. At 2:30 P.M. Hood and Bushrod Johnson's division advanced and became engaged, and continued to drive the Union forces back, crushing the Federal right center, capturing artillery, and seizing the Chattanooga road. The three Confederate divisions soon encountered four fresh divisions of Wood, Davis, Sheridan, and Negley, and were driven back to the east of the road. Stewart had recaptured the battery lost by Cheatham's division, twelve pieces of Federal artillery, and over two hundred prisoners, and several hundred rifles.[11]

On the extreme left Bragg had ordered an attack at Glass's Mill. Slocomb's battery had a artillery duel with a Federal artillery battery on the west side of the river, and under cover of the artillery fire, Confederate General Be Hardin Helm's brigade of Breckinridge's division was crossed over and attacked Union General James Negley's infantry and drove it back. Confedertae General Patrick Cleburne's division, of Hill's corps, which first reached the right, was ordered to attack immediately in conjunction with the force already engaged. This veteran command, under Cleburne, moved to it's work after sunset. Union General George Thomas had move Brannan from his left to his right and was retiring Baird and R. W. Johnson to a better position, when Cleburne took the Yankees completely by surprise, and attacked driving them in great disorder for nearly a mile, and inflicting a very heavy loss. Cleburne captured three pieces of artillery, two stands of colors, and three hundred prisoners. Darkness ended the battle.[12]

The Union troops were given their orders for September 20th. Thomas Corps, with the troops which had reenforced him, was to maintain his line, with Brannan in reserve. McCook Corps was to close on Thomas, his right refused, and covering the position at Widow Glenn's house and Crittenden to have two divisions in reserve near the junction of McCook's and Thomas lines to be able to support either one. Rosecrans line covered the Chattanooga and the Dry

Valley Roads. His line began four hundred yards east of the Rossville Road, on a crest which was occupied from left to right by Baird's division, R. W. Johnson's division, Palmer's division and Reynold's division. They laid behind breastworks of logs in a line running due south and bending back toward the road at each wing. Next on the right of Reynolds was Brannan's division, then Negely's. The line across the Chattanooga road toward Missionary Ridge was completed by Union Generals Philip Sheridan's and Jefferson Davis's divisions of Alexander McCook's Corps: Wood's and Van Cleve's divisions of Crittenden's Corps were in reserve. Col. Robert Minty's cavalry covered the left and rear at Missionary Mills. Union General Mitchell's and Col. John T. Wilder's cavalry covered the extreme right. Rosecrans's Headquarters was at the Widow Glenn's house. [13]

During the night, Bragg ordered his commanders to his camp fire. The whole force was divided into two commands and assigned to two senior officers Lieutenant Generals James Longstreet and Leonidas Polk, the former on the left, the latter on the right. Lt. General Polk was ordered to attack the Yankees on the Confederate extreme right and to take up the attack in succession rapidly to the left. The left wing was to await the attack by the right, take it up promptly when made, and the whole line was then to be pushed against the Union force throughout it's extent. [14]

Also during the night Wheeler was given orders to guard all passes of the mountain and the fords of the river down to Confederate General James Longstreet's left flank, and to attack the Union force at every opportunity. Wheeler's force was concentrated at Glass's Mill. Col. Thomas Harrison's 2nd Brigade was part of Wheeler's Division. His brigade was comprised of the 3rd Confederate Cavalry, 3rd Kentucky Cavalry, 4th Tennessee Cavalry, Eighth Texas Cavalry, 11th Texas Cavalry, and White's Tennessee Battery. White's battery's cannons were brass six pounders from the University of Arkansas.

During the morning hours of September 19th, Wheeler found the ford unguarded, so he quickly hurried Martin's and Wharton's command along the road from the mill until they came to the edge of a large open field, five hundred yards west of the ford. A large Union force, under Col. Eli Long, with the Chicago Board of Trade Artillery were deployed on the opposite bank and skirmishing commenced. White's Tennessee artillery unlimbered and opened fire on the Yankees. Wheeler dismounted his entire corps, crossed the river, and attacked the enemy, hoping that his force might draw troops from the center and thus create a diversion. Wheeler was successful in creating a diversion. The Union force thought Wheeler's advance was a heavy flank movement and reenforced this point heavily. Union Col. Eli Long thought Wheeler's force was a division of infantry. The men of the First Ohio Cavalry also bought into the ruse and thought that Wheeler's troops were Longstreet's infantry. A Lieutenant form General Crook's staff rode up to the First Ohio Cavalry and ordered them to charge. Lt. Col. Valentine Cupp ordered his men to sling carbines and draw their sabers. The Confederates were only three hundred yards away. John Chapin of the First Ohio was a witness and said he saw "three lines of Rebel infantry with loaded guns (which) were before us and coming our way, and we were to charge those bristling walls of steel. I said to Sergeant Irwin, on my left: If this charge is made not a man can come out alive." General Crook arrived on the field and he ordered his men to resist the charge. Chapin and others of the field were quickly relieved that they were not going to make the charge. The troopers dismounted from their horses in order to support a section of the Chicago Board of Trade Battery that was firing canister into the field. The men under Wheeler were now only fifty yards away and charging. The Chicago Board of Trade Artillery limbered up and rode off, and the Ohio troops remounted. Col. Cupp was shot through the bowels and fell off his horse. Chapin was hit with a bullet in his right shoulder, and the bullet lodged against a rib. He too fell off his horse. After a short fight, the Union force wavered. Wheeler charged the enemy and drove them to a largely superior force fully two miles to Crawfish Springs, killing and wounding large numbers and taking thirty five officers and men prisoners, besides the wounded. The Union force states that Longstreet flanked him at this point at the hour Wheeler made the attack. [15]

After the charge, Lt. Dechard of Company D, Eighth Texas Cavalry, was informed that a wounded Union officer wanted to see him. When he saw the man, he said: "Why, it's my old friend, Major Cupp. I am sorry to see you thus." "Lt. Col. Cupp", replied the other, "but I've had my last promotion. You people have got me this time." More than a year before, these officers, each a Lieutenant in command of an escort for a flag of truce, had met. They met again, a few weeks later, under the same circumstances but Cupp was now a captain. After the fight in

Bardstown, Dechard was in command of the guard for the prisoners, and recognized his former acquaintance. "Capt. Cupp, I am glad to see you", said he. "Major Cupp", corrected the prisoner, "but I can not say that I am glad to see you under the circumstances." The dying officer desired Dechard to take his watch and other belongings and send them to his relatives in Ohio, which was done a few days later by flag of truce.[16]

Wheeler was then ordered to move his available force to Lee and Gordon Mills and attack the Union force there. Wheeler arrived at 3:00 P.M., and crossed the river. Union Brig. General Robert Mitchell had formed the brigades of Colonels Ray and Campbell at the edge of a large pasture that lay between the mill and Crawfish Springs. Col. Sidney Post had joined him with his infantry brigade after four days of screening McCook's trains as they labored over the mountains toward McLemore's Cove. Wheeler vigorously attacked the Yankees. By 5:00 P.M. Post's brigade fell back to Missionary Ridge, covering the withdrawal of the trains and ambulances. The Yankees retreated in confusion. Wheeler followed as rapidly as he could, capturing one thousand prisoners, twenty wagons, and a large amount of arms and ordnance stores. After dark Wheeler captured five large hospitals, with considerable supply of medicines, camp equipment, and a great large number of wounded prisoners, besides one hundred surgeons. Wheeler chased the Union force for two hours after nightfall, when Wheeler broke off the chase to feed his horses. Wheeler was totally unaware of the complete Federal rout that was occurring, and that the Federals were now heading for Chattanooga.[17]

Because of a breakdown in communication, the Confederate attack did not begin until 10:00 A.M. The Confederates attack on the right was mainly unsuccessful because of the breastworks, but Union General George Thomas ordered for reenforcements, which weakened the Federal right, until a gap was left. Confederate General James Longstreet entered the gap. Longstreet struck the corps of Union General Thomas Crittenden and Alexander McCook in the flank. The first division to enter the gap was Confederate General Bushrod Johnson's, and began the flank movement to the right. Confederate General John C. Breckinridge and Confederate General Patrick Cleburne attacked the Federal lines. General Forrest dismounted Frank Armstrong's division of cavalry to keep abreast of Breckinirdge and held Pegram's division in reserve. Breckinridge's two right brigades, under Adams and Stovall, met little opposition, but the left of Confederate General Ben Hardin Helm's brigade encountered the left of the Federal breastworks, and was repulsed. Helm was killed during the attack. The command fell to Col. J. H. Lewis, and the brigade was withdrawn. General Breckinridge wheeled his two brigades to the left, and got in the rear of the breastworks. These brigades had reached the Chattanooga road and their skirmishers had pressed past the Cloud's house, where there was a Federal field hospital. The wheeling movement enabled Stovall to gain a point beyond the retired flank of the breastworks, and Adam's brigade advanced father, being in the rear of the entrenchments. Federal reenforcements came up. Adams was severely wounded and fell into Union hands, and the two brigades were pushed back. Beatty's brigade of Negely's division had been the first to come to Baird's assistance. Cleburne had withdrawn his division four hundred yards behind the crest of a hill. Deshler was killed, and his brigade fell to Col. R. Q. Mills. The fight on the right lasted until 10:30 A.M. At 10:10 A.M. Rosecrans ordered McCook to be ready at 10:30 A.M.; Sheridan's division was to support Thomas. This weakened the Federal right. At 11:00 A.M. Stewart's division advanced under an immediate order from Bragg. His three brigades under Brown, Clayton, and Bate advanced with Wood. Stewart marched past the cornfield in front of the Poe's house, two or three hundred yards beyond the Chattanooga road, driving the Yankees within their lines of entrenchments. They encountered a fresh artillery fire on front and flank, heavily supported by infantry, and had to retire. Gists' brigade immediately attacked the logworks which had repulsed Helm, and he was driven back. Liddell had seized the Chattanooga road and was moving behind the breastworks, when a column of the Yankees appeared on his flank and rear, and was compelled to retreat.[18]

At the same time with the advance of Stewart, the heavy pressure on Thomas caused Rosecrans to support him by sending the divisions of Generals James Negley and Van Cleve and John Brannan's reserve brigade. An order to Wood, which Rosecrans claims was misinterpreted, led to a gap being left into which Longstreet stepped in with eight brigades, Bushrod Johnson's brigades, McNair's, Gregg's and Kershaw's, and Laws, Humphrey's, Banning's and Robertson's, which he had arranged in three lines to constitute his grand column of attack. Union General Jefferson Davis two brigades, one of Van Cleve's, and Philip Sheridan's entire division were caught in front and flank and driven from the field. Longstreet now gave order to wheel right instead of the left, and took in reserve the strong position of the Yankees. Five of Union General Alexander McCook's brigades were driven off the field. [19]

Union General George Thomas chose a strong position on a spur of Missionary Ridge, running east and west, and placed General Brannan's division with portions of two brigades of Negley's: Wood's division was placed on Brannan's left. Steedman's division of Granger's Corps came to his aide about 3:00 P.M. His new line was at right angles with the line of breastworks on the west side of the Rossville Road, his right being almost impregnable wall like hill, his left nearly an inclosed fortification. [20]

Confederate General Bushrod Johnson's three brigades in Longstreet's center were the first to fill the gap left by Wood's withdrawal from the Federal right, but the other five brigades under Hindman and Kershaw moved into line and wheeled to the right and engaged in a flank attack. They seized the Federal commander's headquarters at Widow Glenn's, until they found the new Federal line at Snodgrass Hill. Hindman advanced and met success. The brigades of Deas and Manigualt charged the breastworks and rushed over them, and drove Laibolt's Federal brigade of Sheridan's division and drove them off the field. Then General Patton Anderson's brigade of Hindman, having come onto line, attacked and beat back the forces of Davis ,Sherdian, and Wilder in their front, and killed General Lytle, took 1,100 prisoners, 27 pieces of artillery, ordnance trains, etc. Finding no more resistance out on his front and left, Hindman wheeled to the right to assist the forces of the center. the divisions of Stewart, Hood, Bushrod Johnson, and Hindman came together in front of the new line at Snodgrass Hill. [21]

Hindman and Bushrod Johnson organized a column of attack upon the front and rear of Snodgrass Hill. It consisted of Deas, Manigualt, Gregg, Patton, Anderson and McNair. Deas was on the north side of the gorge through which the Crawfish road crosses, Manigualt across the gorge and south, on the crest parallel to the Snodgrass Hill, where Thomas was. The other three brigades extended along the crest with their faces north, while the first tow faced east. Kershaw, with his own and Humphrey's brigade, was on the right of Anderson and was to cooperate in the movement. It began at 3:30 P.M. After 4:00 P.M. the Yankees were reenforced and advanced, but was repulsed by Anderson and Kershaw. At 3 P.M. Forrest reported a strong column was approaching from Rossville. It was Granger's Corps. Cheatham's division was sent in support the Confederate line. General Steedman led the column. Longstreet sent Preston with his division of three brigades under Gracie, Trigg, and Kelley, aided by Robertson's brigade of Hood's division, to carry the heights. At 4:00 P.M. the Confederates advanced. Cleburne ran forward his batteries to within three hundred yards of the Yankees breastworks, pushed forward his infantry. General J. K. Jackson, of Cheatham's division, had a struggle with the fortifications in his front, but had entered them when Cheatham with two more of his brigades, Maney's and Wright's came up. Breckinridge and Walker met with little opposition until the Chattanooga road was passed, when their right was unable to overcome the forces covering the Yankees retreat. Preston gained the heights a half hour later, capturing 1,000 prisoners, 4,500 stand of arms. [22]

Union General George Thomas had received orders from General Granger's arrival to retreat to Rossville, but still held his ground, strongly refusing to do so until nightfall, thus saving the Federals from a great disaster.

Early in the morning on the 21st of September, 1863, Wheeler detached two regiments to pick up stragglers and arms. At 9:00 A. M Wheeler received his first orders from General Longstreet to send a force of cavalry to find the Yankees position. At the same time, Wheeler received orders from Bragg to save the captured property. Wheeler detailed five hundred of his best mounted men under Col. Anderson to comply with General Longstreet's order, with full instructions to report every hour to that officer. Two regiments were already at work collecting stragglers and arms, leaving Wheeler with about 1,700 men.[23]

Just at that time Wheeler received information that his pickets at Owen's Ford had run into a large Yankee force, and was driving back his cavalry from that point. It was also reported that the Yankees had a large train of wagons with them. At the same time, Wheeler saw heavy dust in Chattanooga Valley, which appeared to indicate a movement from Chattanooga along the foot of the mountain toward McLemore's Cove. Wheeler immediately moved over to the Chattanooga Valley, and drove back the Yankees towards Chattanooga, which was the force marching from that place. Wheeler then left the Eighth Texas Cavalry, under Col. Tom Harrison, and his escort to hold the Yankees in check, while with the balance of his command moved up toward McLemore's Cove.[24]

After marching about five miles, Wheeler met a large Union cavalry force, which, seeing Wheeler's dust, had deployed a considerable force in a strong position. Wheeler immediately deployed two regiments and commenced skirmishing. Finding their strong position, Wheeler detached a squadron to turn their right flank. This caused the Yankees to waver, Wheeler then charged in line and also in column on the road, driving the Yankees into confusion. The Yankee cavalry attempted to form a new line with his reserves several times, but Wheeler met him with such force, that the Yankees were stopped and fell back each time, driving the Yankees before them. Wheeler continued the charge several miles, capturing, killing, or dispersing nearly the entire command, said to number two thousand men. Wheeler had a force of only four hundred! Wheeler captured eighteen stand of colors, and secured their entire train, numbering ninety wagons, loaded with valuable baggage. Many of the Yankees who escaped to the adjoining woods were captured the following morning, and only seventy five men, half of whom were dismounted, succeeded in re-joining the Union army. Wheeler also captured a number of arms.[25]

After the Battle of Chickamagua, Giles of the 8th Texas relates the terrible carnage that occurred during those two days of terrible fighting. "Many of the Federal dead and wounded still lay where they had fallen. The air was freighted with a terrible odor, the battlefields commentary on war. The wounded hearing my horses footfalls, began calling me to give some assistance. Dismounting I picked my way to the first one. He desired to be turned over. Another wanted his canteen. The poor fellow had struggled while there was strength and now unable to move further, was out of reach of his canteen...It seemed hundreds were calling. "Are you aware that your own surgeons with their details and ambulances are here uncontrolled on the field." "Oh yes," was the answer, "they come around every day and leave us water a little food and medicine, but it is awful to lie here this way." I mounted and rode off, feeling sad at the fate of these men dying unattended hundreds of miles away from home and loved ones."[26]

During the night, Giles was lost and went to a hospital at the Lee and Gordon's Mill. "I was on that part of the field from which the dead and wounded had been removed, but there was wreck and ruin everywhere. Maimed and groaning horses and no one to waste a load of ammunition to end their suffering; broken gun carriages, the decline of a battlefield."[27]

On the following morning, Wheeler moved to within 1 1/4 miles of Chattanooga, driving the Yankees cavalry behind their infantry. Wheeler remained in this position until night, when Wheeler was ordered to Trenton, preparing to cross the Tennessee River. After one days march, Wheeler received orders to return and sweep up Lookout Mountain to Point Lookout. Wheeler started up the hill with two hundred men.[28]

On arriving at Summertown at dark, Wheeler found one regiment of the Yankees behind some strong barricades. Wheeler dismounted his men to feel their position and charged their flanks, driving the Yankees for some distance. In their retreat, they left several guns, knapsacks, overcoats, and cooking utensils, and their supper, already cooked. Wheeler at this point was informed that his command was stopped at Chickamauga Station. Wheeler with his small command, which numbered one hundred and fifty dismounted men, pressed the enemy off the mountain. After surveying the Yankees works and reporting fully his position to General Bragg, Wheeler proceeded to Chickamauga Station, where he received orders to cross the Tennessee River above Chattanooga. While moving up the Tennessee River, the Rangers saw the 4th Ohio Cavalry on the opposite side of the river. The 4th Ohio's pickets cried out, "Where is Old Ironsides today?," referring to Tom Harrison. One of the Rangers cried out, "At camp. Where is Col. John Kennett?" The 4th Ohio picket cried out, "Oh, the devil, you know where we left him, over at Chickamauga.". These type truces were quite common during the Civil War. Confederates and Yankees would trade with each other anytime there was a lull in battle. The Confederates would trade the Yankees for coffee, and the Yankees very often traded the Confederates for tobacco. They would also trade newspapers and the latest gossip from both sides. [29]

During the night, Wheeler received orders to move toward Charleston to support General Forrest, who was moving upon the Yankees in that direction.

General Wheeler praised General Wharton, and Colonel Harrison for their "zeal, energy, and gallantry during the engagement." Wheeler only had a force of two thousand men during Chickamauga, but managed to capture two thousand prisoners, one hundred wagons, a large amount of property, and eighteen flags. Chickamauga was Bragg's greatest victory. To the frustration of many, he failed to follow it up, and losses were staggering. Bragg listed 2,312 dead, 14,674 wounded, and 1,469 missing or captured. Rosecrans reported 1,657 Union dead, 9,756 wounded, and 4,757 missing or captured. Rosecrans and many survivors began a march for Tennessee that afternoon. Union General George Thomas set up a rear guard at Rossville Gap, holding north through the 21st, then followed the rest of the army into Chattanooga.[30]

On September 29th, Wheeler received orders to cross the Tennessee River with three brigades, Armstrong's, Davidson's, and Hodge's Brigades, which were under General Forrest's command, and the rest of his command, including Wharton's Division. Wheeler's men were exhausted and low on ammunition. They were too far away from the army to get supplies. They were in desolate country, with Union General Ambrose Burnisde threatening their rear and flank. The Tennessee River was to Wheeler's front, and guarded at the point of crossing by an army twice his size, with the Cumberland mountains and Walden's Ridge beyond. Wheeler decided to cross at Cottonport.

On the 30th of September, Wheeler learned that Forrest's commands had just arrived at a point twenty miles from the point of crossing. Wheeler ordered them to the latter place and proceeded there with the commands of Generals Wharton and Martin. The Yankees had occupied the opposite bank and immediately concentrated a force nearly if not quite equal to Wheeler's to resist their crossing. This could be reached as easily by the Yankees as by Wheeler's command. Wheeler determined to cross at the point where the Yankee's were. The three brigades from Forrest only amounted to five hundred men each. They were badly armed, and had a small supply of ammunition, and their horses were in horrible shape, having been marched continuously for three days, and nights without removing their saddles. The men were also worn out, and without rations. General Wharton and Martin came to Wheeler and made urgent protests against their commands being called upon to move in this condition. Wheeler decided to allow the worst horses to be returned to the rear, and with the remainder, crossed in the face of the enemy nearly as large as Wheeler's force. Col. James Hagan, of the 3rd Alabama, was the first to cross the river under Federal fire. Wheeler attacked a regiment of cavalry, which he charged, and drove them back in confusion for three miles. The command marched up the mountain, and the next day reached the Sequatchie Valley. Wheeler decided to do more damage to Rosecrans army by destroying huge wagon trains and stores of supplies. He also would divert the Federals from Brig. General Roddy's cavalry, which were ordered to cross the Tennessee River near Bridgeport.[31]

By the end of September, the Union army was safe in Chattanooga surrounded by Bragg's army. After Wheeler's success during the Battle of Chickamauga, he decided to go on another daring and bold raid in October.

[1]Batchelor-Turner Letters
[2]O.R. Series I-Vol. XXX August 16-September 22, 1863-The Chickamauga Campaign. No 3-Report of Maj. General William S. Rosecrans, U.S. Army, commanding the Army of the Cumberland.
[3]O.R. Series I-Vol. XXX The Chickamauga Campaign. No. 433-Report of Maj. Gen. Joseph Wheeler, C.S. Army, commanding Cavalry Corps.
[4]Ibid.
[5]O.R. Series I-Vol. XXX August 16-September 22, 1863-The Chickamauga Campaign. No 3-Report of Maj. General William S. Rosecrans, U.S. Army, commanding the Army of the Cumberland.
[6]Ibid.
[7]Ibid.
[8]O.R. Series I-Vol. XXX The Chickamauga Campaign. No. 433-Report of Maj. Gen. Joseph Wheeler, C.S. Army, commanding Cavalry Corps.
[9]O.R. Series I-Vol. XXX The Chickamauga Campaign. No. 433-Report of Maj. Gen. Joseph Wheeler, C.S. Army, commanding Cavalry Corps.
[10]O.R. Series I-Vol. XXX August 16-September 22, 1863-The Chickamauga Campaign. No 3-Report of Maj. General William S. Rosecrans, U.S. Army, commanding the Army of the Cumberland.
[11]Cozzins, Peter, This Terrible Sound, The Battle of Chickamauga; The Fight for Chattanooga: Chickamauga to Missionary Ridge; Battles and Leaders of the Civil War.
[12]Ibid.
[13]O.R. Series I-Vol. XXX August 16-September 22, 1863-The Chickamauga Campaign. No 3-Report of Maj. General William S. Rosecrans, U.S. Army, commanding the Army of the Cumberland.

[14] O.R. Series I-Vol. XXX-Report No. 236 Reports of General Braxton Bragg, C. S. Army, commanding Army of Tennessee.
[15] O.R. Series I-Vol. XXX The Chickamauga Campaign. No. 433-Report of Maj. Gen. Joseph Wheeler, C.S. Army, commanding Cavalry Corps.; Cozzins, Peter, This Terrible Sound: The Battle of Chickamauga.
[16] Terry's Texas Rangers, Leonidas Giles, P. 58-64
[17] O.R. Series I-Vol. XXX The Chickamauga Campaign. No. 433-Report of Maj. Gen. Joseph Wheeler, C.S. Army, commanding Cavalry Corps.
[18] Cozzins, Peter, This Terrible Sound, The Battle of Chickamauga; The Fight for Chattanooga: Chickamauga to Missionary Ridge; Battles and Leaders of the Civil War.
[19] Ibid.
[20] Ibid.
[21] Ibid.
[22] Ibid.
[23] O.R. Series I-Vol. XXX The Chickamauga Campaign. No. 433-Report of Maj. Gen. Joseph Wheeler, C.S. Army, commanding Cavalry Corps.
[24] Ibid.
[25] Ibid.
[26] Terry's Texas Rangers, Leonidas Giles, P. 58-64
[27] Ibid.
[28] O.R. Series I-Vol. XXX The Chickamauga Campaign. No. 433-Report of Maj. Gen. Joseph Wheeler, C.S. Army, commanding Cavalry Corps.
[29] O.R. Series I-Vol. XXX The Chickamauga Campaign. No. 433-Report of Maj. Gen. Joseph Wheeler, C.S. Army, commanding Cavalry Corps.; Terry Texas Ranger Trilogy: J. P. Blackburn
[30] O.R. Series I-Vol. XXX The Chickamauga Campaign. No. 433-Report of Maj. Gen. Joseph Wheeler, C.S. Army, commanding Cavalry Corps.; The Civil War Battles of the Western Theater, Bryan Bush.
[31] Campaigns of Wheeler and His Cavalry, 1862-1865

Terry's Texas Rangers

Chapter 11:
Wheeler's First Raid October 1st-9th, 1863

On October 2nd, Wheeler reached Sequatchie Valley, and at 3 o'clock on the following morning proceeded toward Jasper, with 1,500 men. After traveling ten miles Wheeler overtook and captured thirty two, six mule wagons. The 4th Alabama took charge of the wagon train. With one thousand men left Wheeler and his force rode down the valley. [1]

On approaching Anderson's Cross-Roads, Wheelers' force was met by a large Union cavalry force, which Wheeler charged and drove them back. Wheeler found a large wagon train, which extended from the top of Walden's Ridge for ten miles toward Jasper. This train was heavily loaded with ordnance, quartermaster's, and commissary stores. The number of wagons was from about eight hundred to one thousand five hundred. The train was guarded by a brigade of Union cavalry in front and a brigade of cavalry in the rear, and on the flank, were two regiments of infantry. Wheeler formed three columns and attacked the Union regiments of infantry. After a fight, the guards were defeated and driven off, leaving the entire train in their possession. After taking the mules and wagons they needed, they destroyed the rest. While burning the wagons and killing the mules, Wheeler's pickets were attacked on both flanks and the rear. Wheeler repulsed the attack, and he remained undisturbed for eight hours. The three hundred ordnance wagons were set on fire and the explosions were heard in Chattanooga. Rosecrans immediately sent out a force.[2]

Just before dark, as Wheeler was retiring from the field, a large Union cavalry and infantry force moved upon Wheeler's force from Stevenson, skirmishing with their rear until dark.

During the night, Wheeler's force crossed over the Cumberland Mountains, and the next morning joined General Wharton near the foot of the mountains and proceeded to attack McMinnville. Wheeler had ridden forty miles during the night. The Union force was closing in behind, but Wheeler succeeded in capturing the place with an enormous supply of quartermaster's and commissary stores, with fortifications and garrison, which numbered 587 men, with arms, accouterments, and two hundred horses. After taking the works, Wheeler didn't want a fight in the streets, so he demanded that the Yankees formally surrender the town. The 4th Tennessee, U.S. surrendered.[3]

During the day and night, Wheeler's force burned the stores, a locomotive, and a train of cars, on the McMinnville and Manchester Railroad and the bridges over the Hickory Bridge, the Hurricane Creek, and the Collins River.[4]

On the next day, Wheeler's force marched to Murfreesboro, and after making a demonstration upon the town, the force captured a strong stockade guarding the railroad bridge over Stone's River, with it's garrison of fifty two men. The rest of the day was occupied in tearing down the bridge, and burning the railroad ties and track for three miles below the bridge, down the Nashville and Chattanooga Railroad. Captain Kyle with Company F & D, Eighth Texas, was ordered around Murfreesboro and was to reach the railroad leading to Nashville. Once there, he was to capture a train. When he arrived, there was no train, so Captain Kyle captured an oxen train instead. They killed the oxen and converted it to beef.[5]

The following day, Wheeler's force destroyed a train and a quantity of stores at Christiana and Fosterville, and destroyed all the railroad bridges and trestles between Murfreesboro and

Wheeler's First Raid

Wartrace, including all the large bridges at and near Murfreesboro, capturing guards. They also captured and destroyed a large amount of stores of all kinds at Shelbyville, the enemy running from his strong fortification when Wheeler arrived. In Shelbyville some of the Rangers captured a black "Prince Albert" coat from the supplies. They presented the coat to the chaplain of the Eighth Texas. That night, Wheeler ordered Davidson's division to encamp on the Duck River near Warner's bridge, Martin's division two miles farther down, and Wharton's division two miles below Martin's.[6]

During the evening, Wheeler learned that the Yankees, who had been pursuing them, had encamped near Frazier's farm. Wheeler immediately informed General Davidson of the position of the Yankees, and directed him to keep the Yankees observed and to join Wheeler, at Crowell's Mill, should the Yankees move toward him. According to Wheeler, Davidson failed to comply with this order, and on the following morning, General Davidson was attacked by a much larger Union force, under General Crook, who defeated him, capturing a number of prisoners. Davidson was ordered by Wheeler to join him, which he failed to do and even failed to fall back upon Wheeler's main line. He also failed to inform Wheeler in which direction he was falling back upon. Wheeler received two dispatches from General Davidson which indicated that he was moving down from the Duck River, but Wheeler questioned his couriers and ascertained that Davidson was actually moving towards Farmington.[7]

On October 7th, 1863, Wheeler, with nine hundred men, started towards Farmington and arrived at 4 P.M. He was just in time to place General Wharton's division and five regiments of Martin's command in position across the pike, and allowed Davidson's demoralized troops to pass to the rear, when the Union force appeared. Wheeler had ordered Davidson and Col. Thomas Harrison to form in column by fours on the pike and to charge the enemy. General Davidson reported to Wheeler that only three regiments of the Yankee force had been seen during the day. Col. John T. Morgan and his 51st Alabama Partisan Rangers received the first charge from the Federal cavalry, but Morgan fired such a destructive volley that the Yankees juggernaut was temporarily checked. The Federals quickly re-formed and again advanced, approaching within fifty yards of the Confederate line, when Col. Humes poured grape and canister from the cannons into the approaching blue coats, while Blakey of the 1st Alabama and Col. John Hagan of the 3rd Alabama, charged them with a Rebel Yell, driving them back once again. General Davidson had failed to form his columns, and instead moved some distance away. The Union force soon came up in strong force with a division of infantry and a division of cavalry. The cavalry and infantry were armed with Spencer rifles, and were hidden behind large boulders. It began to rain and the artillery smoke drifted down, obscuring the position of the Yankees. The Yankees at one point tried to take the guns under Major Humes, but he made a defense of his battery, and standing by his guns, discharged his pistols, killing Col. Monroe of the 123rd Illinois, who fell thirty feet from where Humes was standing. Wharton and the Rangers charged down the road, and got within seventy five yards of the Union position. The Yankees fired into the Rangers columns, aiming at the horses feet. The volley struck every horse in Company F, except one and a dozen men. Wheeler's force fought them for twenty minutes. Wheeler then decided to charge the line. Wheeler ordered Harrison to charge. Harrison ordered Blackburn to lead the charge. Col. Harrison cried out to Blackburn "Charge them, Rangers!" Col. Harrison moved out to one side and allowed the other companies to pass. They rushed by Harrison and he would say to them, "Follow Blackburn!" Wheeler's command drove back the Yankees for some distance. In this charge Wheeler's horse was shot out from under him and Lt. Col. Cook and Major Christian was wounded. General Wharton's column and their supply train, had now passed the Yankee force and the object for which they fought for was accomplished, Wheeler withdrew his force without being followed.[8]

The Yankees acknowledged 29 killed and 159 wounded, including Col. Monroe of the 123rd Illinois. Wheeler accounts only one fourth that of what the Yankees lost. The Eighth Texas also managed to capture the very expensive and prized weapon; the Spencer rifle. According to Frank Batchelor the Texas Rangers lost twenty killed and wounded in one charge, and claimed that no more than one hundred Rangers were involved in the fight. His horse was severely wounded. General Wharton also had a horse killed at Farmington, but escaped unhurt.[9]

After the battle, Wheeler, and several other officers complimented the Eighth Texas for

111

their gallantry during the battle. Col. Harrison spoke up: "It was no fight at all! I'm ashamed of them! If they can not do better than that I'll disown them!"

A staff officer then added a comment: "I always thought that regiment somewhat overrated anyhow."

This angered "old Tom" Harrison, who got up, shook his finger in the fellow's face and broke out furiously: "Who the hell are you! There is not a man in that regiment who can not kick you all over this yard, sir!"

As he strode off to his horse, he was heard to say: "By _____ I'll curse them all I want to; but I'll be damned if anybody else shall do it in my presence."[10]

The next day Wheeler made a reconnaissance towards Columbia. As soon as the Yankees in the town heard that Wheeler was coming, they burned the stores and evacuated. On the 10th, Stanley's entire corps of cavalry, under General Mitchell, Crook, and McCook continued their pursuit of Wheeler's forces. On that same day, Wheeler reached the Tennessee River at Muscle Shoals, and crossed it without any problems. The Union force arrived just after Wheeler had already crossed. Wheeler notes in his report that one of the limbers belonging to White's battery, which was assigned to Harrison's brigade, blew up, and had to be abandoned. Two howitzers and an old iron cannon had to be abandoned. Wheeler reported that on his raid he managed to capture 1,600 prisoners, and killed and wounded as many of their cavalry as would cover his entire loss. Wharton's division again was appraised for their "accustomed gallantry."[11] According to Frank Batchelor the raid had burned 1,200 wagons loaded with supplies, captured two thousand prisoners, and completely supplied Wheeler's Corps with blankets, boots, hats, pants, coats, and overcoats. "Every article necessary for winter wear" was available to the Rangers. Frank Batchelor also made the comment that the Rangers looked like "a vast caravan of merchants, than soldiers, on returning to Tennessee. Every man had from one to three suits of Yankee clothes, and trinkets of all descriptions."[12]

After Wheeler's Corps crossed the Tennessee River, the Rangers were camped at Decatur, Georgia. The men rested and recouped their horses and dyed their clothes. Since the clothes were Yankee blue, the men had to bleach out the color, and then dye them butternut or grey. Wearing a Union uniform was a good way to get shot as a spy.

While they were at Decatur, Confederate President Jefferson Davis visited the Army of Tennessee. In his speeches he told the Army he intended to drive the Yankees out and reoccupy Tennessee. Frank Batchelor said that he doubted that the army could do it.[13]

Harrison's brigade had become the talk of the Confederate Cavalry Department in the Army of Tennessee especially because of his recent exploits. His brigade routed Watson's Brigade of Federal Kentucky Cavalry and drove them over seven miles capturing their entire train of supplies including three hundred prisoners. They also whipped a division of Stanley's Cavalry at "Owen's Mills" and drove them two miles and captured sixty prisoners.

The Great Raid or October Raid was a great success for Wheeler, Wharton, and Harrison. They had managed to strike a large blow to Rosecrans communications and food supplies , leading to the Union Army sustaining on one third rations. Bragg was hoping to break the will of the Union army in Chattanooga, but time was running out for Bragg and his forces. Disputes among his own Generals and the arrival of Union General Ulysses S. Grant would bring Bragg's dreams of capturing the entire Union army to an end.

[1]Campaigns of Wheeler and His Cavalry 1862-1865; O.R. I-Series XXX Wheeler and Roddey's Raid on Rosecrans Communications. No. 28 Report of Maj. Gen. Joseph Wheeler, C. S. Army, commanding Cavalry Corps, Army of Tennessee.
[2]Ibid.
[3]Ibid.
[4]Ibid.
[5]Terry's Texas Rangers, Leonidas Giles, P. 65-68
[6]Campaigns of Wheeler and His Cavalry 1862-1865; O.R. I-Series XXX Wheeler and Roddey's Raid on Rosecrans Communications. No. 28 Report of Maj. Gen. Joseph Wheeler, C. S. Army, commanding Cavalry Corps, Army of Tennessee.
[7]Ibid.
[8]Campaigns of Wheeler and His Cavalry 1862-1865; O.R. I-Series XXX Wheeler and Roddey's Raid on Rosecrans Communications. No. 28 Report of Maj. Gen. Joseph Wheeler, C. S. Army, commanding Cavalry Corps, Army of Tennessee.; Terry Texas

Rangers Trilogy: J. P. Blackburn; Terry's Texas Rangers, Leonidas Giles, p. 64-68.
[9]Batchelor-Turner Letters; Campaigns of Wheeler and His Cavalry 1862-1865; O.R. I-Series XXX Wheeler and Roddey's Raid on Rosecrans Communications. No. 28 Report of Maj. Gen. Joseph Wheeler, C. S. Army, commanding Cavalry Corps, Army of Tennessee.
[10]Terry's Texas Rangers, Leonidas Giles, P. 65-68
[11]Campaigns of Wheeler and His Cavalry 1862-1865; O.R. I-Series XXX Wheeler and Roddey's Raid on Rosecrans Communications. No. 28 Report of Maj. Gen. Joseph Wheeler, C. S. Army, commanding Cavalry Corps, Army of Tennessee.
[12]Batchelor-Turner Letters
[13]Batchelor-Turner Letter

Chapter 12:
The Knoxville Campaign: The Battle of Lookout Mountain and Missionary Ridge

During the month of November, the Confederate army was in turmoil. Some of Confederate General Braxton Bragg's General's had signed a petition to have Bragg relieved of command. The petition was sent to President Jefferson Davis. Even though Jefferson Davis was ill at the time, he personally took a train to Lookout Mountain to try and solve the dispute between Bragg and his Generals. Bragg and Davis were old friends from West Point, and the Mexican War. Davis decided to keep Bragg in command of the Army which was a fatal mistake. Most of the Confederate Army of the Tennessee had become distrustful of Bragg, and hated his tactics of commanding their army. Many of the soldiers knew that they had won a great victory against the Yankees at Chickamauga, but Bragg would not follow the fleeing Yankees and crush the Union force forever. They were also upset at the way he had handled Perryville. Again the soldiers thought they had won a great victory, but Bragg pulled out. At the Battle of Stones River, many a soldier had heard about the purpose slaughter of the Orphan brigade on the third day of battle. The morale of the men was quickly diminishing.

When Bragg heard that he was still in command of the army, he took revenge on every General that signed that petition. He relieved General Nathan Bedford Forrest of command. He also relieved three Confederate Generals and told them that their services were no longer needed. Another of his targets was General James Longstreet. Longstreet had been one of those that had signed the petition. On November 5th, Bragg sent Longstreet and his twenty five thousand men to Knoxville, Tennessee.

Col. Tom Harrison's brigade, including the 8th Texas, was assigned to General Frank Armstrong's division of cavalry. Frank Armstrong was born in 1835, and was born in Indian Territory. He was the son of an Indian agent. He later became a 2nd Lieutenant in the 2nd Dragoons. When the Civil War broke out, he fought at the Battle of First Bull Run as a Union soldier, but after the battle he signed up for the Confederate army. On August 13th, 1861, Armstrong became a volunteer camp-de-aide, then a Lieutenant and assistant adjutant general; he became a Colonel in the 3rd Louisiana in May 1862, then acting Brigadier General on July 7th, 1862, commanding a cavalry brigade, under Sterling Price's Corps. In September 1863, he became a General of a division under General Forrest's Corps.[1]

In November, Union General Ambrose Burnside was in Knoxville, preparing for the Confederate assault. Bragg could have not afforded to send Longstreet away. Union General Ulysses S. Grant had replaced Rosecrans as commander of the Union force in and around Chattanooga. Grant was assembling a huge Union force, that was now equipped and fresh. Grant was beginning to focus his attention on Lookout Mountain, where most of Bragg's forces had been assembled.

On November 24th, Maj. Gen. William Martin, commanding Longstreet's cavalry, was joined by the 1st and 6th Georgia, and moved his entire force towards Kingston, and tried to take the town. The strength of the Union force in the town was too much for Martin, and he bypassed the town.

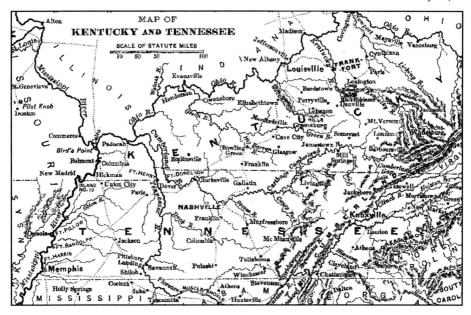

General William Martin was born on March 25, 1823, in Glasgow, Kentucky. He attended Centre College in Kentucky, and then moved to Natchez, Mississippi and became a lawyer. He had a shrewd mind and a forceful voice. In 1861, he organized a troops of cavalry and went to Richmond. In Richmond, his unit became known as the 2nd Mississippi Cavalry with Martin as Major. Early in 1862, Martin was already a Colonel of the Jeff Davis Legion, participated in the expeditions in Virginia, during the Peninsula Campaign. He served as an aide to General Robert E. Lee. After fighting at Antietam he was promoted to brigadier general and was then sent to the West and given a command under General Joseph Wheeler.[2]

During the siege of Knoxville, the Eighth Texas Cavalry were given menial duty. The Union sympathizers around Knoxville were sending supplies on rafts and floating them down to Knoxville by the river. The Yankees in Knoxville would catch the rafts with their booms. It was decided that the Rangers should cut down trees and throw them into the water so that they could float down the river and break the Yankees booms. This began to hurt the morale of the men.[3] While the Rangers were in Knoxville, things were heating up at Lookout Mountain. On November 24th, Union General Joseph Hooker, supported by Union Generals Charles Cruft, Brig. Gen. Peter Osterhaus, and Brig. Gen. John Geary attacked Lookout Mountain. They encountered the small force of 2,694, under Brig. Gen. Charles Stevenson. Most of the infantry under States Rights Gist and William Hardee had been sent to Missionary Ridge. Stevenson could not hold onto Lookout mountain and fell back to Confederate General Patrick Cleburne's position on Missionary Ridge.

With Lookout Mountain, Union General William T. Sherman could bring supplies into Chattanooga without any problems. Sherman had six divisions totaling twenty six thousand men against ten thousand men under Patrick Cleburne and Carter Stevenson. On November 25th, Sherman began his assault on Missionary Ridge. The Federals, under Sherman met heavy resistance at Tunnell Hill. Sherman made several attacks, but failed to dislodge the Confederates. Hooker later arrived at Rossville Gap and attacked the Confederate left. Confederate General John C. Breckinridge was in command of the far left flank. The Federal's routed Breckinridge's men. The Confederate left flank gave way. During this time, Sherman received reenforcements from Union General George Thomas. Thomas sent twenty thousand men to attack the Confederate entrenchments. The Union forces managed to take the first set of entrenchments but could not advance any further. Without orders, Union Maj. Gen. Phil Sheridan rallied the Union forces and pushed up to the second set of entrenchments, and drove up the hill. The Confederates were totally routed. Bragg tried to rally his men, but the damage had been done. They no longer trusted their commander, and yelled curses to Bragg's face, as they were running past him.[4]

When Missionary Ridge fell, Longstreet moved his army to Morristown. Longstreet had to end the siege at Knoxville and take the city before Union reenforcements would arrive from Chattanooga. Longstreet had two divisions of his own corps, McLaws Division under Major General Lafayette McLaws, and John Bell Hood's division under Brig. General Micah Jenkins. Longstreet's artillery corps commander was E. Porter Alexander as well as Major Leydon's artillery, and Major General Robert Ranson's, Jr. Cavalry division from Virginia and a part of Joe Wheeler's cavalry corps. Two cavalry brigades were under Brig. General William Martin and two under Brig. General Frank Armstrong, plus Wharton's First Brigade under Col. Tom Harrison. Altogether Longstreet had fourteen thousand men under his command.[5]

Wheeler's force arrived at Sweetwater, Tennessee on November 11th with portions of four brigades of cavalry and reported to Longstreet.

On November 12th, at Sweetwater, Longstreet revealed to his staff his plan for approaching Burnside's army in Knoxville. His infantry corps, together with his artillery corps, would cross the Tennessee River at Huff's Ferry and advance on Knoxville from the west. Wheeler was to capture the Union force at Maryville and make a diversion of the Yankees flank. He was also to leave sufficient cavalry to guard the Tennessee River from the mouth of Hiwassee to Loudon. Longstreet gave Wheeler information regarding the countryside and how he was to protect his rear and flank should the Yankees attempt a movement across the Holston at Lenoir's Station. The Yankee force at Maryville was estimated to be around five hundred to four thousand men strong.[6]

The next day Wheeler crossed the Tennessee at Motley's Ford with four brigades, two under Martin and two under Armstrong and made a night's march to strike between the Yankees at Maryville and their line of retreat. On approaching Maryville, Wheeler found only the 11th Kentucky Cavalry. Wheeler attacked and captured a few Union cavalry and scattered the rest. He captured one hundred and fifty one men. While Dibrell's brigade was engaged with the 11th Kentucky Cavalry, Col. Frank Wolford, with his brigade, rushed in to help the 11th Kentucky Cavalry and attacked Wheeler's command. Union Col. Wolford was repulsed by Harrison's command of the Eighth Texas and the Eleventh Texas and Third Arkansas. Col. John T. Morgan's brigade along with Harrison's brigade charged the Yankee cavalry and drove them over Little River in the "wildest confusion", capturing eighty five cavalry.[7]

During the night General Longstreet ordered Wheeler to cross Little River, but only if he was successful at Maryville. Wheeler moved over the Little River on the following morning. His entire command crossed over the river by noon. Wheeler pressed the Yankee force, which consisted of Brig. General William P. Sander's, Shackelford's, Wolford's, and Pennebaker's brigades, with one battery of rifled guns, all commanded by General Sanders. After driving them for three miles Wheeler came upon Stock Creek, which was not fordable by horses, and the Union force had partly torn up the bridge. Just beyond the Yankees had taken a strong and elevated position behind a fence inclosing a thick wood, with large fields intervening between the Yankees and Wheeler's position, the ground descending rapidly toward the line occupied by Wheeler's troops. The flanks of the Union force from Little River to Knoxville were protected by a high ridge on their left and the Holston River on their right, thus preventing Wheeler from turning the Yankees position and compelling Wheeler to fight superior forces in positions chosen by the Yankees.[8]

The Yankees began to shell Wheeler's position and the carbines and rifles began to ring out across the fields in Wheeler's direction. Wheeler dismounted nearly half of his command, crossed the creek under cover of a fire from his battery, and drove the left wing on the Yankees from it's strong position. This enabled a detail to repair the bridge while Wheeler pressed on with the dismounted men, compelling the entire line of the Yankees to retreat. Immediately after crossing the creek Wheeler sent General Armstrong to move rapidly up the road with his entire command, which had been in reserve.[9]

In the meantime Wheeler and his force continued to push the Yankees with the dismounted men, driving them from several strong positions. After a delay of more than an hour General Armstrong overtook Wheeler's force, and as soon as his command could be prepared, they charged the Yankees with his command. The Eighth Texas in advance, followed by the 11th Texas, the Third Arkansas on the flanks, the whole supported by Dibrell's Tennessee brigade. The Union line were broken and the entire mass of the Yankees were swept on toward Knoxville. The charge was continued for three miles to within less than half a mile of the river opposite the city. The bulk of the Yankees dashed over their pontoon in their flight into the city. Great numbers scattered over the countryside and many plunged into the river and drowned. Wheeler captured 140 prisoners. Sanders was mortally wounded on the 18th in front of Fort Loudon. He died the next day. [10]

Wheeler was only prevented from following the Yankees into the city by a strong force of the Yankees infantry and artillery in the fortifications on a high hill on the south bank of the river, which opened a heavy fire upon Wheeler's force as they approached. It was now dusk, and the balance of the command was four miles to the rear, so Wheeler decided to withdraw his force to Stock Creek, which was the nearest point at which forage could be obtained. [11]

The next morning the Yankees had strengthened their position and began to fire on Wheeler's men as they advanced. Longstreet sent a message to Wheeler: "Unless you are doing better service by moving along the enemy's flank than you could do here, I would rather you should join us and cooperate." [12] Wheeler decided to march to join the main body of the command. Wheeler received another message from General Longstreet, ordering him to cross the Holston and report to Longstreet on the 17th. Wheeler crossed the Holston near Louisville and reported to Longstreet at 3 P.M. on the 17th. Longstreet had begun to surround the city and Wheeler's force was directed to continue the line from the left of the infantry to the Holston River, upon which his left flank rested, while his right rested upon the Knoxville and Clinton Railroad, giving Wheeler a line of about four miles. This line was kept almost continually skirmishing with the Union soldiers, and the Yankees made no serious attacks against Wheeler's force. Detachments of his command were sent out in their rear and succeed in capturing twelve prisoners, and ten government and two sutler wagons loaded with a large steam cracker baking machine and some clothing and shoes. [13]

The next six days were spent in closely besieging this portion of the line, and engaging the Yankees with both artillery and small arms on several occasions.

On November 19th, Longstreet made plans to attack Fort Loudon, latter named Fort Sanders. It was on a hill that fell off to the northwest, so that a large force could be marched under cover and approach within two hundred yards of the fort without being exposed to view or to fire either from the fort or the adjacent line on either side. All of Longstreet's artillery, thirty four cannons in all, were posted in positions that could hit Fort Sanders and enfilade the adjacent lines. All of the guns were protected by earthworks. [14]

On November 20th, Wheeler's force engaged the Yankees along the whole line. General Micah Jenkins was feeling the Yankees position at the railroad depot about sunset, and Wheeler was ordered to open his batteries about that hour and advance his line of skirmishers.

At 10 P.M. on November 22nd, General Longstreet ordered Wheeler's force to march to Kingston, leaving a brigade to picket and scout upon his left. He was to capture the Union force at Kingston. Half the command fell back seven miles and didn't enter camp until nearly daylight. The roads were so bad that Wheeler only traveled twenty six miles before dark. He was still twenty miles from Kingston. Wheeler and his escort rode to Kingston and found the town reenforced with infantry. [15]

At 3 A.M. the command came up worn out and exhausted, half of the men having lost two nights sleep and they were short of rations. Five of the best regiments were left at Knoxville, and many men were unable to keep up with the command. After an hours rest Wheeler's force encountered Union pickets three miles in front of Kingston. A party was sent out to cut off the pickets but failed. Wheeler pressed on toward the town against the resisting Yankees. Wheeler hoped to reach the town before the Yankees could form up. Upon arriving at the foot of a hill near the town, Wheeler found it covered with long lines of infantry and dismounted cavalry. Wheeler immediately dismounted the Alabama and Georgia regiments, under Martin's division, except one regiment to guard his flanks, and pressed upon the Yankees, who had by this time opened with their artillery and infantry, two of their guns firing 24 pound shells. The Yankees line extended along the crest of the ridge with the concavity being toward Wheeler's men. In order to approach the Yankees it was necessary to advance up a gentle slope through open fields which the Yankees swept by both direct and cross fire. The artillery of Captain Pugh, Wiggins, Freeman with a section of two guns each, kept up a destructive fire on the Federal lines at different points, while Harrison's brigade, with Captain Reese's company, which was Wheeler's escort, made several charges, as well as the Eighth Texas Rangers, who charged in the rear of the Federal batteries, killing a large number and capturing eighty five prisoners. The Federals were driven back to near Knoxville, until they were met by a division of Federal infantry. Wheeler

General Martin and Armstrong also agreed with the withdrawal. At this moment the Yankees charged his right, but were repulsed without being followed by the enemy. [16]

On November 23rd Union General Ulysses Grant made plans to attack Lookout Mountain. Confederate General Bragg ordered Wheeler to report to department headquarters and to turn his command over to General William Martin. Wheeler left for Chattanooga with two divisions, under Armstrong and Morgan's.

On November 26th, Maj. Gen. William Martin, who was commander of Longstreet's cavalry, moved Colonel Tom Harrison's brigade and Russell's 4th Alabama Regiment, of Brig. General John T. Morgan's 1st Brigade, under command of Brig. Gen. John T. Morgan, across the Holston below Knoxville to engage in a demonstration upon the Union lines in Knoxville. The men were dismounted and moved with the infantry on it's left flank. Russell's brigade was engaged, and drove the enemy from their rifle pits upon the side of a difficult ridge. Col. Tom Harrison, on the extreme left, found no Yankees in his front. [17]

On November 29th, Confederate Lt. Gen. Longstreet ordered these two brigades by forced march to re-cross the river. Brig. General Frank Armstrong's force moved with part of his division towards Tazewell to meet a Union advance from that direction.

Reaching the vicinity of Maynardville on the afternoon of the 30th, Martin found General Jone's division skirmishing with the Yankees. It was too late to attack. General Armstrong, with his division, was sent around to the right to reach the rear of the Yankees before daylight. The remainder of Martin's force moved at daylight on Maynardville, but the Yankees had rapidly retreated soon after daylight, leaving a small picket, which was captured. Being joined by Gen. Armstrong, Armstrong's division was pushed toward Clinch River, while General Jone's command was sent to the right to get between the Yankees and the river. A Union force prevented his success. General Armstrong pushed the Yankees in front, and finally he was driven across the river, after being pursued for some time through difficult gorges, which was made more difficult by a frozen stream. [18]

Martin returned to Knoxville, reaching the town on December 2nd. The army on the second night after the siege of Knoxville had been raised, commenced it's retreat toward Rogersville, General Morgan's brigade followed, covering the rear of General McLaw's Division on the south side of the Holston. General Armstrong's division performed the same service on the Knoxville and river roads. The infantry and artillery having passed Bean's Station, Martin was ordered to move to the south side of Holston and cover the railroad and the left flank. [19]

On December 10th, a brigade of the Union cavalry attacked General John T. Morgan's brigade at Russellville, while the greater portion of it was foraging. The Yankees were repulsed by one third of General John T. Morgan's division, leaving dead, wounded, and prisoners in their hands. [20]

Lt. Gen. Longstreet having turned upon the Yankees and attacked them at Bean's Station, Martin was ordered to cross the river and operate in his rear. While engaged in this movement, it was necessary to dislodge the brigade of cavalry guarding May's Ford, in order to cross the river. This was done by the rapid fire which came from artillery from White's Tennessee battery and Wiggin's Arkansas batteries, of Kelley's division. The Yankees lost sixty killed and wounded. [21]

Early the next morning the Yankee pickets were driven in, and before Martin had entirely crossed, he was ordered to move upon the Yankees flank on the Knoxville road, four miles from Bean's Station. The task was accomplished, and a high hill was gained, from which Longstreet's artillery could cover the Yankee's breastworks. With great labor the guns were placed in position and were fired rapidly with effective results. [22]

In the meantime, General John T. Morgan's division was dismounted and moved upon the Union flank. Martin's guns were in sight of, and only four hundred yards from Morgans infantry skirmishers, who were expected to attack in front. Martin's fire was continued for one and a half hours, and the Yankees began to retreat, but was able to detach a large force to hold his men in check, as they were not pressed in front. The infantry did not advance, and Martin's position was held. [23]

The next day Martin moved down the Knoxville and river roads in front of the Union force, who had retreated in the night and after several unimportant skirmishes Martin found them in a strong position, on Richland Creek, holding both roads with a force too great for Martin's cavalry to cope with in a country not at all suited for cavalry operations. [24]

On December 22nd, the command returned across the Holston river and established a picket line from near New Market to Dandridge. Col. Russell's brigade was posted four miles east of

Dandridge. Col. Crews was half way from Morristown to Dandridge and Gen. Frank Armstrong's division was concentrated at Talbott's Depot, on the road leading from Morristown to New Market. Commanders of these divisions were instructed by Martin to attack the Yankee's in the flank or rear if they made an attack upon any of these three positions.

On December 24th Brig. General Samuel Sturgis, commanding the Cavalry Corps, Department of the Ohio arrived at New Market, Tennessee. Union Col. William Palmer, who commanded the 10th Ohio Cavalry, 15th Pennsylvania Cavalry, and the 1st Tennessee Mounted Infantry, arrived from Dandridge with his command. He had captured four prisoners of Morgan's division, who were part of an advance guard to Dandridge. General Sturgis learned from the prisoners that a division or brigade was at Dandridge. Sturgis planned to separate the force at Dandridge from the rest of the force. He planned to move a brigade by Mount Horeb to intercept their retreat, and a brigade with four pieces of artillery on the direct road to Dandridge.

On December 24th, simultaneous attacks were made upon Gen. Frank Armstrong and upon Col. Russell's brigade. After heavy skirmishing Russell was flanked and outnumbered, and was forced to withdraw his pickets from New Market to the eastern side of Mossy Creek. An unexpected attack upon Col. Russell was made by two thousand cavalry under Col. Campbell, 2nd Michigan Cavalry. Russell's brigade was for a moment in confusion, but rallied and repulsed the Union force, who fell back two miles toward Dandridge. Campbell's reported killing eighty or one hundred of the Confederates. Campbell reported twenty or thirty killed of his command.

In the meantime, four regiments of Crew's brigade, six hundred men in all, moved in the rear of Campbell's force. Two of the regiments being in advance made a charge on the Union force and captured their battery.

Support being too far off, the men who made the charge were driven from the guns, and Major Bale, commanding the 6th Georgia, was left dead in the midst of the battery. Two pieces of artillery and the two remaining regiments of the brigade coming up, and the whole command being dismounted, the Yankees were pushed from one position to another, until finally routed. They abandoned one gun and caisson, his dead and wounded, and under cover of night, escaped capture. Col. Russell's brigade should have moved up, but the courier sent with orders failed to reach him. He was watching the movements of five hundred Yankees, who were marching on Crew's right, trying to escape.

The Yankees trying to escape clashed with Crew's men, comprising of the First, Second, Third, and Sixth Georgia Cavalry. The Yankees three times charged Crew's dismounted men in open field and were each time repulsed, but not until, some his men were brought to the ground by clubbed guns. The Yankees were pursued without effect by Col. Russell in the night to New Market.

Union Col. Garrard, who was also sent to Dandridge, engaged near Cheek's Cross roads and lost twelve or fifteen men.

On the 26th, General Samuel Sturgis occupied a line a half mile beyond Mossy Creek, and it was his intention to attack the Confederates, whose line was about three fourths of a mile beyond, and drive them back on their main force. The rain began to fall and threatened to raise the river in his rear, and he was deterred from undertaking a general action. The weather began to clear and about 11 A.M. Sturgis line of skirmishers pushed forward a little and engaged the Confederates but little injury was done on either side. Sturgis artillery opened fire for a little while and was briskly replied to by the Confederate artillery, but the Confederate artillery soon limbered up and retired.

Sturgis thought that the ease with which the Confederates were driven back, taken with the cavalry on their right flank, led him to believe that the Confederates desired to draw him as far as possible toward Morristown with their infantry and Sturgis did not pursue. The position Sturgis occupied was in advance of the roads coming in from Dyer's Ford, from Chucky Bend, and from Dandridge, so he withdrew to the other side of Mossy Creek, so he could command the roads.

While withdrawing, the Confederates attempted to regain some woods on the Morristown road from which they had been driven, when the 4th Indiana charged upon and drove them back, killing several of the Confederates, who then shelled the road and wounded one man.

On the 27th, General William T. Martin tried to dislodge the Yankees from Mossy Creek, but stopped when the couriers could not find Gen. John T. Morgan and without orders, Morgan moved his command, dismounted, from the position Martin assigned him, and made it impossible to carry out his plan to attack Mossy Creek.

Union Brig. General Samuel Sturgis received a report on December 28th that a brigade of

Confederate cavalry was in the area of Dandridge that afternoon. His intelligence reported that the Rebel force was split, and decided to meet and defeat, and possibly capture, this portion of it. He ordered most of his Ohio troopers out toward Dandridge on two roads. In addition, Sturgis pulled the 2nd Brigade out of the line on the Morristown Road and with two guns of the battery, ordered them to move about halfway to Dandridge in the event the two Ohio divisions got into battle. Col. Archibald Campbell, who commanded the First Brigade, First Division, commanded by Col. Edward McCook, was told to spread his brigade to take the place of the men pulled out of the line.

The next morning, on the 29th, Major General William T. Martin and his six thousand men from three cavalry divisions were advancing down the Morristown road. Facing him were the First Brigade, First Division, commanded by Col. Archibald Campbell. The fighting occurred on both sides of the railroad leading from Mossy Creek to Morristown, and continued for one quarter of a mile west of Talbott's Station and ended near the same place they had started from when darkness fell upon the battlefield. The battle began when Gen. John T. Morgan's division was dismounted and formed on the left of the railroad, Gen. Armstrong on the right. The countryside from Talbott's Station to Mossy Creek was composed of open, rolling fields that had been tilled during the past year, and was flanked by high woodlands on each side. Martin could not maneuver the artillery, except near the railroad. Armstrong's division, with the artillery, was moved rapidly upon the Union troops to occupy his attention, while Martin hoped to flank him with Morgan's division on his right. At 9:00 A. M. the pickets of the 2nd Michigan and 1st East Tennessee encountered Martin's forces. The 2nd Michigan and the 1st Tennessee were camped three miles from Mossy Creek, one on each side of the Morristown road. The 9th Pennsylvania Cavalry was ordered two miles back to support the 18th Indiana Battery on the same road. Col. Archibald Campbell, commander of the First Brigade, First Division, fell back. He formed two regiments in line with two battalions Second Michigan, dismounted and retired slowly. Archibald saw Martin and Armstrong trying to flank his command. Both of Martin's two divisions were moving and by the double quick and were driving Col. Campbell back. Campbell's skirmishers kept up a brisk fire, but so did the Confederate artillery. Col. Campbell arrived at a brick house one mile from Mossy Creek.[25]

Up to this time the force opposing Martin was no more than four thousand men, with two batteries. Unfortunately Martin did not know that the 118th Ohio Infantry of Mott's brigade was camped in the town of Mossy Creek. They were marched into thick woods across the road from the Union battery. A section of the 5th Illinois Battery was placed on the right of the Union line, about a half mile away and a little to the rear of Col. Eli Lilly's 18th Indiana battery. They were supported by two hundred and fifty cavalry, who were detachments of the 15th Pennsylvania and the 10th Ohio. [26]

Confederate Col. Crew's brigade was thrown to the right of the railroad, and Gen. Armstrong, with Crew's brigade, was ordered to move up his artillery to within canister range and to charge some woods in his front and that of Col. Crews.

Confederate Col. Russell's brigade had it's right resting on the railroad and his left on the woods. Immediately in his front the Yankees had occupied some barns and outhouses. Martin ordered him to dislodge them. The whole line moved forward. The Yankees were driven back from this position on Martin's left, but by this time some of the Union troopers who had set out for Dandridge had returned and a charge of the 1st Tennessee cavalry upon the Confederate right and Mott's brigade of Union infantry, which was the 118th Ohio Infantry, and the 16th Kentucky, descended upon Crew's brigade and Armstrong's left. Martin's force was forced to yield their ground. The Yankees fixed bayonets and moved into the open field to charge the Georgians and two howitzers some two hundred yards away in his front. Martin wheeled the 7th Alabama Regiment to the right and moved it into a cut of the railroad, securing a good position within fifty yards of the flank of the advancing infantry. The fire from this regiment and a counter-charge by the Georgians soon drove the Yankees into and through the woods, with heavy loss in killed and wounded.[27]

At this time the Union 2nd Brigade, under Col. Oscar LaGrange, arrived and the Yankees were now able to take the offensive, and the entire Union line advanced. Three cavalry charges were upon Russell's left and produced some confusion for a moment. Assisted by the officer's Martin was able to rally the men under a heavy fire from the cavalry and the artillery. For a short time all firing ceased, except from the artillery. Upon reconnoitering the Yankee's position, it was discovered that they were preparing for another attack, and Martin found the Yankees in strong position in his front and overlapping his line on both flanks with three brigades of cavalry, six regiments of infantry and three batteries of artillery in position to sweep the open fields in his front. On the opposite side of the creek in full view, was a reserve of cavalry and infantry. A fresh brigade of cavalry was coming in from the Dandridge road in full view.[28]

Martin's artillery had run out of ammunition, except canister. The division commander reported an average of only five rounds of ammunition for small arms. The 3rd Arkansas, under Col. Tom Harrison's brigade, had fired the last round in it's cartridge boxes, and had been ordered to the rear. The men had been fighting steadily without relief for seven hours. To advance was impossible and to mount and retire on the open fields in daylight before so large a force with such a large force of mounted men would be difficult. The retreat, under heavy fire of artillery and small arms, was carried out in prefect order, the regiments falling back in succession to advantageous points, and then fighting until, having checked the Yankees sufficiently, they could gain another advantage point. Martin's and Armstrong's men were pushed all the way back to Talbott's Station. Darkness ended the battle. [29]

Martin commended Col. Crews and Harrison for their gallantry on the 29th. He also pointed out the "most gallant charge (was) made by the Eighth Texas Regiment." The battle had raged for three hours in which men from both sides were exposed to murderous fire. Total losses for the Union were sixty five men killed, wounded and missing. Losses for the Confederate forces engaged are hard to determine but must have been higher than the Union losses.

By the end of 1863, the Confederate cavalry under Martin was in sad shape. Martin points out that the division and brigade commanders were destitute. They had no shoes, blankets, overcoats, and ragged. They were in great need of clothing. Many of the horses were unshod and the men haven't been paid in six months.[30]

The Knoxville Campaign was a disaster for General Longstreet. He was not able to take Knoxville, he had learned that General Braxton Bragg had been defeated at Missionary Ridge, and that Union General William Tecumseh Sherman was between them and Bragg's army. Longstreet fell back to East Tennessee. Confederate losses were 1,296. Union losses were only 681. The Rangers lost twenty men during the Knoxville Campaign. Texas Ranger Frank Batchelor gave a listing of who was killed and wounded during the Campaign:

Dan Browing killed Nov. 15, 1863, Co. K, Sam Grover, Co. F killed Nov. 15 at Rockford, Tennessee, Jake Godsey, Co. H killed at Mossy Creek December 24th, N. J. Allen Co. D, killed Dec, 29th, Mossy Creek Station, Tennessee, Meredith Odgen Co. G died Dec. 31st at Morristown, Tennessee, Josiah Jackson, Co. A killed Dec. 29th at Morristown, James Langan Co. A killed Dec. 29th at Morristown, W. W. Wells Co. E wounded at Knoxville Sept. 1863, Lt. Black Co. D wounded Nov. 15, 1863 Knoxville Campaign, Capt. John Lowe Co. A wounded Nov. 15, Knoxville Campaign, John Rabb Co. F wounded November 15 at Rockford, Capt. William Jarmon Co. F wounded December 16 at Rutledge, Capt. George Littlefield Co. I severe wound from shell burst, Lt. James Dillworth Co. I wounded December 16th at Rutledge, Richard Torrence Co. H leg shot off December 26 at Mossy Creek.[31]

After the Battle of Mossy Creek, Col. Tom Harrison and his brigade, including the 8th Texas Rangers, were positioned at Pigeon River. The regiment was stationed there for several days on the banks of the stream. The Eighth Texas history tells of an amusing story when the Rangers practical jokes was at it's best. The stream was small but deep. Some two hundred or hundred yards from the banks was a stately home of a wealthy and refined family. The head of the family was away at war, and the house consisted of the wife and three or four daughters. They had secured a house guard to protect them from any harm. Joe Rogers was the guard's name.[32]

The society men of the regiment slipped out after evening roll call to enjoy a game of cards at the house. One night a Lieutenant, a clerk of the quartermaster department, and one or two others, crossed the river on a make shift raft, and were engaged in a game of euchre with the young ladies. Suddenly a cry of "Halt! Halt!" range out on the night air and pistol shots rang out. Out went the lights and the visitors rushed for the doors and windows, knocking over chairs, tables, and even the young women! They rushed to the river, plunged in and swam across to make it to their companies. Sharp orders to "Saddle Up!" were given and the entire brigade was soon in line of battle. Colonel Tom Harrison sent Tom Gill and a small party to investigate the cause for the alarm. Tom passed the house, where all was quite, and immediately set up a picket line. The pickets reported no Yankees had passed their post. Joe Rogers hadn't run with the others at the first alarm. He had gone out back to look for his horse and his equipment. While getting these he heard voices, accompanied by laughter and the voices seemed familiar. Peeping around the house he soon realized the alarm was caused by three Rangers. He reported it to Col. Harrison. The "old man" was furious at first, for the false alarm. However he decided to drop the whole incident, and write it off as a joke gone bad. The men didn't think it was so funny. They were awaken from their sleep for nothing. Frequently at night after the incident, someone would call out: "Who waded Pigeon?" From some other part of the camp the answer would come: "Murray! Brownson!". John Haynie, one of the best soldiers in the regiment, was the leader of the alarmist joke. [33]

Harrison failed to get promoted but General Wharton was made a Major General. The 4th Tennessee, and the 1st Kentucky regiments were taken from Col. Harrison's command. He still had the Eighth Texas, the 11th Texas, and 3rd Arkansas. Matters came to a head with Frank Batchelor and Harrison. While at Knoxville, Batchelor asked Harrison to relieve him from being on his staff. Harrison made no reply. Dr.Thornton quit Harrison's staff without notice. Harrison had to send for Capt. George Decherd, Co. D, who was at the time ordnance sergeant, to come to his assistance to lead the company. "After about a week the old man was terribly out of humor and made some hasty remark about an order I had written when I asked him in the presence of the couriers and staff to relieve me as I desired to return to my Company. We were both mad; after hemming a little he replied: "well Batchelor if you want to go-you may do so." Capt William Sayres told Batchelor that Harrison regretted saying it and begged Batchelor to reconsider it. But Batchelor's wanted to get away from 'the old Bear." Batchelor added: " I wonder that I could for than seven months endure his testiness." The old rival between Harrison and Batchelor came to end. Batchelor never forgave Harrison for installing his nephew to Adjutant, instead of Batchelor[34].

It seems that nerves were beginning to flare. The men were tired and officers were short of hand. Frank Batchelor also reported that Col. Tom Harrison also had a falling out with Major Christian. Frank says that Major Christian was very popular with the men. Christian and Ironsides (Tom Harrison) had some sharp sparring of late in which Major Pat gave back as hard blows as were sent in presence and hearing of the Regiment. In proportion as the men hate the Colonel so they love the gallant Major for his independent course. Col. H. had told his staff he was tired of Maj. C and intended to have him removed, but I think he will find it a job before gets through with it, as the Major is a favorite with General Wharton." Batchelor was commander of his company for the past month and the only commissioned officer present. Lt. Scruggs was left at Morristown, Lt. Tom Burney was also left at Morristown, and Lt. Baylor had not returned. [35]

On January 26th, Gen. John T. Morgan and General Frank Armstrong moved towards Fair Garden Road, between Little East and Middle Forks of Pigeon River and west of McNutt's House. The Union force pushed the Rebel cavalry force to Dickey's. Union Col. Wolford was posted on the Flat Creek road, at a place called Fowler's, and was attacked by Armstrong's Division and was driven back. Col. Israel Garrard, who commanded the 2nd Cavalry Division, was stationed at Tom Evans, on the French Broad, guarding the fords, was ordered down to Wolford's assistance. [36]

The next day, Union Col. Wolford fell back to within two miles of Seierville, and remained there. The Rebel force on the Fair Garden Road was held in position by Col. Archibald Campbell's First Brigade, First Division, and General Samuel Sturgis brought Col. Oscar La Grange's 2nd Cavalry Brigade back to within two miles of Seierville. Col. Garrard remained at Nichol's watching the river road, and Sturgis moved up the troops which were watching the fords below the Little Pigeon to Cannon's, on the Little Pigeon. Learning that Armstrong's force was concentrated on the Fair Garden Road, Sturgis directed Col. Edward McCook, of the First Division, to attack him at daybreak. There was too much fog the next morning, so Sturgis ordered Col. Campbell to charge a ridge occupied by the Confederates on their left, beyond the bend of the Little Pigeon River, near Hodsden's house, which was a key position. Then opening with rifled guns of Capt. Eli Lilly's 18th Indiana battery, his brigade charged the entire Rebel line, driving him for more than a mile. The Rebels took a new position in rear of the creek crossed by McNutt's Bridge, Sturgis ordered Col. Oscar La Grange up the left hand road from Dickey's House toward Fair Garden. The Rebels saw the flanking movement but it was too late to do anything about it, and they fell back. Union General Sturgis then ordered Col. Frank Wolford and Col. Garrard with their commands to hold the position occupied by Col. Edward McCook's division, to prevent the Rebel division of General Armstrong's to re-enforce by any roads leading in the direction of Fair garden. The Confederates under General William Martin and John T. Morgan were pushed back to the intersection of the by-road taken by Col. La Grange on their left flank and the main NewportRoad.[37]

By 4 P.M., Col. Campbell's brigade charged dismounted with the saber and a yell, while La Grange advanced his line within pistol range of the Rebel line. The Rebels opened up with canister shot, but ceased firing and prepared to move his pieces from the field, when Col. La Grange, with the Fourth Indiana Cavalry, charged him with the saber at a gallop, capturing one hundred and fifty prisoners, two rifled 10 pounder guns, one caisson, one ambulance, four flags, arms and horses, all from General John T. Morgan's force. The pursuit was kept up until dark. Col. Wolford and Garrard came in to late to participate in the pursuit of Morgan's force. They were also exhausted from fatigue and no forage.[38]

On January 28th, Sturgis continued the pursuit of Armstrong's cavalry to Swann's Island, above Dandridge. The rout was complete, and General John T. Morgan's brigade was destroyed..

Upon reaching the river, Sturgis sent a reconnaissance to Fain's Island, below Dandridge, where Sturgis found three brigades of Rebel infantry crossing the river. Sturgis determined that it wound be impossible to fight Longstreet's infantry, because Sturgis' horses and men were exhausted. But, before Sturgis left, he would try and destroy Armstrong's cavalry. Sturgis ordered Col. Wolford, supported by La Grange, and left Garrard and McCook to watch the infantry. Armstrong was strongly posted on a heavy timbered bank of the creek on a hill, and fortified himself strongly. Armstrong was also joined by three Rebel regiments of infantry. Col. Wolford's division, supported by Col. La Grange brigade, moved quickly on both sides of the river towards Armstrong's position. Armstrong was driven from the strong position on the ridge, running at right angles with the river near Indiana Creek and compelling Armstrong to fall back behind his breastworks and rifle pits that he had constructed. Col. Wolford succeeded in forcing Armstrong from there on the their extreme left. But reenforcements of three regiments of infantry already engaged, and holding a strong position and was moving his troops across Evan's Ford, six miles below Dandridge, and advancing on Cannon's, three miles from Seierville. Colonel Wolford was ordered to withdraw, followed by Col. La Grange's brigade. Sturgis withdrew his force to Fair Garden.[39]

By February, not only were the Confederates exhausted, but so were the Yankee force, and Longstreet stayed in East Tennessee. The Yankee force surrounded him. Longstreet's force could not move, if he did he ran the risk of running out of forage for his horses. Knoxville could no longer be taken. It was properly defended by Union General Ambrose Burnside, and was heavily fortified with seventy cannons. They also had plenty of supplies for a siege, with fifty thousand pounds of pork and five hundred barrels of flour. If Longstreet tried to cut communications with Chattanooga, and bypassing Knoxville, resistance was ready for him in Union lines from Little Tennessee or the Holston, while reenforcements would have marched from Chattanooga. Plus, Longstreet's communication lines would be open from flank attacks from Knoxville. If Longstreet tried to enter Kentucky through Pound Gap, Pendelton's Gap or Crank's Gap, a column formed of the disposable force at Knoxville, marching rapidly can easily close the gaps in his rear, and capture his trains, while a force may be thrown around by rail from Chattanooga sufficient with that in Kentucky, to destroy him. The best policy for the Yankees was to let Longstreet remain until the objects of the movements farther south are attained and until a offensive could be taken with advantage.[40] The Texas Rangers would not be attached to Longstreet much longer. They would be transferred back to Wheeler's command to participate in the next major campaign of their careers; the Atlanta Campaign.

[1] Who's Who in the Confederacy; Historical Times Illustrated Encyclopedia of the Civil War.
[2] Ibid.
[3] Terry's Texas Rangers, Leonidas Giles, P. 69-80
[4] The Civil War Battles of the Western Theater
[5] O.R. Series I-Vol. XXXI Nov. 4th-Dec. 23rd-Knoxville (Tennessee) Campaign: No. General James Longsrteet, commanding
[6] O.R. Series I-Vol. XXXI No. 76 Maj. Gen. Joseph Wheeler, C. S. Army, commanding

Cavalry Corps.
[7] O.R. Series I-Vol. XXXI No. 76 Maj. Gen. Joseph Wheeler, C. S. Army, commanding Cavalry Corps.
[8] Ibid.
[9] Ibid.
[10] O.R. Series I-Vol. XXXI No. 76 Maj. Gen. Joseph Wheeler, C. S. Army, commanding Cavalry Corps.; Campaigns of Wheeler and His Cavalry 1862-1865.
[11] O.R. Series I-Vol. XXXI No. 76 Maj. Gen. Joseph Wheeler, C. S. Army, commanding Cavalry Corps.
[12] O.R. Series I-Vol. XXXI Nov. 4th-Dec. 23rd-Knoxville (Tennessee) Campaign: No. General James Longsrteet, commanding
[13] O.R. Series I-Vol. XXXI No. 76 Maj. Gen. Joseph Wheeler, C. S. Army, commanding Cavalry Corps.
[14] O.R. Series I-Vol. XXXI Nov. 4th-Dec. 23rd-Knoxville (Tennessee) Campaign: No. General James Longsrteet, commanding
[15] O.R. Series I-Vol. XXXI No. 76 Maj. Gen. Joseph Wheeler, C. S. Army, commanding Cavalry Corps.
[16] Ibid.
[17] O.R. Series I-Vol. XXXI Nov. 4-Dec. 23rd-Knoxville (Tennessee) Campaign: No. 77 Brig. Gen. William T. Martin, C. S. Army, commanding Longstreet's Cavalry.
[18] Ibid.
[19] Ibid.
[20] Ibid.
[21] Ibid.
[22] Ibid.
[23] Ibid.
[24] Ibid.
[25] Series I-vol. XXXI Action at Mossy Creek, Tennessee-No. 4 Report of Col. Edward M. McCook, 2nd Indiana Cavalry, commanding First Cavalry Division; No. 5 Report of Col. Archibald Campbell, Second Michigan Cavalry, commanding First Brigade.; Mossy Creek by John Rowell; O.R. Series I-Vol. XXXI Nov. 4-Dec. 23rd-Knoxville (Tennessee) Campaign: No. 77 Brig. Gen. William T. Martin, C. S. Army, commanding Longstreet's Cavalry.
[26] Mossy Creek by John Rowell
[27] Series I-vol. XXXI Action at Mossy Creek, Tennessee-No. 4 Report of Col. Edward M. McCook, 2nd Indiana Cavalry, commanding First Cavalry Division; No. 5 Report of Col. Archibald Campbell, Second Michigan Cavalry, commanding First Brigade.; Mossy Creek by John Rowell; O.R. Series I-Vol. XXXI Nov. 4-Dec. 23rd-Knoxville (Tennessee) Campaign: No. 77 Brig. Gen. William T. Martin, C. S. Army, commanding Longstreet's Cavalry.
[28] Ibid.
[29] O.R. Series I-Vol. XXXI Nov. 4-Dec. 23rd-Knoxville (Tennessee) Campaign: No. 77 Brig. Gen. William T. Martin, C. S. Army, commanding Longstreet's Cavalry.
[30] Ibid.
[31] Batchelor-Turner Letters
[32] Terry's Texas Rangers, Leonidas Giles. ppgs. 69-80
[33] Ibid.
[34] Batchelor-Turner Letters.
[35] Ibid.
[36] O.R. Series I-vol. XXXII Jan. 26-28, 1864-Operations about Dandridge, Tenn. No. 2 Report so fBrig. Gen. Samuel D. Sturigs, U.S. Army, commanding Cavalry, Army of the Ohio; No. 3 Reports of Col. Edward M. McCook, 2nd Indiana Cavalry, commanding 1st Cavalry Division, Army of the Cumberland.
[37] Ibid.
[38] Ibid.
[39] Ibid.
[40] O.R. Series I-Vol. XXXI Nov. 4th-Dec. 23rd-Knoxville (Tennessee) Campaign: No. General James Longsrteet, commanding

Chapter 13:
The Atlanta Campaign

Col. Harrison's brigade stayed in East Tennessee through the winter and early spring of 1864. In April 1864, Harrison rejoined the Army of the Tennessee, which was now commanded by General Joseph Johnston at Dalton, Georgia. Harrison's brigade in March was made a part of Brig. Gen. William Young Conn Humes division. Humes was born in 1830, and was from Virginia. He attended the Virginia Military Institute and graduated in the top of his class in 1851. He later became a lawyer. Humes served as staff to the line until late 1863. He served as a staff artillerist and was captured at Island No. 10 and exchanged. As a chief of artillery to Wheeler, Wheeler noticed the skill of Humes and gave him the rank of Brig. General commanding brigades at Chickamauga and Knoxville. He quickly rose to divisional command just in time for the Atlanta campaign.[1]

The reason why Wharton was not in command of Harrison's brigade, was that Wharton had a falling out with Confederate General Joseph Wheeler. An episode occurred at Wharton's headquarters in December of 1863, involving a forged order purporting to have been issued by Wheeler. The joke letter backfired in Wharton's face. Wharton's explanation that the order originated as a joke rather than an effort to discredit Wheeler's judgement was not accepted by Wheeler. Wheeler denounced Wharton as a "frontier political trickster." Wheeler sent a letter from Dalton, Georgia to Richmond, Virginia to have Wharton relieved of his command. Wheeler's letter gives more details to the incident. He writes:

> On the receipt of your letter I sent a note to three officers who were in General Wharton's division at the time the false order was written by him or by his sanction, and to which you referred. I called the attention of these officers to the forged order and required them to state what they recollected regarding the circumstances and facts connected with the matter. These officers each made their statements, neither of them knowing that another statement was being made, as they were in different parts of the command. Their statements differ on minor points, but all go to show that the order was written and that it had a bad effect. The facts, as they came to me at the time, were as follows: On the 9th of December last, with the sanction of General (William) Hardee, I ordered General Wharton to move to a point south of Coosa River to recruit, rest, and instruct his command. General Wharton delayed starting with his command for two days. On the receipt of my order to move to the rear an order was written and laid upon the table of his adjutant's office, which order purported to come from me, and directed that Wharton's command should commence picketing on the left of our army and run a line of pickets over Lookout Mountain to the Tennessee River.
>
> Such a disposition would of course have destroyed the horses of the command, as it would have been impossible for them to have been fed.
>
> The command was of course dissatisfied, and abused me as the author of the order, at the same time severely criticizing my judgment in disposing of cavalry. General Wharton came to me and in a laughing way remarked that he got up a joke by having an order published ordering his command to picket on the mountain in order to see how the command would.take it. I fear, however, that he did not mention it to me until he had become convinced that the matter was so public that I would hear of it by other means.
>
> The truth is, General Wharton allowed his ambition to completely turn his head, as his friend in Congress had assured him that he should command the cavalry of this army, he being

one of those politicians (not statesman) who looked upon things we would consider dishonorable as legitimate tricks, and he forgot that he was an officer instead of a frontier political trickster. This state of things has been going on for some time, the object appearing to be to convince his command that he was their friend, while I was not, and also that he was superior as an officer, &c. I regret to state that such things are very contagious and spread to the officers, who sought to cover their own delinquencies by reflecting falsely upon their superiors. I have taken hold of the matter very firmly, and am holding all such officers to a strict account for their conduct, both as officers and honorable men, and it is already having a good effect. I am determined to root out the last vesture of such dealing in this command or fall in the attempt to accomplish this object. I am getting the command to understand the matter, and everything is going on smoothly. I am pleased to state that my efforts to improve and instruct my command are appreciated by both privates and officers, and notwithstanding the misrepresentation made by the disorganizers, they have failed to deprive me of the esteem of my soldiers, which is so essential to success. It is true a few soldiers have by their efforts been induced to believe their false representations, and thus allow themselves to be prejudiced, but I am happy to state they are very few.

Very respectfully,
JOS. WHEELER,
Major-General.[2]

The Confederate Government in Richmond wrote Houston, Texas and Houston's Governor wrote to Wheeler. Wharton was to report to Lt. General Edmund Kirby Smith, who was now commanding the Trans-Mississippi Department.

Harrison's brigade now comprised of the 3rd Arkansas, commanded by Col. Amson Hobson, the Eighth Texas, commanded by Gustavus Cook, and the 11th Texas, commanded by Col. George Reeves. Harrison would remain with Humes Division until the end of the war.

For a month, the Eighth Texas rested at Dalton, Georgia.

On March 18th, 1864, Sherman became commander of all Union forces in the West. Sherman assembled 100,000 men against Joseph Johnston's 45,000 men. He amassed one hundred locomotives, and one thousand cars crammed with supplies for his trip through Georgia. Sherman studied all the maps and censuses for Georgia, because he was going to have his men live off the land, and he needed to know where the most fertile regions were. It was up to Sherman to take Georgia. On May 5th through the 6th, General Joseph Johnston placed his army on the Rocky Face Ridge, which runs north and south, and across Crow Valley, north of Dalton, Georgia. Rocky Face Ridge was eight hundred feet above the valley floor. Sherman sent Union General James McPherson and his Army of the Tennessee (24,465 men) to Snake Creek Gap, an opening through Rocky Face Ridge about twelve miles below Dalton. Sherman also sent Union General George Thomas and his Army of the Cumberland (60,733 men) to Ringgold, about midway to Dalton on the Western & Atlantic Railroad. Maj. Gen. John Schofield was sent with his Army of the Ohio (13,559 men) south via the Tennessee town of Cleveland and followed the east Tennessee & Georgia railroad, which joined the Western & Atlantic at Dalton.[3]

On March 26th, 1864 George Turner of the Texas Rangers died from disease. He was listed as a civil engineer for Col. Harrison staff. Capt. M. G. Turner, George's brother also died from disease.[4]

Maj. Gen. Joseph Wheeler became the commander of the Cavalry Corps during the Atlanta Campaign. On May 6th, Wheeler's force consisted of Col. Major General William Martin's Division, consisting of Allen's and Iverson's brigades; Humes Division consisting of Ashby's, Tom Harrison's and Grigsby's Brigades, and Kelley's Division, consisting of Anderson, Dibrell, William's and Hannon's brigades. His brigades were stretched from Ships Gap, on their left to the Connesauga River, on the right.

For several days previous to the 6th, strong demonstrations were made by the Union army driving Wheeler's pickets with a force varying from a brigade to a division of infantry, with cavalry and artillery. Union General Oliver Howard's corps had marched from Cleveland and taken position in line of battle three miles from Wheeler's headquarters at Tunnel Hill. A portion of Union General John Palmer's Corps had moved through Ringgold Gap and formed upon Howard's right. Union Maj. Gen. John Schofield's (Twenty Third) corps was moving from East Tennessee by way of Cleveland and Varnell's Station to join General Howard. Corse's, Garrard's, Kilpatrick's, McCook's, and Stoneman's divisions of Cavalry were also on the move toward

Wheeler. The Union force were in line six miles from the proposed line of battle of Wheeler's infantry. Wheeler immediately set out to set up roadblocks by cutting down trees in front of the road and passes to slow down the Yankee tide.[5]

On May 6th, the Union force advanced in force near Tunnel Hill; resisted by Wheeler's skirmish line, supported by two regiments. On May 7th, at daylight, a Union force began a determined advance in line of battle one mile in length, with heavy skirmish line in front; stubbornly resisted by dismounted cavalry fighting behind their obstructions and breastworks thrown across the roads at various points north of Tunnel Hill. On reaching Tunnel Hill, Wheeler set up his artillery and immediately told his artillery to open fire on the oncoming Federal line. The Federals were pushed back from several positions. At about 11 o'clock, Wheeler's men were forced to abandon the town, and by three o'clock were driven back to their fortifications, where his infantry line of battle was formed. At dark, Wheeler sent a regiment of Grigsby's brigade to reenforce the picket at Dug Gap.

On May Eighth, the remainder of Col. Andrew Grisgby's brigade was sent to Dug Gap, and with the rest of Wheeler's command moved to the Cleveland road, where he was joined by General Kelly, who had marched from Resaca the previous day. Union General Edward McCook's Cavalry division advanced from Varnell's Station, but after slight skirmishing retired before the command could be brought up into position. Wheeler captured several prisoners. Grigsby's brigade was attacked about 4 P.M. at Dug Gap by John Geary's division of Union General Joseph Hooker's Corps. The Union force made several assaults upon the brigade, which repulsed them with great slaughter, killing and wounding nearly as many of the Yankees as the effective total of Grisby's brigade. Wheeler claims that it was ten Yankees to every Confederate. The next day, on May 9th, Union Col. Edward McCook's division again advanced, supported by infantry. Col. George Dibrell's brigade and part of Allen's brigade were dismounted to keep the Yankees from advancing any further. The Yankees attempted to turn their right, near Rocky Face, but was stopped by Wheeler's escort. On May 10th, the Federals made another movement on the right, pushing down the main Cleveland and Dalton Road. The Yankees pushed back the Confederate pickets. Wheeler placed his troops into position, behind a large field. When the Federals advanced to a safe distance, the dismounted men of Allen's and Dibrell's brigades charged the Yankees by foot, and the Eighth Confederate, and the Eighth Texas Regiments charged mounted, completely routing the Yankees and capturing Col. La Grange, and one hundred prisoners. Wheeler's force also captured one regimental stand of colors and a large number of small arms. Wheeler said in his report that there were about five thousand cavalry supported by infantry. His force consisted of less than nine hundred. "The charge of Wheeler and his Texans was beautiful. In order to get into action they had to cross a morass where only four could go abreast, but they charged in columns of fours, and formed "right into line" as they charged. The result was inevitable, for Sherman had no cavalry which could withstand the onslaught of these men."[6] During the battle Col. LaGrange's horse was wounded and fell on him, pinning him to the ground just at a large farm gate. Texas Ranger John Haynie found Col. LaGrange. Addressing Haynie, LaGrange said: "You have a prize indeed. I am Col. LaGrange. I didn't know that you boys had got down here from East Tenneessee. I knew you as soon as I saw you coming."Haynie helped LaGrange from his horse and led him to Col Tom Harrison. LaGrange said to Harrison: "I was in command of the brigade, and was anxious for the commission of Brigadier General. Had some influential friends who were helping me. My division commander told me to go out, run in the rebel pickets, skirmish a little and send in a report, which he would forward with strong recommendations for my promotion. I came out, ran into the Texas Rangers, and am a prisoner." Harrison told LaGrange: "Only the fortune of war, my young friend. Only the fortune of war."[7] According to another story, when Col. LaGrange was caught it was said that he began to weep. General Wheeler tried to console him and complimented on the gallant fight he had made, to which LaGrange replied: "Yes, General, but General Sherman gave me 2,500 men and told me he would make me a Brigadier General if I captured you-and if I had such men as yours I would have done it!" During the charge, Wheeler lost forty men.[8] Wheeler commended Humes, and Tom Harrison for their actions during the battle of May 27th. "At Varnell's Station less than 1,000 men from Allen's and Dibrell's brigades of Kelly's Divisions, and the Texas Rangers, of Harrison's brigade, Humes division, met and repulsed the attack of a force of cavalry 5,000 strong. At this juncture the gallant Texas Rangers (Col. Cook) and Eighth Confederate Regiment (Col. Prather) charged most heroically into the enemy's ranks, killing and wounding large numbers and capturing over 100 prisoners, including a brigade commander and several other officers. One stand of colors was captured and the enemy completely routed and defeated."[9]

On May 10th and 11th, skirmishing continued along Wheeler's line of defense. Allen's brigade was sent to Resaca, Georgia.

The next day Wheeler's force attacked Brig. General George Stoneman's Corps near Varnell's Station and drove it to Rocky Face Ridge, killing, wounding, and capturing one hundred and fifty Yankees. The Yankees burned four hundred wagons and a considerable amount of commissary stores, in order from them being captured by Wheeler's force. Wheeler had later learned that the Yankees had two divisions which had turned their left flank, moving towards Resaca. Wheeler had to take position on the Oostenaula. [10]

That night, Confederate General Joseph Johnston moved his Army of Tennessee from Dalton to Resaca, Georgia and Wheeler was ordered to relieve the entire line of battle with his cavalry deploying as skirmishers and to cover the movement by slowing down the Federal advance.

On May 13th, before daylight, Wheeler relieved all the infantry skirmishers in their breast works. At daylight the Yankees advanced in force and after several engagements, Wheeler gradually fell back toward Tilton, arriving there at 3:00 P.M.. It was here that Wheeler was reenforced by Confederate General John Brown's brigade of infantry. A large Union force was in Wheeler's front, while a division of the Yankee's infantry turned his left flank, and Wheeler was forced to form his command in a right angle. The Federals attacked both positions with infantry and cavalry, but were repulsed and held in check until 9 P.M.[11]

The next day on May 14th, the Battle of Resaca began. Early in the morning, Wheeler moved out with Kelly's division to encircle the Yankee force. After a severe fight the command was driven back near their works. At 3 P.M. Wheeler then crossed the Connesauga and returned before night to cover his right flank. During the battle Union General John Schofield launched an attack with two divisions against Maj. Gen. Thomas Hindman's Confederate division on the other side of Camp Creek. Union General Jacob Cox attacked on the left, Union Brig. Gen. Henry Judah attacked on the right. Cox captured Hindman's first line of entrenchments at 1:30 PM, but Cox was halted by the Confederates and Cox lost 562 men. On Cox's right, Judah's division got entangled with a division from the Army of the Cumberland that was meant to support him on the right. He didn't halt to reorganize and didn't wait for support troops. Judah ordered a charge across four hundred yards of open ground in the Camp Creek Valley and quickly lost six hundred men. At 4:00 PM, the Confederates in Confederate General John Bell Hood's two divisions attacked Union Brig. Gen. David Stanley on his extreme left. Stanley's 35th Indiana ran but the 5th Indiana artillery stopped the Confederates. Federal General Alpheus Williams reinforcements helped halt the Confederate advance completely. The Confederates had come close to a victory. The fighting ended because of darkness. [12]

On May 15th, Wheeler fought until noon, holding a line of works to which dismounted cavalry had been assigned, but the Federals were making an attempt to turn the Confederate left, crossing the Oostanaula River near Calhoun and at 3 P.M. Wheeler was ordered to Calhoun by General W. H. T. Walker. Wheeler also moved Humes Division, including the Eighth Texas Cavalry, and Allen's brigade to a point on the south side of the Oostanaula. Union General Stoneman's command attacked General William Hardee's hospitals. Wheeler charged Stoneman, defeating him, retaking the hospitals, and pursued the Yankees for two miles, capturing forty prisoners, and two stands of colors. General Sherman ordered Brig. General Thomas Sweeny to cross the Oostanual River at Lay's Ferry. Sherman also ordered a push northwest of Resaca near the mouth of Camp Creek. Union General Schofield moved around the extreme Federal left to make room for Union Major General Joseph Hooker's XX Corps. Hooker would make the attack supported by Howard's IV Corps. Hooker instructed Major General Daniel Butterfield's division to seize the Confederate earthworks and capture Capt. Max Van den Corput's four cannons. Union Col. Benjamin Harrison led his troops down the slope and into the open valley that separated the two ridges. The Indiana troops took the fort. That night under cover of darkness, the Federals took the four guns. Sweeny got across the Oostanaula River and built earthworks. He was attacked by W. H. T. Walker's Confederates, including Wheeler's men, but Sweeny held his ground. Johnston soon realized that he was outflanked again, and his Confederate forces crossed the river and marched southward abandoning Resaca. The Battle of Resaca cost Johnston 2,600 killed, wounded, or captured. Sherman lost 3,500 men, but he had forced Johnston out of his position twice. [13]

At 4 A.M., on May 16th the Yankees having learned that Wheeler's cavalry had retreated from Resaca, shelled the woods in which Allen's brigade was encamped without any injury. At early dawn, Wheeler's skirmishers near the river engaged the Yankees skirmishers, who were crossing the river. Wheeler found on the Calhoun road a full battery of five rifled guns with caissons which had been left by the Confederate army. He immediately ordered sixty men to be dismounted from Allen's brigade and sent them for these guns. They moved to the skirmish line, brought them out, and carried them safely to the rear. Allen's brigade continued skirmishing with the Federal's line, which had been strengthened from the opposite side of the river, and was supported by their artillery from the opposite heights until 12 P.M., when Wheeler ordered it to retire to the main line, which had been formed one mile to the rear of that position. [14]

On May 17th, with Brig. General J. H. Kelly's Division, Col. Tom Harrison's brigade and Brig. General John William's brigade, Wheeler confronted the Yankees, who were advancing on the Calhoun road. They advanced with cavalry, infantry, and artillery. Wheeler opened up on the Yankees with small arms from behind their temporary rail breast works and with two pieces of artillery, forcing the Yankees to deploy their lines. At about 3 P.M., the Yankee cavalry had advanced in his rear, and Wheeler had to fall back to Adairsville. The Yankees moved around Wheeler's left flank on the west side of the creek, which runs near and west of the Adairsville and Calhoun road. General Kelley's division was sent to oppose this force and prevent it from gaining in their rear. Confederate General Benjamin Cheatham's division of infantry also formed in front of Adairsville, along with General William T. Martin's Division and Williams' brigade. Skirmishing was kept up until dark, when Wheeler withdrew the main portion of his command near the town to feed and rest the horses. [15]

Early the next day, on May 18th, Wheeler formed his lines about one mile in rear of the town. The Yankees advanced slowly, skirmishing, but Wheeler held them back until they deployed their lines. Wheeler had to fall back. Wheeler again reformed his lines. Humes Division, along with the Eighth Texas, including Martin's Division was put into line on the Cassville and Adairsville road. Col. G. Dibrell's brigade, Kelly's Division, was put on the Copper Mine road, and Williams brigade, Kelley's Division, was put on the Tennessee Road. The Yankees advanced at 3 P.M. on General Martin's division, but were driven back. At about 7:30 P.M., Wheeler's entire line was withdrawn, leaving the skirmishers in position.[16]

On May 19th, General Johnston withdrew his army from the earthworks during the night and crossed to the south bank of the Etowah. At daylight, Wheeler formed his lines about one mile in front of the infantry line. The Yankees advanced with a heavy line of skirmishers from a woods toward the field in their front. Wheeler opened up two cannons upon the advancing Union force and drove them back. Wheeler was informed that the Yankees were only one mile from Cassville. Wheeler immediately sent for Martin and Kelly to fall back to the town. As the rear of Kelly's line fell back into the town, he was attacked by the Yankees cavalry, which charged his line of skirmishers, but were stampeded by the fire from a second line of Kelly's command and were charged in return by his escort. Wheeler retired his command during the night to the rear of the infantry lines and took position to guard the right flank of the army. General Allen's brigade, Martin's Division, had been ordered from the Kingston road without orders from Wheeler.[17]

On May 20th, Allen's brigade was sent to assist General Jackson's brigade, of Walker's Division. General William H. T. Walker's Division, and with the rest of Wheeler's command guarded all the roads to the right of the railroad leading to Cartersville. The Yankees attacked only his left and were easily held in place. Wheeler's rear retreated across the Etowah River at about 5 P.M., and Wheeler burned the bridge.

On May 23rd, Sherman crossed the Etowah River, west of Alltoona. Wheeler's force was ordered to again cross the Etowah river to Cartersville to ascertain the Federal's strength, location, and movements. At midnight on the 24th, Wheeler was ordered to strike the Yankees rear near Cassville and determine the position of the Yankees. Wheeler was planning to attack a wagon train near Cass Station, when he was handed a message from Col. O. M. Messick, commander of the 11th Texas, Harrison's brigade, stating that they had just drove back the Yankees advance about two miles and a half, capturing horses and one prisoner, who told him that there are three thousand cavalry and fifteen thousand infantry at Cassville. The cavalry was commanded by Federal General George Stoneman. Wheeler decided to attack the wagon train at Cass Station with Kelly's division, using one regiment to hold his right flank on the Kingston road. General Humes division was formed in line of battle in rear of the town to be prepared to

129

reenforce General Kelly if needed, or to cover his retreat or rout. Kelly charged the enemy driving him back, and capturing eighty Union wagons, and they burned the rest of them. While taking the wagons from Cass Station to Cassville, Allen's brigade was attacked by the Federal's. Wheeler placed the Eighth Texas Cavalry and the Second Tennessee Cavalry, of Ashby's Brigade, Humes Division, in position to reenforce Allen while still burning the wagons. The Yankees quickly started to burn some of the new wagons just acquired by Wheeler. Wheeler ordered the Eighth Texas and the Second Tennessee to engage the oncoming Union cavalry. The Yankees charged, and the Eighth Texas and Second Tennessee met them with equal force and drove the Yankees back in confusion for three miles upon the infantry supports near Cartersville. Wheeler continued the charge, killing and wounding the Yankees, and also capturing one hundred prisoners. Wheeler now knew of the Federal position. Wheeler retired back across the river, with his prisoners, wagons, mules, horses, etc.[18] In his official report Wheeler commended the Texas Rangers, and Tom Harrison for their actions at the Battle of Cass Station. "The gallant Texas Rangers and Second Tennessee Regiment supported by the 3rd Arkansas, were promptly placed into position, met and repulsed the enemy's charge; then in turn charged the enemy, driving him upon his infantry support, and capturing nearly 100 prisoners. This affair was one marked of brilliancy."[19]

The next day Sherman had crossed the Etowah and attempted to march around the Confederate left flank toward New Hope Church. He found Johnston in full force at New Hope Church.

On May 26th, Wheeler's force moved from Ackworth to join the main army, and took the position on it's right on the Ackworth and Dallas Road.

The next day on the 27th, the Confederate forces under Confederate General Patrick Cleburne, along with Hannon's, and Allen's cavalry brigades were placed on Cleburne's right flank. All of the men were dismounted and they began to know the way of the spade. They dug massive entrenchments extending for eight hundred yards. General Humes command was held in reserve to attack at any moment along any point of the Confederate entrenchments. At 3 o'clock the line of Confederate skirmishers were driven back by the Federal's cavalry which was advancing up Pumpkin Vine Creek by Widow Pickett's house. A Union squadron was moving towards Humes. A Federal infantry force was also advancing. Wheeler ordered Humes division to bring one brigade to be dismounted to the point of where the Federal infantry was approaching and to hold back his other brigades upon it's right to fill a gap between said position and General Martin's left. The Yankees moved a column up a ravine between Kelly's right and Humes left. A regiment from Humes was ordered to oppose this Union force, but Humes soon had to call up another regiment from his command to hold back the Yankees. While this was going on, Brig. General William Hazen's 2nd Brigade, Third Division, of Federal infantry charged Wheeler's line, but was repulsed by a counter charge of Humes and Kelly's divisions.[20]

During the battle Wheeler captured thirty two prisoners, including one commissioned officer. General Lowrey's brigade, Cleburne's Division, was sent in to relieve Humes brigade. Humes moved to the right, in front of the temporary breastworks. Wheeler stated that he only had eight hundred and twenty two men against General Wood's Third Division, of Major General Oliver Howard's Corps. General Howard was trying to turn Wheeler's right flank, but had failed, with Wheeler holding Howard's force in check until Wheeler was relieved by a division of infantry. Wheeler then moved to the right to guard their right flank. Wheeler captured one thousand stand of arms. The Federals lost between four to five thousand killed, wounded and missing.[21]

On May 28, Wheeler extended to the right, built new earthworks and skirmished with the 14th Corps and Edward McCook's Cavalry and captured thirty prisoners. The next day Wheeler strengthened his works, which was now three miles in length, keeping up rifle fire with the Federal lines. On the 30th the Federals advanced and assaulted the Confederate lines. Wheeler repulsed the Federals. On the 31st, the Federals extended their line to Marietta Road. Wheeler withdrew a portion of his troops from their works and charged them, capturing seventy prisoners.

On June 3rd, Wheeler fought from his breastworks engaging infantry and cavalry under Union General John Schofield. The Confederate front was opposed by infantry corps fortified, while the Confederate right was menaced by their cavalry. The Federal attack was temporarily checked by a severe rain storm. Towards evening the Federals, both infantry and cavalry, charged the Rebel line at two points and were repulsed by the combined firepower of artillery and musket fire. Fifty Federals were captured.[22]

On June 4th, Union General Edward McCook's 1st Division of Cavalry was in Acworth. The main cavalry force under Wheeler, including Col. Tom Harrison's brigade was at Big Shanty. The Union cavalry was moving towards four mountains; Brush Mountain on the Confederate right, Lost Mountain on the Confederate left, and Pine Mountain on the Confederate middle, with Kennesaw Mountain two miles away near Marietta, which was General Joseph Johnston's headquarters. The next day, Union General Garrard's division of cavalry advanced on the Big Shanty road. Wheeler skirmished with the Federal cavalry and then his mounted troops charged and drove the Yankees beyond Big Shanty, capturing forty five men. [23]

On June 9th, the Federals advanced on Wheeler's right with two brigades of infantry and three brigades of cavalry and one battery. The Yankees charged twice, but were repulsed. When darkness fell, the Federals retreated. On June 10th, Sherman received reinforcements, and advanced on Johnston. Sherman had 100,000 men against Johnston's 70,000 men who occupied the hills north of Marietta. Sherman pushed Johnston to Kennesaw Mountain. Wheeler took position near Bell's Ferry and Canton Road. Confederate General Leonidas Polk was killed by Union artillery on June 14th. On June 15th a division of Federal cavalry advanced and attacked the Confederate right at Noonday Creek. The Yankees were repulsed. As they retired, Wheeler charged them in both the rear and flank capturing forty three. [24]

Union General McCook attacked Lost Mountain on June 16th, but the Confederate forces had four guns in entrenchments on the top of the mountain. McCook silenced the four guns with his artillery and managed to reach the first set of barricades on the west side of the mountain, but could go no farther.

On June 17th, McCook chased the Rebel cavalry on the upper road leading to Lost Mountain to Marietta as far as Mud Creek, six miles from Marietta and six miles from Lost Mountain Post Office. A fight broke out at Noonday Creek and the Federals captured the Confederate works. Wheeler moved out, dismounting his men in the woods and engaged the Yankee infantry. The Federals retired, and sixty five men were captured by Wheeler's force.[25]

The next day the Federals attacked the Confederate works at Bell Ferry road and drove them from their works.

On June 19th, the Federals advanced and attacked Wheeler's position at Noonday Creek, near McAfee's farm. The fight lasted two hours, and the Yankees were repulsed. The turning point of the battle was when Wheeler ran two guns on top of a hill, and enfiladed the Union position. [26]

On June 20th, McCook had pushed the Rebels from Marietta and Powder Springs road. General Stoneman's brigades went into Powder Springs after McCook had left, and were driven out by a regiment of Rebels. The Federals on the Canton road attacked and Wheeler was repulsed. Wheeler took three brigades and rode to the Federals rear, and charged mounted, defeating the Federals, killing fifty and captured one hundred and twenty men, two stand of colors, and one hundred and fifty horses. Wheeler lost fifteen killed and fifty wounded. [27]

By June 22nd, the armies were strung out along a line that began north of Marietta, and swung to the west, and then south to a point several miles southwest of the town, near Alley's Creek. Sherman planned to attack at three places-Kennesaw Mountain, Cheatham's Hill west of Marietta, and along Alley's Creek. Sherman left Union General Joseph Hooker's XX Corps and Union General John Schoefield's Army of the Ohio to advance towards Kolb's farm, which was three miles southwest of Marietta. At that same time, Johnston was sending Confederate General John Bell Hood's Corps to advance on Kolb's farm. Hood, on his own orders, decided to attack the Federals. Late in the afternoon, two of Hood's division's emerged from the wood's on both sides of the Powder Springs Road. The Federals already knew of Hood's plans and were expecting his divisions. On the Federal line posted from left to right were the divisions of Brigadier Generals Milo Hascall, Alpheus Williams, and John Geary. Confederate General Carter Stevenson's division, supported by Hindman, attacked the Federals. The Union force had forty cannon and outnumbered the Confederates by eleven thousand men. Stevenson charged and fell back twice, getting within fifty yards of the Union line. Hindman also failed in taking the Federal position. Hood lost one thousand men in this assault, eight hundred and seventy from Stevenson's division alone. Hooker lost three hundred. Hood never reported his losses to Johnston. Sherman brought one hundred and forty cannon to try and break the trench warfare around Kennesaw Mountain and decided to take the mountain by assault.[28]

The next day Wheeler's men engaged the Federals on Beall's Ferry Road, carrying their first line of works. The Federals advanced, but were flanked near McAfee's, and retired. Wheeler created a diversion and prevented them from going after Confederate General Gideon Pillow who was moving to gain their rear.[29]

On June 25th, McCook captured a Captain of the Fourth Tennessee Cavalry, and two men from Harrison's brigade. McCook learned that the Rebel cavalry were passing through Marietta behind Kennesaw, to his left.

At 8:00 AM, on June 27th, Sherman launched his attack on Kenesaw Mountain with an opening salvo from two hundred cannons. The Confederates replied in kind as Union General James McPherson's Army of the Tennessee made the assault on the Confederate right center. About 8:30 AM, three brigades under Union Brig. Gen. Morgan Smith moved east, toward the southern slope of Little Kennesaw Mountain, just below Pigeon Hill. On Smith's right, the Yankees were able to take the rifle pits of General William H. T. Walker's division, and captured one hundred men. Then they started up Little Kennesaw on the left and Pigeon Hill on the right. The main Confederate line was five hundred yards to their front. Smith retreated under heavy fire of cannon and musket and lost five hundred men. At 9:00 A.M., two divisions of Union General George Thomas' Army of the Cumberland moved against the center of the Kennesaw Mountain line. Thomas ordered his five brigades, from Union Generals Jefferson Davis XIV Corps, and John Newton's IV Corps, to attack. On Newton's right, Brig. General Charles Harper's attack had collapsed. Harper took a bullet through his right arm, then one in his chest. His men retreated. Newton's other three brigades lost six hundred and fifty four men and he also fell back. Two brigades under Jefferson Davis attempted to take the Confederate earthworks on Cheatham's Hill. Confederate Major General Benjamin Cheatham's troops were protecting the earthworks. Union Col. Daniel McCook's men got caught in a crossfire between ten Confederate cannon. McCook tried to make a suicidal run at Dead Angle on Cheatham's Hill, and was bayoneted by a Confederate soldier. Union Capt. William Fellows, McCook's brigade inspector, took over command and was shot down. Union Col. Oscar Harmon then took command and he was also killed. Davis took eight hundred and twenty four casualties. McCook's men were ordered to retreat. Sherman lost three thousand men, and gained no ground. Only at Olley's Creek did Sherman claim any degree of success. Schofield already outflanked Kennesaw Mountain, having moved two brigades across Olley's Creek, a mile below Powder Springs road. This put Schoefield to Confederate John Bell Hood's extreme flank. Sherman next moved to the right, forcing Johnston to choose between giving up the Kennesaw line or being cut off from Atlanta.[30]

During the battle, the Federals assaulted Wheeler's earthworks, but were repulsed. The Federals retired to their original line of attack and kept up a fight with artillery and musket fire. The Confederate infantry on Wheeler's right repulsed a assault by two divisions of Federal infantry.

On July 3rd Confederate General Joseph Johnston started a new line at Smyrna, four miles below Marietta. Wheeler's men covered his retreat. Wheeler fought first near Marietta and fought near the State School on the railroad. In this position Wheeler engaged Sherman's infantry for two hours, with ten pieces of artillery and his dismounted cavalry. At night, Wheeler moved to the right and built breastworks on the extension of the Confederate infantry line.[31]

The next day the Federals charged Wheeler's line of works. They were repulsed. Fifty five Federals were captured.

On July 5th the Confederate army fell back to the north bank of the Chattahoochee, where they occupied a heavily fortified position. Sherman sent General Kenner Garrard's cavalry to capture Roswell, sixteen miles upriver and planned to cross above Johnston's fortifications. Wheeler held the Federals in check until the infantry was ready for Sherman's men. The 4th Corps, under Union General O. O. Howard, attacked Wheeler's main line, but were held in check. Wheeler remained with the rear guard, fighting advanced lines of infantry. He crossed over the river. Howard made a attack a mile from Pace's Ferry, charging Wheeler's temporary works. Wheeler's men repulsed the charge. The Federals knew the river was to Wheeler's back and continued the attack, which lasted until 2 P.M., in which Wheeler had his wagon train and horses carried to the south bank of the river.[32]

Wheeler then charged the Federal line and reached the river with his dismounted men and hurried them across the pontoons, cut loose the bridge and swung it around to the south side of the river, just as the Federals in force reached the other bank. Wheeler was the last man to cross and was under heavy fire.[33]

The Atlanta Campaign

On July 6th, General McCook advanced on the Howell and Green's Ferry where it crossed the main Sandtown road. The Confederate infantry had set up breastworks at Sandtown. McCook opened up his artillery and withdrew. Wheeler built breastworks on the river bank and fought the Federals across the other side of the river. He continued the skirmish with the Federals the next day and at dark Wheeler opened up with two batteries on the Federal line.[34]

On July Eighth, Schofield's men crossed the Chattahoochee at Isham's Ford, fortifying the south bank. They continued to cross troops the next day at Isham's Ford and advanced their works some eight hundred yards. On July 9th and 10th, Johnston crossed the Chattahoochee and went into position along Peachtree Creek, a few miles from Atlanta.

On July 11th, the Federals advanced six hundred yards and built a new line of entrenchments. The next day Union General Howard's corps crossed the river, and advanced. On the 14th the Sixteenth Corps crossed at Roswell.

On July 17th, Confederate General Joseph Johnston is replaced with Confederate General John Bell Hood. Confederate President Jefferson Davis was angry over Joseph Johnston allowing the Yankees getting so close to Atlanta. Davis felt that Johnston was not aggressive enough in holding back the Yankee tide. Davis felt that if Atlanta fell it would cause a major blow to the Confederacy. Atlanta was the pride of the South. Atlanta made pistols, rifles, cannon, uniforms, and supplied food to the Confederate troops not only to the West but the East also. It was the bread basket of the South. Atlanta was also a very prosperous city, with major railways running through it. It was know as "The Gateway to the South", and Sherman knew it.[35]

On July 17th and 18th, Wheeler's force, including Col. Tom Harrison and the Eighth Texas Cavalry, were busy in opposing Union General George Thomas forces. Wheeler's force consisted of only 1,600 men. He was also reinforced by Ferguson's brigade of infantry. Confederate General John Bell Hood faced Union General William T. Sherman's army, which was north and east of Atlanta, and Union General George Thomas' army with it's right resting on the Chatttahooche river. Union Generals Schofield and McPherson were to the east trying to reach the Georgia railroad, which was Hood's direct link to the Carolinas and Virginia.

On July 19th, Hood saw a flaw in the Federal lines. He noticed that there was a two mile gap between Thomas and Schofield's lines. Hood planned to attack the Federal gap by sending Hardee's Corps and Stewart to attack Thomas army when it was crossing Peachtree Creek. They were to drive Thomas into the creek, oblique left, and crush his remaining troops. Cheatham's corps was to hold off McPherson and Schofield and then, after Thomas was defeated, Hardee and Stewart would join Cheatham in destroying the other two Federal armies. Because of mistakes in coordinating the attack, the battle didn't begin until two hours past the original time line. During the battle Wheeler's men were engaging McPherson's entire army of three corps. Wheeler and his men fought behind successive lines of breastworks, and repulsed several assaults.[36]

On July 20th, at 4 PM, Hood sent nineteen thousand men into battle. Most of Thomas' Federals had made it across Peachtree Creek when Hardee attacked with four divisions on Thomas' left. Newton's men were hit by Walker's division, and by Bate's. Newton repulsed the Confederate attack on his left and front, but his right was vulnerable. He had a quarter mile gap between Newton's right and the next Union division. Brig Gen. George Maney, of Cheatham's division, poured through this gap. They were counterattacked by troops from Brig. Gen. John Coburn and Col. Ben Harrison and the Confederates fell back. Hardee was going to send Cleburne to attack Thomas' left, but he called off Cleburne's attack and sent him instead to take on McPherson's army when he learned that McPherson was moving on Atlanta, and was threatening to capture Confederate General Joseph Wheeler's cavalry. General Patrick Cleburne arrived with his division of infantry and placed his troops so closely together that only a little more than half of Wheeler's line was occupied by Cleburne's men. While changing position, and before Wheeler's men faced the oncoming Yankees, a attack was made on Wheeler's and Cleburne's front. General Ferguson's infantry, who was on the right, reported to Wheeler that his right flank was being turned. At that same moment, another assault was made by several lines of Union clad soldiers. Ferguson fell back and exposed Allen's brigade, which, with the Georgia brigade, "fought brilliantly", repulsing the assault. Hand to hand fighting broke out along the lines. The Yankees made another assault on Cleburne's and Wheeler's lines and both the Georgia and Alabama brigades, under Allen and Iverson, with the right brigade of Cleburne's division, were forced from their works. After falling back a short distance the Georgia and part of the Alabama brigades, rallied, charged the Yankees, and retook the earthworks, with two officers and twenty privates. Wheeler reestablished his line and maintained his position until relieved late in the day by Cheatham's division. [37]

Confederate General John Bell Hood failed to destroy the Federal army. He had lost 4,796 men. The Federals only lost 1,779 men and were now threatening Atlanta itself.

On the evening of July 21, Hood began the offensive by withdrawing from his outer works, and slipping into the defenses of the city proper. Thinking Atlanta evacuated, Union General James McPherson's advance moved confidently along the Decatur Road on the morning of the 22nd until struck by Confederate skirmishers about two and a half miles from Atlanta. The attackers, two of Hardees divisions under Maj. Gen. W. H. T. Walker and William Bate, came on with great energy. But because of errors by Confederate Generals William Hardee and W. H. T. Walker, they had not marched far enough to the east to clear the Union line and had struck McPherson's left, held by Maj. Gen. Grenville Dodge's XVI Corps. Dodge and his men were also hard fighters, as they proved by repulsing two attacks. During one of the attacks General Walker was killed and soon another casualty occurred. General Blair reported that Brig. Gen. Giles Smith was under attack. McPherson immediately sent John Logan's reserve brigades to plug the gap between Dodge and Maj. Gen. Francis Blair's XVII Corps, on Dodge's right, McPherson rode out to see the gap himself, and on the way back met Patrick Cleburne's division. Captain Richard Beard of the 5th Confederate Regiment ordered McPherson to surrender. McPherson tried to ride off, but Beard ordered his troops to fire on him. The General was hit in the lower back, and would soon die of his wound. [38]

McPherson's death did not ensure a Confederate success. Confederate General William Hardee committed his two other divisions, Brig Gen. George Maney's and Patrick Cleburne's, to a furious, coordinated assault against Blair. Thanks largely to a heavy cannonade, they pushed back Blair's left flank, then moved toward the gap between Blair and Dodge. At the last minute, however, the reserve brigade under John Logan, which had been ordered into the breach by McPherson, slammed the Confederates backward. Hardee's offensive was snuffed out when part of the XVI Corps formed and reestablished the line.[39]

At 3:00 PM, Hood committed Confederate General Benjamin Cheatham's corps, bolstered by five thousand Georgia militia under Maj. Gen. Gustavus Smith, against the Union front. Had this strike been timed to coincide with Hardee's, the Union Army of the Tennessee might have been destroyed, but with Hardee stalled, Maj. Gen. John Logan, who had temporarily re-placed McPherson, secured the front with his own XV Corps and part of Blair's command. Cheatham and Smith penetrated below the line of the Georgia Railroad but were quickly repulsed. Sherman had ordered Wood's division to counterattack and Schofield to mass all the cannons from the Army of the Ohio, twenty in all, on a knoll near his headquarters. General John Logan, now the commander of the Army of the Tennessee, personally led Col. August Mersy's four regiments to the new line north of the Georgia railroad. Four division were now sending seven brigades to counterattack. Supported by thirty cannon, the Union troops overran the Confederate brigades under Arthur Manigault. The Federals managed to restore their original positions, and took back ten artillery pieces that the Confederates had seized earlier.[40]

As Cheatham retreated, Hardee regrouped south of Bald Hill, and Maney's division rallied. Cleburne brought up his reserve brigade as several regiments from Walker's division moved west from Sugar Creek. At 5:00 PM, these units advanced against the southern flank of Giles Smith's division. Smith was hit from the east, west, and south. The Confederates were within fifteen yards of the Federal defenses when the infantry under Col. Harris Lampley charged the earthworks, but Col. Lampley was killed, and Hardee's troops fell back. [41]

At 6:00 PM, Hardee mounted a final attack. Giles Smith pulled back and formed a stronger line. The Confederates charged this new line, but it held firm against them. Cleburne lost forty percent of his men, including thirty of his sixty high ranking officers. Toward evening the fighting died out, but by then over eight thousand Confederates and three thousand seven hundred Union soldiers had been killed or wounded, and Hood's second sortie had failed.[42]

On July 21st, Wheeler moved around to the Yankee's rear to attack him in conjunction with Hardee's force. Hardee ordered Wheeler to attack Decatur at 1 P.M., which was the Yankee's extreme left, and rear. Wheeler found a entire division of infantry well entrenched in the town. Wheeler dismounted his men and moved towards the enemy. The Yankees in turn advanced two regiments of infantry. These two regiments were beaten back and they ran for the works. The Yankees then opened up with their artillery and infantry. Wheeler then threw a force at the

Yankees right and rear and turned his force in to an oblique to the enemy's right. Charges were made against the Union lines. Wheeler took the whole line of earthworks. He captured two hundred and seventy five prisoners, a large number of small arms, one 12 pound gun, one forge, one battery wagon, one caisson, and six wagons. They also captured hospitals, camp equipment, and stores. As Wheeler was carrying off his newly acquired booty, three officer's from Hardee ordered Wheeler to support Hardee's position. He quickly rode to Hardee's position and helped beat back the Union force. [43]

On the 22nd, Wheeler was ordered to pursue the Yankees. He rode forty miles, and learned that the Union cavalry had ridden back to it's main lines. Upon returning to the Confederate main line, Wheeler fell in on the Confederate right, skirmishing with the Yankees until the 27th. On the 27th, Wheeler was ordered to relieve Conf. General Hardee's entire line with his cavalry. Wheeler found that the Yankees were moving on his lines of communication. Wheeler was ordered to pursue, he was relieved and Wheeler rode off in the direction of Union General Stoneman's forces.[44]

Though Confederate General John Bell Hood's savage sortie on July 21st and 22nd failed to wreck a portion of Major General William T. Sherman's army and drive him away from Atlanta, it did, with the help of Atlanta's strong fortifications, block the Union drives on the city from the north and east. Consequently, Sherman looked to the west, deciding to move on the Macon & Western railroad line, the last of John Bell Hood's supply lines still leading into the city. The focus of his attack would be on Lovejoy Station, twenty miles southeast of Atlanta. He would send two separate columns of troops to attack Lovejoy Station, while the Army of the Tennessee would march around Atlanta and attack the railroad between the city and East Point, threatening the Confederate supply line. Sherman hoped that these movements would force Hood to either leave his fortifications and fight him out in the open, or that he would abandon his fortifications and leave the city.[45]

Sherman appointed Major General Oliver Howard to take control of McPherson's Army of the Tennessee. Howard had marched half way around the city when he arrived at Ezra Church and knew there would be trouble from Hood, so he dug in. Grenville Dodge's XVI Corps and Francis Blair's XVII Corps took a north-south line facing east. On Blair's right, Logan's XV Corps extended the line southward in front of Ezra Church and then bent west at a right angle across the Lickskillet road.[46]

Howard was right about Hood. Hood sent four divisions to stop him, one corps was led by Lt. Gen. Stephen D. Lee, the other by Alexander Stewart. On July 28th, Lee met Howard's army. Lee attacked without orders from Hood. Lee sent Brig Gen. John C. Brown against the right of Logan's Corps and Brown lost three commanders during the assault. Lee attacked again and sent Maj. Gen. Henry Clayton against Logan's left wing, but the Federals held.[47]

At 2:00 PM, Stewart arrived and ordered Maj. Gen. Edward Walthall to attack the Union right. At 3:00 PM, Walthall attacked, and three charges were made, but all failed and General W.W. Loring was severely wounded. At 5:00 PM, Walthall and Lee withdrew. The fighting stopped. The Confederates lost six hundred men. In ten days, Hood had lost eighteen thousand men, or nearly one third of his sixty thousand man force.[48]

On July 28th Wheeler relieved General Hardee's entire line of works with his cavalry. While doing so he had discovered that the Yankees had abandoned their position in his front and fallen back to their position north of the railroad. At the same time Wheeler had discovered that a large Federal raiding party under Major General Stoneman had moved toward the Confederate line of communications. Wheeler reported it to Hood, who immediately ordered Wheeler and his force to pursue Stoneman. [49]

By the next day Wheeler had ridden ahead of the Union force of General Kenner Garrard's 2nd Division, which was marching towards Jonesboro, across Flat Creek. Wheeler finding himself outnumbered quickly rode toward the Yankees left. About this time, General Stoneman had ridden towards Covington, with two thousand two hundred men, and heading to Macon. General Wheeler then received a message from Confederate General Francis Shoup, who commanded the artillery under Hardee's Corps, informing him that the Confederate left was threatened by a raid, and that a large force of three thousand Union cavalry were about to attack the Macon railroad, and that General John Bell Hood ordered Wheeler's force to oppose this force. Wheeler sent Ashby's brigade, under General Humes to Jonesboro. Wheeler then ordered Kelly to keep Garrard's division from advancing, along with Dibrell's brigade, and sent Anderson's brigade towards the Jonesboro road. Wheeler arrived in Jonesboro but had learned that the Union force had moved onto the Fayetteville road. General William Jackson, commander of the Cavalry Division under Leonidas Polk, sent Wheeler a message that if he would attack the rear, Jackson would attack the enemy's front.[50]

Wheeler received a message from Brig. General William Jackson: "The enemy moving towards Fayetteville. I am quite certain they are moving back across the Chattahoochee. I have Harrison's brigade in their front at Fayetteville, and am moving now with Ross' brigade to that place. Should the enemy attempt to pass around the place I will gain their front of flank about Newnan. If you can follow and push them in rear it would be well."[51] Wheeler arrived at Fayetteville at midnight, and learned that the Yankees had passed though the town and was within an hour advance of Wheeler. Wheeler quickly rode in advance and took the Yankees rear at Line Creek. The Yankees had destroyed the bridge and were holding the opposite side of the river with troops and strong barricades. Wheeler built a bridge and crossed the river.[52]

At daylight on the 30th, Wheeler received another message from General William H. Jackson: "Since arrival of your courier I received notice from Colonel Harrison that he is opposite the Yankees at Shakerag, three miles from (Fayetteville). The Yankees has gone into camp there. I move at once with Ross brigade." Since Jackson was so far to the rear of Wheeler, Wheeler decided to attack the Union force. Wheeler attacked and the Yankee's were driven from their position, routing their entire line and capturing two hundred prisoners. Wheeler engaged in a running fight, until 9:00 A.M., when the Yankees succeeded by rapid movement in gaining some two miles upon Wheeler's advance. At 12 noon Wheeler was two miles from Newnan and again overtook the Union force, and captured twenty more prisoners. Wheeler up to this point had ridden seventy miles.[53]

About this time, Col. Gustave Cook, Eighth Texas Cavalry, with a portion of his regiment, and Brig. General L. Ross, with two small regiments, each one hundred strong, reported to Wheeler. Wheeler now had seven hundred men. General Jackson and Anderson were still fifteen miles to the rear. Wheeler ordered Col. Ashby's brigade of two hundred men to move through Newnan, and down the La Grange road to get in front of Col. Edward McCook's column. Wheeler then set up pickets and scouts all along the roads leading into Newnan. Wheeler with the remainder of his force numbering three hundred, moved between the railroad and the main La Grange road in hopes of striking the Yankees flank. [54]

After marching three miles, Wheeler found the Yankee force in a dense wood forming a line, the right flank of which was fifty yards in his front. At that moment, Ashby informed Wheeler that he had struck the head of the enemy's column just as it was entering the main La Grange road, three miles and a half below Newnan, and that the enemy was forming into line of battle dismounted. Wheeler dismounted and attacked the Union force in front of him without delay. The Union force in front of Wheeler was ten times his size. Col. Ashby was ordered to engage the Yankees front. Wheeler met some resistance at first, but then the enemy gave way. Wheeler's men then gave the Rebel yell and the entire Union line was thrown into confusion and the Union troops made a disorderly retreat. Wheeler pursued and divided the Yankees forces. In forty minutes Wheeler killed and wounded over two hundred and captured over three hundred, including Col. Harrison of the 39th Indiana, and Col. Torry. He also captured six hundred horses and three stands of colors. [55]

While pursuing the Yankees, Wheeler heard firing in his rear. Ross had left his horses where he had first dismounted. McCook's reserve brigade was attacking Ross brigades horses. Wheeler immediately reached the line, and the 4th Tennessee Cavalry and the Eighth Texas Cavalry charged and drove off the Federals, and recovered all of Ross' horses and captured one hundred Yankees. McCook reformed and made another charge upon Wheeler's line, driving back a portion of his command and throwing the whole of it into confusion. Wheeler rallied his troops and charged the Yankees with two mounted squads and drove them from the field and recaptured General Humes, who was captured by the Federals. The fight had now lasted two hours. [56]

Wheeler again advanced his lines. Wheeler had discovered that the Yankees had now set up a strong position in the edge of a wood, with a large field in front and a deep ravine, only passable at certain points. They also had thrown up strong barricades, and was using their artillery. General Roddey's cavalry brigade, who had been in town, came up with his hundred men, and was placed on Wheeler's left. Roddy strongly advised against not attacking this position. General Wheeler moved his troops to the right and attacked General Edward McCook's left flank. The Yankees began to retreat. Wheeler continued his assault down the LaGrange road upon their flank, cutting off nearly two entire regiments, which surrendered with all artillery, wagons, and ambulances. The entire column was thrown into confusion and a pursuit began. Some three hundred Confederate prisoners were released from their Union captors. General Roddey had retired to Newnan before the battle began. [57]

After pursuing three miles the Yankees had become scattered through the woods and fields. One column under General McCook had moved toward the mouth of New River, and the other under Colonel Brownlow moved on by roads toward the Chattahoochee River, near Franklin. Colonel Bird, who replaced Colonel Anderson was ordered to chase McCook. Wheeler also sent the 3rd Arkansas from Harrison's brigade, and Colonel McKenzie, to gain the front of the Yankees moving toward Franklin. Colonel McKenzie was successful in capturing two hundred prisoners, but Colonel Bird fell asleep during the night and allowed the Yankees to escape across the river. Wheeler arrived before daylight to the river. Wheeler discovered that some four hundred Yankees had escaped. Wheeler crossed the river and continued the chase, and captured the rest of the force, making General Stoneman's cavalry force totally destroyed. General Iverson's brigade, Martin's Division, was successful in their pursuit of General Stoneman and managed to capture five hundred prisoners, some twenty miles from Macon.[58]

Col. Garrard made it back to his army. Col. Edward McCook's column only returned with five hundred men, but none of Stoneman's column returned, with a loss of five thousand men. Wheeler only had a force of three thousand five hundred.[59]

Col. Tom Harrison and Ross were distinguished for their gallantry. Private Basset, of the Eighth Texas, was conspicuous for gallantry during the battle. Wheeler and his force captured 3,200 prisoners, 4,000 horses, rescued 350 Confederate prisoners from McCook, two batteries, two hundred mules, a wagon train and several stands of colors. [60]

[1] Who's Who in the Confederacy; Historical Times Illustrated Encyclopedia of the Civil War.
[2] O.R. Series I-Vol. XXXII-Confederate Correspondence, Orders, and Returns relating to Operations in Kentucky, Southwest Virginia, Tennessee, Mississippi, Alabama, and North Georgia from March 1, 1864 to April 30, 1864.
[3] Civil War Battles of the Western Theater, Bryan Bush
[4] Batchelor-Turner Letters
[5] O.R. Series I-Vol. XXXVIII May 1-September 8, 1864-The Atlanta Campaign No. 713 Reports of Maj. Gen. Joseph Wheeler, C. S. Army, commanding Cavalry Corps, of operations 6-31 and July 17-October 9.
[6] Campaigns of Wheeler and His Cavalry: 1862-1865 Chapter XIII.
[7] Terry Texas Rangers, Leonidas Giles, p. 65-68
[8] O.R. Series I-Vol. XXXVIII May 1-September 8, 1864-The Atlanta Campaign No. 713 Reports of Maj. Gen. Joseph Wheeler, C. S. Army, commanding Cavalry Corps, of operations 6-31 and July 17-October 9.:Campaigns of Wheeler and His Cavalry: 1862-1865 Chapter XIII.
[9] O.R. Series I-Vol. XXXVIII May 1-September 8, 1864-The Atlanta Campaign No. 713 Reports of Maj. Gen. Joseph Wheeler, C. S. Army, commanding Cavalry Corps, of operations 6-31 and July 17-October 9.
[10] O.R. Series I-Vol. XXXVIII May 1-September 8, 1864-The Atlanta Campaign No. 713 Reports of Maj. Gen. Joseph Wheeler, C. S. Army, commanding Cavalry Corps, of operations 6-31 and July 17-October 9.
[11] O.R. Series I-Vol. XXXVIII May 1-September 8, 1864-The Atlanta Campaign No. 713 Reports of Maj. Gen. Joseph Wheeler, C. S. Army, commanding Cavalry Corps, of operations 6-31 and July 17-October 9.:Campaigns of Wheeler and His Cavalry: 1862-1865 Chapter XIII.
[12] O.R. Series I-Vol. XXXVIII May 1-September 8, 1864-The Atlanta Campaign No. 713 Reports of Maj. Gen. Joseph Wheeler, C. S. Army, commanding Cavalry Corps, of operations 6-31 and July 17-October 9.; Civil War Battles of the Western Theater, p. 77
[13] Ibid.
[14] O.R. Series I-Vol. XXXVIII May 1-September 8, 1864-The Atlanta Campaign No. 713 Reports of Maj. Gen. Joseph Wheeler, C. S. Army, commanding Cavalry Corps, of operations 6-31 and July 17-October 9.
[15] Ibid.
[16] Ibid.
[17] Ibid.

[18] Ibid.
[19] Ibid.
[20] Ibid.
[21] O.R. Series I-Vol. XXXVIII May 1-September 8, 1864-The Atlanta Campaign No. 713 Reports of Maj. Gen. Joseph Wheeler, C. S. Army, commanding Cavalry Corps, of operations 6-31 and July 17-October 9.:Campaigns of Wheeler and His Cavalry: 1862-1865 Chapter XIII.
[22] Campaigns of Wheeler and His Cavalry: 1862-1865, Chapter XIII
[23] Campaigns of Wheeler and His Cavalry: 1862-1865, Chapter XIII: Civil War Battles of the Western Theater, p. 77
[24] Ibid.
[25] Ibid.
[26] Campaigns of Wheeler and His Cavalry: 1862-1865, Chapter XIII
[27] Ibid.
[28] Civil War Battles of the Western Theater, p. 78
[29] Campaigns of Wheeler and His Cavalry: 1862-1865, Chapter XIII
[30] Civil War Battles of the Western Theater, p. 78
[31] Campaigns of Wheeler and His Cavalry: 1862-1865, Chapter XIII
[32] Ibid.
[33] Ibid.
[34] Campaigns of Wheeler and His Cavalry: 1862-1865, Chapter XIII: Civil War Battles of the Western Theater, p. 78
[35] Civil War Battles of the Western Theater, p. 80
[36] O.R. Series I-Vol. XXXVIII May 1-September 8, 1864-The Atlanta Campaign No. 713 Reports of Maj. Gen. Joseph Wheeler, C. S. Army, commanding Cavalry Corps, of operations 6-31 and July 17-October 9.
[37] Ibid.
[38] Civil War Battles of the Western Theater, p. 81
[39] Ibid.
[40] Ibid.
[41] Ibid.
[42] Ibid.
[43] O.R. Series I-Vol. XXXVIII May 1-September 8, 1864-The Atlanta Campaign No. 713 Reports of Maj. Gen. Joseph Wheeler, C. S. Army, commanding Cavalry Corps, of operations 6-31 and July 17-October 9.
[44] Ibid.
[45] Civil War Battles of the Western Theater. P. 81-82
[46] Ibid.
[47] Ibid.
[48] Ibid.
[49] O.R. Series I-Vol. XXXVIII May 1-September 8, 1864-The Atlanta Campaign No. 713 Reports of Maj. Gen. Joseph Wheeler, C. S. Army, commanding Cavalry Corps, of operations 6-31 and July 17-October 9.
[50] Ibid.
[51] Ibid.
[52] Ibid.
[53] Ibid.
[54] Ibid.
[55] Ibid.
[56] Ibid.
[57] Ibid.
[58] Ibid.
[59] Ibid.
[60] Ibid.

Chapter 14:
Wheeler's Second Raid

After demolishing Stoneman's cavalry force, Wheeler's force returned to the main Confederate army. Wheeler and his men returned to their positions in the works around Atlanta. Hood later ordered Wheeler to Sherman's lines of communications, destroy them at various points between Marietta and Chattanooga, then cross the Tennessee River, break the line of communication on the two roads running from Nashville to the army; then leave one thousand two hundred men to continue their operations on those roads; then return again striking the railroad south of Chattanooga and join the main army.[1]

On August 9th, Sherman fired more than five thousand shells into Atlanta. Trench warfare began. Sherman decided that the only way to capture Atlanta was to throw his entire army at the Macon & Western Railroad, Atlanta's last lifeline for supplies.

Although Wheeler's men were worn out from constant riding and there was very little food for his horses, Wheeler did what he was ordered to do, and on August 10th, with four thousand men, he left Covington and began his second raid. He first tore up the railroad a few miles above Marietta, near Cassville, and near Calhoun. At Calhoun with Hannon's brigade, he captured a train of cars and destroyed the railroad track. He defeated the Federals, captured a wagon train and a drove of 1,700 cattle. Hannon escorted them to the main army.

On August 14th, General Humes, along with the Eighth Texas Cavalry, and General Kelly's commands attacked and captured Dalton with a large amount of stores and Government property, their trains, two hundred horses and mules, and two hundred prisoners, the balance of the garrison on being driven from the town retreating to a small but strong defensive fortification near the town. Humes and Allen's commands destroyed the railroad for several miles. The stores captured in the town were either taken or destroyed.[2]

When Wheeler's force left Dalton, it was attacked by a large Union force of infantry and cavalry under Major General James Steedman. Wheeler withdrew to Spring Place. The Yankees suffered severe casualties, where as Wheeler suffered only minor losses. Wheeler also managed in capturing one Colonel and wounding General Steedman.[3]

On August 16th, Allen's brigade, Hume's and Kelly's divisions destroyed the railroad for several miles between Resaca and Tunnel Hill,

Wheeler then crossed the Little Tennessee and Clinch. Wheeler learned that the Yankees had made extensive arrangements to gather food for their army from the country along the line of the railroad from Cleveland to Loudon. Wheeler decided to attack the railroad from Cleveland and Charleston so he could deprive the Yankees of their supply route. Wheeler crossed the Hiwasee and captured Athens with a large quantity of valuable supplies, and destroyed the railroad from Charleston to Loudon. During this whole time, Wheeler's force was harassed by Yankee cavalry, who were repulsed each time they attacked.[4]

At Stewart's Landing Wheeler's force attacked and captured a garrison of one hundred men, thirty wagons, and two hundred horses and miles. Wheeler then crossed the Little Tennessee River and continued to French Broad above Knoxville. Wheeler crossed the Holston River, which was guarded by the Yankees, but they were quickly run off. While crossing, Wheeler's force was attacked by Yankee cavalry from Knoxville. The attack was repulsed. Wheeler's force then charged the Yankees cavalry and drove them back to the city with a loss of one hundred men.[5]

After crossing the river and mountain Wheeler destroyed the railroad at various points between Chattanooga and Nashville, captured two trains of cars and a number of small depots of stores including McMinnville. All public property was destroyed, including bridges, blockhouses, stockades, and the railroad. When Wheeler's force approached Nashville, they were attacked by General Lovell Rousseau, who commanded the District of Nashville, including the 3rd Division, 12th Corps, and the 4th Division, 20th Corps, with a superior force of infantry and cavalry. The attack was repulsed. Harrison's brigade charged the Yankees and drove them rapidly for two miles, capturing three stands of colors, a number of prisoners, and arms. He also managed to capture thirty wagons. Wheeler also captured a Federal battery, but the Federals were reinforced by infantry, which prevented Wheeler's men from carrying the guns off the field. The Federals were routed and didn't trouble Wheeler's men again that day. [6]

After two days on the Chattanooga railroad, Wheeler moved over to the Nashville and Decatur road, which he destroyed for several miles. Wheeler also destroyed several loaded trains. During these movements, Union Generals Rousseau, Steedman, and Brig. Gen. Croxton and Granger concentrated their forces and attacked Wheeler's force at Franklin, Lynnville, Campbellville and other points along the route. In every single attack the Yankees were repulsed, even though the Yankee force outnumbered Wheeler's force four to one. During the attacks Union Colonel Brownlow was wounded, and General Kelley was killed. [7]

Wheeler had been behind Union lines for twenty six days. He was low on ammunition and his horses were tired. The wagon train, captured horses, and mules, his own wounded, and unarmed recruits slowed his column down. Wheeler decided to move to a point north of the Tennessee River.

On reaching the Alabama border, Wheeler was ordered back to the Army of the Tennessee again, striking the railroad south of Chattanooga. Confederate General Nathan Bedford Forrest arrived to move into Tennessee. Wheeler ordered one thousand two hundred men to report to General Hood, and moved with the rest of his command to the railroad near Dalton. During his movement towards Dalton, Wheeler destroyed a train of cars, and destroyed the railroad to such an extent that, no train was able to pass over the road for thirteen days. Wheeler received another telegram that he should return immediately to the army, which he did near Cedartown.[8]

During Wheeler's raid, he managed to capture one thousand horses and mules, two hundred wagons, six hundred prisoners, and one thousand seven hundred head of cattle. He also captured twenty trains of cars loaded with supplies, and signed up over three thousand new recruits. Wheeler only lost one hundred and fifty men killed wounded or missing. He caused the Yankees to send their rear to reinforce their garrison's. The Yankees line of communication was destroyed for a longer period than any other cavalry expedition. They broke up depots and fortified posts in Tennessee and Georgia. Wheeler's force rode on average twenty miles a day. During the raid, Wheeler gave high praise to Gen. Humes division, and to Lt. Col. Tom Harrison brigade "for their bravery and faithfulness." [9]

Sherman had to put his entire army on short rations because of Wheeler's raid on the railroad. Wheeler lost one hundred and twenty men.

Back in Atlanta, on the night of August 25th, Sherman pulled his troops from the trenches north and west of Atlanta. One corps, the XX, fell back to the railroad bridge spanning the Chattahoochee River. With his other six corps-the IV, XIV, XV, XVI, XVII, and the XVIII-, sixty thousand men in all, Sherman advanced from the northwest to strike the Macon & Western Railroad, between Rough and Ready and Jonesboro.

On August 30th, Union General O. O. Howard was on the east bank of the Flint River, two miles from Jonesboro. General John Bell Hood didn't realize that the entire Federal army was heading towards the Macon & Western line, and would remain in Atlanta with General Stewart and the Georgia Militia. Hardee would take the other two corps- his and General Stephen D. Lee's- to Jonesboro, with orders to attack the Federals and drive them back across the Flint River.[10]

General Oliver O. Howard had only crossed a portion of his army. The Confederates outnumbered his forces, twenty four thousand to Howard's seventeen thousand. The rest of Howard's troops were still on the far bank of the river. Lee attacked at 2:20 PM, sending his three divisions against Logan's Federal XV Corps. Lee was supposed to wait for Cleburne's troops to engage first. Major General James Patton Anderson led his troops across open terrain and got within eighty yards of the Federal breastworks where Logan's defenders were, but he was repulsed. Reinforcements expected from Col. Bushrod Jones brigade never came. Patton tried to rally his men, but was wounded twice. Lee was being repulsed.[11]

Hardee now advanced with Patrick Cleburne's troops. William Bate's division, now commanded by John C. Brown, charged forward, but was hit by a barrage from a half dozen 12 pound Napoleons. The Confederates took refuge from the cannon fire in a ravine, where they were promptly captured by the 66th Indiana. The division of Confederate General George Maney on Brown's left fell back. On the far left, Cleburne's division, commanded by Brig. Gen. Mark Lowrey, hit the Federal right flank, but his left came under fire from Kilpatrick's cavalry division. Kilpatrick had four artillery pieces and his men were equipped with Spencer rifles. Lowrey charged the Federals, but only one of his units, under Hiram Grandbury continued to assault the Federals. Lowrey's other two brigades then followed suit. The Confederates were driving the Federals back, until Federal reinforcements stopped Lowrey's men and pushed them back. The assault by the other two Confederate divisions of Cleburne's troops had failed. The Confederates lost 1,725 men, 1,300 were lost by Lee alone. The Federals only lost 179 men.[12]

During the afternoon, the Federal columns had managed to cut the Macon & Western Railroad line. By 3:00 PM, Union General Jacob Cox's division had reached the tracks a mile below Rough and Ready.

Hood still believed that the attack would come on Atlanta, so he ordered Hardee to stay in Jonesboro, but wanted him to send Lee's corps back to Atlanta. On September 1st, Lee's corps marched north, and left Hardee defending the army's only supply train. Sherman was planning to attack Jonesboro with his six corps.

Hardee only had thirteen thousand men and they were stretched out in a single line. Hardee's men dug in and built breastworks for the assault they knew would come. Sherman ordered Union General Jefferson Davis' XIV Corps to attack. At 4:00 PM, Davis launched two brigades, but they were repulsed. He then brought up three divisions, and at 5:00 PM, ordered a full assault across a cotton field. The Federals charge overran the earthworks. At this same time, Hood would give the order to abandon the city of Atlanta.[13]

On the left, Govan's brigade began to give way under the massive Federal assault and Govan and his six hundred men soon surrendered. The Federals managed to seize eight Confederate guns. Govan's surrender caused a gap in the line that the Federals rushed through, threatening Grandbury's Texans and Lewis' Kentuckian's. The Confederates fell back, and with reinforcements and massed artillery, they formed a new line which held until darkness settled in and the fighting stopped. Sherman lost 1,300 men.[14]

During the night, Hardee retreated to Lovejoy's Station, six miles farther down the Macon & Western railroad. Stewart's corps and Lee's corps headed towards McDonough. Both were to link up with Hardee at Lovejoy's Station.

On September 2nd, the Confederate rearguard cavalry burned five locomotives, 81 rail cars, and 13 siege guns and shells. Union Major General Slocum, commander of the XX Corps marched into Atlanta, and at 11:00 AM, on September 2nd, Mayor James Calhoun surrendered the city.

By capturing Atlanta, Sherman had not only deprived the Confederacy of a vital arsenal and rail hub, but he had strengthened the will of the Union to continue the War as well. After 128 days and a total of 35,000 casualties in the Confederate army, and nearly as many in his own army, Sherman and his men rested, for they would soon begin the long march to Savannah and the sea.[15]

Although Wheeler, along with the rest of his command, including the Tom Harrison and the Eighth Texas Cavalry, managed to pull off a successful raid in Tennessee and Georgia, it was not enough to stop the relentless Sherman from capturing Atlanta.

[1] O.R. Series I-vol. XXXVIII May 1-Sept. 8, 1864-The Atlanta Campaign. No. 713 Reports of Maj. Gen. Joseph Wheeler, C. S. Army, commanding Cavalry Corps, of operations of 6-31 and July 17-October 9.
[2] Ibid.
[3] Ibid.

⁴O.R. Series I-vol. XXXVIII May 1-Sept. 8, 1864-The Atlanta Campaign. No. 713 Reports of Maj. Gen. Joseph Wheeler, C. S. Army, commanding Cavalry Corps, of operations of 6-31 and July 17-October 9.: Wheeler and His Cavalry: 1862-1865 Chapter XIII.
⁵Ibid.
⁶Ibid.
⁷Ibid.
⁸Ibid.
⁹Ibid.
¹⁰Civil War Battles of the Western Theater, p. 82
¹¹Ibid.
¹²Ibid.
¹³Ibid.
¹⁴Ibid.
¹⁵Ibid

Chapter 15:
March to the Sea Campaign

Even with the Confederate raiding, Sherman was still able to capture Atlanta on September 2nd, 1864. Sherman had brought pontoon engineers, and men whose specific job was to repair the railroads and bridges as quickly as possible, so that his progression to Atlanta would not be slowed down. A major blow had been dealt to the Confederacy. They had lost one their major bread baskets, and their major arsenal in the West. Sherman began to plan for his March to the Sea Campaign. The Confederacy was desperate, they needed to divert Sherman's army away from the rest of Georgia. Confederate General John Bell Hood decided to move towards Nashville, hopefully drawing Sherman's attention. Sherman made Union General George Thomas in charge of taking on Confederate General John Bell Hood's troops. On November 22nd, 1864, Confederate General John Bell Hood's 39,000 Confederates left Florence, Alabama, in three columns commanded by Maj. Gen. Benjamin Cheatham, and Lt. Generals Stephen D. Lee, and Alexander Stewart. Following a plan originated by Hood and approved by Jefferson Davis, they invaded Tennessee to draw Union military attention from the Deep South, crush Maj. Gen. Sherman's Western support for his operations in Georgia and perhaps take the war through Kentucky to the North.[1]

After the fall of Atlanta, Hood had moved the Army of Tennessee northwest in September and October, drawing Sherman and a detached force from Atlanta, skirmishing and wrecking railroads, fighting at Alatoona, and then withdrawing into northwest Alabama. Sherman had followed them west of Rome, Georgia, and unwilling to pursue farther, ordered the IV, XVI, and XXIII Corps to Maj. Gen. George Thomas, at Nashville and returned to Atlanta to begin his March to the Sea. Sherman knew Hood's intent and believed that, reinforced, Thomas would repel him.[2]

Hood and Thomas spent more than twenty days preparing for their parts in the campaign. Hood gathered supplies, reorganized and waited for Maj. Gen. Nathan Forrest's cavalry; Thomas created a cavalry force under Brig. Gen. James Wilson and moved the IV and XXIII Corps from the Chattanooga area to positions west along the Tennessee and Alabama Railroad. The XVI Corps detachment Thomas awaited could not reach him until December. Forrest spent late October and early November raiding Nashville Tennessee's supply lines and wrecking the railroad at Johnsonville.[3]

Forrest joined Hood at Florence, the expedition entered Tennessee, and its columns, traveling miles apart, moved for Columbia, halfway to Nashville. The XXIII Corps, under Maj. Gen. John Schofield and elements of the IV Corps were at Pulaski along the railroad, west of the invading columns. On George Thomas' orders, Schofield raced his force north to Columbia, arriving ahead of the Confederates on November 24th, and covered the bridges over the Duck River astride the invasion route. Federal cavalry sparred with Confederate horsemen from the Alabama line to Columbia. Schofield skirmished around Columbia from the 24th to the 26th until Hood's columns converged on his front. Bridges over the Duck River were destroyed and Schofield's troops withdrew north, covering the fords until Forrest's cavalry crossed at Henry's Mill, on Schofield's left, on the 28th. Wilson sent word to Schofield: "Get back to Franklin without delay."[4]

Union Maj. Gen. David Stanley, commanding IV Corps troops, hurried north to Spring Hill November 29 to hold the town until Schofield's troops passed through. Forrest, with his eastern crossing of the Duck river, threatened the Federal right. Stanley's pickets held him off. Hood failed in his plan to hold the Federals there, circumvent them, and press on to Nashville. He blamed Cheatham for bungled enveloping maneuvers as Schofield slipped through, marching his men from midnight to noon from Spring Hill to Franklin, on November 30th.[5]

When Hood found out that Schofield and his Federals had escaped, he blamed Cheatham. He called all of his officers a bunch of cowards, and said the only way to cure a coward is to throw him into battle. On November 30th, 1864, Hood's men marched over two miles over open ground. They were massacred. Hood lost 11,000 men. He also lost eleven Generals, five of them Major Generals, including Patrick Cleburne. With what he had left of his army he pulled out of Franklin, and proceeded towards Nashville.[6]

Schofield reached Nashville on December 1st. Three divisions, 13,000 men strong, of the XVI corps, under Maj. Gen. Andrew Smith reached Nashville on November 30, from the Trans-Mississippi. Schofield's arrival brought Thomas' strength to nearly 70,000. Hood arrived at the outskirts of Nashville on December 1st. At this point, Hood had only 30,000 men and this number was quickly diminishing. Hood's men were practically starving, they had no food, no clothes, no weapons, or ammunition. Hood faced a well fed, well clothed, and fresh army at Nashville. Nashville was also not an easy city to take. It was on a commanding elevation linked by miles of entrenchments.[7]

On December 15th, Union General George Thomas attacked Hood's entrenchments outside of Nashville. In two days, culminating with the Battle of Shy's Hill, the Army of the Tennessee was totally demolished. Hood lost 6,500 men, the Yankees lost 3,500 men. Hood escaped with Forrest as his rear guard.[8]

During the month of October 1864, Lt. Colonel Tom Harrison's brigade followed Sherman on the rail line north of Atlanta. Harrison remained under Joseph Wheeler's command, under Humes Division.

By October 1st Hood's advance had crossed the Oostanaula and struck the road near Kingston, while Wheeler and his force came upon it near Dalton. He captured two trains and cars and tore up several miles of railroad track. On October Eighth Wheeler met Hood who was marching his army from Allatoona to Northern Georgia. Wheeler and his force forced the Federals to evacuate Rome, Georgia. On October 9th Wheeler crossed the Coosa River with Hood's pontoons and moved with Hood's army around Dalton. Hood's army was now in the rear of Sherman's army and the Confederate cavalry were ordered to guard all approaches to it's front, flanks, and rear.

On October 13th, Wheeler and his force reached the railroad near Resaca. All Confederate troops destroyed the railroad from Resaca to Tunnel Hill, a length of about twenty miles. Dalton was captured, but Hood decided against capturing Resaca. On the 14th Hood withdrew from Dalton, crossing Taylor's Ridge and moved toward Round Mountain Iron Works on the Coosa River. Sherman pursued Hood's army, crossing Oostanaula at Resaca, and penetrated ridges at Snake Creek Gap hoping to strike the flank of Hood's army. Wheeler fought, holding a column of Federals back to allow Confederate troops to pass safely. The Confederate army was withdrawn to Jacksonville and Blue Mountain, Alabama and Wheeler was to send a brigade of cavalry to the Tennessee River with a pontoon train, to create the impression, that Hood was preparing to cross with his army. On the 18th Wheeler was ordered to return and stop Sherman's advance.[9]

Five days later on October 22nd, Hood's rear was ten miles south of Gaylesville, Alabama and Hood ordered Harrison's brigade to reconnoiter in the direction of Rome, Georgia. Harrison obeyed the command and met Wilder's Mounted Infantry Division, which was also advancing. During the ensuing battle between Harrison and Wilder's men, the flag of the Eighth Texas Cavalry was taken by Wilder's men. Leonidas Giles, of the Eighth Texas relates the story as to what exactly happened on that October day. "General Harrison, our old colonel, was in command of the forces composed of ours and Ashby's brigade of mounted infantry and a battery of four guns. For some reason, but contrary to all former usages, our regiment was dismounted and placed near the battery, and Ashby's infantry kept mounted to protect the flanks and lead horses. The fight had barely commenced when it was realized from the immense bodies of infantry in our front that it was a bad one. The battery was ordered to the rear, but just as they were limbered the Yankee cavalry poured in on our flanks and completely enveloped us. I didn't give an order to run nor did I hear an order of any kind, but I soon found myself dodging through and among the Yankees cavalry, who were shouting to us to surrender. We reached out horses, which weren't over 150 yards in the rear, mounted, and after a hasty formation charged out through the enemy and although we made repeated rallies they ran us back about five miles. Why the Yankees didn't capture more of our men is a mystery, as outside of the battery were lost very few prisoners. To give an appropriate name to the battle we called it "Rome Races" for such it was."[10]

In this race the colors furled around the staff and in the oilcloth were lost-not captured."

Major J. J. Wicler, of the 17th Indiana Mounted Infantry, found the Texas Rangers flag the next day.

On October 24th, a large body of Federal cavalry tried to penetrate from Center to Jacksonville. They were driven back..

Hood crossed the Coosa River and established a depot near Round Mountain Iron Works, a distance of thirty three miles from Rome. When Hood reached Dalton, Hood was separated from his depot by seventy miles. Hood left Col. Harrison with five regiments to oppose any advance of Federals from Rome toward the Confederate depot near Round Mountain Iron Works. A large Federal force of both infantry and cavalry attacked and drove Harrison's force back, capturing sixty of his men and two pieces of artillery. The Federals were stopped at a point ten miles from Rome. Harrison lost ten killed, thirty four wounded, and sixty captured.

On November 15th, the 15th, 17th, 20th Corps, and Kilpatrick's Union cavalry left Atlanta in two columns; one on the Jonesboro road and the other on the McDonough road. The 14th Corps reached Atlanta. The Federals headed for Macon. Wheeler placed a portion of his troops in front of a column moving down the Augusta road; kept a portion on the road to Columbus, and the remainder, under Col. Tom Harrison, opposed the direct advance upon Macon.[11]

On November 16th Col. Harrison, with 256 men and two guns, attempted to fight a large force of both infantry and cavalry, and though successful in giving a temporary check, was outflanked by a brigade of Federal cavalry and he had to abandon his two guns, losing thirty prisoners. Wheeler rounded up a few men and fought and repulsed an attack of Federals at Bear Creek Station.[12]

The next day a portion of Wheeler's command arrived from Blue Mountain, and he repulsed the Federal advance upon Griffin. Wheeler only had two thousand men, so it wasn't possible to make a formidable stand to Sherman's march. Wheeler had to make a decision as to what his goals would be since he could not attack Sherman's entire force. He decided to impede and harass Federal columns when practicable; to attack and defeat exposed detachments; to keep the Federals foragers from extending into and despoiling the country, except near main columns; to keep himself and all other officers fully informed of Sherman's movements; to defend all cities along the line of railroad, depots of stores, arsenals, government and other works. Wheeler was senior officer in Georgia and responsible for the defense of that state. He ordered Cobb and G. W. Smith to concentrate their militia and reserves at Macon and prepare fortifications and city for defense. He placed small parties on all approaches to the Federal flanks and rear, keeping his main body engaging their advance. [13]

The next day Wheeler defended and saved the town of Forsyth and the Federals crossed the Ocmulgee River, ten miles above Macon. Wheeler sent Anderson's and Crew's brigades to cross the river at Macon and guard the city from the Federals on the east bank of the Ocmulgee.

On November 19th, Wheeler's force moved towards Macon, Georgia. Upon arriving in Macon, Wheeler found that Lt. General William Hardee had assumed command of the department. Hardee directed Wheeler to move out on the Clinton road and ascertain the enemy's force and location. While marching towards Clinton, both of Wheeler's flanks were attacked by small units, which he drove off. He then moved onto Clinton and found Osterhaus Corps moving through the town. Six men dashed into town and captured Osterhaus servant. A regiment of cavalry charged Wheeler's force. A squad of cavalry pressed in upon Wheeler's line of retreat. The small cavalry force was quickly repulsed and two of Wheeler's regiments came up rapidly to his assistance. Wheeler immediately charged the advancing column and drove it back upon their infantry. They then rallied and charged Wheeler again. Wheeler met this charge and drove the Yankees back toward Clinton.[14]

Wheeler learned from his scouts that a large Union force was moving towards Griswoldville. Col. Crews sent a message to Wheeler stating the Yankees were now moving towards the railroad, and was in pursuit. Wheeler quickly arrived at Milledgeville road and found his artillery engaging the Yankees advance and his infantry in the redoubts ready to receive an attack. The Yankees had already charged up the road and four of them had attempted to capture a gun, but were driven back. Finding large holes in the redoubts that were not protected, Wheeler ordered Tom Harrison's and Hagan's brigades in line, plugging the gaps. After skirmishing for a short while, the Yankees retreated a short distance away.[15]

Under orders from Hardee, Wheeler moved out the next day towards Griswoldville, and drove the Federals out of the town. The next morning Wheeler attacked and drove the Yankees for some distance, capturing sixty prisoners.[16]

It was evident that the Yankees objective was not Macon, so Wheeler moved out towards Oconee, and crossed the river at Dublin and Blackman's Ferry on November 24th. Wheeler moved out towards Station No. 13 on the Central Railroad. The following day, Wheeler's force reached Sandersville. The 14th and 20th Corps had marched from Milledgeville, crossed Buffalo Creek, and were marching upon the town, preceded by cavalry. Wheeler moved out on the lower road, and he sent another force on the upper road. After moving three miles Wheeler was attacked by the Yankees, Wheeler counterattacked and drove the Yankees back for a mile, capturing, killing, and wounding about thirty men, besides capturing horses, mules and one loaded wagon. The next morning, Wheeler's force were slowly driven back toward and finally through the town of Sandersville.[17]

During the evening, Wheeler's pickets, who were under the command of Captain Shanon, informed him that a large Union force of five thousand men under Brig. General Judson Kilpatrick's 3rd Division, had crossed the river on it's way to Augusta. Kilpatrick focused on Augusta because of it's mills, factories, and arsenals, many of which were not protected by fortifications. Wheeler now was hoping to hit Kilpatrick's force hard enough to where he would abandon his plans to sack Augusta. Wheeler learned from his scouts that Kilpatrick had sent five hundred men to Waynesboro to destroy the railroad bridge, which convinced Wheeler that Kilpatrick was definitely heading towards Augusta, not Waynesboro.[18]

Wheeler's force attacked Kilpatrick's rear guards. Horses and arms were captured from the Yankees. Wheeler headed out during the night and attacked and captured Kilpatrick's pickets. In the morning Wheeler rode into Kilpatrick's camp, finding Kilpatrick and his men asleep, and opened fire on them as they lay in bed. According to W. H. Davis, Company F, 4th Tennessee Cavalry, Harrison's brigade, Kilpatrick barely escaped capture by mounting a bareback horse equipped only with a halter. Kilpatrick was staying in a cabin which stood seventy five yards at an angle of forty five degrees to the 4th Tennessee's right from where they had crossed the ravine. Kilpatrick rode away on a sorrel horse only clad in his underclothing, leaving several horses, his gold mounted sword, a pair of ivory handled six shooters, and a handsome saddle. These items were later handed over to General Joseph Wheeler as a gift from Harrison's brigade. One of the horses captured turned out to be a spotted stallion. Wheeler was seen still riding the stallion, when Wheeler and the 4th Tennessee surrendered in 1865.[19]

Wheeler pushed on to Kilpatrick's camp. It took fifteen minutes to drive Kilpatrick's men from their camps, because, according to Davis: "the Yanks fought like emissaries from the infernal regions. They lay in bed and used their seven shooting Spencer carbines and forty five caliber six shooters with deadly effect." Wheeler finally drove Kilpatrick's men back from the main Augusta road and out of his camps, capturing one stand of colors, and badly needed blankets, camp equipment, stores, and clothing.[20]

On reaching Brier Creek Swamp, Wheeler hit the Yankee force so hard that Kilpatrick was forced to turn towards Waynesboro. During the chase the Yankees burned the corn cribs, cotton gins, and large number of barns and houses. Wheeler and his men were able to put out most of the fires, and were able to prevent Kilpatrick's men from burning any more houses.[21]

When Wheeler approached the town of Waynesboro just after dark, the Yankees were just pulling out. The town was set ablaze, but Wheeler and his men quickly put out the flames, except for one building that was too far engulfed. Wheeler then mounted his men and attacked the Yankees, who were now engaged in tearing up the railroad. Wheeler stopped them from their mission, and engaged them most of the night.[22]

About 3:00 A.M. Wheeler sent Humes division, including Col. Tom Harrison's brigade, to move towards the Yankees rear by turning his left flank, he also sent a regiment to gain the rear by turning his right. The units were not able to get into position, and the Yankees were able to pull back. As Wheeler advanced the Yankees charged his line, which Wheeler's force met, and easily repulsed the attack. Wheeler then charged the Yankees flank with Humes and Anderson's division, and attacked the front with the rest of his command, driving the Yankees from their fortified position. The Yankees were totally routed and Kilpatrick was almost captured himself. Wheeler continued the charge until reaching Buckhead Creek, where the Yankees had built barricades on the opposite side of the creek. Wheeler lost one hundred men, while Kilpatrick lost 1,300 men. [23]

By taking advantage of a bend in the creek, Wheeler destroyed the Federal barricades near the bridge, which drove the Yankees out and the bridge soon fell into Confederate hands, though Kilpatrick had set it on fire. It was now 4 P.M. W. H. Davis, Company F, 4th Tennessee Cavalry, under Tom Harrison's brigade, describes what happened next. He writes: *Kilpatrick's advance reached Buck Head Creek, and carefully prepared to fire the bridge spanning it. After crossing it, the application of torches soon had it ablaze. By the dash of "Paul's People" (4th Tennessee, under Paul Anderson) the enemy's rear guard was quickly driven back, and the burning bridge soon recovered from the flames. During this delay Kilpatrick lost no time in erecting rail breastworks, and when we crossed the creek we encountered his outpost within a mile. His first line of works, about two hundred yards in front of the main line, was manned by a dismounted brigade, their right being protected by a mounted regiment in the open, level field, and their left by a dense woodland. "Little Joe"(Joe Wheeler) and "Old Paul" rode at the head of our column, marching in fours. A dense woodland skirted out right, and an open field stretched a quarter of a mile to our left. Arriving within about one hundred yards of the first line, it opened on us a galling fire which threw the head of our column into more or less confusion. An order from General Wheeler to "left front into line" and charge the mounted regiment miscarried, but Jim Blair and myself personally heard the order, and spurred our horses forward to take our places in line. We reached a point within fifty yards of the mounted regiment, every man of whom directed his fire at us. A captain in the enemy's line pointed his sword at us and shouted: "Shoot the _____ scoundrels!" Having no hope of escaping with my life, I dismounted and, turning my horse parallel to their line, rested my carbine across my saddle and took three deliberate shots at him, the third one taking effect in his chest. One of his men seized the reins of his bridle, and another his arm, and conducted him to the rear, whether dead or alive I cannot state. About this juncture Col. Anderson filed the column to the right into the woods, marching to a distance that left our rear opposite the extreme left of the enemy's line. The Tennesseans were followed by Terry's Rangers, and both regiments wheeled into line. The Third Arkansas and Eleventh Texas were aligned to the left of the road in the open. All this was quickly accomplished under a murderous fire. Our buglers blasted the charge, and the entire brigade was hurled at our foes like a thunderbolt. The routing of the bluecoats quickly succeeded our onslaught, and they were driven in wild confusion to the main line, on which was planted a battery of four twelve pound howitzers, which opened a destructive volley of grape and canister. "Little Joe" then sounded a retreat, so as to realign his entire command. Ashby's brigade was on the right, Dibrell's on the left, and Harrison's in the center. Kilpatrick's command was covered by a continuous line of breastworks in crescent shape. Anderson's Tennesseans and Terry's Rangers, being in the timber, proceeded slowly until reaching the open. Meantime the Eleventh Texas and Third Arkansas went by our left flank in as perfect a line as I ever saw on a drill field. Reaching the open, our bugler, Jim Nance, sounded the charge, and at our foe we went like an avalanche, but our entire line was driven back in defeat. Retiring and reforming, a second assault was made with the same result, we both times sustaining fearful loss in men and horses in a hand to hand encounter across the breastworks. We retreated to our former position to reform for the third onslaught. Being in line, Col. Anderson took position in front and center of the regiment, and commanded: "Attention!" Every man ears awaited his command, when he cried out: "Boys, I want every d_____ man in this regiment, when we reach the edge of the woods, to put his horse and go like h_____ to the Yankee breastworks; then abandon your horses, and , with six shooters in each hand, go over and drive the d_____ scoundrels out." From every throat in the line the reply went back" "All right, Colonel. Your people will all be there." Old Jim Nance's bugle's shrill notes sounded "Forward" and with a yell we gain started, not to defeat but to a glorious victory, the howitzers still roaring their uncomfortable refrain, to the successful silencing of small arms.*

Out of the woods, we put spurs to our foaming chargers, and reached the breastworks. Each man, religiously obeying orders, with a six shooter in each hand, commenced scaling the enemy's works in the face of a galling fire. Our foes, quickly perceiving our determination to win or die, were at once discomfited, and beat a retreat, when the wild work of human destruction com-

menced. We went over the breastworks at sunset, using our six shooters very effectively, leaving the field blue with their dead and wounded, and capturing some two hundred prisoners with their horses and arms. Our men fought well to avenge our comrades, whom we had left weltering in their precious blood. We followed in hot pursuit until it became too dark to successfully find our way through the pine and blackjack undergrowth."[24] Wheeler ordered Ashby's brigade to turn the Yankee's left flank and take possession of the Louisville road, upon which the Yankees were retreating. It was getting dark and Ashby by accident got on the wrong road, which allowed the Yankees escape.

During the night Kilpatrick fell back to his infantry. Wheeler placed his pickets along the Brier Creek to prevent the Yankees from attacking Augusta. His main force was moved to Rocky Springs Church.[25]

On December 2nd, the 14th Army Corps and Kilpatrick's cavalry marched upon Waynesboro by the Louisville road. Wheeler attacked the force at Rocky Creek. The Yankees turned and headed towards Thomas Station. Wheeler had to fall back.

On December 3rd, Wheeler attacked the Yankees at Thomas Station, driving the pickets and stopping their destruction of the railroad. After night fall, Wheeler brought up two Napoleon cannons and some dismounted men, crept up to the Union camps and again attacked the Yankees, shelling their camp. At daylight, the Yankees marched upon Waynesboro. Wheeler's force had been sent to forage three miles away. Wheeler quickly concentrated his forces and threw up barricades, while a single regiment held the Yankee force at bay. Wheeler had not even completed his barricade when the Yankees charged his line, which was repulsed. A second, third, and fourth charge was made against Wheeler, each were repulsed and countercharged by Wheeler's men. The Yankees then advanced their infantry, and the cavalry tried to turn Wheeler's flank. Wheeler had no other choice but to fall back, until he reached the town of Waynesboro. The Yankees force became so overwhelming that Wheeler's force had to abandon Waynesboro. The moment Wheeler left his earthworks, he directed Col. Gustave Cook of the Eighth Texas Cavalry and the Ninth Tennessee Battalion to charge the Yankees, meeting and driving back a charge of the Yankees, and the charge was so successful, that the Yankees no longer made any more charges, until Wheeler's force reached a new position north of the town. According to Yankee reports they had now lost fifty killed and one hundred and forty seven wounded. The Yankees stayed in town for three hours and then moved down the Savannah road. [26]

Confederate General William Hardee informed Wheeler that a force had already been sent to block the Savannah road, and that Wheeler and his force were to stay in Augusta to protect the threatened city, and strike the Yankees flank and rear.[27]

On the December 7th, Wheeler attacked the Yankees rear several times, driving them from their positions, and captured one hundred prisoners. During the Yankee attack upon Savannah, they were forced to blockade their rear, frequently building barricades two or three miles in length and destroyed all the bridges on their line of march. The Union forces attacked Wheeler's force by charging within their cavalry, which was met with countercharges and driven back in confusion with heavy losses.[28]

On December Eighth, Wheeler brought up a battery of 12 pound guns and shelled the camp of the 14th Corps, throwing the corps into confusion and causing it to leave camp at midnight, abandoning valuable clothing, arms, etc. Wheeler also captured three wagons and teams, and the Yankees had to burn quite a few others to prevent them from being captured. On that same day, Wheeler captured a dispatch from Union General Slocum to Union General Jefferson Davis giving the location of Sherman's army before Savannah. This dispatch was sent to Hardee. Upon reaching ten miles from the city, Wheeler moved back and crossed the Savannah River, leaving General Iverson's command to watch the Yankees should they move in the direction of Augusta or Western Georgia. On reaching the South Carolina side, Wheeler moved down and was placed in command of the defenses of the New River and adjacent landings of the river, and was ordered to hold the line of communications from Huger's Landing to Hardeeville. The Yankees held the South Carolina side of the river with a division of infantry.[29]

Sherman was now in line of battle before Savannah, his rear protected by fortifications running along the swamps only penetrable on only a few causeways, which the Federals now held, with forts and batteries so strong that an army could hardly expect to take it with any amount of success.

Wheeler decided to join Hardee's forces at Savannah. Wheeler quickly rode to the Savannah River and crossed into South Carolina. Wheeler then traveled to Savannah, and after visiting the troops in the breastworks around the city, returned and took command of the defenses on the Savannah and New Rivers, including Gunbridge and Mongin's Landing, the object was to keep the only line of retreat for the Confederate infantry open. The Federals were not going to make the task easy considering they were approaching the position from three different sides.

The Union army already crossed the Savannah at Izzard's rice plantation. Wheeler attacked and drove them back. Wheeler's lines along the Savannah ran for fifteen miles, and along New River for the same distance. The Federals held an island in the Savannah with artillery, bearing down on the shore. Wheeler held the bank until the 19th, when he visited General Beaureguard. A heavy fire was to be thrown over the slough from the island, driving off the Federal pickets before they could be reinforced.

Wheeler rode to the point and concentrated in their front, fought the Yankees and stopped the advance, though their position on the island prevented them from being dislodged. The Federals were only three miles away from the only causeway in which the Confederate army could escape. Wheeler reinforced all points, fighting all positions, and strengthened his works. He kept back the Federals until the 21st, when the pontoon over the Savannah was completed and the Confederate army withdrew from Savannah.

After the evacuation of the city, on December 20th, Wheeler removed all the guns and ammunition from Tunbridge and Mongan's Landing and New River bridge. He also removed the heavy guns weighing nine thousand pounds each from Red Bluff, along with the ammunition. On December 21st, Sherman entered the city of Savannah thus ending his March to the Sea. Even though Tom Harrison's brigade, along with the rest of Wheeler's cavalry force tried hard to save Georgia, but it was all in vain. Sherman managed to destroy one hundred million dollars worth of property. He also tore up one hundred and ten miles worth of railroad track, and to make sure the South could never use them again he built huge bon fires and laid the rails on top of them and then twisted the rails. Sherman completely destroyed the industrial back bone of Georgia.[30]

During the Savannah Campaign, Wheeler pointed out the gallantry and bravery of Humes Division. He also pointed out the condition of the cavalry by this point in the war. Wheeler stated that his men were eating meat on a stick and baking bread on stone's because they had no cooking utensils. They also haven't been paid for twelve months. He also complained that his men have not gotten the issue of clothing although the infantry had gotten theirs. Wheeler said that his men marched on average about sixteen miles a day, with no wagons, with all rations being foraged and carried on the backs of their horses. During the campaign Wheeler managed to capture four cannons, 1,200 mules, over two hundred wagons, two thousand head of cattle, three thousand cavalry horses with equipment, and four thousand arms. He also destroyed a dozen train cars.[31]

After the fall of Savannah, Wheeler established a line of pickets entirely encircling the Federals army. This line started at the mouth of the Altamaha river, and extending along the banks of the rivers and creeks, crossed the Savannah River at right angles near the mouth of the Ebenezer Creek, from which it ran in a northeast direction, striking the coast near Grahamville.[32]

Wheeler remained in this position for three weeks, being constantly engaged with Federal foraging and scouting parties.

Wheeler was ordered by Hardee to burn all mills, rice and corn as he fell back before the Federal army. Wheeler argued against this policy and Hardee changed his mind. The war was not over and Col. Harrison and the rest of the Eighth Texas Cavalry would go on to fight more battles, although by this point the men were tired, and hungry.

[1] Civil War Battles of the Western Theater
[2] Ibid.
[3] Ibid.
[4] Ibid.
[5] Ibid.
[6] Ibid.
[7] Ibid.
[8] Ibid.
[9] Campaigns of Wheeler and His Cavalry: 1862-1865 Chapter XIII
[10] Terry's Texas Rangers, Leonidas Giles, p. 90-93

[11] Campaigns of Wheeler and His Cavalry: 1862-1865, Chapter XIII
[12] Ibid.
[13] O.R. Series I-Vol. XLIV Nov. 15-Dec. 21, 1864-The Savannah Campaign. No. 157-Report of Maj. Gen. Joseph Wheeler. C. S. Army, commanding Cavalry Corps.
[14] O.R. Series I-Vol. XLIV Nov. 15-Dec. 21, 1864-The Savannah Campaign. No. 157-Report of Maj. Gen. Joseph Wheeler. C. S. Army, commanding Cavalry Corps.
[15] Ibid.
[16] Ibid.
[17] Ibid.
[18] O.R. Series I-Vol. XLIV Nov. 15-Dec. 21, 1864-The Savannah Campaign. No. 157-Report of Maj. Gen. Joseph Wheeler. C. S. Army, commanding Cavalry Corps.; Campaigns of Wheeler and His Cavalry: 1862-1865, Chapter XIII
[19] O.R. Series I-Vol. XLIV Nov. 15-Dec. 21, 1864-The Savannah Campaign. No. 157-Report of Maj. Gen. Joseph Wheeler. C. S. Army, commanding Cavalry Corps.; Campaigns of Wheeler and His Cavalry: 1862-1865, Chapter XIII; Confederate Veteran Vol. XI 1903 P. 8-9
[20] Ibid.
[21] O.R. Series I-Vol. XLIV Nov. 15-Dec. 21, 1864-The Savannah Campaign. No. 157-Report of Maj. Gen. Joseph Wheeler. C. S. Army, commanding Cavalry Corps.
[22] Ibid.
[23] Ibid.
[24] Confederate Veteran, Vol. XI 1903 p. 9
[25] O.R. Series I-Vol. XLIV Nov. 15-Dec. 21, 1864-The Savannah Campaign. No. 157-Report of Maj. Gen. Joseph Wheeler. C. S. Army, commanding Cavalry Corps.
[26] Ibid.
[27] Ibid.
[28] Ibid.
[29] Ibid.
[30] Civil War Battles of the Western Theater; Wheeler and His Cavalry 1862-1865
[31] O.R. Series I-Vol. XLIV Nov. 15-Dec. 21, 1864-The Savannah Campaign. No. 157-Report of Maj. Gen. Joseph Wheeler. C. S. Army, commanding Cavalry Corps.
[32] Wheeler and His Cavalry: 1862-186

Chapter 16:
The War's End: The Battle of Bentonville

After the fall of Savannah, Sherman occupied the city and formulated a plan that would march his army through the Carolinas by feinting on Augusta, Georgia, to the northwest and Charleston, South Carolina, to the northwest, and force the Confederates to divide it's forces in an attempt to defend both cities. Sherman would then advance via Columbia to "either Raleigh or Weldon."[1]

On January 2nd, 1865, Sherman received permission to make his march through the Carolinas. On that same day orders from the Confederate War Department made Wheeler the commander of the Confederate Cavalry Corps consisting of: Iverson's Division, composed of Lewis and Ferguson's brigades; Humes Division, composed of Dibrell's, Ashby's and Harrison's brigades; Allen's Division, composed of Anderson's, Crew's and Hagan's brigades.

On January 14th, 1865, Tom Harrison was made a Brigadier General and was given command of the Eighth Texas, 11th Texas, 4th Tennessee, 3rd Arkansas, and 1st Kentucky. General William Hardee reported to President Jefferson Davis that his effective force in the Carolinas was 3,550 regulars infantry, 3,000 reserves, 1,100 militia, 3,100 heavy artillerists, 1,700 light artillery, and 6,100 cavalry.

By January 15th, Sherman was ready to move on to the Atlantic. Union General O. O. Howard commanded the Right Wing, which was ordered to start from the Thunderbolt, transport his men to Beaufort, South Carolina, and make a move towards the Charleston railroad, at or near Pocotaligo. Union Major General Blair of the 17th Corps was successful in securing the mouth of the Pocotaligo Creek, with easy access to the Hilton Head. The Left Wing was comprised of Union Major General Slocum, and Major General Kilpatrick, who were ordered to rendezvous near Robertsville and Coosawhatchie, South Carolina, with a depot of supplies at Sister's Ferry, on the Savannah River. Because of the heavy rains in January, General Slocum was not able to cross the Sister's Ferry until February. Major Generals Schofield was sent to reenforce the commands of Major General Terry and Palmer, operating on the coast of North Carolina. Sherman sights were on Charleston. [2]

By January 18th, Fort Fisher and the forts at the mouth of Cape Fear River were captured by Admiral David Porter and General Alfred H. Terry. On January 19th, Sherman and his command moved out. On January 22nd, Sherman was heading for Hilton Head from Savannah River to Screven's Ferry. Sherman also laid pontoon boats from Pennyworth's Island to South Carolina bank at Cheves place. Col. Harrison's brigade immediately met resistance from Sherman's men at Frampton place.[3]

By February 2nd, the 15th and 17th Corps of Sherman's army were between Coosawhatchie and Combahee, and advanced to the junction of the Orangeburg and Lawtonville road by the Pocotaligo and Augusta Road. By February 3rd the 20th Corps was moving towards Lawtonville. Union General Phil Sheridan arrived with the 19th Corps at Savannah. On February 1st, 2nd, and 3rd, Wheeler fought the Federals at McBride's bridge, Loper's Crossroads, and on the Lawtonville road. After the battle on the Barnesville Road, Wheeler rode to assist in the defense of River's bridge. Wheeler found the Federals had already crossed the river and gained the rear of the infantry troops. Wheeler charged the Yankees infantry in an open field and drove them back to the river, which enabled the Confederate infantry and artillery to withdraw. In this engagement, the Texas troops under Col. Tom Harrison's brigade, Humes division, were distinguished for their bravery. [4]

The very next day Wheeler again had a severe fight, opposing the Federals advance on Buford's Bridge road. They engaged Wheeler's force near Adam's Ford. On the 6th, Wheeler took a position at Springtown and fought the Federals as they forced the passage of the river. On the 7th, Kilpatrick and three brigades of cavalry charged the pickets at Blackville, but Wheeler with Dibbrell's troops, charged Kilpatrick's cavalry and drove back his entire command. The Federals moved toward Edisto, and Wheeler rode out to meet them. Wheeler kept the Federals from the railroad for two days longer than Hardee had requested. Hardee headed for Charleston. On the 9th, Slocum, with the 14th Corps and 20th Corps and Kilpatrick's cavalry, started for Augusta. Detachments of the 1st, 3rd, and 12th Alabama, under Col. Hagan covered the approaches to Augusta, but were driven to Williston by the Federal force. [5]

On the 10th, Wheeler sent a portion of his force to watch and oppose the 15th and 17th Corps, and after a severe fight, which stopped their progress, he moved with two brigades to place himself in position to defend the city.

The next day, on February 11th, Wheeler was pushed back to Aiken. Wheeler managed to concentrate 2,100 of his men to take on the 14th Corps and Kilpatrick's cavalry. Aiken was thirteen miles from Augusta, and five miles from the factories at Graniteville. Wheeler formed his men in a hidden position in the rear of Aiken. Wheeler planned to attack the Federals while they were temporarily broken up while riding through the town. His left was ordered to swing around and charge the Federals flank, driving them against the railroad and cutting them off from escape. Wheeler's command was formed in columns of squads, so that each column could charge down one of the broad streets of Aiken and engage the Federals in front, while the columns on the left could strike the Federals flank. The Federals entered the town without expecting an attack, a volley was discharged which uncovered Wheeler's position to the Federals. Wheeler charged the Union force at Aiken. Kilpatrick entered the town and charged Wheeler. Wheeler countercharged and drove Kilpatrick in confusion. Wheeler drove him to and beyond his barricades, but Wheeler ran out of ammunition and had to halt to reload. After reloading Wheeler pursued Kilpatrick at full speed to Johnson's Turnout, but Kilpatrick retreated through some woods. Upon reaching the woods, Wheeler found strong fortifications with artillery. Wheeler attacked their flank and their front. Kilpatrick's men dismounted in the works. They were reenforced. Wheeler was sent to Orangeburg, while Allen's division was left in Johnson's Turnout. Wheeler felt that the Yankees were going to attack Augusta, and that this city must be protected because of it's cotton reserves. [6]

During the battle Wheeler captured ninety Federals, and captured several colors. Wheeler lost fifty men during the charge.

Wheeler placed his command between Sherman's army and Columbia. He divided his force on several roads. On the 14th Wheeler charged through a skirmish line of the 14th Corps, captured forty prisoners and broke the main line of battle.

On February 15th, Wheeler's Kentucky and Tennessee troops under Dibbrell were placed at Congaree Creek, where they fought the advance of the Federal 15th Corps, while Wheeler along with the Georgia, Alabama, and Texas troops, rode upon the Federal flank. Sherman ordered General Charles A. Wood, who commanded the leading division, to turn the flank by sending Stone's brigade through a cedar swamp to the left of the Confederate fort. Stone's brigade quickly gained possession of the brigade and fort. The bridge had been partially damaged by fire, and had to be repaired. The 15th Corps was not able to cross the Congaree that night. [7]

Wheeler and his force, including Harrison's brigade, were then ordered to Columbia. He was to cross Broad River and picket the Saluda from it's mouth up ten miles with a portion of his command, while the remainder was ordered to picket the Congaree below the city.

The next day the head column of the 15th Corps reached the bank of the Congaree, but was too late to save the bridge over the river. While waiting for pontoon boats to arrive Sherman could see people running about the streets of Columbia, and small bodies of cavalry. A single gun of Captain DeGress' battery fired at the Confederate cavalry, but Sherman later ordered the shells to land on the State house walls and a few shells at the railroad depot. Sherman instructed General Howard not to cross directly in front of Columbia, but to cross the Saluda at the factory, three miles above, and afterward Broad River, in order to approach Columbia from the north. Within an hour of the arrival of Howard's head column at the river opposite Columbia, the head column of the left wing came upon the scene, and General Slocum was ordered to cross the Saluda at Zion Church, and take the roads direct to Winnsboro, tearing up the railroads and bridges around Alston. Sherman moved toward the Saluda, which allowed the Federals to sweep the sides of the river with artillery and rifle fire. Wheeler tried to resist the movement, but the Federal artillery and infantry under Union General Howard commanded both sides of the banks, and a large body of Union troops was now attempting the cross the stream.[8]

Wheeler decided to concentrate his forces and after heavy fighting managed to oppose the advance toward the Broad River bridge, which was a mile from their point of crossing the Saluda.

General Howard's entire corps crossed the Saluda, near the factory, and moved forward and drove Wheeler to the Broad River bridge. Wheeler dismounted forty men. At the bridge head, while he cheered on his men, he directed his column on the bridge. The bridge was set on fire, and the Federals were now only one hundred yards from his position. In one hour the bridge was totally engulfed in flames. That night Howard made a flying bridge across the Broad River, about three miles above Columbia.

The next day on February 17th, a message arrived for Wheeler to come to the assistance of General Stevenson, who was the commander of the Confederate infantry corps. When Wheeler and his men arrived he found Stevenson in retreat and that the Federals were across the river. Wheeler placed his troops in front of the advancing Yankees and fought a infantry line. By 11 A.M. Wheeler and his men were driven to the junction of the Broad River and Winnsboro Roads. He then turned toward Winnsboro and saw Sherman's men marching into Columbia, South Carolina.[9]

On February 17th, the mayor of Columbia surrendered the city to Col. Stone, 25th Iowa Infantry, commanding the Third Brigade, First Division, 15th Corps. On that same day, the 17th Corps entered Columbia. General Wade Hampton who commanded the rear guard of the Confederate cavalry had ordered all cotton, public and private, to be burned. The cotton that Hampton ordered to be burned spread the flames to the buildings.[10]

The Left Wing of Sherman's army had crossed the Saluda and Broad Rivers, breaking up the railroad around Alston, and all the way to the bridge across Broad River on the Spartanburg road, the main body heading straight for Winnsboro. General Slocum reached Winnsboro on February 21st. Slocum then turned to Rocky Mount, on the Catawba River. The 20th Corps reached Rocky Mount on the 22nd, and crossed the river on the 23rd. Kilpatrick's cavalry crossed over in a terrible rain on the 23rd and moved up to Lancaster, with orders to keep up the delusion that the main assault was to take place at Charlotte, North Carolina.

From the 23rd to the 26th, heavy rains slowed Sherman's army. The 20th Corps reached Hanging Rock on the 26th, and waited for the 14th Corps to get across the Catawba. The Left wing moved towards Cheraw. The Right Wing had broken up the railroad to Winnsboro, and then turned towards Peay's Ferry, where it crossed the Catawba via Young's Bridge, and the 15th Corps by Tiller's and Kelley's bridges. A small force of mounted men under Captain Ducan was to cut the railroad from Charleston to Florence, but was stopped by Butler's division of Confederate cavalry.[11]

On March 1st, Wheeler engaged the Yankees at Wilson's store. On March 2nd, Sherman's 20th Corps encountered Butler's cavalry at Chesterfield. The columns moved towards Fayetteville, North Carolina. The next day the 17th Corps entered Cheraw, the Confederates retreating across the Pedee, and burning the bridge. On March 4th Wheeler encountered Federals near Hornsboro and after a severe fight in which Wheeler captured fifty prisoners, the Federals retreated, leaving camps, and equipment. The next day Wheeler passed through Wadesboro, and reached the Great Peedee at Grany Island the following day. He found the river swollen. He was determined to cross. Wheeler got an old man to pilot him across the ford; but the old fellow got in too deep and downstream he and the horse went until the Rangers pulled him out. The old man would not try again, so Wheeler said he was going across alone. About that time E. H. McKnight, Company K, Texas Rangers, rode down to let his horse drink. James B Nance, 4th Tennessee Cavalry and

McKnight were side by side as the General rode into the water alone. Nance said to McKnight: "Let's go with him." As both the Rangers plunged in with Wheeler, he looked around and saw them and said: "Boys, hold your horses heads upstream and let them float across." Wheeler sank and rose for an entire hour until he made it the other side. They all managed to get to the first island. They proceeded to wrung out the water out of their clothes and boots. Twenty Texas Rangers cavalry from Harrison's brigade also plunged into the torrent. All twenty Texans were swept down river. Other men tried, but only Nance and McKnight succeeded in crossing the stream. Wheeler, Nance and McKnight got across the channels and rode about a mile from the river.[12]

It was late evening and they rode up to a farmhouse to see if they could camp with the farmer that night. The old man said he would like to keep them, but he was afraid to, as the Yankees were watching him. He said he had a son hiding out there who was at home on furlough. He then told them of an old man living on the big road who was friendly to the Yankees and there was not so much danger of his getting burned out if Wheeler and his men got caught there. He gave them details of the place and family; so Wheeler, Nance and McKnight went on and found the old man willing to let them stop for the night. There were three of the family and three blacks.[13]

Wheeler, Nance, and McKnight built a fire in the kitchen to dry their blankets and clothes. Nance and McKnight went to work to dry out while Wheeler kept the old man and family company, as they agreed that he should dry by the old man's fire in the main house and watch him and the women, and Nance and McKnight would watch the black servants. They told the old man that they were Confederates, but did not tell him of what command they belonged to. Nance and McKnight could hear the old man telling Wheeler that Wheeler's cavalry were on the other side of the river and likely to cross as the river went down. The General would agree with him that the cavalry were mighty bad men and would rob and steal everything in sight. The old man said he would have to hide all his stuff the next day, at which Wheeler laughed and agreed with him.[14]

About 12 o'clock a company of the 4th Alabama or 4th Tennessee Cavalry scouts, who had crossed the river up above on a ferryboat, came down the river hunting a place to get food. They stopped and called at the gate, and Wheeler told McKnight to see who it was, so as to give him a chance to get out the back way. McKnight had a hard time to make the Captain understand that Wheeler was at the house, for he said he left Wheeler on the other side of the river; but McKnight finally showed him that he was a Texas Ranger by his boots and Texas spurs, and they went to the house with a detail of his men to watch McKnight. When they got to the door, they peered around the side and said: "Well, General Wheeler, what are you doing here?" Wheeler said: "Looking for Yankees", and the old man of the house became shocked to realize that he had been talking to General Wheeler the whole time.[15]

Wheeler told the Captain to put out a strong picket around the place, so Wheeler, Nance, and McKnight could sleep.

When the men awoke they had a breakfast of butter, eggs, ham and big, fat biscuits. The river fell several feet during the night, and the rest of Wheeler's command crossed. About daylight Captain Shannon's scouts, of the Texas Rangers, came up, but they hardly had time to feed their horses before the picket reported Yankees just down the road robbing a house, and Nance soon sounded his bugle. Shannon's scouts, Wheeler, Nance and McKinght rode to the Federals and made a charge. The Federals were quickly routed. The scouts rode after them and many other Yankees along the road joined in the race for safe quarters. The men of Shannon's scouts tried to out do each other so that Wheeler might see the essential qualifications of a man to be a member of the Shannon's scouts. The chase was kept up until the advancing Federal forces were seen across an open field forming a line of battle, so Wheeler and his small band retreated. The Federals lost thirty five men killed and wounded. As the fight went on one of the scouts called to General Wheeler to tell him something, and the quick response of the General was: "Don't call me General; I'm Private Johnson with you boys today." Wheeler's command soon caught up with him and the whole command marched toward Fayetteville.[16]

At 10 P.M. on the 9th, Wheeler's advance guard, under Capt. Shannon, came upon Kilpatrick's camp. The Union pickets were captured. After consulting with General Wade Hampton, it was

The War's End

determined to make a mounted charge. The roads were muddy by heavy rains and it was daylight before the advance of Humes's and Allen's commands reached their positions. Wheeler arranged for Allen and Humes to charge in five columns upon the Federals, while Capt. Shannon was ordered to take possession of the house in which Kilpatrick was sleeping in. Dibbrell's command was left as a reserve. Three small brigades from Hampton's cavalry, then under General Butler, also took position with Wheeler's men.[17]

Wheeler on his white stallion charged with his men. They headed for the center of the Federal camp, trampling under foot the barely awakened Federals. The other Federals camps suddenly awoke, seized their arms, and the battle began.

Three hundred Federals surrendered, but many attempted to fight or escape. Wheeler soon was surrounded and was personally engaged in a dozen encounters, killing two and capturing a number of Yankees with his own hand.[18]

Kilpatrick's artillery and wagons were captured. The Federals that had formed in front of Wheeler's force were still unbroken. The area was broken and wooded and Wheeler's men soon became separated, which was even made worse when the troopers had to cross a boggy stream on the edge of the Federal camp. Wheeler's force reformed twice and charged the Yankees, who, from a nearby slope were firing volleys upon Wheeler's advancing troops. One of their lines were broken and routed. At this moment General Butler, who had reformed his command, charged. Wheeler raised his hat to these men as they flew by. As Butler's men tore into the fleeing Yankees a solid line of Federals formed in the distance, and approached slowly with a deadly fire forcing Wheeler to retire quickly. General Humes and General Tom Harrison, Col. Hagan, Col. Roberts and Major Farish had all been badly wounded during the attack. General Allen's and Col. Ashby's horses had been shot out from under them. The Alabama brigade lost all it's commanders and every field officer was now commanded by a Captain. Col. King of the Georgia cavalry was killed. The loss of so many officers made it impossible to rally the men for another charge. Wheeler sent numerous messages to Wade Hampton for Dibbrell's troops, but none were heard from and slowly Wheeler's troops left the field. Wheeler's men did manage to carry off four hundred Union prisoners. Wheeler rode to Hampton and Dibbrell, but Sherman's infantry soon arrived on the field, and Hampton advised that the entire force withdraw immediately. Wheeler and Dibbrell fought a delaying action, while the rest of his command fell back toward Fayetteville.[19]

The 14th and 17th Corps reached Fayetteville on March 11th, and skirmished with Wade Hampton's cavalry, which included Wheeler's force, that covered the retreat of Hardee's army, which had crossed the Cape Fear River. On the 12th, 13th, 14th, Sherman passed Fayetteville, destroying the U.S. Arsenal and machinery which had formerly belonged to the old Harper's Ferry Arsenal. Beauregard had been reenforced by Confederate Benjamin Cheatham's corps from the West and by the garrison of Augusta. They had time to move in Sherman's front and flank about Raleigh. Hardee succeeded in getting across Cape Fear River ahead of Sherman, and could complete the junction with the other armies of Johnston and Hoke, and the whole command under Johnston made up the army in front of Sherman, with artillery and infantry.[20]

On March 15th, Sherman's columns moved out from Cape Fear. Sherman accompanied General Slocum, who was preceded by Kilpatrick's cavalry. Kilpatrick skirmished with the Confederate rear guard about three miles beyond, near Taylor's Hole Creek. General Slocum sent forward a brigade of infantry to hold the barricades. The next day the column advanced and encountered the Confederates artillery, infantry and cavalry in an entrenched position in front of the point where the road branches off toward Goldsboro through Bentonville. Hardee in retreating from Fayetteville, had halted in the narrow, swampy neck between Cape Fear and South Rivers, in hopes to hold Sherman to save time for the concentration of Johnston's armies at some point to his rear, namely Raleigh, Smithfield, or Goldsborough. Hardee's force was estimated at twenty thousand men. General Slocum was ordered to hold his position. The 20th Corps, General Williams had the lead, and Ward's division the advance. Ward's division encountered a brigade of Charleston heavy artillery armed with infantry (Rhett's) posted across the road behind a light parapet, with a battery of guns enfilading the approach across a open field. Williams sent a brigade by a circuit to his left that turned the line, and a quick charge broke the brigade which retreated back to a second line better built and strongly held. As Ward's division advanced he encountered a second and stronger line, when Jackson's

155

division was deployed forward on the right of Ward, and the two divisions of Union General Jefferson Davis 14th Corps on the left, well toward the Cape fear. At the same time Kilpatrick was ordered to draw back his cavalry and mass it on the extreme right, and in conjunction with Jackson's right, to feel forward for the Goldsboro road. He got a brigade on the road, but was attacked by McLaws division, but McLaw had to fall back to the infantry. The whole line advanced late in the afternoon and drove the Confederates well within their entrenched lines and pressed them so hard that the next morning the Confederates were gone, having retreated. Wards's division advanced through Averasboro. Kilpatrick was ordered across the South River to the right rear and move up on the east side toward Elevation. Slocum's column was turned to the right, and took the Goldsboro road, Kilpatrick crossing north in the direction of Elevation, with orders to move eastward, watching the flank. Howard's column were taking the roads towards Bentonville and Goldsboro. The Confederate infantry had retreated in Smithfield, and his cavalry retreated across Sherman's front in the same direction. [21]

On the night of the 18th, Sherman was encamped with Slocum's column on the Goldsboro road, twenty seven miles from Goldsboro, about five miles from Bentonville. Wheeler reached Bentonville and placed his troops on the right of Johnston's army.

On March 19th, Major Holmes, of Union General Morgan's command, marched towards Goldsboro, and encountered Dibrell's cavalry. General Carlin's division of the XIV Corps, passed Morgan's division and was also heading down the Goldsboro road. Holmes informed Carlin of Dibrell's cavalry. General Harrison Hobert's brigade, Carlin's division drove back Dibrell's men into the woods. Hobart's brigade was heading straight for Hoke's Confederate Division. When Lt. Col. Cyrus E. Briant's wing of Hobart's brigade approached the Willis Cole's house, he was met by the fire of North Carolina Junior Reserves Brigade and Atkins Battery. Some of Briant's men headed for the protection of the house. Atkins artillery shelled the house, and the Yankees left the house, and ran for the protection of a ravine just north of the Cole field. They were soon joined by Carlin's Second brigade, commanded by General George Buell, which formed on Briant's left. General Slocum ordered Buell's brigade to search out the Confederate right flank.

On Hoke's right was Stewart's Corps, commanded by General William Loring. Lee's Corps, which was on the right of Stewart's Corps, was commanded by Major General Daniel Hill, and Major General William Bate, who commanded Cheatham's Corps.

General Slocum quickly deployed two divisions of the 14th Corps, General Jefferson C. Davis, and brought up on their left the two division of the 20th Corps, General Williams. These he arranged on the defensive and hastily prepared barricades. General Kilpatrick also came up and massed on the left. In this position the Left Wing of the Union army received six assaults by the combined forces of Hoke, Hardee and Cheatham, led by General Hardee himself. The Federals were routed in a few minutes and pushed the Federals out of the temporary barricades. A mile to the rear the 14th Corps rallied on the 20th Corps in a dense growth of young pine trees. In this position the Federal right rested on a swamp, and was covered by entrenchments. The Union troops were pressed back, except on the left. At 6 P.M. the Federal force was greatly increased and the Confederates returned to their first position. [22]

During the days fight Wheeler and his force captured forty prisoners. Wheeler's force was not able to engage the Yankees later in the day because of stream in which it was impossible to cross. [23]

On the morning of the 20th Sherman had a strong line of battle. Confederate General Hoke held the Confederate left, and General Joe Johnston ordered him to refuse his left flank so that he could meet the attack of the oncoming Yankees. Wheeler and Butler's cavalry were moved to the left of the army and to the left of Hoke's force. As Wheeler was moving to the left he was immediately met by a large force of infantry moving up the Goldsboro and Bentonville Road. After a severe fight Wheeler and his force stopped their advance and held them in position until evening, when General Braxton Bragg replaced Wheeler's men by Hoke's division of infantry. Johnston was in a precarious situation, with his flanks resting on no natural defenses, and behind them was a deep and rapid stream called Mill Creek, over which there was only one bridge, which was the only means of escape.

On the 21st, General Schofield entered Goldsboro with no opposition, and General Terry had secured the Neuse River at Cox' Bridge, ten miles above, with a pontoon bridge laid across it and a brigade had already been crossed over, so that three armies were now connected, and the object of the campaign was accomplished.

On the same day General Mower's division, of the 17th Corps, on the extreme right, had moved his corps to the right around the Confederate flank and had almost reached the bridge across the Mill Creek. Sherman ordered a general attack by his skirmishers from left to right.

During the night, Wheeler had managed to build a line of breastworks 1,200 yards long in connection with the infantry. The Eighth Texas were in position in these earthworks. They were resting and eating their rations, when they heard the boom of cannons directly in their rear. Every man listened, for they knew it meant something was serious about to happen. They were right, General Mower's division, of the 17th Corps, on the extreme right of the Union line, were approaching the Mill Creek bridge. General Wade Hampton was informed of the advance of Mower's Corps and he immediately ordered Col. Henderson with Cumming's Georgia brigade to rush to the bridge. He also sent a courier to round up all the mounted men he could find. Capt. "Doc" Mattingly, of Company K, Eighth Texas, commanded about one hundred men responded to Hampton's call. Wheeler galloped up and asked for the commander of the Rangers. He ordered Mattingly, "Capt., mount your men, go fast as you can and charge whatever you find at the bridge." They mounted and raced to the rear. The Yankees were five hundred yards distant in an open field. Here the Rangers halted to close up the column, and for Capt. Mathews to salute General Hardee and staff. Hardee said, "Then execute your order." Capt. Matthews gave the order, " Charge right in front", and with a Rebel yell the Rangers, along with the 42nd Georgia infantry, charged across the five hundred yards of open field upon the Yankee force. The Rangers rode them down and emptied their pistols at close range. The Rangers along with the 42nd Georgia drove the Yankees with ease for about three quarters of a mile until they reached a line of fresh troops, when the force of the charge was ran out by the Rangers, and the Rangers fell back with about two hundred prisoners. Col. Henderson's left flank was now exposed and the Yankees quickly discovered this, advanced their line, which overlapped his right as far as could be seen, and would in a few moments have completely enveloped that flank. Henderson now retreated, with the Eighth Texas being somewhat scattered. The Yankees fell back, halted and did not follow.[24]

In this charge fell mortally wounded, William Hardee, Jr., son of General Hardee. Nearly a year before, he and several boys, had run away from school to join the Rangers, but on account of their extreme youth Col. Tom Harrison sent them back to school. The boy wouldn't remain in school, so General Hardee kept him in his command for several months, but his son wanted to join the famous Rangers. Hardee finally gave into his sons wishes. The boy enlisted in Company D, and fell in his first battle.[25]

After the Eighth Texas and 42nd Georgia fell back, they were placed four hundred yards in the rear of the farthest point to which they had advanced and were placed in position by General Hardee on the right of General Talliaferro, where they remained until 2 o'clock the next morning, when they marched across the Mill Creek bridge and moved to Smithfield.

The Confederates had paid a heavy price they lost 2,606 men. Sherman's loss was 1,595 men killed or wounded.

During the night, Johnston withdrew toward Smithfield. Wheeler covered his retreat.

On the 22nd, Sherman continued to pursue Johnson's men almost two miles beyond Mill Creek, but was halted by Sherman. The Confederate infantry was still in Bentonville, while the Federals pushed on and Wheeler had to bring most of his command into action, and a fight broke out. By 9 A.M. Wheeler had secured a retreat for the Confederate infantry, and by 10 had crossed both Mill and Black Creek, taking a position to meet the Federals advance. The Federal infantry advanced and charged Wheeler. Three color bearers of the leading Union brigade fell within fifty feet of Wheeler's line and the entire Federal force of Sherman's army retreated out of range and didn't renew the pursuit. On that day Sherman was in possession of Goldsboro with it's two railroads back to the sea-ports of Wilmington and Beaufort, North Carolina.[26]

On the 23rd Wheeler marched through Smithfield and took position between Johnston and Sherman's armies, daily engaging the Federals pickets.

On March 27th, Sherman met with Ulysses Grant, Abe Lincoln, George Meade, Ord and others of the Army of the Potomac at City Point. After the meeting, Sherman returned to

New Berne, reaching his headquarters at Goldsboro during the 30th. All three of Sherman's armies converged at Goldsboro. While Sherman was resting his army, events were quickly taking place in Virginia. On April 2nd, Confederate General Robert E. Lee pulled out of the defenses around Petersburg and the road was now open all the way to Richmond, the capitol of the Confederacy. On April 3rd, the Confederate government was fleeing the city. At about 3:00 A.M., a fire began that soon raged out of control, destroying a large area from the James River to the Capitol Square. Five hours later, the Union troops entered Richmond. On April 9th, at a place called Appomattox, in the residence of the McClean house Confederate General Robert E. Lee and Union General Ulysses Grant met to discuss the terms of surrender. Robert E. Lee decided not to carry the war any longer and surrendered his Army of Northern Virginia.

On April 3rd, 1865, at Wayne County, North Carolina, General W. Y. C. Humes Cavalry Division sent a letter to the War Department at Richmond that his corps was dissatisfied with and lacked the confidence in Major General Wheeler, and were upset that they have not been paid, they were half clothed, and their horses were partially shod.

On April 6th, General Joseph Johnston's thirty five thousand infantry and six thousand cavalry were at Smithfield, between Sherman's army and Raleigh.

On April 10th, all the heads of columns were in motion against Johnston's force. Union Maj. Gen. Slocum was taking the two roads for Smithfield; Union Maj. Gen. O. O. Howard was to the right and feigning up the Weldon road to engage the Confederates cavalry; General Terry and Kilpatrick were moving on the west side of the Neuse River and aiming to reach the rear of the Confederates between Raleigh; Gen. Schofield followed Slocum in support. Wheeler and his forces, including Harrison's brigade, were driven by Union forces to Raleigh.

All the columns met within six miles of Goldsboro, and at about 10:00 a.m. the 14th Corps entered Smithfield, the 20th Corps close at hand. Johnston had rapidly retreated across the Neuse River, and having his railroad to lighten up his trains, could retreat faster than Sherman could pursue. The Confederates burned the bridge at Smithfield, but Maj. Gen. Slocum brought up his platoons and crossed over a division of the 14th Corps. On the 13th of April, Sherman reached Raleigh. Wheeler was withdrawing from Hillsboro as the Federals entered the city. Kilpatrick quickly caught up with Wheeler's force. As Wheeler's force came into view, he charged. Wheeler met the Federals with a counter charge, driving Kilpatrick back in disorder for ten miles, capturing a Major of the 13th Pennsylvania Cavalry, who was mortally wounded. Wheeler placed his troops on the Pittsboro and other roads. He skirmished with Kilpatrick's command, which advanced on the Morristown station where after a severe fight, they retreated to Sherman's main army. [27]

The next day Sherman's cavalry reached Durham Station, the 15th Corps reached the Morristown Station, and the 17th Corps reached the Jone's Station. Johnston was retreating rapidly on the roads from Hillsborough to Greensboro. On April 15th and 16th, Sherman had a conference of war with Union General Henry Halleck, whose army was around Burkeville and Petersburg, Virginia. Johnston's only line of retreat was by Salisbury and Charlotte. On April 14th, Johnston sent his first letter for a meeting to surrender the army. Sherman agreed to meet with Johnston in person between their picket lines on the 17th of April, provided the troops remained where they were.[28]

On April 14th Wheeler and his men, including Harrison's brigade, moved towards Chapel Hill, and on the 15th the Federals approached the Haw River Railroad bridge. The Texas Rangers were camped near the bridge. What was left of the Confederate army was crossing the Haw River. A Federal regiment came across the bridge into the edge of the Ranger's camp, while all the men were sleeping, except for five or six men who were getting ready to look for forage. These five or six Rangers quickly took on the Federals, which awoke the rest of the Rangers from their sleep. The Rangers grabbed their shot guns and other weapons and poured a deadly fire into the oncoming blueclad soldiers. The Federals fell back across the bridge. This was the last firing done by Johnston's army. The Rangers had fought the first and last battles of the Army of the Tennessee. [29]

At noon, on April 17th, Sherman and Johnston met for the first time. Their interview according to Sherman was frank and soldier-like, and Johnston told Sherman that further war for the Confederates was useless, that "the cause was lost, and that every life sacrificed after the surrender of Lee's army was the highest possible crime." The conditions that Johnston wanted was that Sherman let him to allay the fears and anxiety of his men, and enable him to maintain control over them until they could return to their homes, thereby saving the State of North Carolina the devastations inevitably to result from turning his men loose and unprovided on the spot, and other pursuit across the State. Also he wanted to embrace in the same general proposition the fate of all the Confederate armies that remained in existence. Sherman didn't have the authority to approve of Johnston's demands but he felt that there was a chance for peace. Sherman also thought that he should no longer push his concession for unconditional surrender on a General that was so frank with his inability to cope with Sherman's army. If he were to not accept Johnston's surrender it would be "cowardly and unworthy" of him and his men.[30]

General Johnston felt it was unworthy of him to speak for the armies in Texas. They agreed to meet the next day. Sherman returned to Raleigh and conferred with his Generals. Johnston also returned to his army. He told the Texas cavalry it would be their own decision if they wanted to surrender. If they didn't want to surrender they could join General Taylor in Louisiana. Captain "Doc" Mathews was twenty three years old and he felt that he was too young to surrender the unit, so each company was returned to it's own commander with authority to surrender, or leave as it saw fit. Only two hundred and forty eight men were present for duty the next day before surrender.[31]

About fifteen to eighteen men of Company F, Eighth Texas Rangers, decided not to surrender and headed for home. At 1 o'clock in the morning, they were headed for Mobile, Alabama. They went through Greensboro, North Carolina. Colonel Harrison, who had been injured at the Battle of Averysboro, and was using a house to re-cooperate in Greensboro, had heard that these men were heading in his direction and he called for the men to come to the house. The men arrived and stood outside the house. Harrison came to the door in his crutches. Harrison made a speech. He commended Company F for their movement heartily and said he regretted only that he was unable to accompany them. Then many tears and benedictions were made. Harrison bade the men of Company F, including Blackburn, "Godspeed with god's blessing" and a loving farewell to his faithful comrades who "were the heroes of 300 battles."[32]

On the following day, Sherman met with Johnston. Johnston assured Sherman that he would disband the armies for the states of Alabama, Mississippi, Louisiana, and Texas, as well as those in his immediate command, namely North Carolina, South Carolina, Florida, and Georgia.

On April 18th, Sherman agreed to Johnston's proposals, and a armistice was signed between the two men. On April 23rd, Sherman learned that his armistice with Johnston was denied and that he must inform Johnston that hostilities would be renewed within 48 hours. On April 26th, Order No. 62, would be issued to the troops terminating the truce and for all his armies to be ready to march at 12 P.M.. General Grant had orders from the President to direct military movements, and Sherman explained to Grant the exact position of the troops, and he approved it, but did not relieve Sherman of command. On the 25th, Sherman received another letter from Johnston asking for another interview. Grant approved, and urged Sherman to accept. Sherman told Johnston that he would meet with him on April 26th at 12 noon. Johnston arrived at 2 P.M., a train accident delayed from arriving sooner. Johnston signed the final terms of capitulation. Sherman took the letter back to Grant and Grant approved of the terms. Even though Sherman was lambasted in the newspapers for his allowing Johnston to surrender with dignity, Sherman was overjoyed with is decision. Sherman said that the "country was saved from further ruin and devastation...without the loss of one single life to those gallant men who had followed me from Mississippi to the Atlantic, and without subjecting brave men to the ungracious task of pursuing a fleeing foe that didn't want to fight."[33]

On April 26th, 1865, their were less than one hundred and fifty men left in the Texas Rangers, out of a regiment that once numbered 1,173.

On April 28th 1865, Wheeler wrote his last order, which was a farewell address to his men. The letter is as follows:

"Gallant comrades: you have fought your fight. Your task is done. During a four years struggle for liberty you have exhibited courage, fortitude and devotion. You are the victors of more than 200 sternly contested fields. You have participated in more than a thousand conflicts of arms. You are Heroes! Veterans! Patriots! The bones of your comrades mark battlefields upon the soil of Kentucky, Virginia, North Carolina, South Carolina, Georgia, Alabama, and Mississippi. You have done all that human exertion could accomplish. In bidding you adieu, I desire to tender my thanks for your gallantry in battle, your fortitude under suffering and your devotion at all times to the holy cause you have done so much to maintain. I desire also to express my gratitude for the kind feelings you have seen fit to extend toward myself and to invoke upon you the blessing of our Heavenly Father, to whom we must always look in the hour of distress. Brethren, in the cause of freedom, comrades in arms, I bid you farewell."[34]

The last Ranger unit to finally surrender was on May 26th, by Captain Tom Weston, Company H, who commanded ninety men. They accepted their paroles and headed for home.

Terry's Texas Rangers had fought the first battle of the Civil War at Woodsonville, Kentucky and the last battle of the Civil War near the Haw River, in North Carolina.

The war was over. Now it was time for the country to heal.

Tom Harrison served his country with valor and courage. During his career, he would win praise from General Frank Armstrong, who would call him "the best Colonel of cavalry in the army." He took part and led his men in some of the most hotly contested battles of the Western Theater. Harrison never let the enemy take him by surprise and never suffered his command to be attacked without notice. During the war, he was wounded three times, once seriously, and had five horses shot out from under him. Many Confederate Generals sang the praises of the Rangers. Albert Sidney Johnston before his untimely death said: "With a little more drill you are the equals of the old guard of Napoleon." General Hardee said of the Rangers: "I always feel safe with the Rangers to my front." General Braxton Bragg once said: "There is no danger of a surprise when the Rangers are between us and the enemy." President Jefferson Davis said: " The Terry Rangers have done all that could be expected or required of soldiers."

The Texas Rangers "were the safest and swiftest horsemen, the surest and best shots, and of the coolest and bravest men that ever charged a battery."

A poem was written about the Rangers that reflected the twilight of their careers:
"Their shivered swords are red with rust.
Their plumed heads are bowed;
Their proud banner, trailed in dust,
Is now their matrial shroud."[35]

[1]The Battle of Bentonville, March 19-21 Blue & Gray, Dec. 95 Mark Bradley
[2]O.R. Series I-Vol. XLVII Jan. 1-April 26, 1865-The Campaign of the Carolinas. No. 1 Reports of Maj. Gen. William T. Sherman, U.S. Army, commanding Military Division of the Mississippi.
[3]Wheeler and His Cavalry, Chapter XIII; O.R. Series I-Vol. XLVII Jan. 1-April 26, 1865- The Campaign of the Carolinas. No. 1 Reports of Maj. Gen. William T. Sherman, U.S. Army, commanding Military Division of the Mississippi.
[4]Wheeler and His Cavalry, Chapter XIII
[5]Ibid.
[6]Ibid.
[7]Wheeler and His Cavalry, Chapter XIII; O.R. Series I-Vol. XLVII Jan. 1-April 26, 1865- The Campaign of the Carolinas. No. 1 Reports of Maj. Gen. William T. Sherman, U.S. Army, commanding Military Division of the Mississippi.
[8]Ibid.
[9]Ibid.
[10]O.R. Series I-Vol. XLVII Jan. 1-April 26, 1865-The Campaign of the Carolinas. No. 1 Reports of Maj. Gen. William T. Sherman, U.S. Army, commanding Military Division of the Mississippi.
[11]Ibid.
[12]Scouting with Wheeler, Confederate Veteran, Vol. XXVI p. 344; The Last Roll, Confederate Veteran XXVI, p. 360; Scouting with Wheeler, Confederate Veteran Vol. XIX, p. 72
[13]Ibid.
[14]Ibid.
[15]Ibid.
[16]Ibid.
[17]Wheeler and His Cavalry; O.R. Series I-Vol. XLVII No. 304 Reports of Lt. Gen. Joseph Wheeler, C. S. Army, commanding Cavalry Corps, of operations Jan. 3-April 15.

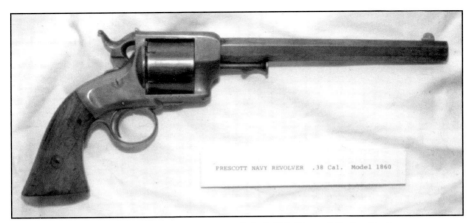

A) Prescott Navy Revolver .38 Cal. (Ft. Harrod Collection)

B) Colt New Model Pistol .36 Cal. Patent 1862. (Ft. Harrod Collection)

B) Detail of chamber of Colt .36 Cal. (Ft. Harrod Collection)

Above: B) Colt New Model Pistol .36 Cal. Patent 1862. Below: C) Colt Sidehammer (rare) .31 Cal. Patent 1855. (Ft. Harrod Collection)

D) Allen & Thurber Pepperbox six-shot .31 Cal. Model 1845 Worchester (Ft. Harrod Collection)

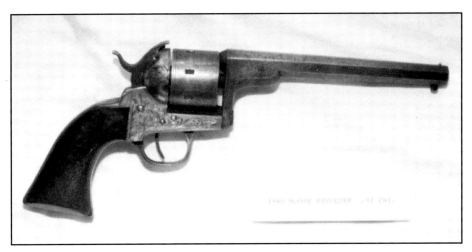

E) 1860 Moore Revolver .32 Cal. (Ft. Harrod Collection)

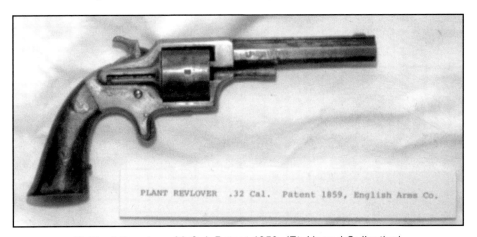

F) Plant Revolver .32 Cal. Patent 1859, (Ft. Harrod Collection)

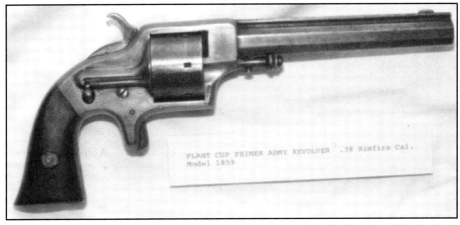

F) Plant Cup Primer Army Revolver .38 Rimfire Cal. Model 1859. (Ft. Harrod Collection)

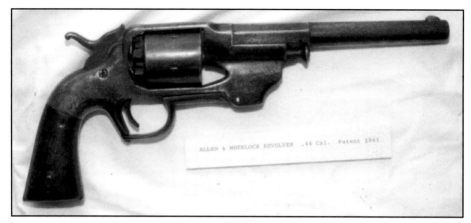

G) Allen & Wheelock Revolver .44 Cal. (Ft. Harrod Collection)

H) Lematt Revolver (Ft. Harrod Collection)

I) Cooper Navy Revolver .36 Cal. (Ft. Harrod Collection)

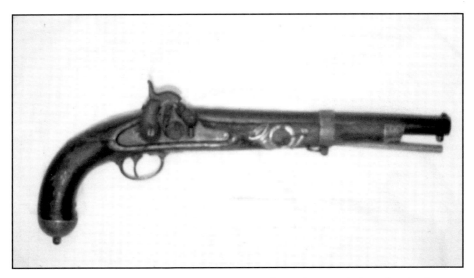

Flintlock conversion to percussion. Notice the infantry hat symbol on the stock, more than likely used by Confederate Cavalry. (Ft. Harrod Collection)

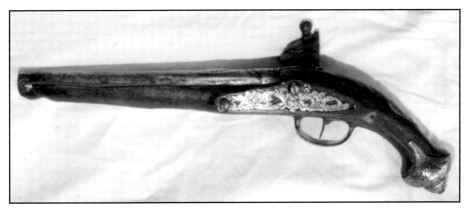

Flintlock with ornate silver inlays on the butt and lock plate, many of these outdated pistols were converted to percussion, since there was a lack of updated arms in the Confederacy when the war broke out. (Ft. Harrod Collection)

Top view of Flintlock. (Ft. Harrod Collection)

Cedar Snagg's Flag, 1st Tennessee Cavalry, participated with the Rangers in the Battle of Bardstown. (Special thanks to John Bersoe and the Tennessee State Museum)

Reproduction of 1861 Texas Rangers Flag

Reproduction of 1863 Texas Rangers Flag

Reproduction 5th Texas Infantry flag; according to C.C. Jefferies, the design may have been used by the Rangers for a flag they owned.

Reproduction of an unknown Texas Infantry flag. Again, this type of design may have been used by the Texas Rangers

18 Ibid.
19 Ibid.
20 O.R. Series I-Vol. XLVII Jan. 1-April 26, 1865-The Campaign of the Carolinas. No. 1 Reports of Maj. Gen. William T. Sherman, U.S. Army, commanding Military Division of the Mississippi.
21 Ibid.
22 Battles and Leaders of the Civil War; The Battle of Bentonville, by Wade Hampton; The Battle of Bentonville, Mark Bradley.
23 Wheeler and His Cavalry; O.R. Series I-Vol. XLVII No. 304 Reports of Lt. Gen. Joseph Wheeler, C. S. Army, commanding Cavalry Corps, of operations Jan. 3-April 15.
24 Terry's Texas Rangers, Leonidas Giles, p. 94-98; Terry Texas Rangers Trilogy, J. P. Blackburn; Wheeler and His Cavalry: 1862-1865, Chapter XIII
25 Ibid.
26 Wheeler and His Cavalry; O.R. Series I-Vol. XLVII No. 304 Reports of Lt. Gen. Joseph Wheeler, C. S. Army, commanding Cavalry Corps, of operations Jan. 3-April 15.
27 Wheeler and His Cavalry; O.R. Series I-Vol. XLVII No. 304 Reports of Lt. Gen. Joseph Wheeler, C. S. Army, commanding Cavalry Corps, of operations Jan. 3-April 15. ; O.R. Series I-Vol. XLVII Jan. 1-April 26, 1865-The Campaign of the Carolinas. No. 1 Reports of Maj. Gen. William T. Sherman, U.S. Army, commanding Military Division of the Mississippi.
28 O.R. Series I-Vol. XLVII Jan. 1-April 26, 1865-The Campaign of the Carolinas. No. 1 Reports of Maj. Gen. William T. Sherman, U.S. Army, commanding Military Division of the Mississippi.
29 Terry's Texas Trilogy. J. P. Blackburn.
30 The Memories of Union General William T. Sherman
31 Terry's Texas Rangers Trilogy, J. P. Blackburn, p. 173.
32 Ibid.
33 The Memories of General William T. Sherman
34 O.R. Series I-Vol.
35 Confederate Veteran, Terry's Texas Rangers, Vol. XV, 1907, p. 49

Chapter 17:
Twilight on Brilliant Careers

After the Civil War, in 1866, Tom Harrison was chosen Judge of his Judicial District, and served until after the Throckmorton Government was set aside and a Provisional Government was established by the United States. In the campaign of 1872, he was chosen by the Democratic Party as one of the Presidential State electors. He became a district judge and anti-Reconstruction Democrat. While married to Sallie McDonald, Harrison had five children: Hallie E., Thomas, who became a stock trader; James A, who became a city attorney; Mary Lou; William Kelley, a graduate of the United States Naval Academy and became a officer in the United States Navy. Thomas Harrison died in Waco, Texas in 1891. [1]

Nathan Bedford Forrest after the war devoted his life to farming and business interests, but he would never amount the wealth that he had before the Civil War. He personally equipped and feed his soldiers, which after four years of war, had broke his fortune. Forrest would give rise to myth and legend for his exploits during the Civil War and would be counted as one of the greatest Civil War Cavalry Generals the South ever had. Forrest died in Memphis, Tennessee on October 29th, 1877. [2]

After the war, Joseph Wheeler became a cotton planter in Alabama, entered politics, and served in the U.S. House of Representatives from 1855-1900. During the Spanish-American war, Wheeler was appointed a major general of volunteers by President McKinley. The appointment was hailed through the country as a healing of the wounds of the Civil War. Wheeler commanded a cavalry division, in his division were the Rough Riders under Theodore Roosevelt. Wheeler's son, who was attending West Point, would serve as his adjutant. Wheeler would participate in the Santiago expedition and took part in the Battle of San Juan Hill. He was sent to the Philippines in command of brigade but soon returned to the U.S. to be commissioned a brigadier general in the Regular Army as of Sept. 10th, 1900. He retired on his 64th birthday, living in Brooklyn, New York, until his death on January 25th, 1906. [3]

In 1864, John Wharton was sent to report to Confederate General Edmund Kirby Smith who was the commander of the Trans-Mississippi Department. Wharton fought in the Battle of Pleasant Hill and Mansfield, and was given high praise for his actions during these two battles. It was during one of these battles, that Wharton had a falling out with Col George Baylor, who commanded a cavalry battalion at the Battle of Mansfield. Baylor criticized Wharton for the useless sacrifice of men in that action. Wharton took offense at such remarks. Matters got worse when Wharton was given a furlough and Baylor was not. The final straw was when the army underwent reorganization and Wharton sent David Terry, brother of Colonel Terry, to take charge of Baylor's command. Baylor went out to find Wharton. On April 6, 1865, Wharton was in Houston, riding in a buggy, heading for the train station, to take a train to Hempstead, along with him was a man named Harrison. Wharton had gone back to Texas on his furlough. the buggy was stopped and Wharton came face to face with Baylor. Baylor insulted Wharton, but before the men could get into a fight, Harrison slapped the horses with his whip and away went the carriage. Wharton wanted to turn around and see Magruder about the matter. Together Wharton and Harrison proceeded to Magruder's hotel room, in the Fannie Hotel. Magruder wasn't in, but Baylor was there. The men began to argue again. Wharton came at Baylor with his fists, and Harrison got in between the two men to prevent them from fighting. Baylor drew his pistol and fired underneath Harrison's arm and shot Wharton. Wharton cried "Oh, oh!", turned around several times and gradually sank to the floor. He stretched himself out on his back, placed his hands across his breast and in a few minutes he was dead. His body was taken back to his home at Eagle Island in Brazoria County, Texas. Wharton had no children and no living relatives. His name would fade into history. Unfortunately his grave is even gone. No trace of it is left. [4]

Frank Armstrong after the war settled in the Southwest, working on the Texas Overland Mail Service, then serving successfully as U.S. Indian inspector and assistant commissioner of Indiana affairs. He died in Bar Harbor, Maine on September Eighth, 1909.[5]

William Humes returned to Memphis after surrendering with General Johnston. Humes resumed his law practice. Later he transferred his office to Huntsville, Alabama, where he died on September 11, 1882.[6]

[1] Who's Who in the Confederacy; Historical Times Illustrated Encyclopedia of the Civil War
[2] Ibid.
[3] Ibid.
[4] C. C. Jeffries Terry's Texas Rangers
[5] Who's Who in the Confederacy; Historical Times Illustrated Encyclopedia of the Civil War
[6] Ibid.

Chapter 18:
Flags of Terry's Texas Rangers:

Terry's Texas Rangers carried two known flags and probably at least two other suspected patterns for their war career. The first pattern was the Bonnie Blue Flag. The flag has a medium blue wool bunting field upon which was placed what was once a yellow star that has faded to an off white. The star is bunting as well. Over the star in painted yellow letters is the phrase "Terry's Texas Rangers" applied on the field in the following measurements: Terry's-2 1/2 and 1 7/8 inches high, Texas-2 inches and 1 1/2 inches high. Rangers-2 inches and 1 1/2 inches high. The differences in the letters are the first letters of each word are taller. The flag was attached to the staff by a double back leading edge that is 1 1/4 inches wide in sleeve for. The flag overall is 23 1/2 inches on the hoist by 32 inches on the fly.

This flag was captured in the Battle of Woodsonville, December 17, 1861. Col. Terry was killed in the battle when he was shot by a member of the 32nd Indiana Infantry. The flag currently is the collection of the Chicago Historical Society. (*Reproduction shown on page 166*)

The second documented flag of Terry's Texas Rangers was made by Miss Flora McIver and Miss Robbie Woodruff, who were living in Nashville, Tennessee at the time. On September 20th, in Florence, Alabama, the flag was presented to Col. Gustave Cook, of the Eighth Texas Regiment. The material was used was a blue silk dress of Miss McIver's and was lined with a white satin wedding dress. The flag was based on the famous Hardee pattern. The field was a parrellogram made of dark blue silk with a white silk circular disc in the middle. A red silk Maltese cross with pointed ends, and not reaching the outer edges of the circle, was in the middle of the disc. Their cross was adorned with eleven gold embroidered five pointed stars with open centers, which was sewn on with white silk floss. On one side of the field and around the cross there was embroidered in Roman unical letter are the word's "Ducit amor Patriae-Terry's Texas Rangers" made of dark blue silk floss; and on the other side, "God defend the right Terry's Texas Rangers." The overall flag dimensions are the disc is 15 1/4 inches in diameter, the cross is two inches wide and eleven inches by eleven inches in length to the points on the ends.; the stars are 1 1/8 inches across the points; the mottos are 3/4 inches high and the units designation is 1 1/8 inches high. The flag was presented at an evening dress parade by Miss McIver's brother, John S. McIver, and the speech was made by Col. Gustavous Cook. The old flag was sent back to Texas.[1] (*Reproduction shown on page 167*)

During the "Rome Races" in Rome, Georgia in 1864, the flag was lost and captured. Leonidas Giles relates the story: "General Harrison, our old colonel, was in command of the forces composed of ours and Ashby's brigade of mounted infantry and a battery of four guns. For some reason, but contrary to all former usages, our regiment was dismounted and placed near the battery, and Ashby's infantry kept mounted to protect the flanks and lead horses. The fight had barely commenced when it was realized from the immense bodies of infantry in our front that it was a bad one. The battery was ordered to the rear, but just as they were limbered the Yankee cavalry poured in on our flanks and completely enveloped us. I didn't give an order to run nor did I hear an order of any kind, but I soon found myself dodging through and among the Yankees cavalry, who were shouting to us to surrender. We reached out horses, which weren't over 150 yards in the rear, mounted, and after a hasty formation charged out through the enemy and although we made repeated rallies they ran us back about five miles. Why the Yankees didn't capture, more of our men is a mystery, as outside of the battery were lost very few prisoners. To give an appropriate name to the battle we called it "Rome Races" for such it was.[2]

In this race the colors furled around the staff and in the oilcloth were lost-not captured."

On May 18th, 1898, a Union soldier named J. J. Wicler, who was a Major commanding the 17th Indiana Volunteer Mounted Infantry, wrote a letter to the Terry's Texas Ranger Association. Wicler had met H. W. Graber, a former member of the Texas Rangers, and Wicler told Graber that they found the Rangers flag the day after the engagement. The Major was commanded by the General to take two companies and move through the woods on the right of their line to a certain point where a country road intersected the main river road then occupied by their brigade. Just before coming into the main road Wicler picked up a package or roll of something, threw it over his saddle, and on his return to the main command examined the package, and found it to be the Terry's Texas Rangers flag in the case. It seems to slipped off the staff and been lost in that way. The flag was in the possession of the 17th Indiana and was returned directly to Louisville and sent by express to Indiana. Since the flag was found and not captured, Wicler felt the flag should be returned to the Rangers. In March 1899, through a special act of the Indiana Legislature, it passed that the flag should be returned to the Texas Rangers and $250.00 was alloted to defray the costs of shipment. The flag was taken to Dallas, Texas by Governor Mount of Indiana, accompanied by his staff and members of the legislature and the Grand Army of the Republic. The flag was returned to the Terry's Texas Rangers during their reunion in Dallas on October, 1899. [3]

In C. C. Jeffries book on the Texas Rangers, he mentions that there was another flag given to the Rangers in the summer of 1862. The makers were Miss Eliza Groce and Annie Jefferson of Hempstead, Texas, just fifty miles north of Houston. The flag was a parrellogram in form. The field was composed of deep red French merino, having ten broad bars of blue silk running crosswise on either side. Upon these were twelve white stars, and one large one where they met at right angles in the center. It was ornamented with a neat tasseled border. A graceful blue streamer flew from the top of the flagstaff, bearing on one side the inscription "We conquer or die" ,and on the other "Terry's Texas Rangers" with two words separated by a five pointed star with the word "Texas" printed between it's points. The care of the flag was entrusted to Ensign Albert C. Jones.[4] *(Reproduction shown on page 168)*

Other flags that might have been used by the Rangers after the loss of their first flag may have been a First National pattern flag, used by many Western Theater units, such as Confederate General John Hunt Morgan. This pattern was very popular for regimental colors. Another flag that may have been used by the Rangers was the Confederate battleflag, issued in the spring of 1864. It is a rectangular flag. The cavalry versions were usually the same as the infantry issues although some were smaller. This type of flag was mentioned but not described in the book "A Terry Texas Ranger-The Life Record of H. W. Graber." At some point before September 1864, they must have either lost their flag, packed it away or their flag was so badly damaged they retired it.

[1]Confederate Veteran: The Texas Ranger's Flag, p. 159; Greg Biggs Essay: Flags of Terry's Texas Rangers
[2]Terry's Texas Rangers, Leonidas Giles.
[3]Confederate Veteran: The Texas Ranger's Flag, p. 159; Greg Biggs Essay: Flags of Terry's Texas Rangers
[4]C. C. Jeffries, Terry Texas Rangers.; Greg Biggs Essay: Flags of Terry's Texas Ranger

Terry's Texas Rangers

Chapter 19:
Pistols and Carbines

E. H. McKnight's .44 caliber Dance Army Revolver, Serial No. 25. and his Terry's Texas Rangers badge (see page 49) which was presented to him at a reunion in 1899. Edward McKnight was a member of Terry's Texas Rangers, Eighth Texas Cavalry, Company K. H e was born on December 4th, 1841 in Washington, Mississippi. He was a deacon of the Baptist Church, in which he served in this capcity for forty years. After the war, McKnight went to Oklahoma on Thanksgiving Day in 1889 and first settled near Eldorado. In 1893 he moved to McKnight and helped build up a good church. The latter part of his life was spent at Hollis. McKnight was married to Miss Katherine Munford in October 1865, and had eleven children. He also had twenty three grandchildren and seven great grand children. He also left three brother at Roswell, New Mexico. Edward died on June 9, 1918 in Hollis, and was buried in the McKnight Cemetery. .He also received the Southern Cross of Honor.

McKnight's J. H. Dance & Brothers Revolver was made in Columbia, Texas. It is a dragoon Type Percussion Revolver, .44 caliber. There were only 275 to 350 of these weapons ever made. The revolver is a six shot with part octagon, part round barrel. It has one piece walnut grips, blued finish, with brass gripstraps left bright.

The J. H. Dance & Brothers company began making the revolvers in 1862, since the need for firearms was so great that the Governor of Texas granted exemption for the company's work force from military service. The factory was later moved from Columbia to a new site a few miles away. Following the move the manufacture of revolvers was not resumed. (Revolver and Badge Courtesy of Donald Bryan) (Resource Flayderman's Guide to Antique American Firearms, 6th Edition)

Illustrations of the following are found on pages 161-164

(A) Prescott Navy Reolver,.38 caliber, five groove rifling. Edwin A. Prescott of Worcester, Massachusetts and Norwich, Connecticut, an ex-employee of Ethan Allen, was the patentee and maker of these .38 caliber rimfire cartridge revolvers. His design was granted patent #30,245 on October 2, 1860, and manufacture of the revolvers began in his Worcester, Massachusetts armory. Once the revolvers were made they were distributed by Merwin & Bray. Prescott was hoping for a lucrative government contract for his new revolver. Unfortunately the weapon was an infringement upon the Rollin White patent, which was assigned to Smith & Wesson, and production on the Prescott Revolver was stopped in 1863. No records exist indicating that any were ever bought or issued by the Federal government. Some of the Prescott revolvers are known to have been carried and used by Union officers and enlisted men during the Civil War. The number of these revolvers produced is not known but the consensus seems to be that it did not exceed several hundred. Of that amount about 25% had iron frames and 75% brass frames.

(B) Colt New Model Pistol, .36 caliber, patent 1862- Between 1862 to 1872 there were 25,000 produced. The Colt New Model had a round, roll engraved cylinder (stagecoach hold up scene) octagonal barrel, and hinged loading lever of the Pocket Navy. It was a five shot with different barrel lengths of 4 1/2, 5 1/2, and 6 1/2.

(C) Colt Model 1855 Sidehammer, .31 caliber-The Side Hammer Colts are known as the Root Models, since E. K. Root patent of 1855 illustrated a prototype pistol with distinctive side mount hammer. A unique feature to the Root was a pattern of grooves on the cylinder surface, cut precisely to engage an aperture attached to the hammer. On cocking, this hammer connection would revolve the cylinder to the next chamber for firing. Only a handful of these prototype pistols survived. A better technique of turning cylinders was an internal hand attached to the hammer. To align each chamber for firing, a stop was devised which did not engage the cylinder itself, but rather slots on the back end of the cylinder pin. Access to the internal mechanism was only by removing a plate on the left side of the frame and pulling off the stocks. There were 40,000 pistols made in .28 and .31 caliber between 1855 till 1870. All pistols were 5 shot.

(D) Allen & Thurber Pepperbox, .31 caliber, Model 1845- One of the best known of the pre war firearm gun makers was Ethan Allen of Massachusetts. Allen started making cutlery in Milford, Massachusetts in 1831, and in 1837 he move his factory to Grafton and started to manufacture pistols. His first patent was highly successful pepperbox. Allen's pepperbox was a double action lock which made his gun the fastest firing handgun in the world, far better than Colt revolver for more than a decade. Loaded and primed in advance, one of these double action pistols could be drawn and fired in a single action. The bar hammer was streamlined so that there were no rough contours to catch in the belt or clothing, and the charges in the extra barrels gave assurance that there were shots in reserve if the first should miss. Allen moved his business to Worcester, Massachusetts in 1847. For twenty five years Allen was in partnership with his brothers in law Chalres T. Thurber and later Thomas Wheelock. Between 1856 till 1864, the company was known as Allen & Wheelock.

(E) 1860 Moore Revolver, .32 caliber, The front loading revolvers that probably had the largest sales were those that fired teat cartridges. These revolvers were manufactured by Moore's Patent Fire Arms Company, Brooklyn, New York and alter by the National Firearms Company, Brooklyn. The dealers of these weapons told the public not to buy the new Smith and Wesson revolvers that had been flooding the market, but to buy the Moore revolver since the Smith and Wesson left the cartridge heads fully exposed at the rear. They argued that the explosive force of the powder acted backward as well as forward, and that energy was wasted and bullet velocity reduced by having the chamber wide open at the rear, with only a weak recoil shield to back the cartridge and protect the shooter. The teat cartridges were made in .45 caliber and .32 caliber.

(F) A. Plant Revolver .32 Caliber, Patent 1859 and B. Plant Cup Revolver, .38 caliber rimfire Model 1859-The revolvers were made by the Plant's Manufacturing Company, New Haven, Connecticut. The patent was issued July 12th, 1859 to Willard C. Ellis and John N. White of Springfield, Massachusetts. The weapon had a cylinder chamber that was not entirely bored through, sot hat a small round opening was formed at the rear to permit the tip of the hammer to pass through and strike within the hollowed base of the cartridge. This construction left at the rear of the chamber an annular ring, or shoulder, which served adequately as a recoil shield. The earlier, hinged frame has a fixed ejecting rod. This anchored to the barrel, and removal of waste cases requires taking the cylinder out of the frame so a chamber may be pushed over the rod. The early cartridges had a narrow flange projecting outward at right angles a the bullet end. This flange was to give a hold for removing the exploded shell.

(G) Allen & Wheelock revolver .44 Caliber, Patent 1861-By 1861 Ethan Allen had made corrections to his Allen & Wheelock Revolver. The side hammer was gone and a center hammer was put in it's place. The cylinder pin was removed from the back of the frame to the front. The center hammer revolvers were made in .36 and .44 caliber. From 1861 till 1862 seven hundred and fifty .44 caliber center hammer revolvers were made and about five hundred Navy Models were made. When the Civil War broke out the Ordnance Department bought five hundred and thirty six Allen revolvers for $9,130.50. In December 1861, the Ordnance Department bought on the open market 198 Allen revolvers from William Read & Sons of Boston. The weapons cost about $22.00 a piece amounting to $4,356.00. About 338, .36 caliber revolvers were also purchased. It's known that the .44 Allen & Wheelock Revolvers were used by the 2nd Michigan Cavalry, 3rd Michigan Cavalry, and the Eighth Pennsylvania Cavalry. By the end of the war, there were 38 Allen revolvers in storage at the New York Arsenal. In 1901, 38 revolvers were sold to Francis Bannerman for $26.27 each. Allen died in 1871, and Wheelock died in 1864. Allen added two sons in laws, Sullivan Forehand and Henry Wadsworth. In 1871, the company became known as the Forehand and Wadsworth Company, and in 1902 it became the Hopkins & Allen Manufacturing Company. The center hammer fires a lip cartridge, in which the fulminate is concentrated in a small prominence on the cartridge rim. The chambers are bored through as in rimfire revolvers. A small cut to hold the lip of the cartridge was made in the rear of the cylinder a the edge of each chamber mouth. It was necessary to place each cartridge so the lip would fit into the cut prepared for it.

(H) LeMatt-.42 caliber, lower chamber .63 caliber-Jean Alexandre Francois LeMat was a French born physician and Colonel on the staff of the Louisiana governor. He was granted an American patent in October 1856 for a two barrel pistol combining features of both revolver and shotgun. A nine shot .42 caliber cylinder, aligned to a standard barrel, revolved upon a central grapeshot barrel of .63 caliber. A moveable hammer nose fired either barrel at will. Under a partnership with soon to be Confederate General P. G. T. Beauregard, some three hundred were made in New Orleans. The revolver was never officially adopted by the U.S. even though it was approved by the Military board. The partnership between Beauregard and LeMat soon dissolved. In 1861, LeMat along with Charles Girard moved their factory to Paris, France and contracted with the Confederate Army and Navy. Some 2,200 guns were made in Paris. In 1864, the factory was moved to Birmingham, England and another 1,000 pistols were produced. All percussion revolvers are considered Confederate.

(I) J. M. Cooper & Co., Philadelphia, Pennsylvania Navy Revolver, .32 caliber-Made between 1864 to 1869. About 15,000 of these weapons were made. It was a five shot, 4", 5" or 6" octagonal barrel. It was privately purchased, since there are no known government contracts.

Resources
Early percussion Firearms, Lewis Winant, William Morrow & Company New York, 1959.
Civil War Guns-William Edwards, Thomas Publications, 1997
Encyclopedia of Firearms, Harold Peterson
The Colt Heritage, R. L. Wilson, Simon and Schuster, 1979
Flayderman's Guide to Antique Firearms, 6th Edition.

Carbines
Illustrations of the following ar found on page 96

1. Spencer Carbine Model 1863: The Spencer carbine was invented by Christopher Spencer in 1860, and founded the Spencer Repeating Rifle Company, of Boston, Massachusetts. The Spencer was one of the most widely used and popular firearms, and was one of the deciding factors in the Union winning the War. It was used mainly for cavalry use. The carbine was a .52 caliber rimfire, 22" barrel, with six groove rifling. The Spencer used an all metallic cartridge with a built in primer. The magazine allowed the user to fire seven rounds in thirty seconds. [1]

2. Spencer Carbine Model 1865: Same as the Spencer Carbine 1863 except it was a .50 caliber instead of a .52 caliber.

3. Model 18S5 Colt Repeating Carbine: The Colt Repeating carbine was made between 1856 to 1864. They came in 36, 44, and 56 calibers, and came in five or six shot cylinders. Barrel lengths varied between 15", 18", and 21". All barrels were round in shape with semi octagonal breech. The Colt Repeating Carbine was basically a large version of the Colt revolver. Elisha Root, Colt's armory superintendent, was a major contributor to the weapon's design. The weapon was loaded by firmly seating each chamber with a cone shaped bullet that came in a paper cartridge, with the lever action ramrod. The nipples at the back of each chamber had to be fitted with a percussion cap. During the Civil War, the U.S. government purchased only 4,712 of the Colt Repeaters. One major problem with the Colt repeater was the tendency for all cylinders to ignite at once. The 21st Ohio were armed with Colt Repeaters at the Battle of Chickamauga, and many of the Confederates during the battle thought the regiment was an entire division. [2]

4. Model 1855 "First Model" Sporting Rifle: The Model 1855 was manufactured between 1856-59. It came in .36 caliber, six shot cylinder. The barrel length varied between 15" and 18" in the carbine size, and 21", 24", and 27" and 30" in the rifle. Round in shape and semi octagonal at the breech. It was the first of Colt's production of revolving firearms in Hartford, Connecticut, and one of the few sidehammers longarm groups to be individually serial numbered. [3]

5. Cosmopolitan Carbine: The Cosmopolitan Carbine was made by the Cosmopolitan Arms Company of Hamiton, Ohio, which was owned by E. Gwyn and A. C. Campbell. it came in a .52 caliber, percussion, breechloader. It had a 19' round barrel with an octagonal section at the breech The distinctive feature was the hammer. Only about 1,140 were made and were delivered to cavalry units of Illinois and delivered in June of 1862. They were also issued to the 5th and 6th Illinois cavalry. It was loaded by unlatching the trigger guard, which depressed the breechblock's forward section and unsheathed the cartridge chamber. [4]

6. Gallager Carbine: The Gallager Carbine was made by Richardson & Overman, of Philadelphia. There were about 23,000 of these weapons made. It came in a .50 caliber, was percussion capped, breechloader. It was a single shot, with the barrel sliding forward to load. It had a 22 1/4 round barrel. The Gallager saw extensive use during the Civil War. Among the cavalry units known to have used the Gallager were the 3rd, 4th, 6th Ohio, the 13th Tennessee, and the 3rd West Virginia. It was the most inexpensive carbine on the market, costing only $30 dollars. The U.S. Government purchased about 18,000 of these rifles between 1861 to 1864. [5]

7. & 8. Ballard Carbine: It was among the most famous of American single shot breechloading carbines. It was invented by Charles H. Ballard of Worcester, Massachusetts in 1861. The Ballard was manufactured by five different firms. They were Ball and Williams; Dwight, Chapin & Company, R. Ball & Company; Merrimack Arms & Manufacturing and Brown manufacturing Company. Six thousand carbines made during the Civil War went to fill contracts. The State of Kentucky bought 4,600 of the carbines. New York bought five hundred of the carbines in 1863. They came in a .44 rimfire, 22 1/8" part round part octagonal. Units to have used the Ballard were the 13th and 45th Kentucky cavalries. To load the weapon the user pushed the curved trigger guard lever forward, freeing the breechblock from the barrel, and then dropped a .44 caliber copper rimfire cartridge into the chamber, returned the trigger guard lever to it's former position. [6]

9. Remington Rolling Block: The Rolling Block was made between 1867 to 1888. Over one million of these weapons were made during that time period. Although a post war weapon, the original concept for the single shot Breech Loading Carbine was in invented in 1865. It came in a 46 and 50 caliber rimfire. It had a 20" round barrel fastened with a single barrel band. It was Remington's earliest production longarms chambered for metallic cartridge ammunition. They were also the last type arms supplied to the Union government on contract prior to the ending of the Civil War. Later the Civil War Remington's were equipped with the Rolling Block. [7]

10. Two Trigger Wesson Rifle, Second Model: The Wesson Rifle was made between 1859 to 1888 at Worcester, Massachusetts. Frank Wesson was granted a patent in October 1858 for a breech locking bolt, the breech elevating spring and wedge shaped recess in the standing breech to accommodate the rim of a metallic cartridge. The Wesson Two Trigger came in a .22, .32, .38, and .44 caliber. The weapon shown is a .32 caliber, and barrel lengths came in 24" to 28". [8]

11. Allen Drop Breech Rimfire Rifle: The Allen Drop Breech Rimfire Rifle was made by Allen & Wheelock, Ethan Allen & Company, between 1860 to 1871. About 2,000 of these weapons were made during this time period. They came in a variety of calibers ranging from 22 to 44 rimfire. It was a single shot weapon with a part round, part octagonal barrel. Lengths varied from 23" to 28". The breech opened by lowering the trigger guard, the motion ejecting the empty cartridge, hammer cocked manually. [9]

---

[1] Flayderman's Guide to Antique Firearms, 6th Edition, p. 518; Atlas Editions, Spencer Rifles
[2] Flayderman's Guide, p. 78; Atlas Editions, Colt Repeating Rifles
[3] Flayderman's Guide, p. 78
[4] Flayderman's guide, p. 507; Arms & Equipment of the Union, p. 54.
[5] Flayderman's Guide, p. 508; Arms & Equipment of the Union, p. 57
[6] Flayderman's Guide, p. 125-126; Arms & Equipment of the Union, p. 63
[7] Flayderman's Guide, p. 152-53.
[8] Ibid., p. 228-229
[9] Flayderman's Guide, p. 60

References

Books

Terry Texas Rangers Trilogy, State House Press, Austin, Texas, 1996.
Memorial and Biographical History of McLennan, Falls, Bell, and Coryell Counties, Texas, 1893, Texas State Archives.
Terry's Rangers, C. C. Jeffries, Vantage Press, Inc., New York, N.Y., 1961.
Terry's Texas Rangers, Eighth Texas Cavalry, C.S.A., An Address by Lester Fitzhugh, March 21, 1958.
Terry's Texas Rangers, Leonidas Giles, The Pemberton Press, Austin, Texas, 1967
The Campaigns of Lt. Gen. General Nathan Bedford Forrest and of Forrest's Cavalry, General Thomas Jordan and J. P. Pryor, Da Capo Press, New York, 1996, originally published 1868.
The Orphan Brigade: The Kentucky Confederates Who Couldn't Go Home, William Davis, LSU Press, 1980.
Who's Who in the Confederacy, Stewart Sifakis, Facts on File, New York, 1988.
Historical Times Illustrated Encyclopedia of the Civil War, Patricia Faust, 1986, Harper & Row, New York.
The Charles C. McCormick Papers, Colonel, 7th PA. Cavalry, Transcribed by Larry K. Fryer.
Pottsville Miner's Journal, The Civil War Letters of the 7th Pennsylvania Cavalry, Interpreted by Larry Fryer.
Batchelor-Turner Letters 1861-1864 Written by two of Terry's Texas Rangers. Annotated by H.J. H. Rugeley. 1961, The Steck Company, Austin, Texas.
Battles and Leaders of the Civil War.
Cozzens, Peter, This Terrible Sound: The Battle of Chickamauga, University of Illinois Press, 1992.
Dodson, W. C., Wheeler's Confederate Cavalry Association, Campaigns of Wheeler and His Cavalry, 1862-65, Hudgins, Publishing, Co., Atlanta, 1899, reprinted 1997 Morningside.
Starr, Stephen, The Union Cavalry in the Civil War, Volume III, The War in the West, 1861-1865, Louisiana State University Press, Baton Rouge and London, 1985.
They Rode with Forrest and Wheeler; John Fisher, Mcfarland & Co., Inc., Publishers, 1995.
Graber, Henry: A Terry Texas Ranger: the life Record of H. W. Graber/new introduction by Thomas W. Cutrer, Austin, Texas, Texas State House Press, 1987.
Confederate Military History Extended Edition, Wilmington, NC., Broadfoot Publishing Company.
History of Kentucky, Judge Charles Kerr, William Elsey Connelley, and E. M. Coulter, Volume II, The American Historical Society, 1922.
The Rebellion Record: A diary of American Events, Edited by Francis Moore, New York, 1866.
Sword, Wiley, Shiloh: Bloody April, Morningside Bookshop, 1988, Dayton, Ohio
Daniel, Larry, Shiloh: The Battle that Changed the Civil War
Early Battles in Kentucky: The Road to Shiloh, Time Life Books.
Civil War Cards
Civil War Battles of the Western Theater, Bryan Bush
Wild Riders of the 1st Kentucky Cavalry

Letters

The Pearce Collection: The Issac Fulkerson Letters, Navarro College, 3200 West 7th Ave., Corsicana, Texas 75110
The Cyrus Love Letters, Mary Counts Burnett Library, Texas Christian University
The Civil War Letters of John Rabb
The Civil War Letters of Henry S. Bunting, Texas State Library and Archives Commission

Articles

Civil War History, With Terry's Texas Rangers: The Letters of Dunbar Affleck, edited by Robert W. Williams, Jr. and Raplh A. Wooster, Vol. 9, 1963.
Surrender or Die, William Brooksher and David Snider.
Blue & Gray Magazine: The Battle of Mill Springs

Confederate Veteran Magazine

Confederate Veteran, Vol. XI, 1903, Davis, W. H., Company F, Fourth Tennessee Cavalry, Cavalry Service under Gen. Wheeler.
Confederate Veteran, W. H. Davis, Kilpatrick's Spotted Horse.
Confederate Veteran, Terry's Texas Rangers, Monument to that Gallant Cavalry Regiment.
Confederate Veteran, The Texas Ranger's Flag.
Confederate Veteran, Sensations in Kentucky Backwoods, McDonald, Ward, Fourth Alabama Cavalry, Powderly, Texas.
Confederate Veteran,-Vol. XXVI-Scouting with Wheeler-by Ed Kennedy
Confederate Veteran-Vol.XIX-Scouting with Wheeler-by E. H. McKnight
Confederate Veteran-Vol. XXVI-The Last Roll-Edward McKnight
Confederate Veteran-Vol. VIII-1900-Reminiscences of Fighting in Kentucky, by L.S. Ferrell, Number One, Tennessee.
Southern Bivouac, The Texas Rangers, A. P. Harcourt.
Greg Biggs Essay: Flags of Terry's Texas Rangers

Official Records of the Civil War

O.R. Series I-Vol. II The Bull Run or Manassas Campaign, Va.
No. 100 Report of Gen. James Longstreet, C. S., commanding the 4th Brigade.
O. R. Series I-Vol. IV
Chapter XII Correspondence, Orders, & Returns Relating Specially to Operations in Ky, Tenn., from July 1 to Nov. 19, 1861, Confederate Correspondence, Etc. #4
O.R. Series I-Vol. VII Dec. 17, 1861, Action at Rowlett's Station, (Woodsonville) Green River, Ky.
No. 3 Col. August Willich, 32nd Indiana
No. 4 Brig. Gen. Thomas Hindman, C. S. Army, with congratulatory orders from Maj. Gen. Hardee.
O.R. Series I-Vol. X Pittsburgh Landing, or Shiloh, Tenn
No. 180 Report of Col. Preston Pond, Jr., 16th Louisiana Infantry, commanding Third Brigade
No. 185 Report of Captain William H. Ketchum, Alabama Battery.
No. 229 Report of Col. John A. Wharton, Texas Rangers Unattached
Appendix April 8, 1862 Reconnaissance from Shiloh Battlefield. Report of Thomas Harrison, Texas rangers, unattached
Skirmish on Elk River, Tenn., Report No. 2 Lt. Col. Woodward, First Kentucky Cavalry (Confederate)
O.R. Series I-Vol. XVI
No. 8 Report of Lt. Col. John C. Parkhurst, 9th Michigan Infantry
O.R. Series I-Vol. XXVIII
No. 12 Report of Brig. Gen. N. B. Forrest, C. S. Army, commanding Cavalry Brigade.
No. 1 Report of Brig. Gen. Thomas Wood, U.S. Army, of skirmish at Little Pond.
No. 2 Report of Capt. Henry R. Miller, 18th Ohio Infantry, of skirmish at Short Mountain Crossroads.
No. 3 Report of Col. Edward P. Fyffe, 26th Ohio Infantry, skirmish at Little Pond.
O.R. Series 1-Vl. XVI/1 Battle of Perryville or Chaplin Hills, Ky.
No. 31
Oct. 4th Skirmish near Bardstown, Ky. Report of Maj. Gen. George H. Thomas, U. S. Army.
O.R. Series I-Vol. XLVII/1 [S#98] No. 1 The Campaign of the Carolinas
O.R. Series I-Vol. XLVII/1 [S#98] No. 293 The Campaign of the Carolinas
O.R. Series 1-Vol. XLVII/1 [S#98] No. 292 The Campaign of the Carolinas
O.R. Series 1-Vol. XLVII/1 [S#98] No. 301 The Campaign of the Carolinas
O.R. Series 1-Vol. XLVII/2 [S#99]
O.R. Series 1-Vol. XXXVII/2 [s#73] No. 383 The Atlanta Campaign
O.R. Series 1-Vol. XXXVIII/2 [S#73] The Atlanta Campaign No. 399
O.R. Series 1-Vol. XXXVIII/3 [S#74] The Atlanta Campaign No. 713
O.R. Series 1-Vol. XXX/2 [S#51} No. 28
O.R. Series 1-Vol. XXXI/1 [S#54] No. 7
O.R. Series 1-Vol. XXXI/1 [S#54] No. 10
O.R. Series 1-Vol. XXXII/1 [S#57] No. 3
O.R. Series 1-Vol. XXXII/1 [S#57] No. 3
O.R. Series 1-Vol. XXXII/1 [S#57] No. 2
O.R. Series 1-Vol. XXXII/1 [S# 57] No. 1
O.R. Series 1-Vol. XXXII/1 [S# 57] No. 2
O.R. Series 1-Vol. XXXII/1 [S# 57] No. Jan. 10-11, 1864-Scout from Near Dandridge to Clark's Ferry, Tenn. Report of Col. William Palmer, 15th Penn. Cavalry
O.R. Series 1-Vol. XXXI/1 [S# 54] No. 77
O.R. Series 1-Vol. XXX/2 [S# 51] No. 433

O.R. Series 1-Vol. XXIII/1 [S# 34] No. 5
O.R. Series 1-Vol. XXIII/1 [S# 34] No. 84
O.R. Series 1-Vol. XXIII [S# 34] No. 101
O.R. Series 1-Vol. XXIII/1 [S# 34] Abstract from "Record of Events" Second Brigade, Second Cavalry Division, Department of the Cumberland, commanded by Col. Eli Long.
O.R. Series 1-Vol. XXIII/1 [S# 34] No. 92
O.R. Series 1-Vol. XXIII/1 [S# 34] No. 6
O.R. Series 1-Vol. XXIII/1 [S# 34] No. 5
O.R. Series 1-Vol. XXVI/2 [S# 42] Confederate Correspondence, Orders and Returns to Operations in West Florida, Southern Alabama, Southern Mississippi, Louisiana, Texas, and New Mexico. From May 14 to December 31, 1863 #18
O.R. Series 1-Vol. XXII Appendix, No. 923
O.R. Series 1-Vol. XXXII The Stone's River Campaign, No. 811
O.R. Series 1-Vol. XXXII The Stone's River Campaign, No. 966
O.R. Series 1-Vol. XVII Confederate Correspondence, No. 781
O.R. Series 1-Vol. XXXII, No 81
O.R. Series 1-Vol. XXII, P. 626
O.R. Series 1-Vol. XXVIII, P. 810
O.R. Series 1-Vol. XXIII/1 [S# 34] March 19th-Skirmish near College Grove, Tenn. Report of Brig. Gen. John A. Wharton, C. S. Army.
O.R. Series 1-Volume XXX/1 The Chickamauga Campaign. No. 3 Report of Maj. William S. Rosecrans, U.S. Army, commanding the Army of the Cumberland.
O.R. Series 1-Volume XXXI-November 4-December 23, 1863-The Knoxville Campaign. No. 76-Report of Maj. Gen. Joseph Wheeler, C. S. Army, commanding Cavalry Corps.
O.R. Series I-Volume XXXI-The Knoxville Campaign-No. 77-Report of Maj. Gen. William T. Martin, C. S. Army, commanding Longstreet's cavalry.
O.R. Series I-Volume XXXI-December 24-28, 1863-Operations near Mossy Creek and Dandridge, Tenn., No.2-Reports of Brig. Gen. Samuel Sturgis, U.S. Army, commanding Cavalry Corps, Department of the Ohio.

Special Thanks

Many of the firearms shown in this book may be seen at the **Old Fort Harrod State Park**. Old Fort Harrod State Park commemorates the first permanent European settlement west of the Alleghenies. In March 1774, Captain James Harrod and thirty-two determined, brave men left Pennsylvania, and set out for Kentucky to claim lands and make a settlement. After a long and adventuresome journey, on June 16, 1774, Harrod and his men laid out a town, naming it Harrodstown. Today, Old Fort Harrod is a replica of the original. Enjoy a "living history" experience as you visit the cabins and blockhouses, complete with pioneer furnishings, where costumed craftspeople perform tasks such as weaving, basketry, woodworking, broom-making, and blacksmithing. Children will especially enjoy meeting the creature residents – cattle, sheep and turkey – in the fort corral! "Living History" with craftspeople and animals mid April thru October.

Fort open year-round, admission charged, group rates available. (Closed Thanksgiving, Christmas week, and Mondays in January)

8:30 a.m. - 5:00 p.m. March 16 - October 31
8:00 a.m. - 4:30 p.m. November 1 - March 15

Mansion Museum: This Greek Revival home was built by Major James Taylor in 1830. Museum displays include Civil War history, McIntosh Gun collection, and Indian artifacts.

9:00 a.m. - 5:30 p.m. March 16 - October 31
8:30 a.m. - 5:00 p.m. November 1 - March 15

About the Author

Bryan Bush was born in 1966 in Louisville, Kentucky and has been a native of that city ever since. He graduated with honors from Murray State University with a degree in History and Psychology. Bryan has always had a passion for history, especially the Civil War. He has been a member of many different Civil War historical preservation societies, has consulted for movie companies and other authors, coordinated with other museums on displays of various museum articles and artifacts, has written for magazines, such as *Kentucky Civil War Magazine*, and *North/South Trader*, and worked for many different historical sites, and has always fought hard to maintain and preserve Civil War history in the Western Theater. In 1999, Bryan published his first work: *The Civil War Battles of the Western Theater*, which was given good reviews by *North/South Magazine*, and *Kentucky Monthly*. *Kentucky Monthly* said Bryan Bush "has with his first book created a needed addition to any serious Civil War library." The book remains one of Turner Publishing's better sellers of Kentucky history. Bryan has been a Civil War reenactor for seven years, portraying a artillerist. For five years Bryan was on the Board of Directors and curator for the Old Bardstown Civil War Museum and Village: The Battles of the Western Theater Museum in Bardstown, Kentucky. For the last two years Bryan has been co-chairman for the Battle of Corydon.

$39.95

Also By BRYAN BUSH:
The Civil War Battles of the Western Theatre

- ❖ History of the 14 major battles in the West
- ❖ Complete order of battles
- ❖ 700 photos, maps, charts, and illustrations, featuring full color, rare and never seen artifacts, uniforms, weapons and accessories, such as John Hunt Morgan's ruby-crusted pistols and NINE Orphan Brigade uniforms!
- ❖ 8 1/2 x 11, 225 pages

To request a copy, write to:
Civil War Battles of the Western Theatre
Turner Publishing Company
P.O. Box 3101
Paducah, KY 42002-3101

Civil War Battles of the Western Theatre: $39.95
Shipping & Handling: (first book) $5.00, (each additional book) $3.50

Order over the phone: 1-800-788-3350
(270) 443-0121

Or on the Web at: www.turneronline.com

Index

Symbols
105th Ohio 59
10th Indiana 19
10th Michigan 83
10th Mississippi 44
10th Ohio 84, 119, 120
11th Kentucky 116
11th Texas 76, 79, 84, 97, 98, 104, 116, 122, 126, 129, 147, 151
123rd Illinois 111
12th Alabama 152
12th Corps 140
12th Tennessee 57
13th Arkansas 12
13th Indiana 43, 44
13th Kentucky 177
13th Louisiana 28
13th Pennsylvania 158
13th Tennessee 177
14th Army Corps 148
14th Corps 85, 101, 102, 130, 145, 146, 148, 152, 153, 155, 156, 158
14th Iowa 26
14th Texas 76
154th Tennessee 13
15th Corps 145, 151, 152, 153, 158
15th Mississippi 19
15th Ohio 16
15th Pennsylvania 88, 119, 120
15th Wisconsin 67
16th Corps 133
16th Kentucky 120
16th Louisiana 26
17th Corps 145, 151, 152, 153, 155, 157, 158
17th Indiana 52, 145, 43, 173
18th Indiana 120, 122
18th Louisiana 26, 27
18th Ohio 41, 42
18th Regulars 43
19th Alabama 71

19th Confederate 103
19th Corps 151
19th Louisiana 28
19th Ohio 72
19th Tennessee 19
1st Alabama 57, 111, 152
1st Arkansas 28
1st Brigade 13, 70, 74, 116, 118, 120, 122
1st Cavalry 57, 66
1st Confederate 69
1st Corps 28
1st Division 10, 120, 122, 131, 153
1st East Tennessee 122
1st Georgia 36, 38, 39, 115, 119
1st Kentucky 19, 34, 37, 46, 57, 59, 61, 87, 122, 151
1st Louisiana 43, 71
1st Middle Tennessee 67
1st Mississippi Rifles 7
1st Ohio 19, 104
1st Platoon 59
1st Squadron 69
1st Tennessee 119, 120, 166
1st Texas Rangers 35
20th Corps 85, 101, 102, 140, 145, 146, 151, 152, 153, 155, 156, 158
20th Mississippi 44
20th Tennessee 19
21st Corps 85
21st Kentucky 72
21st Ohio 176
22nd Alabama 71
22nd Indiana 67
23rd Kentucky 72
24th Ohio 72
25th Alabama 71
25th Illinois 66, 71
25th Iowa 153
25th Missouri 21
26th Alabama 71

26th Ohio 40, 43
29th Mississippi 44
2nd Arkansas 86
2nd Brigade 26, 28, 104, 120, 130, 156
2nd Cavalry 57, 122
2nd Corps 28
2nd Div. 10, 28, 74, 135
2nd Georgia 36, 38, 39, 46, 57, 67, 69, 70, 79, 119
2nd Kentucky 72, 88
2nd Michigan 119, 120, 175
2nd Minnesota 19
2nd Mississippi 115
2nd Tennessee 130
30th Illinois 71
30th Ohio 72
31st Indiana 28
32nd Indiana 2, 5, 14, 17, 172
33rd Kentucky 43
33rd Ohio 59
35th Indiana 72
38th Tennessee 26, 28
39th Alabama 71
39th Indiana 16, 136
3rd Alabama 57, 108, 111, 152
3rd Arkansas 116, 121, 122, 126, 130, 137, 147, 151
3rd Brigade 26, 28, 103, 153
3rd Confederate 69, 81, 88, 104
3rd Corps 28
3rd Division 28, 72, 130, 140, 146
3rd Georgia 57, 119
3rd Indiana 46
3rd Kentucky 99
3rd Louisiana 114
3rd Michigan 175
3rd Minnesota 37, 38
3rd Mississippi 26
3rd Ohio 84, 177
3rd West Virginia 177

42nd Georgia 157
42nd Illinois 66
44th Indiana 72
44th Mississippi 44
45th Kentucky 177
49th Ohio 16
4th Alabama 43, 44
4th Alabama 110, 154
4th Alabama 10, 118
4th Corps 132
4th Georgia 36, 38, 39
4th Illinois 32
4th Indiana 119, 123
4th Kentucky 19, 37, 46
4th Louisiana 28
4th Michigan 67
4th Ohio 46, 69, 84, 107, 177
4th Tennessee 20, 41, 46, 47, 48, 57, 66, 79, 104, 110, 122, 132, 136, 146, 147, 151, 153, 154
50th Indiana 44
51st Alabama 111
53rd Ohio 26
58th Indiana 43
59th Illinois 67
5th Arkansas 85
5th Confederate 134
5th Illinois 120, 177
5th Indiana 128
5th Kentucky 99
5th Wisconsin 67
66th Indiana 141
66th Indiana 43, 44
69th Ohio 76
6th Arkansas 86
6th Confederate 57
6th Georgia 115, 119, 177
6th Kentucky 57, 72
6th Ohio 177
74th Illinois 67
74th Indiana 43, 44
75th Illinois 69
77th Ohio 32
7th Alabama 44, 120
7th Arkansas 86
7th Mississippi 44

7th Pennsylvania 37, 59, 67
81st Indiana 66, 71
83rd Illinois 78, 79
86th Indiana 72
89th Indiana 43, 44
8th Arkansas 86
8th Confederate 57, 127
8th Indiana 43
8th Iowa 29
8th Kansas 66
8th Kentucky 37
8th Pennsylvania 175
8th Texas 17, 48
8th Wisconsin 66, 71
99th Ohio 72
9th Michigan 37, 38, 41
9th Mississippi 44
9th Ohio 19
9th Pennsylvania 120
9th Tennessee 148

A
Abbott 44
Aberdeen 7
Ackworth 130, 131
Adairsville 129
Adams 31, 34, 35, 61, 100, 105
Adam's Ford 152
Adrian 57
Affleck 47, 57, 59, 62, 69, 71, 73, 74
Aiken 152
Alabama Cav. 41
Alatoona 143
Alexander 116
Alexandria 39, 83, 101
Allatoona 144
Allen 57, 121, 126, 127, 128, 129, 130, 132, 139, 151, 152, 155, 174, 175
Alley's Creek 131
Alltoona 129
Alpine 101, 102
Alston 153
Altamaha River 149
Altamont 36, 40

Ammen 30
Anderson 9, 26, 47, 48, 57, 61, 88, 106, 110, 126, 135, 136, 137, 141, 145, 147, 151
Antietam 115
Antioch Station 40, 83
Appler 26
Appomattox 158
Arkansas Inf. 13, 14
Armstrong 54, 105, 108, 114, 116, 118, 119, 120, 121, 122, 123, 160, 171
Army of Northern Virginia 99, 158
Army of Tennessee 63, 68, 81, 85, 97, 112, 114, 125, 126, 128, 132, 134, 135, 140, 144, 143, 158
Army of the Cumberland 68, 85, 126, 128, 132
Army of the Mississippi 41, 46, 57
Army of the Ohio 41, 63, 126, 131, 134
Army of the Potomac 157
Ash 32
Ashby 69, 126, 130, 135, 136, 144, 147, 148, 151, 155, 172
Ashland 76
Athens 35, 101, 139
Atkins 156
Atlanta 94, 132, 133, 134, 135, 139, 140, 141, 143, 144, 145
Atlanta Campaign 6, 123, 125, 126
Attack on Dover 78, 79, 81
Auburn 83
Augusta 146, 148, 151, 152, 155
Averasboro 156
Avery 102
Ayer 65

B
Bacot 41
Baird 101, 102, 103, 104, 105
Baker 81
Bale 119
Ballard 177
Bankhead 12
Banning 106
Bar Harbor 171
Barboursville 63
Bardstown 4, 45, 46, 47, 48, 63, 105, 181
Barren Fork 40
Basset 137
Batchelor 14, 15, 17, 20, 21, 22, 23, 34, 48, 59, 65, 66, 73, 74, 75, 98, 100, 111, 112, 121, 122
Bate 105, 133, 134, 141, 156
Battle 19
Battle Creek 101
Battle of Averysboro 159
Battle of Bardstown 41, 48, 166
Battle of Belmont 13
Battle of Bentonville 5, 6, 151
Battle of Bull Run 5
Battle of Cass Station 130
Battle of Chickamauga 100, 101, 107, 108, 176
Battle of Corydon 181
Battle of Dover 76
Battle of First Bull Run 114
Battle of First Manassas 8
Battle of Fort Donelson 35, 36
Battle of Fort Henry 35, 36
Battle of Liberty 6, 83

Battle of Lookout Mountain 6, 114
Battle of Manassas 9
Battle of Mansfield 170
Battle of Mill Springs 20, 23, 54
Battle of Monterey 7
Battle of Mossy Creek 121
Battle of Munfordville 45
Battle of Murfreesboro 73, 74, 75
Battle of Perryville 6, 56, 59, 63, 72, 89, 90
Battle of Pleasant Hill 170
Battle of Resaca 128
Battle of Rowelett's Station 17
Battle of San Juan Hill 170
Battle of Shiloh 5, 6, 25, 32, 34, 36
Battle of Shy's Hill 144
Battle of Stone's River 51, 65, 67, 69, 71, 73, 75, 77, 85, 114
Battle of the Fallen Timbers 32, 34
Battle of Wildcat Mountain 18
Battle of Woodsonville 2, 50, 172
Baylor 122, 170
Bayou Teche 8
Bean's Station 118
Bear Creek 101, 145
Bear Wallow 21
Beard 134
Beatty 72, 105
Beaufort 151, 157
Beaumont 8, 10, 68
Beauregard 8, 26, 30, 31, 34, 35, 149, 155, 176
Bedford City 36
Bedford County 81
Beech Grove 18, 20
Bell Station 20

182